D0600668

THE IMPACT OF ECONOMIC POLICIES ON POVERTY AND INCOME DISTRIBUTION

Evaluation Techniques and Tools

THE IMPACT OF
ECONOMIC POLICIES
ON POVERTY AND
INCOME DISTRIBUTION

Evaluation Techniques and Tools

François Bourguignon

Luiz A. Pereira da Silva

Editors

A copublication of the World Bank and Oxford University Press

© 2003 The International Bank for Reconstruction and Development / The World Bank

1818 H Street, NW
Washington, DC 20433
Telephone 202-473-1000
Internet www.worldbank.org
E-mail feedback@worldbank.org

All rights reserved.
First printing August 2003

1 2 3 4 06 05 04 03

A copublication of the World Bank and Oxford University Press.
Oxford University Press
198 Madison Avenue
New York, NY 10016

The findings, interpretations, and conclusions expressed here are those of the authors and do not necessarily reflect the views of the Board of Executive Directors of the World Bank or the governments they represent.

The World Bank cannot guarantee the accuracy of the data included in this work. The boundaries, colors, denominations, and other information shown on any map in this work do not imply on the part of the World Bank any judgment of the legal status of any territory or the endorsement or acceptance of such boundaries.

Rights and Permissions
The material in this work is copyrighted. No part of this work may be reproduced or transmitted in any form or by any means, electronic or mechanical, including photocopying, recording, or inclusion in any information storage and retrieval system, without the prior written permission of the World Bank. The World Bank encourages dissemination of its work and will normally grant permission promptly.

For permission to photocopy or reprint, please send a request with complete information to the Copyright Clearance Center, Inc., 222 Rosewood Drive, Danvers, MA 01923, USA, telephone 978-750-8400, fax 978-750-4470, www.copyright.com.

All other queries on rights and licenses, including subsidiary rights, should be addressed to the Office of the Publisher, World Bank, 1818 H Street, NW, Washington, DC 20433, fax 202-522-2422, e-mail pubrights@worldbank.org.

ISBN 0-8213-5491-4

Library of Congress Cataloging-in-Publication Data
The impact of economic policies on poverty and income distribution : evaluation
    techniques and tools / edited by François Bourguignon, Luiz A. Pereira da Silva.
        p. cm.
    Includes bibliographical references and index.
    ISBN 0-8213-5491-4
        1. Economic assistance—Evaluation. 2. Poverty. 3. Income distribution.
    I. Bourguignon, François. II. Silva, Luiz A. Pereira da.

HC60.I4146 2003
339.4'6—dc21

                                                    2003053508

Contents

Introduction

Part I. Microeconomic Techniques

Part II. Macroeconomic Techniques

Conclusion

Tables, Figures, and Boxes

Figures

Boxes

Foreword

Development is about fundamental change in economic structures, about the movement of resources out of agriculture to services and industry, about migration to cities and international movement of labor, and about transformations in trade and technology. Social inclusion and change—change in health and life expectancy, in education and literacy, in population size and structure, and in gender relations—are at the heart of the story. The policy challenge is to help release and guide these forces of change and inclusion. But how can policymakers assess whether what they have done, or what they are doing, is right?

Since the 1970s public economics has placed the serious analysis of growth at the center of its agenda. It has shown how to integrate growth and distribution—in simple terms, the size of the cake, and the distribution of the cake—rigorously into the discussion of public policy, both theoretically and empirically. This is an achievement of great importance. What is needed today is research that will extend this analysis of size and distribution to the more dynamic questions of change and inclusion. Standard public economics has made a vital step forward by moving beyond traditional welfare theory and examining problems of constraints on policy that arise from limitations on information. It has helped to discuss the role of the state and to view the provision of public goods both as a political process and as a budget process. But because our perspective on development has changed, our theories and tools for evaluation of policies must also change.

In the past two decades we have begun to look beyond incomes to health and education. Indeed, we now look beyond the basic elements of human well-being and see freedom as part of development. We see the state not as a substitute for the market, but as a critical complement. We have learned that markets need government and government needs markets—and that government action is crucial in enabling people to participate in the growth process and to take advantage of economic opportunities. Economic growth is the most powerful force for the reduction of income poverty. Countries that have reduced income poverty the most effectively are those that have grown the fastest, and poverty has expanded most widely in countries that have stagnated or fallen behind economically.

At the same time, we now know that social cohesion is an important foundation for sound policies and institutions. Societies function more effectively when poor people are empowered with the ability to shape the basic elements of their own lives. Empowerment thus requires not only that people be educated and healthy, but also that they be effective participants, which, in turn, depends on information, accountability, and the quality of local organizations.

These are the dimensions along which public economics, applied to development and analytical tools for evaluating development policies, must evolve. In recent years much progress has been made in evaluating the impact of public programs. New methods have emerged, and existing tools have been improved. Still more is needed, and more will be done. Yet, before these innovations bear fruit, the existing tools must be used more extensively and systematically so that policymakers can clearly see how the choices they make accelerate growth and inclusion and thus reduce poverty. It is the objective of this volume to make these tools for evaluating the effect of policies on poverty available to practitioners, decisionmakers, and scholars in the field of development.

This toolkit results from an extensive collaborative effort between practitioners and researchers in government, universities, aid agencies, NGOs, and other development institutions to build and test various techniques to evaluate the poverty and distributional impact of economic policy choices. The resulting "tools" assembled in this volume represent the most robust, best-practice techniques available for conducting poverty and distributional analysis of a broad range of policies. These tools encompass methods that can be applied to various situations and policy experiments and that allow countries to better quantify tradeoffs in alternative scenarios when exploring ways to reduce poverty.

Analyzing the effects of economic policies on poverty and its distribution requires that these effects be linked at some point to the corresponding changes in income and expenditure of *individual* households as observed in household surveys. This is probably the most important lesson of this volume. It shows that one may go quite far using existing tools and, in particular, making more intensive use of existing household surveys than is currently the case for analyses of the poverty and distributional effects of macro- and microeconomic policies.

This volume also proposes directions for an ambitious but necessary research agenda. First, there is a need to develop more empirical surveys and gain a better analytical understanding of the dynamics of the investment climate, individual preferences, and political reform. We hope that more work using microeconomic data at the firm level—proposed at the end of this volume—will prove to be a fruitful direction for future research. Second, the work presented here suggests that more research is needed to improve the integration of macroeconomic models and the models of household behavior as captured in household surveys. Such an integration is obviously crucial when the distributional incidence and macroeconomic effects of key policies are being studied—as with taxation, trade barriers, and many aspects of public spending—but also when major structural reforms are being evaluated.

This volume is not the end of the road. Innovative research is under way that will permit analysts to go further and solve difficulties raised throughout these pages. Yet, this volume is an important milestone in our effort to provide empirical tools that match the development challenges faced by policymakers and to satisfy their need to evaluate complex public actions. Ultimately, the quality of the tools used depends on the intensity with which they are applied, and their use depends on their quality.

Nicholas Stern
Chief Economist
The World Bank

Acknowledgments

This volume originated from a joint initiative by Nicholas Stern, Chief Economist of the World Bank, and Stanley Fischer, then First-Deputy Managing Director of the International Monetary Fund. It began with a series of workshops aimed at reviewing existing techniques for evaluating the poverty and distributional impact of various policies available for development, and was discussed both in national and international circles by national policymakers, multilateral institutions, the international community of donors, NGOs, and academics. The work was conducted under the overall guidance of Nicholas Stern. Gobind Nankani and Frannie Leauthier brought the World Bank's operational and training perspective. Ian Goldin and John Page managed the discussions inside the World Bank, with the help of Ines Garcia-Thoumi.

Naturally, this volume is above all the sum of the authors' contributions, and they must be the first to be thanked, both for their own work and for the comments they provided on their colleagues' work.

The volume also benefited from comments, suggestions and peer review by Pierre-Richard Agénor, Benu Bidani, Shahrokh Fardoust, Hippolyte Foffack, Alan Gelb, Norman Hicks, Roumeen Islam, Jeny Klugman, Phillippe Le Houerou, Phillippe Guimarães Leite, Michael Lewin, Jeffrey Lewis, Tamar Manuelyan-Attinc, Ernesto May, Brian Ngo, Martin Rama, Anne-Sophie Robillard, Sudhir Shetty, and Joachim Von Amsberg.

Alexandre Padolina Arenas, Aline Coudouel, and Stefano Paternostro assisted with the electronic and Web site version of this volume.

Roula I. Yazigi, Lucie Albert-Drucker, and Bilkiss Dhomun provided administrative support. Martha Gottron was the copy editor, and Kim Kelley was the production editor for this publication.

Acronyms and Abbreviations

CDD	community-driven development
CES	constant elasticity of substitution
CGE	computable general equilibrium
CPI	consumer price index
DD	double difference
DECRG	Development Economics Research Group (World Bank)
DHS	Demographic and Health Survey
FGT	Foster-Greer-Thorbecke
FPM	Financial Programming Model (FPM)
FSC	Fiscal Sustainability Credit
GAMS	General Algebraic Modeling System
GDP	gross domestic product
GIS	Geographic Information System
HIMS	Household Income Microsimulation
HIPC	heavily indebted poor country
IEA	Integrated Economic Accounts
IES	Income and Expenditure Survey
IFPRI	International Food Policy Research Institute
IVE	instrumental variables estimator
JSIF	Jamaica Social Investment Fund
KDP	Kecamatan Development Program (Indonesia)
LAV	linkage aggregate variable
LCU	local currency unit
LES	Linear Expenditure System
LFS	Labor Force Survey
LSMS	Living Standards Measurement Study

MDG	Millennium Development Goals
MS	microsimulation
NSS	National Sample Survey (India)
OLS	ordinary least squares
PAMS	Poverty Analysis Macroeconomic Simulator (Excel EViews application)
PDC	poverty depth curve
PETS	Public Expenditure Tracking Survey
PFP	Policy Framework Paper
PIC	poverty incidence curve
PNAD	Pesquisa Nacional por Amostra de Domicilios (Brazil)
PovStat	Poverty Projection Toolkit (Excel-based software)
PPA	Participatory Poverty Assessment
PPP	purchasing power parity
PPV	Pesquisa Sobre Padroes de Vida (Brazil)
PRA	Participatory Rural Appraisal
PRGF	Poverty Reduction and Growth Facility (IMF)
PRSP	Poverty Reduction Strategy Paper
PSM	propensity-score matching
QSDS	Quantitative Service Delivery Survey
RH	representative household
RRA	Rapid Rural Appraisal
SAM	social accounting matrix
SEWA	Self-Employed Women's Association (India)
SimSIP	Simulations for Social Indicators and Poverty (Excel-based software)
SNA	System of National Accounts
SUSENAS	Survei Sosial Ekonomi Nasional (Indonesia)
UPP1	Urban Poverty Project 1
UPP2	Urban Poverty Project 2
VAR	vector autoreggression
ZCCM	Zambia Consolidated Copper Mines

Introduction

Evaluating the Poverty and Distributional Impact of Economic Policies: A Compendium of Existing Techniques

François Bourguignon and
Luiz A. Pereira da Silva

How do economic development policies affect poverty and distribution? In recent years that question has become a major focus of national and international approaches to development policies. To be fair, the debate on economic development policies has more or less continuously intertwined growth and distribution issues, but never before have evaluations of the effects been so systematic or so prominent an element of the debate. This new approach is particularly evident in the emergence of a set of multiple development goals that explicitly go beyond the narrow focus on aggregate output maximization. One example is the Millennium Development Goals forged by the member countries of the United Nations. Another is the Poverty Reduction Strategy Papers (PRSPs), the cornerstone of the concessional lending by the International Monetary Fund (IMF) and the World Bank to low-income countries.[1] PRSPs are explicitly aimed at reducing poverty and meeting several social goals rather than exclusively maximizing economic growth. By definition then, they require "poverty and distributional analysis" of a set of recommended economic policies and strategies. Even though economic and social objectives are usually complements, they may produce tradeoffs; for example, the pace of growth may have some influence on the distribution of economic and social welfare, and vice versa. The demand for more poverty and distributional analysis that results from this change of focus is pressing. It comes from practically all quarters: civil society, national governments, nongovernmental organizations, bilateral aid agencies, international development agencies, and international financial institutions.

Whether reforms concern fiscal or monetary policy, shifts in particular expenditures such as education or health, trade liberalization, financial sector liberalization, government decentralization, or the regulation of utilities, economists and social scientists working on developing countries are increasingly asked both to figure out the likely aggregate effect of these policies and their effect on various social groups—as well as their impact at the individual household level. A casual observation of the decision process in national governments and international development institutions reveals that such evaluations are not being conducted systematically, at least not for all the policy changes most frequently discussed in developing countries since the 1980s (box I-1). One reason may be that until recently poverty reduction was not included in the evaluation criteria. Another reason is technical: poverty and distribution evaluation techniques were not widely used because they were not easily accessible or were unsatisfactory on theoretical grounds, or because lack of relevant data simply made them difficult to implement.

Indeed, analysts who evaluate the poverty and distributional impacts of economic policies face a big challenge. Because poverty is essentially an individual feature, they must necessarily operate at the microeconomic level. Thus they require information or predictions on how individuals, rather than the whole population or even any particular broad aggregate group, are likely to fare under the policy being investigated. Such an analytical tradition exists in the public finance literature under the heading *incidence analysis*. The goal of incidence analysis is to evaluate how particular individuals or households are affected by a change in the tax system or in the accessibility of public services. However, this "micro-oriented" approach is far from relating immediately and directly to the macroeconomic policies and structural reforms listed in box I.1.

This volume is a compendium of techniques currently available for evaluating the impact of economic policies on poverty and distribution of living standards. Experienced practitioners and researchers will realize that these techniques are not original or novel. All the techniques reviewed here are widely or increasingly

Box I.1 Recurrent Economic Policy Issues in Developing Countries

Public Finance

Public expenditures, such as shifting the allocation of public spending to specific public programs that affect particular sectors or targeted groups through cash and/or in-kind transfer policies, loan guarantees, microfinance, or the provision of various types of infrastructure

Tax policy, including changing tax bases, bands, or rates of direct and indirect taxes and subsidies

Management of pension and public insurance systems, including health and unemployment insurance

Pricing of publicly provided goods and services

Structural Reforms

Liberalization and/or regulation of specific markets, including labor and basic commodity markets

Trade liberalization, through the elimination of tariff and nontariff barriers and other preferential agreements; and adherence to WTO rules

Financial sector reforms, including regulation of the banking sector, openness of the capital account, availability of microcredit, and adherence to international financial codes and standards (such as those of the Bank for International Settlements, or BIS)

Public sector management, including the delivery of services, quality, and targeting of services

Private and public governance reforms, including adherence to international standards

Restructuring, privatization, and regulation of public utilities, infrastructure, and other firms

Decentralization and reforms in intergovernmental institutional relations

Civil service reforms, including the size and composition of public sector employment

Land reform, such as negotiated voluntary land transfers

Environmental regulation, including pollution control and enforcement

Macro Policies
(Alternative Frameworks and Responses to Shocks)

Fiscal policy, including appropriate deficit levels, controlling for cyclicality

Monetary policy, including Central Bank independence, inflation targeting, and interest rate policies

Exchange rate regimes (fixed, crawling-peg, or floating), and effects of a real devaluation

Public debt management, including the size and composition of public sector liabilities

used by academics and policy analysts. The review thus stops short of discussing the cutting-edge field of distributional evaluation of micro- and macroeconomic policies. Cutting-edge analytical techniques will be the subject of a forthcoming volume. We deliberately made this choice to prevent readers from embarking on techniques with uncertain and ambiguous results. The originality of this first volume comes from its attempt to organize the analytics of all these techniques around the common thread of incidence analysis, and to show that this basic microeconomic evaluation tool can be used in many and very different ways to evaluate a wide range of macroeconomic policies with some potential impact on poverty.

The annex at the end of this volume provides a short summary of the tool discussed in each chapter, including rationale for using that technique or tool; the main policy reforms that it can address; its most important requirements (data, timeframe, skills needed to develop an application, and software supporting the tool); and the team of experts who are familiar with the tool. This summary description of the tools covered in this volume is part of a broad effort to provide guidance and a roadmap for practitioners who want to conduct poverty and social impact analysis.[2]

Incidence Analysis as the Core Evaluation Framework for Poverty and Distributional Analysis

Incidence analysis is a concept that is rooted in public finance. Its policy applications began with the study of the welfare impact of taxation and were extended subsequently to that of public spending. For taxation, it consists of identifying those economic agents that actually bear the cost of a particular tax, those who gain from it, and the amount each group will gain or lose in terms of some metric of welfare. The same issues arise with regard to social benefits and other transfer programs—who gains, who loses, how much. There are two main difficulties behind this exercise. First, gainers and losers may not be those who at first sight nominally benefit from the transfer or pay the tax. Behavioral and market responses to taxes and transfers may shift their burden or their benefits to other agents through partial or general equilibrium mechanisms. For example, an indirect tax paid by producers may be partly or fully shifted onto consumers. Second, the identification of the gainers and losers is made difficult by the natural heterogeneity among individual economic agents, even when they belong to some apparently well-defined sociodemographic group such as "unskilled urban workers" or "small farmers."

Evaluating the effect of economic policies on poverty has much to do with tax-benefit incidence analysis. However, poverty incidence analysis is more complex because it involves explicitly ranking gainers and losers of a policy against their initial individual welfare levels or poverty status or, equivalently, concentrating on gains or losses of poor people. Also because the policies being evaluated may be different from a standard tax or subsidy, the issue of identifying direct and indirect gains or losses may also be much more complicated.

Identifying the poor in a population in order to gauge the poverty incidence of a particular policy requires the use of household- or individual-level data. This need arises because the heterogeneity underscored earlier implies that no single easily observable and analytically relevant attribute is strictly equivalent to poverty. Poor people can be found in virtually all categories of agents that economic analysis can distinguish. As a result, poverty incidence analysis must begin at the microeconomic level to identify those individuals who gain or lose because of a specific policy. Indeed, a common feature of the evaluation methods reviewed in this volume—whether they focus on microeconomic or macroeconomic phenomena—is that they are always somehow connected with individual or household information coming from various types of sample surveys. Most of these are nationwide labor force and household expenditure surveys, but some are ad hoc surveys undertaken to evaluate specific policies or programs. Designing and taking surveys are a necessary first step in poverty evaluation and must be considered as part of the evaluation methodology. Chapter 7 is devoted to this issue.

Measuring the *actual* monetary flows between the government (central or local), and the individuals, households, or entities that provide services directly to households is another type of data problem confronting analysts. A substantial discrepancy often exists between flows that are budgeted, flows that are actually disbursed, and flows that actually reach the intended target, whether the target is a specific group of households or a specific geographic area of the country. Of course, the second and third kinds of flow are the ones that must be taken into account in incidence analysis. Following the full path and examining the behavior of microeconomic agents responsible for managing and monitoring these policies are often necessary to understand where reallocation or leakages take place. These issues, which have a great deal to do with policy governance in general, are taken up in chapter 9.

Objectives and General Organization of the Volume

Relying on this proximity of incidence analysis and poverty evaluation techniques, the practical objective of this volume is to make the most current poverty evaluation instruments accessible to all analysts. The 15 chapters of this book give a full account of existing basic techniques and the principles on which they are built, together with illustrative applications and practical tips on implementation. Each chapter refers systematically to recent case studies where the use of these methods can be best appreciated. At the same time, both the presentation and the discussion are intended to be as nontechnical as possible, although some technicality is unavoidable.

Two caveats apply to the practical use of the techniques described here. First, in many instances, using one technique alone allows only a partial evaluation of the poverty impact of a particular policy. A more comprehensive view may be obtained by using various techniques at the same time—or possibly by devising original methods based on existing techniques but better adapted to the policy under analysis. Likewise, evaluating the poverty impact of a "complex" set of policies generally requires using various techniques at the same time. For this reason, this volume provides some leads to cover these more complex cases. They should prove valuable in handling policy issues not directly concerned with the techniques being reviewed.

Second, we acknowledge that the set of poverty evaluation techniques currently available has serious gaps and weaknesses. Although we are confident about the relevance of the general incidence approach, some policy reform areas cannot be evaluated with the tools described here (see our conclusions at the end of this volume).[3] Moreover, even for simple reforms, building a rigorous bridge between microeconomic phenomena taking place at the household level and modeling at the macroeconomic level is recognized as one of the big challenges of economic analysis. Some tools do exist to handle "micro-macro" policy issues, and the most widely used ones are indeed reviewed in this volume. But they are imperfect and may be unsatisfactory for particular applications. In some instances, solutions have been proposed in the literature, but not enough practical experience has been gained to make them suitable for systematic use. Therefore, no attempt is made in this volume to include either all economic policies with some possible impact on poverty and the distribution of welfare or all possible evaluation techniques. We review here only those that seemed to be broadly applicable and to have acquired some robustness, noting the gaps they leave and, more generally, the limits of these standard techniques. Filling some of the gaps and reducing the limitations are left for a further volume.

The tools reviewed in this volume are organized in two parts and in each part arranged according to the policy being considered, the perspective taken, or their level of complexity. The chapters in part 1 are exclusively microeconomically oriented and are devoted to the effects of public expenditures, taxation, and redistribution policies on poverty and the distribution of economic welfare. The chapters in part 2 focus on macroeconomic policies and the links that may be established between macroeconomic modeling and the distribution of economic welfare. The unifying link between the two parts is the *systematic* reliance on microeconomic data sets that describe the distribution of economic welfare in the population, that is, household surveys of various types. As it turns out, the incidence analysis developed in part 1 may also be used—albeit with more difficulty— to evaluate macroeconomic policies, which modify consumption and factor prices (including their own labor) that households face much as tax and subsidy policies do. Moving to macroeconomic instruments, such as fiscal or exchange rate policy, from these changes in prices and factor rewards may require the analyst to take nontrivial steps in modeling or to make strong simplifying assumptions. In addition, other dimensions of individuals' economic environments must also be taken into account, which actually makes evaluation of macroeconomic policies more than the straight generalization of incidence analysis.

Each chapter discusses both a specific policy evaluation technique and a particular policy instrument or situation to which the technique is adapted. The authors of each chapter carefully note the limitations of the tools currently in use and the risks of pushing them too far outside their limit of validity.

The techniques reviewed in both parts of this volume require the user to make some methodological choices at the outset, depending on the perspective adopted for poverty evaluation, the data at hand, the economic modeling capacity available, and the nature of the policy being studied. Having these constraints and issues in mind should help users of this volume make the appropriate choice for evaluating a specific policy in a particular context.

Using the Incidence Framework at the Microeconomic Level

Because poverty incidence analysis is initially focused on the microeconomic level, it is important to evaluate the immediate or direct impact of a policy on households and individuals as accurately as possible. Even though this initial impact may quite possibly be modified by market mechanisms induced by behavioral responses, it is unlikely to be dominated by these indirect effects. Moreover, this second round of effects may be difficult to study at the same level of disaggregation as direct effects. This is the reason why direct microeconomic incidence analysis, possibly including direct behavioral responses, is so important. It also explains why techniques that rely on this approach are best suited to evaluate policies with a marked direct impact on households, such as reforms in the tax system or in the structure of public spending, including cash or in-kind transfers.

It is not suggested, however, that second-round effects be neglected. Indeed, the indirect effects that arise from the behavioral responses of microeconomic agents through market mechanisms might be sizable. They may directly affect household welfare by modifying the price system, the returns on productive assets, and the overall conditions of the labor market. The distributional incidence analysis of those changes that take place at the aggregate level is the subject of the second part of the volume.

The policies with some directly observable or easily conjectured impact at the household or personal level are typically tax, transfer, and, more generally, public spending policies. Poverty incidence analysis may be more or less difficult and more or less detailed depending on the nature of the tax or public expenditure being considered and the way in which policies are actually implemented. For example, evaluating the direct poverty impact of some transfer policy conditional on some individual or household characteristic requires only observing those characteristics as well as knowing the welfare status of households. But an evaluation may also require information on possible differences between the official transfer rules and the actual implementation. Observing or inferring the actual impact of a policy may be more difficult in other instances. Evaluating the impact of building infrastructure in an area, such as a road or a sewer line, may require knowing who is using it or likely to use it, information that is not always available in the data sources.

Several chapters in part 1 are defined by the policy being evaluated: taxes in chapter 1, public spending in chapter 2, and multifaceted community programs in chapter 5. Other chapters are defined by the perspective that is adopted. For example, the implementation issues mentioned earlier are dealt with in chapter 9. Other perspectives are also considered. Incidence analysis may take an accounting or behavioral approach, it may be ex ante or ex post, it may be quantitative or qualitative, and it may be concerned with the average or the margins. All these conceptual distinctions are important for knowing whether a given evaluation technique is appropriate for dealing with the problem at hand. They are discussed next.

Accounting versus Behavioral Approaches

The simplest type of incidence analysis is the *accounting* approach. *Who* pays *what* to the state, *who* receives *what* from it? In some cases, that information may be obtained directly from sample surveys that ask about cash transfers, income taxes, or the use of certain public services. Some inference may be necessary, however. A value may have to be imputed to public services being consumed; transfers or taxes may not be directly observed in surveys and may have to be figured out indirectly. Indirect methods involve applying official eligibility rules or official income tax schedules or imputing indirect taxes paid through observed spending.

Accounting approaches stop at that point. They ignore possible behavioral responses by agents that may modify the amounts they actually pay or receive; an accounting approach would not detect tax evasion, for example, resulting from an increase in income tax rates. Better said, these approaches are limited to *first-round effects* and disregard second-round effects attributable to behavioral responses. In contrast, *behavioral approaches* try to take those responses into account. An individual may decide to work less than otherwise to avoid losing her eligibility for a means-tested transfer, parents may decide to send their children to school to take advantage of free school lunches, or they may pay more attention to their children's health if a public dispensary is built in the neighborhood. Accounting for behavioral responses is important for poverty incidence analysis since changes in behavior may compound or, more rarely, mitigate the first-round effects revealed by the accounting approach. The difficulty, of course, comes in identifying the behavioral response and its determinants in order to integrate it properly into the analysis.

Behavioral considerations are also important in valuing public services for potential users. Offering free public education in a village means more to a household that was initially sending its children to a school 10 kilometers away from the village than to a household whose children were initially not enrolled. Finding the right value of a free public service for actual users may thus require estimating the "demand" for that service, or, equivalently, the "willingness to pay" for the service. Behavioral responses are discussed in various chapters and dealt with explicitly in chapters 3, 5, and 6.

Ex Ante versus Ex Post Analysis

Economic policies may be evaluated and monitored either before they are enacted (or implemented)—ex ante—or after they have been in place for some period of time—ex post. Ex ante evaluation involves quantitative techniques that try to *predict* the various effects of policies including those on distribution and poverty. It is also crucial to evaluate policies ex post to actually *observe* and precisely identify the direct and indirect effects of a policy to see whether the actual effects were those expected—and perhaps to reform those policies that did not produce the intended effects.

The distinction between ex ante and ex post analysis may not seem crucial for the accounting approaches mentioned earlier, which simply ignore all behavioral responses to the policy being evaluated. For example, one may evaluate ex ante the impact on poverty of some prospective means-tested cash transfer program by computing for each household in a sample survey the change in its welfare attributable to the program. If implementation were to proceed as described in official documents, and if behavioral response were ignored, then the results of the evaluation would be the same whether it was conducted before or after the policy or the reform was implemented. Matters would be quite different if the implementation of a policy involved some departure from the official intention; for example, one need only look at public finance where disbursed expenditures frequently differ from the budgeted expenditures. The same would be true where the actual effect of the policy depended on whether targeted households actually seized the opportunities offered to them by the policy (the take-up rate). Actual transfers to households and the characteristics of beneficiaries may be observed ex post if the necessary data channels have been collected, as described in chapters 5, 7, 8, and 9. It is much more difficult to figure the size of these corrections on an ex ante basis.

Even when implementation issues are ignored, the difference between ex ante and ex post approaches is more significant when complex behavioral responses are taken into account. Ex post approaches try to compare individuals or households before and after some policy change, or households involved in some specific program with households not involved in the program. In both cases, one might assume that observed differences would reflect the direct effect of the program or the policy reform as well as all possible second-round behavioral effects. An important issue in this respect is whether households in the program or those concerned by the reform may be considered as randomly selected in the population or as self-selected. This issue is discussed in detail in chapter 5.

Ex ante approaches that take into account behavioral responses rely necessarily on some structural modeling of household behavior in the field under scrutiny, such as labor supply or occupational choices, demand for schooling, or demand for health services. These models must be able to predict the likely response of households to a change in the set of alternatives offered to them because of the program or the reform being analyzed. At the same time they must be consistent with the characteristics and the behavior of the households as they are observed in the sample survey used as a data base. Examples of the use of such models are given in chapters 3 and 6.

Average versus Marginal Effects

The incidence of public spending on poverty may be evaluated taking into account all expenditures in a specific field such as primary education or health care. Within an accounting, ex post framework, one may thus reach conclusions such as the poorest 20 percent of the population receives 25 percent of public spending in primary education and 15 percent of spending on health care. Does this mean that switching some expenditures from health care to primary education would improve the lot of the poor?

The answer is not necessarily yes. The preceding figures show who benefits from public spending *on average*. They say nothing about the effect of expanding, or contracting, public spending in a particular field *at the margin*. Expanding or contracting spending may involve giving access to health care or primary education to some part of the population that did not benefit from these services initially. But that part of the population is rarely a random sample of the population who originally had access to these services. To be sure, expanding primary education in a poor country will predominantly affect the poorest segments of the population because school enrollment is likely to be initially close to 100 percent for the rich and the middle class. But that might not always be the case for other public services, such as tertiary education or electrification. Identifying this marginal incidence and making the distinction with average incidence is important in evaluating the actual impact of policy reforms on poverty. This does not mean, however, that average incidence is irrelevant in such a context. For example, evaluating the poverty impact of a policy consisting of improving uniformly the quality of education for *all* children already enrolled clearly calls for an average incidence analysis. An explicit treatment of marginal incidence analysis is given in chapter 3.

Qualitative versus Quantitative Approaches

Poverty, or more generally distributional incidence analysis, tends to be quantitative because poverty is often defined in terms of some measurable concept such as income or expenditure per capita. In such a framework, it makes sense to talk about the "bottom" 20 or

40 percent of a population in terms of its income or expenditure shares and how its (real) income or expenditure may be modified by taxation and various components of public spending. But, of course, social public spending and social programs have many dimensions that cannot be reduced to an income measure but that are nevertheless important in defining and evaluating the incidence of poverty. Dealing with all these dimensions in quantitative terms is virtually impossible. Hence the importance of approaching incidence analysis also from a qualitative point of view. This is the subject of chapter 8.

Partial versus Universal Coverage and the Spatial Dimension of Public Spending

Incidence analysis and prospective policy evaluation based on household surveys may be limited by the information available in these surveys. In particular, policies with some important geographical dimensions—road construction, irrigation, or electrification, for example—may be difficult to evaluate because household samples typically cover a limited number of localities. Statistical techniques that match data in censuses with those found in household surveys permit dealing partly with that difficulty. The analysis may then proceed *as if* it had a universal rather than a partial coverage of the population. These techniques and the possibilities offered by the extensive poverty maps they allow to draw are discussed in chapter 4.

Using the Incidence Framework at the Macroeconomic Level: Links between Macroeconomic and Microeconomic Techniques

In contrast to part 1 of the volume, which is focused on microeconomic techniques, part 2 considers techniques for evaluating economic policies that affect poverty through changes in the volume (growth), the structure (sectoral composition), and the parameters (prices, factor rewards) of the macroeconomy. These techniques can be seen as an extension of the microeconomic analysis where all effects on behavior and market equilibriums are taken into account. In such a perspective, indirect tax reforms or large public expenditure programs are indeed likely to have sizable macroeconomic effects. But macroeconomic phenomena may affect prices, factor rewards, and other parameters through very different channels, including foreign trade, the financial sector, and monetary and

fiscal policies. In all cases, evaluating the poverty effect of macroeconomic policies may require the analyst to move beyond the
straight incidence analysis reviewed in part 1. Not only may macroeconomic phenomena affect the main parameters behind incidence
analysis through very different channels, but they are also likely to
affect some dimensions of household welfare that were previously
left aside. That is especially true for changes in income-generation
mechanisms either through the labor market or through returns on
nonlabor assets.

The "ground floor" of the analysis can be found in the relationship between economic growth and poverty in aggregate models.
From a distributional point of view, this may be considered the first
level of the analysis because the macroeconomic framework gives
no information whatsoever on inequality-related variables. Of
course, inferences about the impact on (absolute) poverty are possible if one is willing to make some necessarily arbitrary assumption
about changes in the distribution. Two simple tools adapted to this
class of models are discussed in chapter 10.

The next chapters move on to disaggregated models. Several
possible linkages between poverty analysis based on household survey data grouped into so-called "representative households" and
different classes of macroeconomic models are presented. First, in
chapter 11 the household survey data are linked to a macroconsistency accounting framework with a simple representation of the
labor market. Second, in chapter 12 the focus is shifted to the distribution and poverty impact on producers and consumers observed
in a microeconomic database of changes in prices and quantities
produced in a set of related markets under partial equilibrium
assumptions. Third, in chapter 13 the micro-macro linkage is done
with a simple three-sector general equilibrium model with flexible
prices and wages. Fourth, in chapter 14 the link is made through
social accounting matrices (SAMs), which are useful for showing
how different household groups derive their incomes from different
sources and their spending patterns. Finally, in chapter 15 the linkage is established with a wider class of disaggregated general equilibrium models.

Regardless of its type—macroconsistency or general equilibrium—the main role of the macroeconomic models described in
part 2 is to produce a set of macroconsistent changes of commodity
and factor prices that can be used to extend the poverty incidence
approach of part 1. Indeed, it is essentially through these channels
that macroeconomic policies may affect the various components of
consumption and revenue of individuals and households.

The extension of the microeconomic incidence framework to a macroeconomic level is important when the indirect effects of economic policies that arise from the behavioral responses of microeconomic agents through market mechanisms are sizable. These effects may directly affect household welfare by modifying the price system, the returns on productive assets, and the overall conditions of the labor market. For instance, a change in the structure of indirect taxation may induce a sectoral reallocation of resources with some effects on the structure of earnings or self-employment income. A tax incidence analysis that focused only on the effects of changing consumer prices could thus miss the mark if it were not supplemented by an analysis at the macroeconomic level.

The general approach, outlined in this part, consists of decomposing these effects and of generalizing the standard incidence analysis of public spending and taxation to cover some, but not all, of the macroeconomic policy issues listed in box I.1. To accomplish this, we suggest a three-layer methodology for evaluating the poverty effect of economic policies. The bottom, or micro, layer (individuals in the household survey) consists of a microsimulation analysis, based on household microeconomic data, that permits analyzing the distributional incidence not only of changes in social public spending or taxation but also of changes in the structure of consumer prices and earnings, or more generally in the income-generation behavior of households caused by some macroeconomic policy or shock. The top, macro aggregate, layer includes aggregate macroeconomic modeling tools that permit evaluating the impact of exogenous shocks and policies on aggregates such as gross domestic product (GDP), its components, the general price level, the exchange rate, the rate of interest, and the like, either in the short run or in a growth perspective. The intermediate, meso, layer consists of tools that permit disaggregating the predictions obtained with the top layer into price, earning, employment, and asset returns in various sectors of activity and various factors of production.

For the analysis to be conducted consistently between these three layers, they should be linked with each other in some consistent way. For instance, studying some change in public spending in education at the bottom level should modify the rate of growth of the economy in the top layer as well as the structure of activity and of factor remunerations in the intermediate layer. In turn those latter changes should affect the household income generation model in the bottom layer. Unfortunately, available analytical equipment for such a full integration of these three analytical layers is far from complete. Techniques covered in this part of the volume typically cover part of this general framework.

The Relationship between Growth and Poverty in Aggregate Models

Any change in poverty may be decomposed into changes in growth (what is attributable to the uniform growth of income) and changes in distribution (what is attributable to changes in relative incomes), see Datt and Ravallion (1992). Without information on changes in distribution, likely changes in poverty resulting from changes of x percent in aggregate household income may be calculated by multiplying all incomes or consumption expenditures observed in a household survey by x. This provides an extremely simple way of mapping growth into poverty reduction. In terms of the incidence analysis reviewed in the first part of the volume, this procedure is equivalent to assuming that the rewards of all factors owned by individuals or households rise by x percent.

Chapter 10 reports on two procedures based on this principle. In the first one the calculation can be made in the absence of household survey data. All that is required is a set of assumptions on the distribution of income across specific groups of households. An Excel-based spreadsheet software—the SimSIP simulator—has recently been built and made available to exploit that idea. This simulator should be useful to analysts who do not have access to the unit-level records of household surveys but do have information by level of income, as often provided, for example, in published reports from national statistical offices.

Another similar procedure based on household survey data can be found in PovStat. PovStat is an Excel-based program that can simulate poverty measures under alternative growth scenarios and over a user-specified projection horizon. Poverty projections are generated using country-specific household survey data and a set of user-supplied projection parameters for that country. The program can also handle exogenous distributional changes that would accompany growth provided they can be parameterized in an adequate way. PovStat may also handle some rough sectoral disaggregation of GDP growth in terms of both mean household income and sectors of employment.[4] The program offers a wide variety of options in specifying projection parameters as well as an output datasheet capability.

Linking Household Survey Data to Macroeconomically Consistent Accounting Frameworks with a Simple Representation of a Labor Market

As suggested by the example of PovStat, the preceding techniques for evaluating the incidence of growth on poverty could conceptually be generalized to disaggregate representations of growth by sector or social group, or both. One need only observe the growth of specific sectors or be able to predict them with the appropriate modeling tools. Then, knowing the distribution *within* these sectors or groups, the same mechanism as above could be used to estimate the expenditure or income of households within a group and then to estimate the change in poverty in the entire survey sample. In terms of incidence analysis, it is now assumed that all the factors owned by households operating in a given sector have their rewards raised in the same proportion as given by GDP per capita in that sector in the macroeconomic model.

This is the method used in chapter 11 by the Poverty Analysis Macroeconomic Simulator, or PAMS, model. An Excel-EViews package, PAMS uses as a starting point a macroeconomic framework taken from any macroeconomically consistent model (for example, the "traditional" World Bank RMSM-X) and disaggregates production into economic sectors (such as rural and urban, tradable and nontradable, formal and informal). Each sector, in turn, is assumed to employ only one type of labor extracted from the available household survey (regrouping individual observations into representative groups of households defined by the labor category of the head of the household). PAMS' labor market, disaggregated by economic sector, projects labor demand, which depends on the growth of sectoral output, and unit labor cost for the relevant sector. Given the disaggregation by sector and skills explained above, PAMS then recalculates income growth for each labor category and feeds these growth rates back into the household survey.

The usefulness of all the preceding tools lies essentially in their simplicity. This simplicity entails some problems, though. First, the way in which macroeconomic levers produce changes in sectoral income per capita is oversimplified. Second, assumptions about changes in the distribution within sectors are totally arbitrary. For instance, no account is taken of the fact that the structure of factor rewards may change within sectors or that households are differently affected by a change in the structure of consumption prices. Finally, the treatment of the distributional effects of changes in sectoral structures is oversimplified. In particular, it is assumed that movements between representative groups or sectors being considered in the analysis are distribution neutral, which seems unlikely in reality.

Poverty Analysis with Partial Equilibrium (Multimarket) Models

The approaches described so far rely on the assumption of fixed prices that is present in most of the macroconsistency frameworks. Besides the effect of real unit labor cost on labor demand and the effect of the real exchange rate on aggregate exports in PAMS, changes in relative prices are ignored even though they directly affect household welfare on the consumption side and household income on the production side. This approach can be misleading when evaluating the effects of some policies that aim precisely at reallocating output more efficiently and assessing the poverty impact of such moves.

Another route to link policy changes to their effect on households' real income—and thus on poverty and distribution—is to use a different class of model where prices are flexible. There are two main classes of such models in the literature. The first comprises sophisticated computable general equilibrium (CGE) models, with goods and factor markets modeled explicitly and wages, prices, and private income determined endogenously. The second class neglects some of these indirect general equilibrium effects and focuses only on a set of interrelated markets where the policy under study is likely to have its main effects. This approach has been used primarily in analyzing the agricultural sector and agricultural commodities. The approach has the advantage of simplicity, but it also has the (unknown since not calculated) disadvantage of putting aside potentially large indirect economic and social effects of policies.

The use of such "multimarket models" for poverty and distribution analysis is discussed in chapter 12. Whether they are called "limited general equilibrium" as in Mosley (1999) or "multimarket partial equilibrium" as in Arulpragasam (1994), these models focus the analysis on the combination of direct effects and indirect effects through price and quantity changes in a small group of commodities or factors with strongly interlinked supply and demand. They are most appropriate for the evaluation of policies that change the relative price of a specific good—for example, the removal of a subsidy or the elimination of a tariff or quota. The indirect effects explicitly modeled are those resulting from relative price responsiveness of demand and supply in markets for substitute goods.

Once the direct effect on a market (or markets) of a policy reform is identified, one can also figure out (through data examination, survey of experts, or other prior knowledge) which other markets are strongly interlinked in demand or supply with the markets in which the direct effect is measured. The next step is to rely on household survey information to estimate the shares of expenditures that are affected by these changes through own-price and cross-price elasticities of demand for the entire set of interlinked markets. Producer survey information is used to derive estimates of own-price and cross-price elasticities of supply for the set of interlinked markets. These estimates are combined to create a system of demand and supply functions, and price- or quantity-clearing is imposed for each good in the system of equations. This closure is made consistent with the observed macroeconomic outcomes by requiring the resulting equilibrium to duplicate international relative prices and trade flows in each good and other national statistics for the base year chosen. The impact of the policy reform in this system of equations is then calculated by introducing the desired policy change. Relative prices and quantities produced and consumed domestically are derived for this new equilibrium. The derived relative prices and quantities are combined with household survey information, households often being both consumers and producers, to determine the marginal impact of the policy reform on the incidence and depth of poverty.

Poverty Analysis with a Simple Computable General Equilibrium Model

Suppose now that available evidence suggests that the policies being assessed have large indirect and second-round effects. A partial equilibrium approach such as the one described above would be inadequate to measure the poverty and distributional consequences of such policies. A general equilibrium approach is necessary.

Chapter 13 explores what can be done with what probably is the simplest computable general equilibrium model of a complete economy. This is the 1-2-3 model, by Devarajan and others (2000); the model name stands for one country, two sectors, three commodities (such as exports, domestic goods, and imports). This is a static model (that is, it has to be "fed" with an exogenous growth path), but one of its important aspects is that it captures the effects of macroeconomic policies on two critical relative prices, namely, the real exchange rate and the real remuneration rate of (wage) labor, and on the allocation of resources between tradable and nontradable sectors. Another important aspect is that the calibration of the model is relatively easy using national accounts data and simple assumptions of equilibrium in labor and capital markets. The model's simulations predict the effect of several types of macroeconomic policies on wages, sector-specific employment, self-employment income and profits, and relative prices that are mutually consistent.

The link with poverty analysis is provided by plugging the model's projected changes in prices, wages, and profits into available data on labor and profit income and on commodity demands for representative groups of households (or deciles of the welfare distribution). In principle, the impact on each household in the sample can be calculated so as to capture the effect of the policy under study on the entire distribution of income. Thus changes in various poverty measures can also be reported. In short, the 1-2-3 framework allows for a forecast of welfare measures and poverty outcomes consistent with a set of macroeconomic policies and of their effect on key macroeconomic variables such as the real exchange rate or the sectoral allocation of employment.

Poverty Analysis with Social Accounting Matrices (SAMs) Approaches

The "simplest" CGE model described above has obvious limitations. For example, some policies will affect specific categories of workers and specific economic sectors within the broad aggregates of the 1-2-3 approach, but the approach itself cannot measure these specific changes. Much energy since the 1980s has been dedicated to developing disaggregated models that would permit simultaneous analysis of changes both in the structure of the economy due to some specific macroeconomic policy and in the distribution of income within the population.

For more than three decades social accounting matrices have been used as an integrating framework for data belonging to separate spheres—national accounts, social accounts, household surveys, and so forth—and as a basis for modeling the social consequences of macroeconomic policies. A SAM is usually quite explicit in portraying the structural features of an economy, in particular how different household groups derive their incomes from different sources and their spending patterns. Chapter 14 sets out the basic framework of a SAM and shows how it has been used to compute Keynesian-like multipliers to help assess the impacts of policy and external shocks on household incomes and expenditures and on poverty. SAM-based models show how the incomes of a particular household group, say, small-scale farmers, may be affected by an increase in, say, textile output. The method identifies all the various paths or channels of transmission of the effects of policies, from origin to destination. For instance, it may be that an increase in the income of unskilled workers arises directly, through the hiring of unskilled labor in some unskilled-labor intensive sector, or indirectly, through a stimulus from increased spending on food crops, the increased production of which also needs unskilled labor (Thorbecke 1995). Structural path analysis computes the importance of the various paths relative to the global influence.

One major limitation of SAM multipliers, however, is their implicit reliance on fixed price Keynesian-like mechanisms. This has several drawbacks for the analysis of poverty, including the difficulty of separating out whether the predicted change in the mean income of a household group is due to price and wage or employment effects.

*Poverty Analysis with More Disaggregated CGE Models
Using the Representative Household Approach*

Since the pioneer work by Adelman and Robinson (1978) for Korea
and by Lysy and Taylor (1980) for Brazil, many CGE models for
developing countries combine a highly disaggregated representation
of the economy within a consistent macroeconomic framework with
a description of the distribution of income through a small number
of representative households meant to represent the main sources of
heterogeneity in the whole population with respect to the phenomena or the policies being studied. Models were initially static and
rigorously Walrasian. They are now often dynamic—in the sense of
a sequence of temporary equilibriums linked by asset accumulation—and often depart from Walrasian assumptions to incorporate
various macroeconomic features, or "closures," as well as imperfect
competition features.

Several representative households are necessary to account for
heterogeneity among the main sources of household income—or
among the changes in income—attributable to the phenomena or the
policies being studied. Despite the need for variety, the number of
representative households is generally small, however, usually fewer
than 10. The representative households are essentially defined by the
combination of the productive factors they own: farmers, rural wage
workers, skilled urban workers, unskilled urban workers in the formal sector, and so forth. Although simple, this disaggregation
methodology has proved to be very useful and has allowed many
insights into a variety of issues. With time, this approach led to an
increasing degree of disaggregation of the production and the
demand sides of the economy, of the degree of heterogeneity among
agents (by explicitly considering that households within a representative group were heterogeneous but in a "constant" way), of the
specification of government transfers and other types of expenditure,
and of the structure and the functioning of factor and good markets.

CGE models with representative household groups already have
a long history in taxation incidence analysis. In effect they may be
considered as the logical extension of the microeconomic incidence
analysis of the type reviewed in the first part of this volume to general equilibrium effects and to aggregate household groups.[5] However, the same models could be extended to provide inputs, such as
the precise consumption price vector, sectoral employment levels,
and the like, to conduct incidence analysis of taxation at the household level, as seen in part 1, rather than with representative groups.
Another important field of application of CGE modeling with representative household groups is concerned with the distributional

effects of trade reforms (for a recent example, see Yao and Liu 2000). Non-Walrasian models, which incorporate some description of the financial sector, have also been used extensively since the 1990s to study the distributional effects of macroeconomic stabilization and structural adjustment (Bourguignon, Branson, and de Melo 1992; Decaluwé and others 1998; and Agénor, Izquierdo, and Fofack 2001).

Chapter 15 illustrates this macroeconomic approach to distributional issues by presenting the structure of a standard CGE model combining sectoral disaggregation and representative household groups. Such models are calibrated on the basis of a social accounting matrix, which provides the definition of factors, activities, commodities, and institutions incorporated in the CGE model. The model itself is written as a set of simultaneous equations that describe the behavior of producers and consumers. These equations also include a set of constraints that correspond to equilibrium conditions in the various markets for factors and commodities, as well as for some macroeconomic aggregates (savings-investment balance, the budget of the government, and the current account of the balance of payments).

Like SAM multipliers, standard CGE with representative household groups cannot account for heterogeneous effects of a given policy within a heterogeneous group. Thus, they may miss important sources of change in poverty. Also, they do not quite comply with the three-layer structure for linking microeconomic and macroeconomic aspects of the poverty effect of policies. With the CGE and SAM models, as well as with simpler approaches like PAMS, SimSIP, or PovStat, it is clearly the bottom layer that is unsatisfactorily handled in the sense that a large part of microeconomic heterogeneity is simply ignored.

Various attempts are being made to resolve this problem, and progress will eventually remedy this weakness.[6] As mentioned earlier, however, it is not the intention of this volume to cover research currently under way at the cutting edge of poverty evaluation techniques. The chapters presented here are more practical in that they describe techniques and tools on which some experience has already been accumulated in common work that World Bank teams have been conducting for years with governments in client countries, academic researchers, bilateral aid agencies, and nongovernmental organizations.

That the tools described in this volume are not yet of universal or systematic use in the poverty evaluation of development policies shows the need to give them more exposure. At the same time, inherent weaknesses may explain why the use of these tools is not more widespread. Greater reflection on these weaknesses was thus also necessary. We hope that this volume will achieve both objectives— and that the analytical tools summarized here will be more widely used in the future. This is a necessary step in establishing firm ground upon which to develop new tools that will fill the gaps in the existing tools and will respond to unmet demand.

Notes

1. Poverty Reduction Strategy Papers (PRSPs) are the new general policy documents elaborated by the governments of developing countries that want to access concessional resources from the International Monetary Fund (IMF) and the World Bank. The PRSPs replaced in 1999–2000 the Policy Framework Papers (PFPs) written by the staff of the IMF and the World Bank in consultation with governments.

2. Other general presentations of instruments that are available for poverty and social impact analysis can be found at www.worldbank.org/poverty.

3. For example, it is still difficult to analyze the poverty effect of reforms such as "privatization" or "land reform," which involve changes in ownership of assets. Similarly, there are dynamic effects (such as the accumulation of human capital through education) or the effects on agents' expectations (such as improvement in "investment climate") whose transmission mechanisms into income and expenditures of households are not fully understood.

4. SimSIP, which stands for Simulations for Social Indicators and Poverty, does the same but using standard decomposability properties of some inequality or poverty measures rather than the original microdata.

5. In effect, this may have been one of the first uses of computable general equilibrium models, but these tended to concentrate on industrial countries; see, for example, Shoven and Whalley (1984). For an excellent application of this framework to developing countries, see the model of Devarajan and Hossain (1998) for the Philippines.

6. See in particular Chen and Ravallion (2002) and Bourguignon, Robillard, and Robinson (2002).

References

The word *processed* describes informally reproduced works that may not be commonly available through library systems.

Adelman, Irma, and Sherman Robinson. 1978. *Income Distribution Policy: A Computable General Equilibrium Model of South Korea.* Stanford, Calif.: Stanford University Press.

Agénor, Pierre-Richard, Alejandro Izquierdo, and Hippolyte Fofack. 2000. "IMMPA: A Quantitative Macroeconomic Framework for the Analysis of Poverty Reduction Strategies." World Bank Institute, Washington, D.C. (www.worldbank.org/wbi/macroeconomics/modeling/immpa.htm).

Arulpragasam, Jehan, and Carlo del Ninno. 1996. "Do Cheap Imports Harm the Poor? Rural-Urban Tradeoffs in Guinea." In David Sahn, ed., *Economic Reform and the Poor in Africa*. Oxford, U.K.: Oxford University Press.

Bourguignon, François. 2003. "The Growth Elasticity of Poverty Reduction: Explaining Heterogeneity across Countries and Time Periods." In T. Eicher and S. Turnovsky, eds., *Inequality and Growth*. Cambridge, Mass.: MIT Press.

Bourguignon, François, W. Branson, and J. DeMelo. 1989. "Macroeconomic Adjustment and Income Distribution: A Macro-Micro Simulation Model." OECD Technical Paper 1. Organisation for Economic Co-operation and Development, Paris.

Bourguignon, François, Anne-Sophie Robillard, and Sherman Robinson. 2002. "Representative vs. Real Households in the Macroeconomic Modeling of Inequality." International Food Policy Research Institute, Washington, D.C. Processed.

Chen, Shaohua, and Martin Ravallion. 2002. "Household Welfare Impacts of China's Accession to the WTO." Paper presented at the Fourth Asia Development Forum, Seoul, Korea, November 3–5, 2002. In *East Asia Integrates: A Trade Policy Agenda for Shared Growth*. Washington, D.C.: World Bank. Forthcoming.

Datt, Gaurav, and Martin Ravallion. 1992. "Growth and Redistribution Components of Changes in Poverty Measures: A Decomposition with Applications to Brazil and India in the 1980s." *Journal of Development Economics* 38 (April): 275–95.

Datt, Gaurav, and Thomas Walker. 2002. "PovStat 2.10: A Poverty Projection Toolkit, User's Manual." World Bank, Washington, D.C. Processed. (www.poverty.worldbank.org/library)

Decaluwé, Bernard, A. Patry, and L. Savard. 1998. "Quand l'eau n'est plus un don du ciel: Un MEGC appliqué au Maroc (When Water Is No Longer a Gift of God: A CGE Applied to Morocco)." *Revue d'Economie du Developpement* 0 (3-4, December): 149–87.

Devarajan, Shantayanan, and Shaikh I. Hossain. 1998. "The Combined Incidence of Taxes and Public Expenditures in the Philippines." *World Development* 26(6): 963–77.

Devarajan, Shantayanan, William R. Easterly, Delfin S. Go, C. Petersen, L. Pizzati, C. Scott, and L. Serven. 2000. "A Macroeconomic Framework for Poverty Reduction Strategy Papers." World Bank, Washington, D.C. Processed.

Lysy, Frank J., and Lance Taylor. 1980. "The General Equilibrium Model of Income Distribution." In Lance Taylor, E. Bacha, E. Cardoso, and Frank J. Lysy, eds., *Models of Growth and Distribution for Brazil*. Oxford, U.K.: Oxford University Press.

Mosley, Paul. 1999. "Micro-Macro Linkages in Financial Markets: The Impact of Financial Liberalization on Access to Rural Credit in Four African Countries." Finance and Development Research Programme Working Paper 4. University of Manchester, Manchester, U.K. Processed.

Shoven, John B., and John Whalley. 1984. "Applied General Equilibrium Models of Taxation and International Trade: An Introduction and Survey." *Journal of Economic Literature* 22(3): 1007–51.

Thorbecke, Erik. 1995. *Intersectoral Linkages and Their Impact on Rural Policy Alleviation: A Social Accounting Approach*. Vienna: United Nations Development Organization.

Wodon, Quentin, Krishnan Ramadas, and Dominique van der Mensbrugghe. 2002. "SimSIP Poverty: Poverty and Inequality Comparisons Using Group Data." World Bank, Washington, D.C. Processed. (www.worldbank.org/simsip)

PART I

Microeconomic Techniques

1

Estimating the Incidence of Indirect Taxes in Developing Countries

David E. Sahn and Stephen D. Younger

The distributional impact of the public sector's budget is a topic of enduring interest for economists and policymakers. The more recent literature on developing countries has focused almost exclusively on the expenditure side of the budget, as discussed in chapter 2. But the few available studies on tax incidence in developing countries show that some tax policies have redistributive impacts—both positive and negative—of a size comparable to the effects of the more commonly studied social sector expenditures, justifying more equal attention from analysts interested in understanding the distributional consequences of public policies.

The methods that we describe for tax incidence analysis are intuitive and computationally straightforward. They have practical limitations, which we address in the final section of this chapter. But one conceptual limitation should be addressed up front: these methods are useful only for analyzing the equity consequences of public policy. Yet good policy analysis requires consideration of both equity and efficiency consequences, and not necessarily in that order. Consequently, the type of analysis described here is only one input to a complete analysis of tax policy.

The Technique and Theoretical Background

The *MIT Dictionary of Modern Economics* defines tax incidence as describing "those who suffer a reduction in their real income resulting from the imposition of a tax." (Pearce 1986, p. 192). To accomplish this description, we use survey data to determine individual households' loss and then show how that loss is distributed across the households in the sample. To measure each household's loss from a tax, we rely on basic duality theory. A household's expenditure function, $y = e(p,u)$, is the minimum amount of money that it must spend to generate utility level u given a vector of prices p for all goods and services consumed. A household's compensating variation for a tax increase is the amount of income that it would need to keep its utility constant in the face of any price changes caused by the tax:

$$(1.1) \qquad CV = e(p_1,u^0) - e(p_0,u^0)$$

where zero indicates the initial state and one indicates the state after the tax change.

Clearly, if we could estimate the household's expenditure function, we could easily calculate the compensating variation and thus know how much real income declines as a result of the tax. Unfortunately, that is a difficult task, both in terms of data and analysis, and the methods that we use avoid it entirely by approximating the compensating variation. Consider for the moment the case in which the tax change affects only one price, p_i. Recall that by Shephard's lemma, the derivative of the expenditure function with respect to p_i is the compensated demand function for good i. The Taylor expansion of equation 1.1 is therefore

$$(1.2) \qquad CV \approx x_i^c(p^0,u^0) * \Delta p_i + \frac{1}{2} * \frac{\partial x_i^c(p^0,u^0)}{\partial p_i} * \Delta p_i^2 + \dots$$

where $x_i^c(p^0,u^0)$ is the compensated demand function and Δp_i is the change in the price of p_i caused by the tax increase. The first term in the Taylor expansion is the change in expenditure that the household would have to undertake to keep utility constant without changing its demand for good i (or any other), that being the initial quantity consumed times the price change. This is a first-order approximation to the compensating variation. Put otherwise, the compensating variation of a *marginal* change in the price of a good is simply the change in the consumption budget that is necessary to keep the consumption basket constant. In other words, the demand response to the tax may be ignored as a first approximation.

We can graph this approximation by noting that the difference in expenditures noted in equation 1.1 is equal to the integral of the compensated demand function from p_0 to p_1, again by Shephard's lemma.

$$CV = e(p_i^1, u^0) - e(p_i^0, u^0) = \int_{p_0}^{p_1} x_i^c(p, u^0)\,dp_i$$

This integral is the area to the left of the compensated demand function in figure 1.1, shown as ABDE. The first term in the Taylor expansion in equation 1.2 is equal to the area ACDE, the original quantity consumed times the price change. The second term is the triangle BCD. Higher-order terms would capture the curvature of the demand curve.

The only information generally used in incidence analysis is the first-order approximation, area ACDE. As such, behavioral changes that the tax change might induce are not accounted for.[1] We simply observe the existing pattern of demand, multiply it by a hypothesized price change, and use the result as an estimate of each household's loss in real income. Finally, if a change in tax policy changes more than one price, all the first-order terms in equation 1.2 for goods whose price changes are summed together. While such an approach cannot tell us anything about the efficiency consequences of the tax change—those depend entirely on its behavioral consequences—it has been found to be a reasonably satisfactory shortcut for the study of a policy's distributional impact.

Figure 1.1 Compensating Variation for an Ad Valorem Tax on Good i

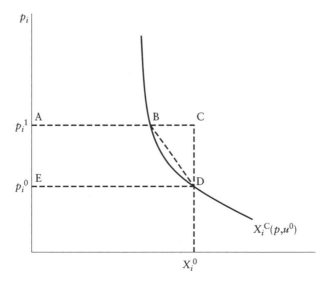

Source: Authors' illustration.

How to Do a Tax Incidence Analysis

Most analyses of indirect tax incidence are concerned with the share of taxes paid by different groups. For such analyses, the only data necessary are a variable that defines the groups and an estimate of the taxes paid by each group, where "taxes paid" is understood to be the loss in real income described above. The most common source of these data is a nationally representative household survey such as a Living Standards Measurement Survey (Grosh and Glewwe 2000) or a household income and expenditure survey. (Summaries of these surveys, as published by national statistical agencies, might suffice if they are disaggregated according to the grouping of interest.)

Usually, the groups are defined by welfare levels—poor and non-poor, or each quintile of the welfare distribution—so a variable is required that ranks people by welfare, and the preferred choice in the vast majority of studies is household expenditures per capita or per adult equivalent. But other groupings are possible, such as geographic location (by political region or urban-rural breakdown), gender, ethnicity, or age cohort. In all cases, these variables are almost always readily available for each individual or household in the survey data.

Estimates of the taxes paid by each group are more difficult, and it is helpful to explain first what to do with such an estimate, returning to the question of how to get it later. The simplest sort of comparison notes that group A pays so much of a particular tax, group B so much, and so forth. For the most common case, where we want to group people by welfare status, the groups might be poor and nonpoor, or people in each quantile of the welfare distribution. But in fact, it is easy to make a much more attractive comparison based on the theory of welfare dominance, which also offers the advantage of involving individual agents rather than groups of agents.

The theory of welfare dominance provides general criteria that allow us to conclude that one distribution of welfare is better than another for broad classes of social welfare functions (Saposnik, 1981; Shorrocks, 1983; Foster and Shorrocks, 1988; Yitzhaki and Slemrod, 1991; Lambert, 1993). One particular application of this theory is particularly useful for tax incidence analysis. Shorrocks (1983) shows that if the generalized Lorenz curve for one distribution of welfare is everywhere above the generalized Lorenz curve for another, then the first distribution is preferable to the second under any social welfare function that is increasing in the welfare variable, anonymous, and equality-preferring.[2] By increasing we mean that a larger value of the welfare variable, w_i, is better than a smaller one for each individual i, that is, there is no satiation. By anonymous we mean that the welfare function does not pay attention to the identity of each person in the ordering or to whether a person changes position from one ordering to another. By equality-preferring we mean that if a distribution is generated by taking an existing distribution and transferring a small amount of welfare from a better-off individual to a worse-off one, the new distribution is preferred to the old. The generality of this comparison makes it quite attractive. To carry it out, we need to construct only two generalized Lorenz curves, one before the tax and one after, and then see if one curve is clearly above the other.

In practice, however, we have found it useful to use a slightly more restrictive condition. If we assume that the tax (change) of interest has no efficiency consequences, then the mean of the distribution of tax payments will be constant, allowing the use of Lorenz curves rather than generalized Lorenz curves. In addition, the Lorenz curves tend to be quite close together, even for major tax changes, so that visually, it is more attractive to work with concentration curves, defined as

$$C(i) = \left(\sum_{k=1}^{i} T_k \bigg/ \sum_{k=1}^{n} T_k \right)$$

which is the same formula as the Lorenz curve with the total tax paid substituted for welfare. Note that observations remain ordered by welfare, not by taxes paid, so that $C(i)$ gives the share of taxes paid by the poorest i/n households or individuals in the sample. If the concentration curve for a tax is everywhere below the Lorenz curve of income/welfare, then increasing that tax by a small amount and refunding the proceeds in proportion to welfare (the Lorenz curve) will increase social welfare for all social welfare functions that are increasing, anonymous, and equality-preferring. Similarly, if the concentration curve of one tax is everywhere below that of another tax, then increasing the first tax slightly and reducing the second tax such that total tax revenue is unchanged will improve social welfare for the same class of social welfare functions (Younger and others 1999).

Note that it is possible to make poor-nonpoor comparisons based on Lorenz and concentration curves, and also comparisons of each quantile's share, but the use of the entire distribution is more general than either of these comparisons and equally easy to calculate. Standard errors for these curves are more difficult to calculate (Davidson and Duclos 1997), but a specialized software package, DAD, is now available to do this.[3]

Calculating Taxes Paid by Households or Groups

We now return to the question of evaluating the cost to a given household of an ad valorem tax. Economists since David Ricardo have recognized that the statutory incidence of tax—those who have to transfer the tax to the government—is not the same as the economic incidence of the tax—those whose real purchasing power declines because of the tax. Much of public economics involves understanding exactly how different statutory taxes are shifted among various agents, based on models of their behavioral responses to the taxes. The type of empirical tax incidence study that we describe here ignores all but the simplest aspects of this theory. Typically, we assume that indirect taxes on goods are shifted entirely to consumers, a standard result if markets are competitive and the taxes apply only to final sales (or value added). This assumption ignores any effect that the taxes may have on firms' welfare (or rather, the welfare of the firm's owners) and, more important, any cascading of taxes through the economy's production structure. For import duties, we usually assume that all prices, including those for domestically produced goods of the same type, rise in proportion to the duty rate. Again, this is true in the simple case where markets are competitive and the country is small (although in this case we should note that some of the benefits of the tax go to domestic producers rather than the government).[4]

In addition to deciding whose purchasing power actually declines when a tax is increased, we also need to calculate how much they lose. In the simplest of cases, where taxes are collected according to the letter of the law, this calculation is straightforward for ad valorem taxes. The tax paid is simply the tax rate times the pretax value of expenditures:

$$(1.3) \qquad\qquad T_{i,j} = t_j p_{i,j} x_{i,j} = \frac{t_j}{1+t_j} e_{i,j}$$

where $T_{i,j}$ is household i's total loss in purchasing power for a tax on good j; $p_{i,j} x_{i,j}$ is household i's pretax amount of expenditure on good j; t_j is the tax rate; and $e_{i,j}$ is the post-tax amount of expenditure on good j. The fact that $T_{i,j}$ is proportional to $e_{i,j}$, the expenditure that would be reported in a household survey, is convenient, for reasons that we come to shortly.

Unfortunately, taxes are not paid according to the letter of the law, both because of corruption and because many transactions in developing countries occur in informal markets not subject to the government's tax handles, which are almost always formal sector firms or goods passing through the port. In Madagascar, for example, we found that actual value added tax (VAT) collections were about 8 percent of formal sector value added in 1995, even though the official VAT rate was 25 percent. And of course, formal sector value added is relatively small in Madagascar. Even if we assume that tax evasion and avoidance occur in such a manner that the result is an equiproportional increase in market prices for all consumers that is something less than the statutory tax rate, we face the practical problem of deciding what tax rate to use in equation 1.3. Our sense is that probably the best one can do without expending considerable resources is to gather information on tax revenues and tax bases from the authorities and use the ratios as estimates of the "effective" tax rate for that particular tax.

There is one case in which this problem can be avoided. If we assume that a tax's incidence is proportional to expenditures, whatever the proportion, for all households, then we can simply use observed expenditures in equation 1.3, because the proportion cancels out of the numerator and denominator. This only works, however, for one tax rate. Any attempt to combine two or more items with different tax rates requires that the calculation of taxes paid be made.

Examples of Application

There is an emerging body of literature examining household tax incidence in developing countries that follows the framework presented above. Most recently, using data on expenditures from the 1992 Integrated Household Survey, Chen, Matovu, and Reinikka (2001) conduct a welfare dominance analysis of tax incidence in Uganda. They find that the tax structure was progressive before reforms and remained so after reforms, indicating that the burden of tax reforms had not fallen disproportionately on the poor. Most individual tax categories were also progressive before reforms, with the exception of the excise tax on paraffin (kerosene), which is heavily consumed by poor households. Export taxes on coffee, one of Uganda's main exports, remained highly regressive, as the burden of the tax is shifted to relatively poorer rural farmers. Petroleum taxes (except paraffin) remained progressive.[5] The study concludes that reducing export taxes on coffee and taxes on paraffin would benefit the poor. Other tax reforms implemented in the 1990s were generally pro-poor. The pay-as-you-earn tax remains the most progressive tax, as it applies to the formal sector where the nonpoor are employed. The study also finds that substituting value added taxes for sales taxes does not necessarily worsen the welfare of the poor, since most goods consumed by the poor were zero-rated.

A similar study by Younger and others (1999) examines household tax incidence in Madagascar. The study finds that most taxes are progressive, with the exception of kerosene taxes and export duties on vanilla. It proposes that a movement away from trade taxes and toward broadly based value added or income taxes would be both more equitable and efficient, since they would apply to the formal sector where the nonpoor are employed. It also concludes that taxes on petroleum products (except kerosene, which is used heavily by the poor) are highly progressive and also provide a good tax handle for the government. Thus, it proposes concentration of duties on gasoline and reduction of duties on kerosene. Similar to the finding on export duties on coffee in Uganda, this study also finds that export duties on vanilla are more regressive than many other taxes, because the burden is passed on to vanilla producers who are rural farmers and not as wealthy as the population in general. Thus, the study concludes that a movement away from export duties would have a positive distributional impact.

Using data from the 1988 Ghana Living Standards Survey, Younger (1993) presents a tax incidence analysis from Ghana. Its findings are similar to those from the studies conducted in Uganda and Madagascar—broad-based taxes are either proportional (sales taxes) or progressive (income and property taxes), and a greater reliance on broad-based taxes would improve both equity and efficiency. Petroleum taxes are proportional or slightly progressive, even after taking into account the intermediate effects (such as on the cost of the public transit sector). However, the tax on kerosene, used heavily by poorer households, is regressive. As in the above-mentioned cases, this study also finds that the export duty on cocoa in Ghana is regressive, placing an undue burden on rural farmers, and should be reduced to address equity considerations.

In the context of ongoing tax reforms in Papua New Guinea, Gibson (1998) discusses the impact of introducing VAT on consumer welfare. The paper uses a variant of the proposed technique, where the "distributional characteristic" of each good is defined as a measure of how heavily its consumption is concentrated among the poor.[6] Gibson argues that instead of removing existing distortions by virtue of being a uniform consumption tax, a VAT introduces new distortions through the proposed "merit-good" exemptions: on financial services, health and educational services, and public road transport. Using data from the 1996 Papua New Guinea Household Survey, Gibson also finds that the proposed exemptions are on commodities whose consumption is not concentrated among the poor, including axes, bush knives, and garden tools; school fees and children's clothing; pots and pans; and salt, rice, and tinned fish. He proposes that exemptions on rice and tinned fish fulfill both merit-good and poverty alleviation objectives and may be better candidates for VAT exemptions.

Using data from the 1993 Living Standards and Development Survey for South Africa, Alderman and del Ninno (1999) employ a similar methodology to assess how well VAT exemptions have been targeted and also rank commodities in terms of tax efficiency and equity, as well as the impact of exemptions on household food consumption. They estimate the ratio of the "welfare cost" to the "revenue benefit," which gives a cost-benefit ratio to assess commodity-specific exemptions.[7] A ratio larger than one indicates that the welfare cost is greater relative to the revenue generated, which indicates that the commodity is a good candidate for tax exemption. They find that maize, which is currently exempted from VAT, is the best choice for low tax rates from the standpoints of equity, efficiency, and the impact on the nutritional intake of the poor. In contrast, they find that lower tax rates on fluid milk, which is currently exempted from VAT, and meat, for which an exemption has been proposed, are not good instruments for achieving equity or nutritional objectives. This reflects the importance of maize in the consumption bundle of the poor, in contrast to other commodities, and the fact that, for example, a tax exemption on maize and milk would have the same effect on total revenues. Thus, a maize exemption would have a more positive impact on the nutrient consumption of those at the bottom end of the income distribution for a comparable cost in terms of forgone revenues. They also find that tax exemptions for beans, sugar, and kerosene have favorable rankings from the viewpoint of equity.

Ahmad and Stern conducted much of the pioneering work on tax incidence during the 1980s for India and Pakistan. Using 1979–80 data, Ahmad and Stern (1984) show that taxes on cereals, fuel, and "light" are less socially desirable relative to a tax on clothing for social welfare functions that are averse to inequality. In one exercise, they show that raising the tax on cereals by one rupee and lowering the tax on sugar and gur by one rupee maximizes revenue, while holding the welfare of all households constant. In another, they show that reducing the tax on cereals and increasing the tax on sugar while holding revenue constant increases the welfare of the poorest rural household.

In a later study on India, Ahmad and Stern (1987) examine the effect of replacing a number of direct and indirect taxes on consumption with a simple, proportional, value added tax. Using data from 1979–80, the authors find that switching to a VAT would be equivalent to reducing the real expenditures of the poorest rural households by as much as 6.8 percent and increasing those of the richest rural households by more than 3 percent. Similarly, the real expenditures of the poorest urban households are reduced by about 4.8 percent, whereas those of the richest are increased by 4.2 percent. This indicates that the welfare of the poor would be reduced if a proportional VAT replaced existing indirect consumption taxes.

Ahmad and Stern (1987, 1991) also use a marginal analysis to compare the distributional impact of taxes on income with that of taxes on commodities.[8] At higher levels of inequality aversion, they find that an extra unit of revenue is socially much more desirable if it comes from a tax on income rather than from a tax on cereals. In addition, the authors conclude that at higher levels of inequality aversion, import duties are the most attractive form of indirect tax revenue.

Ahmad and Stern (1990) conduct a similar study on marginal tax reform in Pakistan. First, under the assumption that shadow prices of goods are proportional to producer prices, where the shadow price represents the increase in the value of the social welfare function when an extra unit of public sector output is made available, the authors show that at higher levels of inequality aversion, wheat and pulses—which consume a large proportion of poor households' budgets—are not desirable candidates for sources for additional tax revenue, whereas housing, fuel, and light are. After relaxing the assumption that shadow prices are proportional to producer prices, the authors similarly find that goods such as wheat and pulses are not desirable candidates for additional tax revenue at high levels of inequality aversion. However, when shadow prices are incorporated for goods with high shadow prices, their desirability as candidates for taxation changes. For example, rice becomes a relatively more attractive candidate for taxation than it is when shadow prices are not taken into consideration. The reason, as the authors explain, is that rice has a high shadow price relative to the market price (since it is an exportable), which implies that the government should discourage domestic consumption of this valuable commodity by taxing it. In conclusion, the authors say that holding other things constant, a good is a less desirable commodity for a tax increase if its consumption is concentrated among the poor, if it has a low shadow price, and its demand is more price elastic in terms of revenue increase.

Ahmad and Stern (1991) also assess the utility of introducing a VAT in Pakistan to address distributional and revenue concerns. They state that a single-rate VAT for developing countries is inappropriate, since a number of agricultural sectors cannot be covered under a uniform VAT. The authors suggest, however, that a tiered VAT system with zero rating for exports, exemptions for the agricultural sector, a standard rate of 10 percent, and a luxury rate of 20 percent, together with excises, could be revenue-neutral while having a progressive impact on income distribution.

General Evaluation and Operational Hints

The great advantage of the methods for tax incidence analysis discussed here is their simplicity. With a standard household survey, an analyst who is familiar with the tax system and market structure of a country can usually obtain a sensible estimate of a tax's incidence in a few hours. The requisite programming skills are minimal, and a convenient software package, DAD, is available that calculates concentration curves and other summary measures of incidence easily, with standard errors.

The simplicity of the results—"group k pays x percent of tax (change) j"—is also attractive to a broad public interested in economic policy. Even those who find most economic analysis incomprehensible (or nonsensical) can easily understand the meaning and the relevance of this type of result.

Of course, simplicity often comes with inaccuracy. There are several potential sources of inaccuracy in these methods. First, because the methods do not take into account behavioral responses to a tax change, they provide only a first-order approximation of a tax's true incidence. As such, they are more appropriate for the analysis of marginal changes (what happens if the VAT is raised from 15 percent to 16 percent?) than for large policy changes (what happens if a VAT is substituted for import duties?). We are not aware of a literature that tries to calibrate how inaccurate these methods might be in analyzing the incidence of large tax changes in developing countries, although Banks, Blundell, and Lewbel (1996) found that first-order approximations of a change in the United Kingdom's VAT from 0.0 to 17.5 percent (the actual rate) were inaccurate.

A second source of inaccuracy is the use of simple assumptions about how statutory taxes translate into economic incidence. Almost uniformly, markets are assumed to be competitive so that buyers bear the burden of all consumption taxes. More egregiously, questions of tax avoidance through informal markets or corruption are mostly ignored, even though the ratio of actual taxation to expenditures is often a small fraction of the amount that the statutory rates suggest should be collected. Unfortunately, considerably more complex analysis of the behavior of both consumers and producers in the relevant markets is required to address these limitations (see chapter 12 on multimarket models). Tax avoidance also complicates the analysis of taxes that ostensibly have the same tax rate. If evasion differs across products, then even estimation of a uniform VAT faces the problems of aggregation across commodities with different effective tax rates.

A third source of inaccuracy comes from the fact that many indirect taxes, even those like the VAT that are intended to fall only on final sales, are effectively levied on intermediate goods. In these cases, even with the simplifying assumptions of competitive markets, one must take into account the nature of production in the economy to understand the incidence of the tax for consumers. While it is possible to approximate these indirect effects using only an input-output table (Rajemison and Younger 2000), most analyses use a computable general equilibrium model with the consequent increase in complexity and cost. This issue is handled in detail in chapters 13 and 15. An obvious recommendation, then, is that the methods are better applied to taxes whose burden clearly falls directly on consumers, advice that excludes taxes such as excise duties on petroleum products and import duties on production inputs that are important in developing countries.

Given the uncertainty about effective tax rates in developing countries, another recommendation is that these methods are more likely to be accurate when considering taxes on individual goods or on sets of goods where effective tax rates are likely to be similar. That is because in these cases one does not need to know the tax rate, only that it is proportional to expenditures. Most analyses can then be conducted using only the household expenditure information.

Finally, we reiterate our caution from the introduction: these methods are about equity, but tax policy analysis must also consider both economic and administrative efficiency. It must be clear in particular that if demand responses may be ignored as a first approximation when evaluating the welfare effects of a small change in indirect taxation, that is not the case for total tax receipts. Examining the impact of large changes in tax receipts requires going beyond a first approximation to model economywide behavioral responses to the policy changes.

Notes

The authors of chapter 1 thank Ruchira Bhattamishra for her research assistance.

1. The second term in equation 1.2 does account for induced behavioral changes, the move up the demand curve. Including it in our calculation

would yield an improved, second-order approximation to the compensating variation, but it requires estimating a demand system.

2. The generalized Lorenz curve is defined by

$$L(i) = \left(\sum_{k=1}^{i} w_k \bigg/ \sum_{k=1}^{n} w_k \right) * \mu(w)$$

where $L(i)$ is the generalized Lorenz ordinate and $\mu(w)$ is the mean of the distribution W. In words, the generalized Lorenz curve plots the cumulative share of individuals in the sample (indexed by i) on the X-axis against the cumulative share of the welfare variable multiplied by its mean on the Y-axis. The Lorenz curve is identical but not scaled by the mean.

3. DAD is available on the Web at http://132.203.59.36:83/.

4. We are not aware of an analysis that tries to calculate this aspect of an import duty's incidence across households.

5. Taking into account the intermediate effects of a petroleum tax diminished the progressivity of this result.

6. The welfare effect of a marginal price change is given by the weighted sum of each household's consumption of the taxed good(s). The weights reflect the social marginal value of consumption by each household, with higher weights given to consumption by the poor.

7. The "welfare cost" is based on the change in the unit cost of the commodity multiplied by a welfare weight (with more weight being put on the cost to poorer consumers) aggregated across all households. The "revenue benefit" is based on the change in revenue from the new tax, aggregated across all goods and all households.

8. The commodities chosen for taxation are those with low demand elasticities.

References

The word *processed* describes informally reproduced works that may not be commonly available through library systems.

Ahmad, Ehtisham, and Nicholas Stern. 1984. "The Theory of Reform and Indian Indirect Taxes." *Journal of Public Economics* 25(3): 259–98.

———. 1987. "Alternative Sources of Government Revenue: Illustrations from India, 1979–80." In David Newbery and Nicholas Stern, eds. *The Theory of Taxation for Developing Countries*. Oxford, U.K.: Oxford University Press.

———. 1990. "Tax Reform and Shadow Prices for Pakistan." *Oxford Economic Papers* 42(1): 135–59.

———. 1991. *The Theory and Practice of Tax Reform in Developing Countries*. Cambridge, U.K.: Cambridge University Press.

Alderman, Harold, and Carlo del Ninno. 1999. "Poverty Issues for Zero Rating VAT in South Africa." *Journal of African Economies* 8(2): 182–208.

Banks, James, Richard Blundell, and Arthur Lewbel. 1996. "Tax Reform and Welfare Measurement: Do We Need Demand System Estimates?" *Economic Journal* 106: 1227–41.

Chen, Duanije, John Matovu, and Ritva Reinikka. 2001. "A Quest for Revenue and Tax Incidence." In Ritva Reinikka and Paul Collier, eds., *Uganda's Recovery: The Role of Farms, Firms and Government.* Washington, D.C.: World Bank.

Davidson, Russell, and Jean-Yves Duclos. 1997. "Statistical Inference for the Measurement of the Incidence of Taxes and Transfers." *Econometrica* 65: 1453–65.

Foster, James E., and Anthony F. Shorrocks. 1988. "Poverty Orderings." *Econometrica* 56: 173–77.

Gibson, John. 1998. "Indirect Tax Reform and the Poor in Papua New Guinea." *Pacific Economic Bulletin* 13(2): 29–39.

Grosh, Margaret E., and Paul Glewwe, eds. 2000. *Designing Household Survey Questionnaires for Developing Countries: Lessons from Fifteen Years of the Living Standards Measurement Study.* Washington, D.C.: World Bank.

Lambert, Peter. 1993. *The Distribution and Redistribution of Income: A Mathematical Analysis.* 2d ed. Manchester, U.K.: Manchester University Press.

Pearce, David W. 1986. *The MIT Dictionary of Modern Economics.* 3d ed. Cambridge, Mass.: MIT Press.

Rajemison, Harivelo, and Stephen D. Younger. 2000. "Indirect Tax Incidence in Madagascar: Estimations Using the Input-Output Table." CFNPP Working Paper 106. Cornell University, Cornell Food and Nutrition Policy Program, Ithaca, N.Y. Processed.

Saposnik, Rubin. 1981. "Rank-Dominance in Income Distributions." *Public Choice* 36: 147–51.

Shorrocks, Anthony F. 1983. "Ranking Income Distributions." *Economica* 50: 3–17.

Shoven, John B., and John Whalley. 1984. "Applied General Equilibrium Models of Taxation and International Trade: An Introduction and Survey." *Journal of Economic Literature* 22(3):1007–51.

Yitzhaki, Shlomo, and Joel Slemrod. 1991. "Welfare Dominance: An Application to Commodity Taxation." *American Economic Review* 81:480–96.

Younger, Stephen D. 1993. Estimating Tax Incidence in Ghana: An Exercise Using Household Data." CFNPP Working Paper 48. Cornell University, Cornell Food and Nutrition Policy Program, Ithaca, N.Y.

Younger, Stephen D., David E. Sahn, Steven Haggblade, and Paul A. Dorosh. 1999. "Tax Incidence in Madagascar: An Analysis Using Household Data." *World Bank Economic Review* 13: 303–31.

2

Analyzing the Incidence of Public Spending

Lionel Demery

This chapter is about public spending and how to assess who benefits from it. It describes benefit incidence analysis, highlights good practice, and provides some guidance on how to estimate and interpret its results. Public subsidies are justified on a number of grounds. Market failure and the presence of pure public goods call for government intervention on *efficiency* grounds. But the case for public subsidies is also based on *equity* considerations. Helping the poor escape from poverty has traditionally been considered a responsibility of the state. The provision of basic services for the poor is one of the most effective instruments governments have to achieve this objective. But it is not the only one. The analysis in this chapter is based on the following premises:

• First, public expenditures can be effective in reducing poverty only when the *policy setting* is right. It is hardly worth increasing spending on primary education for girls if distortions in labor markets prevent female school graduates from securing employment. It is futile to increase spending on agricultural extension or research if overvalued exchange rates make agricultural activity unprofitable. Pro-poor expenditures must be accompanied by pro-poor policies.

• Second, it is assumed that the public expenditure process (including budget management, accountability, transparency, and so on) is based on outcomes and impacts and not just on line items and inputs. Simply spending money on the provision of a service, without attending to the efficiency with which that spending generates services and to the impact on the intended beneficiaries, is not what is recommended here (see Filmer, Hammer, and Pritchett 1998 and chapter 9 in this volume).

• Third, public policy in general, and public expenditure decisions in particular, must be based on a sound understanding of the needs and preferences of the population at large. The provision of public services should be viewed as a collaboration between governments, on the one hand, and households on the other. To make this collaboration effective, there must be a two-way flow of information, with governments constantly "listening" to households, and households, in turn, being informed of government objectives and their rights under explicit contracts or covenants. This chapter is concerned with one dimension of the information flow: how can governments be informed about the needs and behavior of their clients, especially the poor? Who indeed benefits from public spending?

The Problem

Economists have long been interested in measuring the benefits that are derived from public spending. For government expenditures that simply involve income transfers, such measurement is not problematic, since the monetary value of the benefit received is clear. The problem arises when governments subsidize the provision of goods and services and particularly when governments take on responsibilities to provide them. When such services are provided by the state, it is much more difficult to measure the benefit obtained by users of the service. In standard microeconomic theory, the price is usually taken as a good measure of value. But for pure public goods, and for private goods that are provided by the state, price is not a good guide. Sometimes no price is charged, but this does not mean that the service is not valued. Even when prices are charged, the provision of the service is often rationed, so that the price paid does not necessarily reflect its value to the consumer. Yet in deciding which services to provide, and to gain some idea of which groups in society benefit, some (monetary) measure of the distribution of the benefits derived from publicly provided services is called for.

The Solutions

Much recent work stems from Aaron and McGuire (1970), who set out the basic principles to be followed in assessing how public expenditures benefit individuals. They argued that a rationed, publicly provided good or service should be evaluated at the individual's own valuation of the good (the individual's demand, or *virtual,* price). Such prices will vary from individual to individual. But the difficulties inherent in estimating these valuations (reviewed by Cornes 1995) led to less demanding approaches, in which publicly provided goods and services are valued at their *marginal cost* (Brennan 1976). Since then, the literature has been characterized by two broad approaches. The first emphasizes the measurement of *individual preferences* for the goods in question, based on refinements of the Aaron and McGuire methodology—what van de Walle (1998) terms the "behavioral" approach. These analyses are well founded in microeconomic theory, but they are data demanding, requiring, for example, knowledge of the underlying demand functions of individuals or households. The second approach is *benefit incidence* analysis, which combines the cost of providing public services with information on their use in order to generate distributions of the benefit of government spending. This has become an established approach in developing countries since the pathbreaking work by Meerman (1979) on Malaysia and by Selowsky (1979) on Colombia. Note that because this analysis calls for information on the use of subsidized public services (or the receipt of public transfers), it can be applied only to "assignable" public expenditure—subsidies on private goods and services. The fact that most government spending cannot be readily assigned to individuals (being nonrival in nature) means that incidence analysis can cover only a small proportion of the public budget (typically around one-third of the budget). It should also be noted that incidence analysis does not deal very well with issues of service *quality.* This issue is taken up in chapters 8 and 9 of this volume. Finally, this chapter is concerned with the *average* incidence of public spending. In other words, how does existing spending affect the distribution of income? The incidence of changes in public spending—the marginal incidence—is distributed quite differently. Marginal incidence is reviewed in chapter 3.

The Technique: What Is Benefit Incidence?

Benefit incidence shows who is benefiting from public services and describes how government spending affects the welfare of different groups of people or individual households. It does this by combining information about the *unit costs* of providing those services (obtained usually from government or service-provider data) with information on the *use* of these services (usually obtained from the households themselves through a sample survey). In effect, the analysis imputes to those households using a particular service the cost of providing that service. This imputation is the amount by which household income would have to increase if it had to pay for the service used.

Taking the example of government spending on education, this imputation can be formally written as:

$$(2.1) \qquad X_j \equiv \sum_{i=1}^{3} E_{ij} \frac{S_i}{E_i} \equiv \sum_{i=1}^{3} \frac{E_{ij}}{E_i} S_i$$

where X_j is the amount of the education subsidy that benefits group j, S and E refer respectively to the government education subsidy and the number of public school enrollments, and the subscript i denotes the level of education (three levels are specified in equation 2.1—primary, secondary, and tertiary).[1] The benefit incidence of total education spending imputed to group j is given by the number of primary enrollments from the group (E_{pj}) times the unit cost of a primary school place, plus the number of secondary enrollments times the secondary unit cost, plus the number of tertiary enrollments times the unit cost of tertiary education. Note that S_i / E_i is the *mean* unit subsidy of an enrollment at education level i.

The *share* of total education spending imputed to group j (x_j) is:

$$(2.2) \qquad x_j \equiv \sum_{i=1}^{3} \frac{E_{ij}}{E_i} \left(\frac{S_i}{S} \right) \equiv \sum_{i=1}^{3} e_{ij} s_i$$

It can be seen that this share depends on two major determinants:

- The e_{ij}'s, which are the shares of the group in total service use (enrollments in this case). These reflect *household behavior.*
- The s_i's, or the shares of public spending across the different types of service, reflecting *government behavior.*

Understanding how the benefits of public spending are distributed, and doing something about it, therefore requires an understanding of how both governments and households behave—including how they are constrained in making choices.

Equation 2.2 defines only one unit subsidy for each level of service. In some applications regional and other (ethnic) variations in subsidies are also taken into account. Equation 2.2 would then become:

$$x_j \equiv \sum_{k=1}^{n} \sum_{i=1}^{3} \frac{E_{ijk}}{E_i} \left(\frac{S_{ik}}{S} \right) \equiv \sum_{k=1}^{n} \sum_{i=1}^{3} e_{ijk} s_{ik}$$

where the k subscript denotes the region specified in the unit cost estimate, there being n regions. For simplicity the k subscript is dropped throughout, although in some countries this distinction is important. A variant of this approach bypasses the need for estimating the unit subsidy and focuses only on whether a service is used or not. For each service, households are assigned an "accessibility dummy" taking the value of unity for those that used the service, and zero for those that did not (the s_i's are set to unity). The distribution of this dummy across income groups provides a measure of the equity of service provision.

Examples of Benefit Incidence Analysis

There is now a large literature on the benefit incidence of government spending (Demery 2000). Here I emphasize mainly the benefit incidence of spending of the social sectors (health and education). One good example is selected from each sector to illustrate the nuts and bolts of estimating the incidence of public spending.

Education Spending

The incidence of education spending in Indonesia is taken to illustrate the methodology (see World Bank 1993 and van de Walle 1992). Table 2.1 provides estimates of the benefit incidence of education spending in Indonesia. The format of the table is important. The highlighted columns reflect the e_{ij}'s—the shares of the quintiles in the use of services. The highlighted row shows the s_i's—the allocation of public spending across the services.

These results indicate:

• The poorest quintile benefits most from the primary schooling subsidy and least from tertiary spending. The opposite pattern applies to the richest quintile.

• The *combination* of the two sets of ratios (the e_{ij}'s and s_i's) determines the overall benefit incidence of education spending. Given the quintile shares of enrollments and the allocations of public spending across the subsectors, the poorest quintile is shown to gain just 15 percent of total education spending, compared with 29 percent for the richest quintile. The fact that lower-income groups hardly use secondary and tertiary education services (which together absorb just under two-fifths of the education budget) means that their share of the education budget is significantly less than that of the richer groups.

• Although spending on primary education is well targeted to the poor, education spending as a whole is not. The Indonesia findings were based on mean unit subsidies for each education level. Disaggregating subsidies further can change the results (box 2.1).

Table 2.1 Benefit Incidence of Public Spending on Education in Indonesia, 1989

| | Primary | | Secondary | | | | Tertiary | | All education | | |
| | | | Junior | | Senior | | | | | | Subsidy as share of total household expenditure |
Quintile	Per capita (Rp)	Share of subsidy (e_{ij}) (%)	Per capita (Rp.)	Share of subsidy (e_{ij}) (%)	Per capita (Rp.)	Share of subsidy (e_{ij}) (%)	Per capita (Rp.)	Share of subsidy (e_{ij}) (%)	Per capita (Rp.)	Share of total subsidy (%)	
1	2,179	22	179	7	56	3	0	0	2,414	15	12
2	2,111	22	354	14	107	6	1	0	2,573	17	9
3	2,094	22	508	19	210	11	17	1	2,830	18	8
4	1,828	20	684	26	424	24	88	7	3,025	20	6
5	1,285	14	867	34	956	56	1,168	92	4,274	29	5
Indonesia	1,892	100	523	100	358	100	264	100	3,037	100	7
Memorandum: Government spending:											
(millions of Rp)	300,124		83,017	56,738	41,885	436,764					
% share (s_i)		62	17	12	9	100					

Source: World Bank (1993).

• But the benefit incidence is *progressive*, because the subsidy received by the poor represents a larger share of the income (or total expenditure) of the poor compared with higher income groups (see the final column in table 2.1).

USING GRAPHICS.   Graphical presentation of benefit incidence results can be helpful in showing how targeted and progressive subsidies are. Figure 2.1 reports the Lorenz curve for Indonesia in 1989. This curve tracks the cumulative distribution of total household expenditures (or welfare) against the cumulative population ranked by per capita expenditures. The figure also shows the concentration curves of education subsidies.[2] A comparison of these curves conveys some important messages. These curves are statistical estimates and as such allow for the estimation of standard errors (Davidson and Duclos 1997). That in turn allows testing of whether these curves are statistically different—having different ordinates (box 2.2). Comparisons with the Lorenz curve reveal how *progressive* or *regressive* the subsidy is. Concentration curves lying above the Lorenz curve are progressive, in that they indicate that the subsidy is more equally distributed than income (or expenditure in this case). As a proportion of total income, poorer groups gain more than the better-off. By comparing the concentration curves with the 45° diagonal, analysts

Figure 2.1 Indonesia, Benefit Incidence of Education Spending, 1989

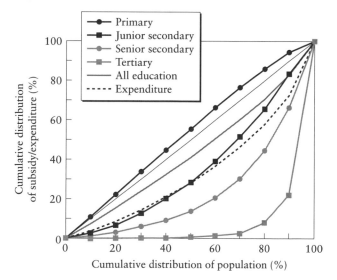

Source: World Bank (1993).

Box 2.1 Aggregating Unit Subsidies May
Mask Inequality

Where spending is very unevenly distributed geographically (or in other ways), the use of aggregate unit subsidies can mask inequality in public spending. But it need not. Two examples that illustrate this point are given here. In both South Africa and Madagascar, it was possible to disaggregate unit subsidies on education. In South Africa Castro-Leal (1996) obtained five levels of unit subsidy based on the budgets of the different "Houses" of government, were divided along racial grounds. Unit subsidies varied enormously. The primary education subsidy varied from just Rand 708 for Homeland Africans to R 3,298 for whites. Despite these differences, enrollment rates were high, even among the poorest groups receiving the lowest subsidy. The net primary enrollment rate among Homeland Africans in the poorest household quintile was 85 percent in 1994 (compared with 90 percent for whites).

In Madagascar, it was possible to distinguish unit subsidies in the six main regions of the country. The primary unit subsidy varied from FMG 34 to FMG 71 (World Bank 1996). Enrollment rates were low for the poor. The net primary enrollment rate in the poorest population quintile was just 27 percent, compared with 72 percent for the richest quintile. This low rate might be a result of the lower unit subsidies in some regions. So in contrast to South Africa, unit subsidies did not vary as much in Madagascar, but enrollment rates declined sharply at low-income levels.

Two estimates of the benefit incidence of education spending are reported in the box table. One is based on the disaggregated unit subsidies, while the other is computed using an average unit subsidy at each education level. In South Africa the aggregation of unit subsidies makes a significant difference to benefit incidence. Whereas the poorest quintile is shown to gain just 19 percent of primary spending in 1994 using race-specific unit subsidies, the share increases to 26 percent if the unit subsidy is averaged across races. The share going to the richest quintile is halved when aggregate unit subsidies are employed. For education spending as a whole, the use of mean subsidies makes it appear as though each quintile received roughly its proportionate share of the education budget. But in actual fact, the poorest quintile gained only 14 percent and the richest 35 percent of total education spending when unit cost variations between the races were taken into account.

The Madagascar estimates tell a quite different story. Here, the use of national average unit subsidies (at each level of schooling) changes the benefit incidence estimates only marginally compared with the use of region-specific unit subsidies. The differences are literally matters of decimal points. Why the difference with South Africa? Three factors explain this different outcome. First, the unit subsidies were far more variable in South Africa, reflecting as they did, the years of the apartheid regime. Although significant, the variations in unit subsidies in Madagascar were modest in comparison. Second, the population within the quintiles was distributed across regions in Madagascar, so that there was some variability in the unit subsidies within quintiles. In South Africa the population in the poorest quintile was almost entirely black, so that only the lowest unit subsidy applied. Third, enrollment rates were uniformly high in South Africa, whereas in Madagascar the variations across income groups were significant. It is likely that the lower enrollment rates among the poorer groups in Madagascar resulted from the lower unit subsidies allocated to them. Thus when national average unit subsidies are used, although the unit subsidy variations are missed, their effects on the enrollment patterns across income are captured and reflected to some extent in the benefit incidence estimates (through the e variables).

Benefit Incidence of Education Spending in South Africa and Madagascar (percent)

Population quintile	Share of primary subsidy		Share of secondary subsidy		Share of tertiary subsidy		Share of education subsidy	
	Dis-aggregated unit subsidies	Mean unit subsidy	Dis-aggregated unit subsidies	Mean unit subsidy	Dis-aggregated unit subsidies	Mean unit subsidy	Dis-aggregated unit subsidies	Mean unit subsidy
South Africa (1994)								
1	18.9	25.8	11.5	18.8	6.1	6.1	14.1	19.9
2	17.7	23.3	15.0	22.6	9.9	10.0	15.4	20.7
3	16.5	19.7	16.3	22.7	14.0	14.3	16.0	19.7
4	19.1	17.8	18.6	19.4	22.9	22.5	19.6	19.1
5	27.8	13.5	38.6	16.6	47.2	47.1	34.9	20.3
Madagascar (1993)								
1	16.8	17.2	1.9	2.0	0.0	0.0	8.2	8.3
2	24.6	24.7	12.3	12.3	1.6	1.6	15.1	15.2
3	21.3	21.0	14.8	15.3	0.6	0.6	14.3	14.0
4	23.0	23.1	29.2	28.9	9.2	9.2	21.3	21.4
5	14.4	14.0	41.8	41.5	88.6	88.6	41.2	41.0

Sources: Castro-Leal (1996); World Bank (1996).

can judge the *targeting* to poorer groups. If the curve lies above the diagonal, it means that the poorest (say) quintile gains more than 20 percent of the total subsidy (and the richest quintile, less than 20 percent). Distributions below the diagonal signify weaker targeting.

In Indonesia the primary subsidy was well targeted and progressive, the concentration curve lying above the diagonal. The senior secondary and tertiary subsidies were not only poorly targeted (being below the diagonal), but also regressive (below the Lorenz curve). The junior secondary subsidy concentration curve crosses the Lorenz curve, so it is difficult to judge its progressivity. The overall education subsidy was not well targeted but was progressive.

BENEFIT INCIDENCE AND NEEDS.   Poorer households gain a large share of the primary subsidy in part because they have a disproportionate share of primary-school-age children. Their needs for such services are therefore greater than others. In Indonesia, for example, 24 percent of primary-school-age children came from the poorest population quintile, and only 14 percent from the richest quintile. Judged against this need, the poorest quintile's share of the primary education subsidy (at 22 percent) does not appear quite so equitable. The different demographic characteristics of the quintiles should be taken into account when interpreting benefit incidence. If the welfare indicator used to rank households is sensitive to these demographic characteristics, the results can be profoundly affected. Using household expenditures per adult equivalent (rather than per capita) often gives a completely different ranking of households and changes the demographic characteristics of the quintiles (and the benefit incidence of education spending). In Ghana, for example, the poorest quintile (based on a ranking by per capita expenditure) gained 22 percent of primary education spending in 1992. But with households ranked by adult equivalent expenditure, the share falls to just 17 percent (Demery 2000).

HOUSEHOLD SPENDING.   Households must incur out-of-pocket expenses to obtain the in-kind subsidy embodied in education services, and these should be incorporated into benefit incidence analysis. Some can be considered as *transactions costs* (such as transport expenses), while others add to the benefit that is obtained from the service (such as spending on books or extra tuition). Together these costs can represent a serious burden, especially to low-income households. Although benefit incidence refers only to the distribution of the public subsidy, it is often useful to incorporate into the analysis household spending on the service, to obtain a full accounting of the service involved. Doing so often uncovers other layers of

---

Box 2.2 Significance Tests for Differences between Concentration Curves

Judging whether or not one subsidy is more equally distributed than another involves comparing two concentration curves. Such curves are usually based on sample data and are subject to sampling errors. For any one concentration curve to dominate another (that is lies above it at every point), there has to be a statistically significant difference between the curves. Davidson and Duclos (1997) derive the standard errors needed for such an assessment. The more common approach would be to reject the null hypothesis of nondominance if the difference between any one pair of ordinates is statistically significant and none of the other pairs of ordinates is statistically significant in the opposite direction. How many ordinates should be selected in such a choice—and should these ordinates be defined for every decile or quintile? Taking wide quantiles (say, quintiles) makes the test less demanding. Finer disaggregation (say, percentiles) cannot be taken too far because of the problem of small samples within each quantile. There is also the problem that differences between ordinates at the extremes of the distribution are rarely statistically different, which has led Howes (1996) to exclude the extremes in the dominance test. In their comparisons of concentration curves, Sahn and Younger (1999) exclude the top and bottom five percentiles of the distributions, and compare 20 equally spaced ordinates from the 5th to the 95th percentiles.

---

inequality, in addition to those found through the benefit incidence of the public subsidy.

A useful way to set out the household education accounts is given in table 2.2. Household spending *per capita* is decomposed into two components—household spending *per student*, and *students per capita* (that is, the percentage of students in the population of each group). This reveals that the main reason why the richer quintiles spend more per capita on education lies not in the fact that they have significantly more children in school, but that they spend more on *each student*. Spending per student by households in the top quintile was almost ten times greater than spending by households in the poorest quintile. As a result, these private expenditures dominated spending among the top quintile, exceeding the government subsidy. But for all other quintiles, the government subsidy was by far the most important source of financing. This finding means that the provision of state-subsidized education services is more unequal than the benefit incidence of the subsidy would suggest—children

Table 2.2 Household and Government Spending on Public Schooling in Indonesia, 1987

| Quintile or region | Average household spending per student (Rp.) | Percent of students in quintile population (%) | Per capita spending | | | | | Total |
| | | | Household spending | | Government spending | | | |
			Rp. per capita	Percent share	Rp. per capita	Percent share		Rp. per capita
1	584	25	146	8	1,602	92		1,749
2	984	26	255	13	1,762	87		2,017
3	1,398	27	374	23	1,227	77		1,601
4	2,196	27	594	32	1,260	68		1,854
5	5,619	29	1,632	53	1,471	47		3,104
All Indonesia	2,147	27	600	29	1,465	71		2,065
Urban	4,180	31	1,288	42	1,781	58		3,069
Rural	1,348	25	342	20	1,346	80		1,688

Source: van de Walle (1992).

from better-off households not only get a large share of the state subsidy, they receive even greater benefits (relative to those from poorer households) from their private spending.

Health Spending

As with education, one good example of the benefit incidence of health spending is taken to illustrate the nuts and bolts—health spending in Ghana in 1992. Unit subsidies for health care were not readily available, and so a "mini public expenditure review" was undertaken to obtain estimates in five regions (four predominantly rural and one urban).[3] These estimates revealed significantly higher recurrent public spending per patient in the capital city than elsewhere, as well as on inpatient hospital-based care. Information on the use of health facilities was subject to two survey problems. With illness being self-reported in the household survey, its incidence was greater among the rich than the poor, reflecting only perception biases. And the survey did not pick up the relatively rare events of inpatient hospital care. In all probability, the household survey underestimated both the incidence of illness among poor people (though not necessarily their use of health facilities) and the use of inpatient services by the better-off urban populations.

Combining the unit subsidies with the use patterns reported in the household survey reveals very unequally distributed health spending in Ghana (table 2.3). Recall that the highlighted columns indicate the e_{ij}'s and the highlighted rows show the s_i's. The findings suggest the following:

• The poorest quintile made little use of all publicly provided health facilities compared with the better-off. Health spending at all levels was very poorly targeted to the poor. The poorest quintile obtained just 12 percent of overall health spending with little variation across health subsectors.

• But as with education in Indonesia, the health subsidy was progressively distributed. For the poorest quintile it represented 3.5 percent of total household expenditure, compared with just under 2 percent for the richest 20 percent.

• A major source of the inequality in the benefit incidence of health spending in Ghana was clearly the gender dimension (Demery 2000). Although females gained more than males from hospital-based services overall, this gender advantage applied only to the top two quintiles. For the remaining population, a bias *against* females was suggested. The low share of the poorest quintile in total health spending was attributable in large part to the lack of use of hospital-based health services by poor females. Of the outpatient subsidy

Table 2.3 Benefit Incidence of Public Spending on Health, by Quintile and Level, Ghana, 1992

Quintile	Primary facilities		Hospital outpatient		Hospital inpatient		All health		
	Per capita subsidy (Cedis)	Share of subsidy (e_{ij}) (%)	Per capita subsidy (Cedis)	Share of subsidy (e_{ij}) (%)	Per capita subsidy (Cedis)	Share of subsidy (e_{ij}) (%)	Per capita subsidy (Cedis)	Share of total subsidy (%)	Subsidy as share of total household expenditure
1	661	10	1,079	13	555	11	2,296	12	3.5
2	1,082	17	1,242	15	741	14	3,065	15	3.1
3	1,202	19	1,432	17	1,058	20	3,692	19	2.8
4	1,460	23	1,564	19	1,203	23	4,228	21	2.3
5	1,966	31	2,883	35	1,666	32	6,515	33	1.8
Ghana	1,274	100	1,640	100	1,045	100	3,959	100	2.4

Memorandum: Government spending:

(m Cedis)	18,987		24,437		15,568		58,992		
% share (s_i)	32		41		26		100	87	7

Notes: The Cedi is the official currency of Ghana. For details of meaning of e_{ij} and s_i, see text.
Source: Demery and others (1995).

received by males, 17 percent went to males in the poorest quintile. Their female counterparts gained just 10 percent. It is therefore impossible to understand the unequal benefit incidence of health spending in Ghana in 1992 without reference to these critical gender differences.

HOUSEHOLD SPENDING.   Households must incur out-of-pocket expenses to gain subsidized health services and, as with education, these need to be taken into account to obtain a full accounting of the financing of health care and how the quintiles might be differently affected. A useful construct to assess the burden of this spending is the *affordability ratio*. This ratio compares household spending per health visit with per capita nonfood expenditures of the household. In the Ghana illustration, the former is simply total household spending on fees and medications for each visit to a publicly subsidized facility (table 2.4).

The burden of health care is significantly greater for the poor than for the better-off in Ghana. Out-of-pocket expenses for even an outpatient visit amount to more than 5 percent of nonfood household spending per capita. Gertler and Van der Gaag (1990) suggest that any ratio higher than 5 percent would imply too heavy a burden, since typically the price elasticity of demand exceeds unity at prices above this level. Hospital-based care is therefore likely to be particularly burdensome for the poorest quintile in Ghana.

Table 2.4 Affordability Ratios for Publicly Subsidized Health Care in Ghana, 1992

Quintile or region	Household spending per visit (Cedis)[a]			Percent of nonfood expenditure		
	Hospital			Hospital		
	Outpatient	Inpatient	Clinics	Outpatient	Inpatient	Clinics
1	1,352	9,753	989	5.4	38.8	3.9
2	1,452	7,746	796	3.5	18.7	1.9
3	1,510	6,776	843	2.7	12.2	1.5
4	1,764	14,235	1,252	2.3	18.3	1.6
5	1,744	20,834	941	1.0	12.4	0.6
Ghana	1,606	13,750	957	2.2	18.6	1.3
Urban	1,916	11,598	1,167	1.7	10.2	1.0
Rural	1,355	14,919	856	2.5	27.7	1.6

a. Includes fees and medication costs only.
Source: Demery (2000).

Comprehensive Coverage of Government Spending

The above estimates focus on spending on two important sectors—
education and health. Benefit incidence estimates can also be
obtained for other items of government spending, including social
assistance and other transfers, subsidies for other services (such as
agricultural extension), and subsidies of private goods (such as food
or fuel subsidies). The decision of how comprehensive a benefit incidence study should be clearly depends on the objectives of the analysis and on the available data. The earlier work by Meerman (1979)
and Selowsky (1979) sought to be as comprehensive as possible and
yet was finally restricted by the data and the time constraints of the
study. Meerman distinguished between public expenditure items
that were, as he put it, potentially "chargeable" to households. He
classified spending into items that were not chargeable in principle
(such as defense, administration, and debt service), those chargeable
in principle but not in practice, and those chargeable in practice and
reported in his work. Items not chargeable amounted to 40 percent
of total government spending. Items that were charged in his study
represented one-third of total government spending. The study,
therefore, failed to deal with about a quarter of total spending,
which was chargeable in principle.

Most studies fall short of estimating the full fiscal impact on
income groups, because they do not deal with the revenue side of
the account. Adding the revenue side can change the picture quite
significantly. Within the framework of a computable general equilibrium model with representative households (see chapter 15),
Devarajan and Hossain (1995) provide estimates of full fiscal incidence for the Philippines. This study covered three main expenditure items that had potentially redistributive roles—education,
health, and infrastructure, representing 30 percent of total government spending (about the same coverage as the Meerman study).
Although spending in the social sectors was allocated according to
household utilization, as described above, the study was obliged to
adopt ad hoc allocation rules for infrastructure. These results (table
2.5) show the following.

• Taxation was marginally regressive, due mainly to the effect of
indirect taxes.

• Expenditures, especially education subsidies, were very progressively distributed.

• The fiscal system in the Philippines was shown to be progressive mainly because of the incidence of spending rather than taxation. Combined, the fiscal system implied net subsidies to the poorest and increasing rates of net taxation with higher decile orders.

Table 2.5 Net Fiscal Incidence in the Philippines, 1988–89 (Percentage share of gross income of decile)

Household decile	Taxation	Government expenditure						Net fiscal incidence	
		Health	Education	Infrastructure		Total			
				(a)	(b)	(a)	(b)	(a)	(b)
1	20.8	7.3	20.9	18.7	3.3	46.9	31.5	26.1	10.7
2	20.5	3.5	10.0	8.7	3.4	22.2	16.9	1.7	−3.6
3	20.1	2.8	7.8	6.9	3.4	17.5	14.0	−2.6	−6.1
4	20.0	2.3	6.2	5.9	3.3	14.4	11.8	−5.6	−8.2
5	19.8	2.0	5.1	5.1	3.2	12.2	10.3	−7.6	−9.5
6	19.9	1.7	4.1	4.4	3.2	10.2	9.0	−9.7	−10.9
7	20.1	1.5	3.4	3.8	3.3	8.7	8.2	−11.4	−11.9
8	19.7	1.2	2.5	3.2	3.2	6.9	6.9	−12.8	−12.8
9	19.7	0.9	1.8	2.4	3.3	5.1	6.0	−14.6	−13.7
10	19.6	0.02	0.04	0.05	3.4	0.1	3.5	−19.5	−16.1

Note: Benefit incidence of infrastructure spending is allocated in equal absolute amounts under (a) and equal percentages under (b).
Source: Devarajan and Hossain (1995).

• Exactly how progressive the system was depended on how infrastructure spending was treated. The two (ad hoc) alternatives presented in the table give slightly different degrees of progressivity.

Operational Hints for Calculating Benefit Incidence

Estimating the benefit incidence of public spending involves four steps.

Step 1: Estimating unit subsidies. The unit cost of providing a service is defined as total government spending on a particular service divided by the number of users of that service (for example, total primary education spending divided by primary enrollment, or total outpatient hospital spending divided by outpatient visits). Estimating the cost of providing a service is not as easy as it sounds. The following issues usually have to be resolved:

• Should capital as well as recurrent spending on the service be included? Most recent studies cover only recurrent spending, but if capital spending is included, one must use only the service flows from that spending and not the principal itself.
• How should administrative spending be incorporated? It is usually allocated using ad hoc rules (such as pro-rata allocations).
• How is cost recovery treated? That depends on whether the fees are returned to the treasury (in which case they are netted out from gross spending to get the public subsidy). But if they are retained by the providers (the schools or clinics), they should not be netted out since they enhance the flow of finance to the providers.
• Where do the data on service use come from? Usually official data on use (enrollments, visits to health facilities, and the like) are weak. Most applications use data from household surveys, but exactly how they are combined with official data can affect the results.
• Should regional and other variations in unit costs be taken into account? The answer depends on whether one thinks these variations reflect benefits to households or just different transactions or delivery costs. But using disaggregated unit costs can make a big difference to the results.

As mentioned earlier, some analysts consider that the estimates of unit subsidies are not sufficiently accurate for policy analysis, and they assume that all unit subsidies are equal to unity. This assumption then focuses the attention of the analysis on the use of the service, rather than the level of the subsidy and the imputed income transfer (see Younger 2003 for an example of such an approach).

Step 2: Identifying users. Information on who uses the service is usually obtained from a household survey. Even when the data from schools and clinics on service use are good, they are not much use for benefit incidence. One needs to find out which types of household get the service (rich or poor, male- or female-headed, size of household, occupation of members, and so forth), and this information is not usually obtained from clinics and schools. Two issues invariably arise:

• Biases in the data: for example, biases arising from the self-reporting of illness, and the "rare event" problem, with sample surveys failing to find such events (such as university enrollments).

• Matching data sources: information in the household survey does not always match public expenditure data. Typically surveys identify the facility used by the household (a private or public school, a hospital, or a clinic, for example), so that the challenge is to estimate the unit costs of the facility using the public accounts.

Step 3: Aggregating users into groups. To describe how the benefits from public spending are distributed across the population, it is usually helpful to combine or aggregate individuals or households into groups.[4] The most common grouping is by income. This enables the policymaker to judge whether the distribution is progressive or regressive. Individuals are ranked according to income, usually proxied by the per capita expenditure of the household to which they belong. This ranking procedure can be complex. For example, the welfare measure on which it is based needs to include subsistence consumption and account for price variations across regions. Using different welfare measures (for example, using household expenditure per adult equivalent rather than per capita) can affect the results significantly. It is customary to group individuals into deciles or quintiles, although other groupings are possible—poor or nonpoor, for example. Note that for services provided to individuals (such as school enrollments), it is better to use population quintiles. But for those provided to households (such as sanitation, water, electricity), household quintiles may be appropriate.

Analyzing benefit incidence by income or expenditure quintile means that the survey from which the information on service use is obtained must also gather the data needed to calculate the welfare measure. Often surveys that collect the latter (such as budget surveys) do not obtain information on service use. And surveys that are designed to get data on service use do not get information on the income or expenditure of the users. The Living Standards Measurement Study survey design (and its African cousin, the Integrated Survey) provide the needed data. Recent approaches that use asset and household characteristic data to "instrument" for income can be used to rank households (see, for example, the application of factor analysis to Demographic and Health Survey data by Stifel, Sahn, and Younger 1999).

Other groupings can be as important for policy purposes. These include region, rural or urban location, poor or nonpoor, occupation of household head, and ethnicity. An important grouping that is usually ignored in the literature is *gender*, even though gender differences often hold the key to understanding why the targeting of public spending is so weak. In many countries this weak targeting stems from household decisions discouraging females from seeking medical care and girls from attending schools (Demery 2000).

Step 4: Accounting for household spending. Households must incur out-of-pocket expenditures to gain access to subsidized government services. Such spending extends beyond the cost-recovery contributions that might have been netted out in the unit subsidy discussed above. Whereas benefit incidence refers solely to the distribution of the public subsidy, providing a full accounting of financing a service—to account also for household or private spending— can give further policy insight into the extent of inequality in the sector concerned. Experience has shown that households contribute substantially to service provision despite the large government subsidies involved, and that this contribution increases with income. The burden of these out-of-pocket costs (especially to low-income households) can discourage the use of the services and lead to poor targeting of the government subsidy.

Interpretations and Limitations of Incidence Analysis

Having dealt with the nuts and bolts, we now come to the more challenging part—the interpretation of the results. Benefit incidence is a powerful instrument. When presented to government officials and policymakers, it can have a profound effect on how a given country situation is perceived. It is therefore all the more important for analysts to take great care in drawing only valid inferences from their results. The concern in this section is to highlight what benefit incidence analysis tells us—and what it leaves unresolved.

Limited Coverage

First, benefit incidence cannot hope to be exhaustive in its coverage of public expenditure. Studies that sought to be comprehensive in their treatment of government accounts managed to include only about one-third of them. And to achieve that coverage, some fairly heroic assumptions were made to assign expenditures to individuals. The fact that most government spending is not assignable (being nonrival in nature) means that benefit incidence simply cannot be exhaustive.

An Exercise in Current Accounting

Equations 2.1 and 2.2 were identities. That is because benefit incidence is best regarded as an exercise in *accounting*. These accounts concern only *current* flows—the long-run or capital-account effects being ignored.[5] And they are based on current *costs*. They measure how much the current income of households would have to increase if the households had to pay for the subsidized services at full cost. Thus the conclusions that can be drawn from the analysis are limited in a number of ways.

First, the analysis does not necessarily measure the benefits households and individuals receive. The reason why the approach is termed *benefit* incidence is simply to distinguish it from *expenditure* incidence. The benefit flows to *recipients* of government services are distinguished from the income flows government spending generates to the *providers* of those services and other government administrators. This distinction should not be taken, however, to imply that benefit incidence analysis is an accurate tool for measuring benefits to service recipients. Perhaps a better term to describe the technique is *beneficiary* incidence since that term avoids the suggestion that true benefits are measured but simply conveys the message that spending is imputed to the beneficiaries.

Second, since the exercise does not take into account any long-run effects of government spending on the beneficiaries, its results must be interpreted accordingly. At best, benefit incidence provides clues about which components of government spending have the greatest impact on the current income and consumption levels of households. Can income redistribution be effected through subsidized government services, rather than through direct income or consumption transfers? When the World Bank (1993) investigated how well targeted government spending was in Indonesia by comparing the benefit incidence of a selection of expenditure items (on health, education, and subsidies for kerosene and diesel fuel), it was really simply asking the question: which expenditure items are most effective in transferring current income (or expenditure) to the poorest households? The finding that spending on health centers was the most targeted expenditure item is to be judged purely from this perspective. Spending on health centers is recommended only because it is more efficient at transferring income to the poor. From the perspective of benefit incidence, health spending has no special attributes that make it more deserving than any other commodity. Thus, the finding that 12–13 percent of health spending reaches the poorest quintile in Ghana may seem a remarkably high figure to some, since governments would be hard pressed to find another commodity where consumption by the poorest quintile approaches such a large share of total consumption.

Why then might others consider that the 13 percent share is really far too low? Clearly, such an opinion is based on the belief that health is not just another commodity and that the government provision of such a good should be much more targeted to the poor—not simply to redistribute current consumption to such groups, but to raise health standards and help in achieving a permanent escape from poverty. There is nothing in the technique that makes health (or education or water or any other service) different from any other subsidized commodity or other method of income transfer. To bring out the special nature of expenditures in these sectors, analysts must go beyond incidence analysis. So, for example, Hammer, Nabi, and Cercone (1995), having established the benefit incidence of health spending in Malaysia, go on to show that such spending is critical to health *outcomes*, and that is what makes the targeting of such spending to the poor all the more important. Benefit incidence may give some measure of targeting efficiency, but the basis for such targeting does not go beyond the objective of redistributing current income.

Are Unit Costs Good Proxies for Values?

Even within the confines of the current accounting framework, a major limitation surrounds the use of average costs or subsidies as a valuation tool. Only under fairly heroic assumptions (as initially expounded by Brennan 1976) can average costs be taken as reasonable proxies for values.[6] Even then, they can represent only the *average* values placed on services, and they ignore differences in values across households. By ignoring individual preferences, the use of costs fails to recognize an important component of values. As Cornes (1995, p. 84) put it, "It cannot capture the fact that a sick individual with no children may benefit from a diversion of public expenditure from education to health while a healthy family with children may lose out."

One of the main practical problems analysts face in using costs as proxies for values arises from the inefficiency of the public sector. The observed structure of costs may have as much or more to do with government inefficiency as with society's value orderings.

What Is the Counterfactual?

Table 2.5 defines how far benefit incidence analysis can go. By comparing income distributions before accounting for tax and spending incidence, an assessment can be made of the pre- and post-fisc distributions, and thereby of the net effect of government interventions on the distribution of current incomes. But note, the prefisc distribution was taken as the currently observed income distribution. Is this really the appropriate counterfactual to take for assessing fiscal incidence? For it to be acceptable, the observed income distribution must be shown to be unaffected by government spending and taxation—in other words, relative prices and relative primary income flows must not be particularly sensitive to government interventions. These assumptions will rarely if ever apply, so the true counterfactual (what the income distribution would be in the absence of government taxation and spending) will not be observed.

There are many reasons why observed household income (or expenditures) will be affected by government spending. The provision of services by the state can influence household spending decisions, in some cases displacing private spending and in others augmenting it (van de Walle 1995). For instance, government spending on secondary education may have the effect of reducing private spending on such schooling, and government subsidies in health may induce households to spend on transportation to seek care. Moreover many programs, such as agricultural subsidies, are actually designed to influence incomes. Similarly, changes in private transfers between households may be induced through government subsidies. Evidence suggests that such crowding out of private transfers may be quantitatively important (Cox and Jimenez 1992). Despite these problems with the counterfactual, most analysts are obliged to use observed per capita expenditure (or per capita income) as the prefisc distribution with which to compare benefit incidence, mainly because there is really very little alternative; see chapter 3 for these alternatives.

Marginal versus Average Benefit

Benefit incidence provides a *description* of the situation as it is and does not handle policy experiments (counterfactuals) very well. It says very little about what would happen if governments increase spending significantly on certain categories. The existing pattern of demand for services is useful only for analyzing certain types of policy change—specifically changes that would affect only existing users in proportion to their current level of use—such as a change in user fees. But more commonly, changes in expenditure will have complex effects. As Younger (2003, p. 3) puts it, policymakers

> implicitly view public services as rationed, and they think of increased public expenditures that relax the rationing constraint. In this case, the benefits do not go, by definition, to existing beneficiaries, so the standard method, which maps out the concentration of existing beneficiaries in the welfare distribution, is misleading.

It is important therefore to distinguish the average benefit incidence from the marginal incidence—the latter incorporating the distributional effects of changes in coverage.

The *marginal* gains are likely to be distributed quite differently from the average incidence. Lanjouw and Ravallion (1999) use cross-sectional data to assess the extent to which the marginal benefit incidence of primary school spending differs from average incidence. They regress the "odds of enrollment" (defined as the ratio of the quintile-specific enrollment rate to that of the population as a whole) against the instrumented mean enrollment ratio (the instrument being the average enrollment rate without the quintile in question). The estimated coefficient indicates the extent to which there is early capture by the rich of primary school places. Under that circumstance any increase in the average enrollment rate is likely to come from proportionately greater increases in enrollment among the poorer quintiles. That would lead to higher marginal gains to the poor from additional primary school spending than the gains indicated by the existing enrollments across the quintiles. Whereas the poorest quintile gains just 14 percent of the existing primary education subsidy in rural India, it would most likely receive 22 percent of any additional spending. This result suggests that caution is needed in drawing policy conclusions from average benefit incidence results. The distributional impact depends on how the money is actually spent.

Long on Problems, Short on Answers

The treatment of the *proximate* determinants of the benefit incidence of government spending to a particular group distinguished two main factors—government spending allocations (s_i) and household behavior (e_{ij}). These were combined to generate a current accounting of government spending. Yet benefit incidence says little if anything about the *fundamental* determinants of these two components—especially about household behavior. Incidence analysis can thus be said to be helpful in identifying problems, but not particularly useful in providing solutions.

Consider the gender incidence of education spending. The fact that girls often gain little from education spending is attributable almost entirely to the decisions by households not to send their girls to school—even to primary school. Incidence analysis has traced the problem but does not provide the answer. That must be found in an understanding of the enrollment behavior of households. Unfortunately, incidence analysis itself says very little about how to change such behavior. It takes existing patterns of behavior as given. Benefit incidence has posed the problem very graphically but has not

provided the solution.[7] As a practical and operational matter, benefit incidence is usefully viewed as one input into a program of policy analysis that goes into greater depth on both the public expenditure and household use aspects. Such a program could include public
expenditure tracking, identifying leakage from the system that
reduces the benefits to consumers. Information on the views of the
beneficiaries about the service provided would also complement
incidence analysis. These data could come from qualitative empirical methods (see World Bank 1995 for an example from Ghana), or
from structured surveys such as the Core Welfare Indicators Questionnaire. The studies by Hammer, Nabi, and Cercone (1995) on
Malaysia, and Fofack, Ngong, and Obidegwu (2003) on Rwanda
are examples of such a comprehensive approach.

I do not mean to suggest that benefit incidence studies never provide any answers. There are cases where the problem of weak targeting to the poor clearly lies in inappropriate budget allocations
within a sector, such as education spending in Indonesia (see table
2.1). Here is a case where benefit incidence clearly signals the direction in which policy should go. Finally, it is important to be aware
that government spending decisions and household behavior are not
independent of each other. Governments may well be responsive to
behavioral changes. And certainly a change in government subsidies
induces behavioral responses by households. One of the most powerful uses of public spending incidence is to track changes over
time—showing whether public spending changes (for example in
the context of the Heavily Indebted Poor Countries (HIPC) debt initiative and the Poverty Reduction Strategy Paper (PRSP) reforms)
improve the targeting of public subsidies to poorer groups. Younger
(2003) discusses how to analyze the incidence of such changes in
public spending.

Notes

1. Incidence is presented here in terms of groups. But, of course, groups
may be defined as single individuals or households.

2. A concentration curve has the same formula as the Lorenz curve, but
with the subsidy benefit substituted for the welfare measure.

3. For a more systematic treatment of issues linked to the measurement
of unit subsidies, see chapter 9.

4. Analysts increasingly have access to unit record data, and so incidence is estimated at the individual or household level. But to understand
whether there are systematic differences in the distribution of the subsidies
across the population, it is analytically (as well as presentationally) helpful
to aggregate households into groups.

5. Note that capital *spending* by the government can be incorporated into the technique, but not the effects on the capital accounts of households (their human capital, for example).

6. These assumptions require that public goods are optimally supplied so that on average marginal costs would equal the arithmetic mean of all the individual marginal valuations—and of course that marginal cost would equal average cost.

7. The solution to problems of this sort involves estimating a behavioral model. On this, see chapters 3 and 6.

References

The word *processed* describes informally reproduced works that may not be commonly available through library systems.

Aaron, Henry, and Martin C. McGuire. 1970. "Public Goods and Income Distribution." *Econometrica* 38: 907–20.

Brennan, Geoffrey. 1976. "The Distributional Implications of Public Goods." *Econometrica* 44: 391–99.

Castro-Leal, Florencia. 1996. "Poverty and Inequality in the Distribution of Public Education Spending in South Africa." PSP Discussion Paper 102. World Bank, Poverty and Social Policy Department, Washington, D.C. Processed.

Cornes, Richard. 1995. "Measuring the Distributional Impact of Public Goods." In van de Walle and Nead (1995).

Cox, David, and Emmanuel Jimenez. 1992. "Social Security and Private Transfers: The Case of Peru." *World Bank Economic Review* 6(January): 155–69.

Davidson, Russell, and Jean-Yves Duclos. 1997. "Statistical Inference for the Measurement of the Incidence of Taxes and Transfers." *Econometrica* 65: 1453–66.

Demery, Lionel. 2000. "Benefit Incidence: A Practitioner's Guide." World Bank, Poverty and Social Development Group, Africa Region, Washington, D.C. Processed.

Demery, Lionel, Shiyan Chao, René Bernier, and Kalpana Mehra. 1995. "The Incidence of Social Spending in Ghana." PSP Discussion Paper Series 82. World Bank, Poverty and Social Policy Department, Washington, D.C. Processed.

Devarajan, Shantayanan, and Shaikh I. Hossain. 1995. "The Combined Incidence of Taxes and Public Expenditures in the Philippines." Policy Research Working Paper 1543, World Bank, Policy Research Department, Washington, D.C. Processed.

Filmer, Deon, Jeffrey Hammer, and Lant Pritchett. 1998. "Health Policy in Poor Countries: Weak Links in the Chain." Policy Research Working Paper 1874. World Bank, Policy Research Department, Washington, D.C. Processed.

Fofack, Hippolyte, Robert Ngong, and Chukwuma Obidegwu. 2003. "Rwanda Public Expenditure Performance: Evidence from a Public Expenditure Tracking Study in the Health and Education Sectors." Africa Region Working Paper 45. World Bank, Washington, D.C. Processed.

Gertler, Paul, and Jacques Van der Gaag. 1990. *The Willingness to Pay for Medical Care: Evidence from Two Developing Countries*. Baltimore: Johns Hopkins University Press for the World Bank.

Hammer, Jeffrey, Ijaz Nabi, and James A. Cercone. 1995. "Distributional Effects of Social Sector Expenditures in Malaysia, 1974 to 1989." In van de Walle and Nead (1995).

Howes, Stephen. 1996. "The Influence of Aggregation on the Ordering of Distributions." *Economica* 63(250): 253–72.

Lanjouw, Peter, and Martin Ravallion. 1999. "Benefit Incidence, Public Spending Reforms, and the Timing of Program Capture." *World Bank Economic Review* 13(May): 257–73.

Meerman, Jacob. 1979. *Public Expenditure in Malaysia: Who Benefits and Why?* New York: Oxford University Press.

Sahn, David E., and Stephen D. Younger. 1999. "Dominance Testing of Social Expenditures and Taxes in Africa." IMF Working Paper WP/99/172. International Monetary Fund, Fiscal Affairs Department, Washington, D.C. Processed.

Selowsky, Marcelo. 1979. *Who Benefits from Government Expenditure?* New York: Oxford University Press.

Stifel, David, David E. Sahn, and Stephen D. Younger. 1999. "Inter-Temporal Changes in Welfare: Preliminary Results from Ten African Countries." CFNPP Working Paper 94, Cornell University, Cornel Food and Nutrition Policy Program, Ithaca, N.Y. Processed.

van de Walle, Dominique. 1992. "The Distribution of the Benefits from Social Services in Indonesia, 1978–87." Policy Research Working Paper 871. World Bank, Country Economics Department, Washington, D.C. Processed.

———. 1998. "Assessing the Welfare Impacts of Public Spending." *World Development* 26(March): 365–79.

van de Walle, Dominique, and Kimberly Nead, eds. 1995. *Public Spending and the Poor: Theory and Evidence*. Baltimore: Johns Hopkins University Press for the World Bank.

World Bank. 1993. "Indonesia: Public Expenditures, Prices and the Poor." Report 11293-IND. World Bank, Country Department III, East Asia and Pacific Region, Washington, D.C. Processed.

————. 1995. "Ghana: Poverty Past, Present and Future" Report 14504-GH. World Bank, West Central Africa Department, Washington, D.C. Processed.

————. 1996. "Madagascar: Poverty Assessment." Report 14044 (vols. I and II). World Bank, Central Africa and Indian Ocean Department, Washington, D.C. Processed.

Younger, Stephen D. 2003. "Benefits on the Margin: Observations on Marginal versus Average Benefit Incidence." *World Bank Economic Review* 17(1): 89–106.

3

Behavioral Incidence Analysis of Public Spending and Social Programs

Dominique van de Walle

The ways in which participants and other agents respond to a program can matter greatly to its distributional outcomes. For example, recipients of a transfer payment may change their labor supply or savings choices such that the net income gain is less than the amount of the transfer. Or the behavior of intervening agents (local governments in decentralized programs, for example) may be such that the incidence of a change in aggregate spending differs from the average incidence.

This chapter discusses some simple tools for introducing behavioral responses into the analysis of the incidence of public spending or policy changes. The chapter looks at ways of incorporating two quite distinct types of responses: first, those of the direct participants and the people they interact with; and second, the responses of administrative or political agents.

The approaches to incorporating behavioral responses reviewed in this chapter tend to be *ex post* in that they study interventions that have already occurred, though often drawing implications for future policies. They also tend to be *nonstructural*, in that they do not trace all the behavioral interlinkages that may be involved, but focus instead on the final "reduced form" relationships between outcomes and interventions. More structural approaches to *predicting* the marginal incidence of reforms not yet implemented are discussed in chapter 6.

Assumptions about Behavioral Responses Do Matter

The key issue for all incidence analysis is how to define the counter-factual of what the income (or other welfare indicator) of beneficiaries would be in the absence of the program. Only then can one determine how individuals should be ranked so as to infer program incidence. It is only by seeing the incidence of benefits according to how poor people would have been without them that the distributional impact of the benefits can be known.

So an appropriate indicator is needed to identify the poor. In conventional benefit incidence analysis of cash transfers or in-kind transfers whose cash value has been imputed, the without-intervention position is often assumed to be given by the welfare indicator (such as expenditures per capita) less the monetary value of the benefits secured from the publicly provided good or program under study. Implicit in this practice is the strong assumption that there is no replacement through household behavioral responses. Surely there are underlying behavioral impacts of the benefits one is assigning. By the same token, the opposite assumption—treating post-transfer consumption as the welfare indicator for assessing incidence—is equally suspect. Ideally, one would like to subtract the intervention amount but add in the replacement income households would have achieved through their behavioral responses had they not benefited from the intervention.

Note that in the case of in-kind programs for which no imputed value has been included in consumption or income aggregates (as is commonly the case for public education and health programs), one does not of course have to net them out in calculating the without-intervention position. However, the issue of behavioral responses also arises for such programs; consumption or income may well be very different in the absence of publicly provided health or education, for example.

The assumptions made about behavioral responses can matter greatly to the conclusions one draws from any benefit incidence study. Naturally, this is an empirical issue. Table 3.1 highlights the potential sensitivity of the incidence of average mean per capita transfers in Yemen in 1998. The table gives incidence results under two assumptions (fully excluding or fully including transfer incomes when assigning households to pre-intervention deciles). When deciles are defined net of transfers, the results suggest that transfers are well targeted to the very poorest households. The opposite conclusion is reached when deciles are instead defined on the basis of post-transfer expenditures: transfer income is concentrated in the richest decile. Conclusions about targeting and incidence clearly depend on how the counterfactual is defined.

Table 3.1 Distribution of Net Public and Private Transfers in Yemen in 1998 under Different Assumptions about the Propensity to Consume out of Transfers (Yemeni rials)

Welfare indicator	Per capita expenditures net of transfers (net mean per capita transfers)			Per capita expenditures with tranfers fully included (net mean per capita transfers)		
1998 National deciles	Rural	Urban	National	Rural	Urban	National
1	14,757	32,942	17,347	1,181	1,651	1,233
2	3,169	5,482	3,552	1,625	2,055	1,696
3	2,290	4,165	2,671	1,650	2,468	1,818
4	2,158	3,925	2,528	2,331	2,311	2,327
5	2,237	2,718	2,346	1,985	3,200	2,252
6	985	2,601	1,352	3,246	3,693	3,350
7	1,777	3,153	2,106	3,039	4,658	3,443
8	1,294	3,172	1,780	5,138	4,948	5,090
9	1,475	3,987	2,146	4,860	6,400	5,288
10	1,749	2,023	1,851	10,777	11,915	11,217
Total	3,358	5,139	3,770	3,358	5,139	3,770

Note: Deciles are formed by ranking the population by household per capita expenditures under different assumptions about the propensity to consume out of transfers. Net transfers are calculated from income and expenditure on transfers identified in the Yemen Republic Household Budget Survey—namely, income from *zakat*, retirement, and pensions; local and foreign remittances; and payments from government organizations minus transfers given on *zakat*, aid to dependents, other gifts, and donations. Total household expenditures includes spending on transfers, so that only transfer income needs to be netted out to get at the "net" amounts.

Source: van de Walle (2002a) using the 1998 Yemen Republic Household Budget Survey.

The current consumption gains to a participant can differ from the monetary value of a program's benefit level for several reasons. The program can affect savings, labor supply, and schooling choices, and it can also affect private transfers received. Without identifying the precise "structural" channel, the most direct approach to incorporating such responses is to see how much consumption changes when benefits are received.

Recognizing the importance of the behavioral responses (as illustrated in table 3.1), a few studies have explored the issue using panel data. An example can be found in Ravallion, van de Walle, and Gautam (1995), who use panel data for Hungary to estimate the marginal propensity to consume out of social income.[1] This estimate is then used to determine the net gain to consumption from social transfers and to construct the counterfactual consumption level without intervention. This process allows a behavioral incidence analysis.

In a similar vein, van de Walle (2002c) estimates the marginal propensity to consume out of social income for Vietnam, where household surveys for 1993 and 1998 contain a panel of 4,308 households. Consumption of household i at time t (t = 1993, 1998) (C_{it}) is assumed to be represented as an additive function of public transfers (T_{it}), observed household characteristics (X_{it}), and time varying (δ_t) and time invariant (η_i) latent factors:

$$(3.1) \qquad C_{it} = \alpha + \beta T_{it} + \gamma X_{it} + \eta_i + \delta_t + \varepsilon_{it}$$

There are a number of potential problems with estimating β with this equation. An endogeneity concern arises if, as is likely, transfers are correlated with time invariant household characteristics [$\mathrm{cov}(T_{it}\eta_i)$ $\neq 0$], as could result from purposive targeting to the long-term poor. Endogeneity also arises if transfers are correlated with time-varying determinants of consumption [$\mathrm{cov}(T_{it}\delta_t) \neq 0$ or $\mathrm{cov}(T_{it}\varepsilon_{it}) \neq 0$]. That would occur if transfers target those who suffered a shock or simply if transfer eligibility changes—for example, because of the death of a pension-receiving elderly household member.

There is likely to be heterogeneity in the behavioral response across households. Differences in the impact of the transfers associated with observable differences in the characteristics of individuals can be introduced by adding appropriate interaction effects in equation 3.1, so that it takes the form:

$$C_{it} = \alpha + (\beta_0 + \beta_0 X_{it})T_{it} + \gamma X_{it} + \eta_i + \delta_t + \varepsilon_{it}$$

One can also readily introduce random differences in impacts not correlated with the program assignment. There are also nonparametric methods (that do not need to postulate a parametric regression equation for the outcome variable); these methods are reviewed in chapter 5. However, for the purpose of this exposition, attention is confined to the simplest parametric model in equation 3.1.

A double differencing model, where all variables are expressed in first differences, purges the estimate of fixed effects and thus deals with the first source of endogeneity. Equation 3.1 becomes

$$\Delta C_{it} = \beta \Delta T_{it} + \gamma \Delta X_{it} + \Delta \delta_t + \Delta \varepsilon_{it}$$

With only two rounds of data, the term $\Delta \delta_t$ becomes an ordinary intercept term in a regression of the change in consumption on the change in transfers.

In the Vietnam example, this regression was initially run assuming that $\gamma \Delta X_{it} = 0$ (characteristics do not change or do not have any effect), giving the standard "double difference" estimate of the consumption impact of transfers. This specification gives a β estimate of 0.45 with a heteroscedasticity and clustering-corrected t-statistic of 4.3. A number of different regressions are run that control for time-varying household characteristics and the possibility that there are omitted variables that alter over time and affect transfers (using an instrumental estimator), and that test for possible heterogeneity in impacts. However, none of the estimates for the propensity to consume out of social income are significantly different from the initial simple double difference estimate of 0.5 (van de Walle 2002c).

The study thus uses consumption expenditures net of half of the value of transfer receipts as its ranking welfare indicator. Interestingly, though perhaps completely coincidentally, the Hungary study also estimates a marginal propensity to consume out of transfer incomes of 0.5 (Ravallion, van de Walle, and Gautam 1995) and, in a slightly different context, Jalan and Ravallion (2003) estimate about 50 percent income replacement for public transfers in Argentina.

These examples are for cash transfer programs. However, the same points apply to in-kind transfers such as publicly provided health or education. Then one would model consumption or income as a function of participation in such programs. The same issues of endogeneity bias naturally arise, and the panel data methods described above offer an approach to addressing these issues.

Marginal Incidence Analysis

Another example of a behavioral incidence analysis is what is sometimes called "marginal incidence analysis," where one measures the incidence of actual increases or proposed cuts in program spending. This approach departs from standard benefit incidence analysis that attempts to estimate how the *average* benefits from public spending are distributed at one point in time. The latter can be deceptive about how changes in public expenditures will be distributed. It is possible, for example, that the political economy of incidence means that the rich tend to receive a large share of the inframarginal subsidies, while the poor benefit most from extra spending. Ravallion (1999) provides a model of the political economy of fiscal adjustment that can generate such an outcome.

Using Single Cross-Sectional Data to Infer Marginal Incidence

The simplest way to identify marginal incidence is to compare average incidence across geographic areas with different degrees of program size. This is essentially the method of Lanjouw and Ravallion (1999), who used data from India's National Sample Survey (NSS) for 1993–94. This survey includes standard data on consumption expenditures, demographics, and education attainments, including school enrollments. This particular NSS round also asked about participation in three key antipoverty programs: public works schemes, a means-tested credit scheme called the Integrated Rural Development Programme, and a food-rationing scheme called the Public Distribution System. The data on participation in these programs can be collated with data on total consumption expenditure per person at the household level.

Sampled households in the NSS were ranked by total consumption expenditure per person normalized by state-specific poverty lines. Quintiles were then defined over the entire rural population, with equal numbers of people in each. So the poorest quintile refers to the poorest 20 percent of the national rural population in terms of consumption per capita.[2] The analysis was done at the level of the NSS region, of which there are 62 in India, spanning 19 states; each NSS region belongs to only 1 state. So, for any given combination of quintile and program, the participation rates across the 62 NSS regions were regressed on the average participation by state (irrespective of quintile). The results provide estimates of the marginal incidence of participation across quintiles and indicate that expansion of primary schooling would be very pro-poor in contrast to average incidence figures that suggest the opposite. With regard to the poverty schemes, additional spending would be significantly more pro-poor than suggested by the average incidence of participation.

Although the technique requires a cross-sectional household survey only, it must contain information on program participation at the household level and sufficient regional disaggregation and variance in participation for estimation to be possible. The main concern with using a single cross-sectional survey is that there may be important state-level differences in the propensity to reach the poor that are correlated with levels of social spending. One method for revealing marginal incidence in a way that is more robust to latent heterogeneity in local political factors is to assess incidence at two or more dates. This can be done using two cross-sections or panel data (if they are available) on households or regions.

Marginal Incidence Analysis Using Repeated Cross-Sectional Data

Take the example of spending on education, and the case where two consecutive cross-sectional surveys are available with information on households with children attending school in both years. Each enrolled child is assumed to receive the same subsidy in a schooling level i. The change in quantile specific participation in education between the two years can then be represented by

$$(3.2) \qquad E_{ij2}/E_{i2} - E_{ij1}/E_{i1} \qquad j = 1, 2, \ldots$$

where E_{ijt} is the number of children in a given level of schooling i in welfare quantile j, at date $t = 1, 2$, and E_{it} is total school enrollment in that level at date t. Alternatively this can be interpreted as the marginal incidence of spending on education between the two years where enrollments are multiplied by the appropriate subsidy level as in chapter 2. In the following the same simplified notation E is used to refer to both representations. E_{jt}/E_t can be interpreted as the share of total enrollments or education spending that goes to quantile j through the school attendance of its children. The expression in equation 3.2 shows the change in each quantile's share of enrollments or spending. Alternatively, one might want to know the share of a given quantile in the total change in enrollments or education spending as given by:

(3.3) $$(E_{j2} - E_{j1}) / (E_2 - E_1)$$

The above approach can be applied to health care, social transfers, and other public spending programs for which participation at the household or individual level can be identified and—if one wants to identify public spending amounts—a benefit value attributed. The important point is that there may be a big difference between average incidence at a point in time (as indicated by E_{j1}/E_1 or E_{j2}/E_2) and the marginal incidence defined by equation 3.2 or 3.3.

A number of studies have examined ex post marginal incidence in this way. Early examples looked at whether changes during the 1980s were pro-poor for Indonesia's public health sector and Malaysia's health and education sectors (van de Walle 1994; Hammer, Nabi, and Cercone 1995, respectively) and found that they were. Another study looked at the changing incidence of cash transfers in Hungary (van de Walle, Ravallion, and Gautam 1994). A more recent example includes Younger (2001, 2002) for Peru.

The method has limitations. Simple comparisons of incidence at different points in time do not reveal which factors are responsible for marginal incidence patterns. For example, a key question is often to what degree government policy, as opposed to income growth, can be credited with improvements in equity. The Malaysia study (Hammer, Nabi, and Cercone 1995) supplements the incidence analysis with more detailed analysis of the underlying mechanisms. Success in the education sector is attributed to the government's policy of ethnic targeting, while pro-poor improvements in the health sector are attributable to the private sector's increasing ability to attract wealthier households. Another limitation is that when the distribution of the underlying population alters between periods— due, for example, to urbanization—the technique is unable to disaggregate incidence results over time geographically, information that is typically of interest.

In implementing ex post marginal incidence analysis, an issue arises concerning the definition of the quantiles j. Is it changes in the amount going to the relatively poor or to the absolute poor that is of interest? The two could be quite different depending on how absolute poverty is changing. Some studies simply define quantiles specific to each date, so that they are not strictly comparable. This approach helps answer questions concerning changes in incidence for, say, the bottom 20 percent of the population at any one date. But often the interest is in how the amounts received, conditional on real income, have changed. Then one would want to fix the cutoff boundaries in real income space rather than in relative income space. When a panel is used to study the incidence of the changes in social spending, households can be ranked by three different definitions of welfare, which can be loosely viewed as delineating the initial, new, and long-term poor—namely, the welfare indicator in the initial period, the welfare indicator in the later period, and the mean over both years (see table 3.2 for an example of the first two).

Marginal Incidence Analysis Using Panel Data

Two studies have explored the dynamic marginal impacts of public expenditures using ex post benefit incidence with data that follow the same households over time. Using a panel of Hungarian households for 1987 through 1989, Ravallion, van de Walle, and Gautam (1995) devise a methodology to examine how well the social safety net protected vulnerable households from falling into poverty versus how well it promoted households out of poverty. The essential idea is to simulate a counterfactual joint distribution of the welfare indicator over time without the change in transfers, using econometric methods similar to those described above.

Similar techniques were used in a study of the safety net in Vietnam (van de Walle 2002b). Poverty fell quite dramatically in Vietnam, and there was a clear expansion in the total outlays going to social welfare programs between 1993 and 1998. These events provide an interesting backdrop for a number of questions concerning marginal incidence: Was the expansion pro-poor? What role did transfer programs play in the reduction in poverty? Does the revealed instability over time in who gets transfers reflect the system's response to changing household circumstances?

An important role for the public sector in a poor rural economy like Vietnam is to provide protection for those who are vulnerable to poverty due to uninsured shocks. The typical incidence picture is uninformative about whether transfers perform such a safety net function. The static average incidence may not seem particularly well targeted, but it may be deceptive about the degree to which

Table 3.2 Distribution of Social Transfer Income
in Vietnam (percent)

Net quintiles	Share of 1993 transfers	Share of 1998 transfers	Share of total transfer increase 1993–98
1993			
1	13.3	13.1	12.8
2	15.2	15.5	15.7
3	16.9	17.5	17.9
4	21.2	22.4	23.4
5	33.3	31.6	30.2
Total	100.0	100.0	100.0
1998			
1	15.3	15.7	16.0
2	14.0	15.4	16.6
3	20.5	19.6	18.9
4	19.8	19.9	20.0
5	30.4	29.3	28.5
Total	100.0	100.0	100.0

Note: National population quintiles are constructed using per capita expenditures
net of half of social transfers.
Sources: 1993 and 1998 Vietnam Living Standards Survey.

outlays, coverage, and changes over time were perhaps correlated to
poverty-related shocks and changes in exogenous variables.

Table 3.2 ranks households by two definitions of welfare as discussed above—namely, per capita expenditures (net of half of transfers) in the initial period and the same welfare indicator in the later
period—and presents a comparison of the average incidence of social
income receipts in both years and the marginal incidence of the
spending increase. The former is expressed as the percent of total
social income going to each quintile, while the latter is given by the
percent of the total increase going to each group. In this particular
case, little difference is found between the average and marginal inci-
dences for either definition of welfare. Expansion was more or less
proportional to base-year receipts across groups. The evidence does
not suggest that the poor were specifically targeted by the program
expansion.

Were changes in transfers responsive to poverty-related shocks?
Table 3.3 presents information on mean changes in transfers
received by panel households classified into a three-by-three matrix.
Households ranked into terciles of their initial 1993 level of per
capita consumption (low, middle, or high) are cross-tabbed against
the change in their consumption between the two dates categorized
by whether consumption fell, stayed more or less the same, or rose

Table 3.3 The Incidence of Changes in Transfers by Initial
Consumption and Changes in Consumption over Time

Initial consumption	Fall in consumption	Consumption stayed the same	Large rise in consumption
Low			
Percent receiving transfers	34	27	27
Per capita change, Vietnamese dong	111,901	246,476	241,658
Number of households	80	506	848
Middle			
Percent receiving transfers	32	30	30
Per capita change, Vietnamese dong	408,469	251,619	296,513
Number of households	240	422	772
High			
Percent receiving transfers	33	36	32
Per capita change, Vietnamese dong	481,618	343,329	367,991
Number of households	496	221	720

Note: The population is ranked into three equal groups based on 1993 per capita expenditures net of half of transfers and cross-tabbed against the level of their change in consumption over time net of half the change in transfers. The first number gives the percentage of households in the cell that received transfers in 1998. The second number gives the per capita amount, in Vietnamese dong, of the change in transfers received by those with positive receipts only. The final number gives the number of households in the cell. Changes in transfers refer to changes in amounts received from social insurance, social subsidies, and school scholarships.

Source: van de Walle (2002b) using the 1993 and 1998 Vietnam Living Standards Survey.

significantly. The results strongly suggest that the programs were unresponsive to consumption shocks. Neither starting out poor nor experiencing negative consumption shocks appear to have elicited a response from social welfare programs.

The study also examines the role transfers played in the impressive reduction in poverty that occurred over this period. The panel structure is exploited to evaluate how well the safety net performed dynamically following the approach proposed in Ravallion, van de Walle, and Gautam (1995). In comparing joint distributions of consumption expenditures, such as with and without policy changes, the approach tests a policy's ability to protect the poor (PROT) and its ability to promote the poor (PROM). It indicates which distribution offered more protection and which offered more promotion and allows a calculation of the statistical significance of the difference.

The baseline joint distribution of consumption in the two years is presented in table 3.4. Households are classified into four groups according to whether they were poor or nonpoor in both years, and whether they escaped or fell into poverty over the period. There is evidence both of a large drop in poverty and of considerable persistent poverty.

What was the effect of transfers on poverty? To answer this question, it is necessary to simulate the counterfactual joint distribution without transfers; as in the static incidence calculations, this is done by subtracting half the transfers received in each respective year from consumption in that year. Table 3.5 shows that transfers have negligible impact on poverty. Without them, an additional 1 and 2 percent of the population would have been poor in 1993 and 1998, respectively. Neither the degree of promotion or protection is statistically different from zero.

One can also assess the impact of changes in transfers between the two dates by simulating the joint distribution had there been no changes. Alternatively one could compare the current distribution relative to a simulated uniform allocation of actual 1998 social income across the entire population to see if better targeting could have improved impacts on poverty incidence. A number of targeting scenarios can be tested.

Table 3.4 The Baseline Discrete Joint Distribution (percent)

	1998		
1993	Poor	Nonpoor	Total
Poor	33.54	26.58	60.12
	(55.78)	(44.22)	100
Nonpoor	4.84	35.04	39.88
	(12.14)	(87.86)	100
Total	38.38	61.62	100

Note: The population is ranked into poor and nonpoor groups based on actual per capita expenditures at each date and cross-tabbed. The first number in each cell gives the percentage of total population who were in that row's poverty group in 1993 and that column's group in 1998. Numbers in parentheses give the proportion of each row's population that is in each column's group in 1998, or the transition probability.

Source: van de Walle (2002b) using the 1993 and 1998 Vietnam Living Standards Survey.

Table 3.5 Joint Distribution without Transfers (percent)

1993	1998		
	Poor	*Nonpoor*	*Total*
Poor	35.21	25.88	61.09
	(57.63)	(42.37)	100
Nonpoor	5.15	33.76	38.91
	(13.24)	(86.76)	100
Total	40.36	59.64	100

Note: The population is ranked into poor and nonpoor groups based on their simulated without transfer per capita expenditures (minus 0.5*transfers) at each date and cross-tabbed. Ability to protect the poor (PROT) = 0.31(0.66); ability to promote the poor (PROM) = 0.70(0.74). z-scores in parentheses, with critical values: 1.96 (2.58) at the 5 percent (1 percent) level.

Source: van de Walle (2002b) using the 1993 and 1998 Vietnam Living Standards Survey.

The Vietnam analysis concludes that transfers had a negligible bearing on poverty outcomes and failed to protect those who faced falling living standards during this period. By contrast, the Hungary case study found that cash benefits protected many from poverty even though it helped few escape poverty. The policy reforms examined were more successful at reducing transient than persistent poverty. Such evidence on dynamic performance is of key value in designing effective safety nets.

Marginal Incidence Analysis Using Geographic Panel Data

Another strand of the literature has focused on tracking the incidence of public spending across geographic areas over time. This approach does not require household-level panel data. Instead, the idea is to aggregate cross-sectional data geographically (typically these will be subnational governmental areas such as provinces) and then compare incidence over time. Local governments will differ in their preferences for redistribution and be heterogeneous in other unobserved ways. By allowing for geographic fixed effects in incidence, the method can study incidence and its determinants robustly to such latent heterogeneity. Ravallion (1999) illustrates this approach using province-level panel data on the incidence of a social program in Argentina.

The first step is to estimate benefit incidence, or a summary measure of incidence, for each geographic area at each date. For this purpose one might use household survey data or data for very fine geographic areas; for example, Ravallion uses the empirical relationship between program spending and the local poverty map across local government areas ("departments") within each province of Argentina. The poverty map uses the percent of households with unmet basic needs at departmental level based on census data. The spatial variances in both spending and poverty incidence within each province are exploited to measure targeting performance.

This estimation entails running an OLS regression for each province of spending allocations across departments against poverty incidence. The regression coefficient gives a "targeting differential" interpretable as the mean difference in spending between the poor and nonpoor (Ravallion 2000). This regression is done for all dates for which spending allocations are available. Thus a panel can be formed of these targeting differentials by provinces and over time.

Next the province- and date-specific targeting differentials are regressed on per capita spending allocations to the provinces in a regression that pools all dates and provinces and includes a province fixed effect to capture province-specific factors that affect targeting. This estimation allows one to see what happens to targeting performance during program expansions and cutbacks. Ravallion (1999) finds that during a retrenchment period in Argentina's Trabajar program, a $1 cut in average spending reduced the targeting differential by $3.55 on average. Hence, cuts were accompanied by worsening targeting performance.

Conclusions

Ignoring behavioral responses to public spending or social programs can yield deceptive assessments of incidence because one does not correctly assign beneficiaries to the pre-intervention distribution. For example, by subtracting the full amount of a transfer received, one overestimates how poor beneficiaries will have been in the absence of the intervention. Similarly, if one ignores the influence of the political economy on the assignment of beneficiaries and the incidence of program spending allocations, one can arrive at severely biased estimates of impacts and hence incidence.

This chapter has reviewed some relatively simple methods that can help address these deficiencies of nonbehavioral incidence analysis. There is a large literature on reduced-form regression-based methods in which one essentially regresses the relevant outcome measure (income, for example) on program allocations with relevant controls. With household panel data one can exploit changes in program spending over time to obtain estimates that are robust to potential endogeneity of the program assignment across units (provided the endogeneity is fully reflected in time-invariant factors).

These methods can be made more sophisticated, such as by incorporating heterogeneity in impacts and allowing for more complex forms of endogeneity in program assignments or spending levels. Once one knows the impact on incomes, one can then work out what the income or other welfare indicator of program participants would have been in the absence of the intervention and so estimate the incidence of spending relative to that counterfactual.

Marginal benefit incidence analysis is another important example of how behavioral responses through the political economy of incidence can be incorporated. It can provide valuable information for charting the course of pro-poor reforms in public spending. The method can be implemented using a single cross-sectional survey, but access to two or more consecutive household cross-sectional surveys with information on program participation usually provides estimates that are more robust. Household or regional panel data allow an even richer analysis of policy and spending changes. By examining actual changes ex post, these methods provide a reality check for the results of methods that attempt to approximate or predict reality ex ante.

Notes

1. The marginal propensity to consume out of social income can also be estimated using regression methods on a cross-section, but depending on how well one can control for heterogeneity, the results are likely to be biased by omitted variables. With a uniform benefit level, a third approach is to use propensity-score matching with a single difference estimator (as in Jalan and Ravallion 2003). The advantage of the latter is that a model or structure does not need to be imposed.

2. Note that, although this study does not allow for behavioral responses on the part of individuals and households in determining the welfare ranking indicator as above, there is nothing that prevents it from doing so.

References

The word *processed* describes informally reproduced works that may not be commonly available through library systems.

Hammer, Jeffrey, Ijaz Nabi, and James Cercone. 1995. "Distributional Effects of Social Sector Expenditures in Malaysia, 1974 to 1989." In Dominique van de Walle and Kimberly Nead, eds., *Public Spending and the Poor: Theory and Evidence*. Baltimore: Johns Hopkins University Press.

Jalan, Jyotsna, and Martin Ravallion. 2003. "Estimating the Benefit Incidence of an Antipoverty Program by Propensity Score Matching." *Journal of Business and Economic Statistics* 21(1): 19–30.

Lanjouw, Peter, and Martin Ravallion. 1999. "Benefit Incidence, Public Spending Reforms, and the Timing of Program Capture." *World Bank Economic Review* 13(2): 257–74.

Ravallion, Martin. 1999. "Is More Targeting Consistent with Less Spending?" *International Tax and Public Finance* 6: 411–19.

———. 2000. "Monitoring Targeting Performance When Decentralized Allocations to the Poor Are Unobserved." *World Bank Economic Review* 14(2): 331–45.

Ravallion, Martin, Dominique van de Walle, and Madhur Gautam. 1995. "Testing a Social Safety Net." *Journal of Public Economics* 57: 175–99.

van de Walle, Dominique. 1994. "The Distribution of Subsidies through Public Health Services in Indonesia 1978–87." *World Bank Economic Review* 8(2): 279–309.

———. 2002a. "Poverty and Transfers in Yemen." Middle East and North Africa Working Paper Series 30. World Bank, Office of the Chief Economist, Middle East and North Africa Region, Washington, D.C. Processed.

———. 2002b. "The Static and Dynamic Incidence of Viet Nam's Public Safety Net." Policy Research Working Paper 2791. World Bank, Development Research Group, Washington, D.C. Processed.

———. 2002c. "Viet Nam's Safety Net: Protection and Promotion from Poverty?" World Bank, Development Research Group, Washington, D.C. Processed.

van de Walle, Dominique, Martin Ravallion, and Madhur Gautam. 1994. "How Well Does the Social Safety Net Work? The Incidence of Cash Benefits in Hungary 1987–89." Living Standards Measurement Study Working Paper 102. World Bank, Washington, D.C.

Younger, Stephen D. 2001. "Benefits on the Margin." Cornell University, Department of Economics, Ithaca, N.Y. Processed.

———. 2002. "Public Social Sector Expenditures and Poverty in Peru." In Christian Morrisson, ed., *Education and Health Expenditure, and Development: The Cases of Indonesia and Peru*. Paris: Organisation for Economic Co-operation and Development, Development Center Studies.

4

Estimating Geographically Disaggregated Welfare Levels and Changes

Peter Lanjouw

Welfare levels tend to vary among the regions of almost every country of the world. Poverty is rarely distributed evenly within a country; particularly in the developing world, where pockets of severe deprivation are no rare occurrence. The existence of such poor areas can result from differences in geographic capital—biophysical endowment, access to infrastructure and markets, and so forth—as well as from government policies, such as migration policies or the distribution of centrally allocated resources.

In the face of such geographic heterogeneity, successful policy-making requires a good information base. For instance, an understanding of poverty and inequality levels at detailed spatial scales is a prerequisite for fine geographic targeting of interventions aimed at improving welfare levels. Decentralization in many countries has meant that decisionmaking for poverty alleviation programs is shifting from central government to regional or local levels. However, local decisionmaking, the design of the decentralization processes, and even the decision whether to pursue further decentralization should be based on reliable, locally relevant information on living standards and the distribution of wealth. In most countries such information is not readily at hand.

The problem of a lack of locally relevant poverty information is well known. Two main types of welfare-related information sources are available to policymakers. *Household surveys* often include a detailed income or consumption expenditure module, or both. However, because of relatively small sample size, the collected information is usually representative only for broad regions of the country. *Census data* (and sometimes large household sample surveys) are available for all households (or very large samples of households) and can provide reliable estimates at highly disaggregated levels such as small municipalities, towns, and villages. But censuses do not contain the income or consumption information necessary to yield reliable indicators of the level and distribution of welfare such as poverty rates or inequality measures.

Recent research has explored a technique that addresses the problem of lack of local data on poverty and inequality.[1] This method combines survey and census data to estimate consumption-based welfare indicators for small geographic areas such as districts and subdistricts, that is, a *poverty map*. Testing of the method using data for a growing number of developing countries indicates that statistically reliable estimates of poverty and inequality are attainable at encouragingly fine levels of spatial detail.

This research is closely related to the literature on small area statistics, which is also concerned with deriving estimators of population parameters at disaggregated levels using multiple data sources (for surveys, see Ghosh and Rao 1994 and Rao 1999). Empirical Bayes and best linear unbiased prediction models have been used to estimate the relationship between observables and a variable of interest at the unit record level. Together with the distribution of population covariates, these models are used to construct a "synthetic" estimator of an unobserved population parameter—a total, a mean, or more recently, proportions (see, for example, Malec, Davis, and Cao 1999). The synthetic estimator is typically used to "give strength" to a direct, sample-based estimator for the target area by lowering its variance. The current research extends this literature by developing estimators of population parameters that are nonlinear functions of the underlying variable of interest (unit-level consumption or income) and that derive from the full unit-level distribution of that variable. Following through on this extension leads naturally to the consideration of semi-parametric techniques for calculating synthetic estimates, as is done here. Finally, the focus of the attention here is almost entirely on areas where no direct sample information is available.

Data sets have been combined to fill in missing information or avoid sampling biases in a variety of other contexts. Examples in the econometric literature include Arellano and Meghir (1992), who estimate a labor supply model combining two samples. They use the U.K. Family Expenditure Survey to estimate models of wages and other income conditioning on variables common across the two samples. Hours and job search information from the much larger Labour Force Survey is then supplemented by predicted financial information. In a similar spirit, Angrist and Krueger (1992) combine data from two U.S. censuses. They estimate a model of educational attainment as a function of school entry age, where the first variable is available in only one census and the second in another, but an instrument, birth quarter, is common to both. Lusardi (1996) applies this two-sample instrumental variable estimator in a model of consumption behavior. Hellerstein and Imbens (1999) estimate weighted wage regressions using the U.S. National Longitudinal Survey but incorporate aggregate information from the U.S. census by constructing weights that force moments in the weighted sample to match those in the census.

The method described in this chapter combines household and census data using statistical procedures aimed at taking advantage of the detailed information available in household sample surveys and the comprehensive coverage of a census. Using a household survey to impute missing information in the census, poverty and inequality are estimated (as opposed to directly measured) at a disaggregated level based on a household per capita measure of expenditure, y_h. The idea is straightforward. First a model of y_h is estimated using the sample survey data, restricting explanatory variables to those that can be observed and linked to households in both sets of data. Then, letting W represent an indicator of poverty or inequality in some locality, the expected level of W is estimated given the census-based observable characteristics of the population of interest using parameter estimates from the "first-stage" model of y.

Progress to date has been encouraging and has prompted the implementation of the method in a growing number of developing countries. In addition exploration of extensions of the poverty mapping methodology is moving forward along a variety fronts. Elbers and others (2002a) apply the methodology to two household surveys, rather than a household survey and census, so as to impute into one survey a welfare indicator from another. Mistiaen (2002) explores the feasibility of applying poverty mapping techniques to evaluate geographic distribution of the *impact* on poverty of policy reforms. Efforts are also currently underway to explore the feasibility of producing "maps" expressed in terms of alternative notions of welfare (nutritional status, health).

Box 4.1 The Basic Steps of Poverty Mapping:
An Overview

The poverty map methodology involves detailed analysis of two main sources of data: a household survey, and the population census. In the first stage of the analysis, the two data sources are subjected to very close scrutiny with an eye toward identifying a set of common variables. In the second stage, the survey is used to develop a series of statistical models that relate per capita consumption to the set of common variables identified in the preceding step. In the final stage of the analysis, the parameter estimates from the previous stage are applied to the population census and used to predict consumption for each household in the population census. Once such a predicted consumption measure is available for each household in the census, summary measures of poverty (or inequality) can be estimated for a set of households in the census. Statistical tests can be performed to assess the reliability of the poverty estimates that have been produced. If the estimates are judged not to be sufficiently reliable, it may be necessary to return to the first stage for further experimentation with the model specification. Alternatively, it may be necessary to increase the number of households over which the poverty measure is estimated (issues of statistical reliability will guide whether the poverty map can be reliably produced at the region, district, or subdistrict level).

The three stages of analysis occur in sequence. The work involved in these stages is distinct, but the outputs of the first two stages are each key inputs into the subsequent stage. If the first stage cannot be satisfactorily carried out (for example, because of problems with the data), there is no point in continuing on to the second stage. And similarly, if the statistical models of the second stage are not satisfactory, there is no point in continuing on to the third stage. The poverty map exercise thus requires that progress be periodically assessed and evaluated. One cannot rule out the possibility that the exercise may need to be abandoned before it is completed.

The First Stage

The first stage in the poverty mapping exercise involves a rather painstaking comparison of common variables across the household survey and the population census. The idea here is to identify variables at the household level that are defined in the same way in both the household survey and the census. It is important that this common subset of variables be defined in exactly the same way across the two data sources. The only way to check this is to look at means and percentiles for each of the variables in both data sources and ensure that in terms of these means and percentiles the variables are virtually identical across the data sources. One can make this check rigorously, on the basis of statistical tests of differences, or informally, by simply making visual comparisons.

A concurrent exercise that can be carried out in parallel to the exercise described above is the compilation of a database at a level of aggregation higher than the household, which can be inserted into the household level census and the household survey databases. One of the methodological concerns in the poverty mapping exercise is that the common pool of household variables will not suffice to capture unobserved geographic effects, such as agroclimatic conditions or quality of local government administration, which might still be very important in predicting household-level consumption. In an effort to proxy these unobserved factors, it is useful to merge, say, district or subdistrict data that have been compiled separately into both the census and the household survey. These subdistrict data may comprise a wide range of variables (for example, construction of schools, public spending figures, infrastructure availability, and population estimates).

The Second Stage

Assuming that the two tasks described above yield a good and reasonably large set of common household-level variables, supplemented by a series of additional variables at a slightly higher level of disaggregation, the decision can then be made to proceed to the second-stage analysis. This stage involves the econometric estimation of models of consumption on the set of household-level and community variables. Most likely, a different model will be estimated for each stratum in the household survey data set, possibly separately for rural and urban areas. A large number of diagnostic tests need to be carried out, and a large number of different specifications are likely to be experimented with. It is possible that there will be a need to return to the *zero-stage* analysis to verify the construction of certain variables, to transform some variables, or to seek ways to add to the set of available regressors.

The Third Stage

Successsful completion of the second-stage analysis permits one to take the parameter estimates and attendent statistical outputs to the third stage. This stage is associated with the imputation of consumption into the census data at the household level and the estimation of poverty and inequality measures at a variety of levels of spatial disaggregation. Software has been developed that allows this phase of the work to be carried out mechanically

Once the poverty map exercise has been completed for all regions in the country, the resulting databases that provide estimates of poverty and inequality (and their standard errors) at a variety of levels of geographic disaggregation can be projected onto geographic *maps* using GIS (Geographic Information Systems) mapping techniques. This involves the application of GIS software (such as ARCView), which merges information on the geographic coordinates of localities such as the district or subdistrict with the poverty and inequality estimates produced by the poverty mapping methodology.

The Technique

Survey data are first used to estimate a prediction model for consumption, and then the parameter estimates are applied to the census data to derive poverty statistics. A key assumption of the methodology is thus that the models estimated from the survey data apply to census observations. This assumption is most reasonable if the survey and census years coincide. In this case, simple checks can be conducted by comparing the estimates to basic poverty or inequality statistics in the sample data. If different years are used but the assumption is considered reasonable, then the welfare estimates obtained refer to the census year, whose explanatory variables form the basis of the predicted expenditure distribution.

An important feature of the approach applied here involves the explicit recognition that the poverty or inequality statistics estimated using a model of income or consumption are statistically imprecise. Standard errors must be calculated. The following subsections briefly summarize the discussion in Elbers, Lanjouw, and Lanjouw (2002, 2003).

Definitions

Per capita household expenditure, y_h, is related to a set of observable characteristics, x_h:[2]

$$\ln y_h = E(\ln y_h \mid x_h) + u_h$$

Using a linear approximation, the observed log per capita expenditure for household h is modeled as:

(4.1) $\ln y_h = x_h^T \beta + u_h$

where β is a vector of parameters and u_h is a disturbance term satisfying $E(u_h \mid x_h) = 0$. In applications we allow for location effects and heteroskedasticity in the distribution of the disturbances.[3]

The model in equation 4.1 is estimated using the household survey data. We are interested in using these estimates to calculate the welfare of an area or group for which there is no, or insufficient, expenditure information. Although the disaggregation may be along any dimension—not necessarily geographic—the target population is referred to as a "county." Household h has m_h family members. Although the unit of observation for expenditure is the household, we are more often interested in welfare measures based on individuals. Thus we write $W(m, X, \beta, u)$, where m is a vector of household sizes, X is a matrix of observable characteristics, and u is a vector of disturbances. Because the disturbances for households in the target population are always unknown, the expected value of the indicator is estimated given the census households' observable characteristics and the model of expenditure in equation 4.1.[4] This expectation is denoted as $\mu = E(W \mid m, X, \xi)$, where ξ is the vector of all model parameters, including not only the coefficients β, but also the parameters describing the variance and the heteroskedasticity of the disturbance terms. In constructing an estimator of μ_v, the unknown vector ξ is replaced with consistent estimators, $\hat{\xi}$, from the first-stage expenditure regression. This yields $\hat{\mu} = E(W \mid m, X, \hat{\xi})$. This expectation is generally analytically intractable, so Monte Carlo simulation is used to obtain the estimator, $\tilde{\mu}$.

Estimating Error Components

The difference between $\tilde{\mu}$, the estimator of the expected value of W for the county, and the *actual* level of welfare for the county may be written:

$$W - \tilde{\mu} = (W - \mu) + (\mu - \hat{\mu}) + (\hat{\mu} + \tilde{\mu})$$

Thus the prediction error has three components: the first resulting from the presence of a disturbance term in the first-stage model that implies that households' actual expenditures deviate from their expected values (idiosyncratic error); the second resulting from variance in the first-stage estimates of the parameters of the expenditure model (model error); and the third resulting from using an inexact method to compute $\hat{\mu}$ (computation error).[5]

 • *Idiosyncratic Error.* The variance in the estimator resulting from idiosyncratic error falls approximately proportionately in the number of households in the county. That is, the smaller the target population, the greater is this component of the prediction error, and there is thus a practical limit to the degree of disaggregation possible. At what population size this error becomes unacceptably large depends on the explanatory power of the expenditure model and, correspondingly, the importance of the remaining idiosyncratic component of the expenditure.
 • *Model Error.* The part of the variance attributable to model error is determined by the properties of the first-stage estimators. Therefore model error does not increase or fall systematically as the size of the target population changes. Its magnitude depends on the precision of the first-stage coefficients and the sensitivity of the indicator to deviations in household expenditure. For a given county its magnitude will also depend on the distance of the

Table 4.1 Estimated Poverty Incidence in Ecuador, 1990

	Number of households			
Estimates	*100*	*1,000*	*15,000*	*100,000*
Headcount	0.46	0.50	0.51	0.51
Standard error	0.067	0.039	0.024	0.024
Idiosyncratic variance/				
total variance (%)	75	25	4	2

Source: Elbers, Lanjouw, and Lanjouw (2002).

explanatory variables for households in that county from the levels of those variables in the sample data.

 • *Computation Error.* The variance in the estimator attributable to computation error depends on the method of computation used and can be made as small as desired with sufficient resources.

The relationship between precision of the poverty estimates and the population size of the locality for which the estimate is being produced can be readily observed it table 4.1. The table estimates the incidence of poverty in four populations (constructed out of random draws from the 1990 census population of the rural coastal region of Ecuador) comprising, respectively, 100, 1,000, 15,000, and 100,000 households. The estimated incidence of poverty in these four populations is identical (by construction), but the precision of the estimate improves sharply as the population increases in size. This pattern arises from the relationship between population size and idiosyncratic error, described above. In the smallest population, the idiosyncratic error accounts for about 75 percent of the total variance around the poverty estimate (which corresponds to a standard error of 6.7 percentage points). As the population increases in size from 100 to 1,000, the overall standard error declines markedly, and the contribution attributable to the idiosyncratic error also declines sharply. When the population is as large as 100,000 households, the idiosyncratic error has virtually declined to zero, and the overall standard error is effectively composed only of model error.[6]

An Example: Public Health Spending and the Geography of Poverty in Madagascar

Figure 4.1 presents two maps of Madagascar. The first depicts the spatial distribution of public spending on (nonsalary) health spending

Figure 4.1 Health Spending and Poverty in Madagascar

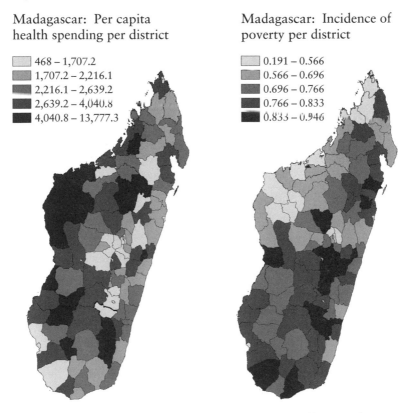

Madagascar: Per capita health spending per district

☐ 468 – 1,707.2
▨ 1,707.2 – 2,216.1
▨ 2,216.1 – 2,639.2
▨ 2,639.2 – 4,040.8
■ 4,040.8 – 13,777.3

Madagascar: Incidence of poverty per district

☐ 0.191 – 0.566
▨ 0.566 – 0.696
▨ 0.696 – 0.766
▨ 0.766 – 0.833
■ 0.833 – 0.946

Notes: Health spending refers to per capita nonrecurrent public expenditures in 2000 Malagasi francs (US$1 is approximately FMG 6,000). Poverty data are for 1993, the year of the last population census.

Source: Galasso (2002).

by district (*fivondrona*) in 2000. The second depicts the *fivondrona*-level poverty map of Madagascar in 1993, the year of the most recent population census (Mistiaen and others 2002). Mistiaen and others (2002) demonstrate that predicted poverty measures in Madagascar's 111 *fivondronas* are generally estimated with levels of precision that are comparable to province-level estimates in the household survey. The gain from implementing this methodology is thus an increase in disaggregation from six provinces to 111 *fivondronas* without incurring any penalty in terms of precision.[7]

Experience: Some Case Studies

Poverty mapping techniques are being applied in a rapidly growing number of countries. These exercises are yielding valuable new insights into the geographic distribution of poverty and inequality within countries. The basic methodology is also proving to be quite flexible and can be readily extended and applied to other policy-relevant questions.

The Spatial Distribution of Poverty

A recent paper by Demombynes and others (forthcoming) takes three developing countries, Ecuador, Madagascar, and South Africa, and implements the poverty mapping methodology in each to produce estimates of poverty at a level of disaggregation that to date has not generally been available. The countries are very unlike each other—with different geographies, stages of development, quality and types of data, and so on. Nonetheless the paper demonstrates that the methodology works well in all three settings and can produce valuable information about the spatial distribution of poverty within those countries that was previously not known.

The paper demonstrates that the poverty estimates produced from census data are plausible in that they match well the estimates calculated directly from the country's surveys (at levels of disaggregation that the survey can bear). The precision of the poverty estimates produced with this methodology varies with the degree of disaggregation. In all three countries considered, the method yields satisfactorily precise estimates of poverty at levels of disaggregation far below that allowed by surveys.

The paper illustrates how the poverty estimates produced with this method can be represented in maps, thereby conveying an enormous amount of information about the spread and relative magnitude of poverty across localities, as well as about the precision of estimates, in a way that is quickly and intuitively absorbed also by nontechnical audiences. Such detailed geographical profiles of poverty can inform a wide variety of debates and deliberations, among policymakers as well as civil society.

Finally, the paper notes that perceptions about the importance of geographical dimensions of poverty are themselves a function of the degree of spatial disaggregation of available estimates of poverty. The smaller the localities into which a country can be broken down, the more likely one will conclude that geography matters.

The Spatial Distribution of Inequality

A paper by Elbers and others (2002b) implements the poverty mapping methodology to produce disaggregated estimates of inequality in Ecuador, Madagascar, and Mozambique. Just as Demombynes and others (forthcoming) show for poverty, the paper demonstrates that inequality estimates produced from census data match well the estimates calculated directly from the country's surveys (at levels of disaggregation that the survey can bear). Again, in all three countries considered, the inequality estimators allow one to work at a level of disaggregation far below that allowed by surveys.

Interest among policymakers regarding local distributional outcomes has risen in recent years with the growing recognition that community-level income inequality can influence the extent and nature of capture of local government by local elites and thereby affect the impact of decentralization initiatives (Bardhan 2002). Similarly, in a recent review of experience with community-driven development, Mansuri and Rao (2003) suggest that community-based targeting (whereby communities are asked to assist in the targeting of the poor within their communities) may be hampered by high levels of heterogeneity in living standards within those communities. In the study by Elbers and others (2002b), inequality in Ecuador, Madagascar, and Mozambique is decomposed into progressively more disaggregated spatial units, and even at a very high level of spatial disaggregation the contribution to overall inequality of within-community inequality is found to be very high (75 percent or more). This finding illustrates the danger of simply assuming that living standards at the local level are more equally distributed than at the national level. However, it is also shown that a high within-group decomposition result does not suffice to indicate that all communities in a given country are as unequal as the country as a whole. The paper shows that in all three countries examined, the amount of variation in inequality across communities is considerable. Many communities are rather more equal than their respective country as a whole, but many communities are not, and some may even be considerably more unequal. These findings may have important implications for the design of decentralized financing, for the design and implementation of policies, and for the success of community-driven development initiatives.

Given the spatial variation in inequality the paper explores some basic correlates of local-level inequality in the three countries. Consistent patterns are observed. In all three countries, geographic characteristics are strongly correlated with inequality, even after controlling for demographic and economic conditions. The correlation with geography is observed in both rural and urban areas. In rural areas population size and mean consumption at the community level are positively associated with inequality, indicating that smaller and poorer communities in rural areas tend to be more equal. In urban areas this pattern is not observed—smaller and poorer neighborhoods are as unequal as rich ones. In both rural and urban areas, populations with large shares of the elderly tend to be more unequal.

Survey to Survey Imputations: A Case Study of Brazilian Inequality and Poverty

A recent paper by Elbers and others (2002a) imputes a measure of consumption from a relatively small household survey in Brazil, the Pesquisa Sobre Padroes de Vida (PPV), fielded in 1996, into the much larger and more widely used Pesquisa Nacional por Amostra de Domicilios (PNAD) household survey for the same year. The purpose is to estimate measures of welfare, such as poverty and inequality, defined in terms of consumption, at levels of disaggregation that are permitted by the PNAD data set.[8] Standard errors on the consumption-based point estimates in the PNAD are shown to be quite reasonable—certainly compared with the standard of typical household surveys. These standard errors reflect not only the errors produced in the standard poverty mapping approach but also the fact that the PNAD survey, into which consumption is imputed, is a sample survey, not a census.

This exercise was undertaken to address a concern in the literature regarding PNAD-based distributional analysis. Although the PNAD underpins virtually all national-level analyses of poverty and inequality in Brazil, concerns have been raised that the income measure in this survey might suffer from serious biases. In particular it is feared that the PNAD income concept does not capture well incomes accruing from informal sector and self-employment activities (Ferreira, Lanjouw, and Neri 2003).

The paper by Elbers and others (2002a) finds that poverty and inequality, estimated on the basis of consumption in the PNAD, tend to be much lower than estimates based on the income concept. This is not necessarily an indictment of income-based analysis, however, as the two concepts of welfare are different and should not be expected to yield the same quantitative estimates. To the extent, however, that consumption is viewed as a more appealing indicator of welfare, the results do suggest that Brazil is less of an outlier, in terms of inequality and poverty, compared with other countries in the world, than is commonly thought. It should be noted, in addition, that differences in estimates of poverty and inequality between the PNAD and the PPV are not attributable to noncomparability of these two surveys. The PNAD consumption-based estimates are very close to those that obtain with the PPV.

Income and consumption-based analysis of the PNAD is found to result in broadly similar qualitative conclusions regarding the spatial distribution of poverty and inequality. In only a few cases do differences appear across the two approaches that merit further attention. First, according to the consumption criterion, there is a clear basis for viewing metropolitan areas in the northeast as less poor than other areas. This distinction is less clear-cut according to the income criterion. Second, within rural areas in the northeast, rural Paraiba is the least poor state according to the PNAD consumption criterion but the third poorest state according to the PNAD income criterion. Third, the PNAD consumption criterion finds that metropolitan areas in the northeast are markedly more equal than other urban areas in this region. The PNAD income criterion finds the reverse. Fourth, the consumption-based approach reflects much more strongly than the income-based one the contribution of differences in average incomes across states to overall rural inequality.

Mapping the Impact of Policy Reforms

In an ongoing research project, the poverty mapping methodology is adopted to explore the impact of macroeconomic policy reforms at unprecedentedly low levels of spatial disaggregation. In a preliminary study, Mistiaen (2002) simulates the impact on poverty in urban Antananarivo, Madagascar, of a 15 percent decrease in the price of rice (roughly equivalent to the elimination of the import tariff in that country in 1993) by recalculating net consumption expenditures based on these new prices. To provide a short-run benchmark, he considers the case of a perfectly elastic labor supply and assumes that nonfood prices and other incomes remain constant; thus the impact of a marginal change in food prices depends on whether the household is a net consumer or a net producer of food.

Mistiaen (2002) compares the poverty map based on the "post-reform" consumption measure against the poverty map based on the original consumption definition, and finds evidence of considerable variation in the magnitude of poverty impacts across neighborhoods in urban Antananarivo. Thus, not only is there substantial variation in well-being among small areas, but these results also suggest that the microeconomic-level welfare impact of macroeconomic-level policies can exhibit a considerable degree of geographic heterogeneity.

A number of methodological issues must be resolved before the "impact mapping" approach can be mainstreamed. An important issue currently under scrutiny concerns the proper treatment of interdependence between actual and simulated expenditures and the implications this interdependence will have for the precision of the small area impact estimates. Looking forward, the methodology seems to offer a promising route toward linking macroeconomic-level policy reforms to microeconomic-level poverty impacts. While the work to date has focused on rather simple policy reforms and has assumed away many plausible behavioral responses, there is ample scope for elaboration in the simulation scenarios, once outstanding methodological concerns are resolved.

Final Remarks

The poverty mapping methods outlined in this chapter are potentially of value in analyzing the geographic incidence of public spending and its impact in reducing poverty. It is important to restate, however, that implementation of the method is predicated on the availability of unit-record-level household survey *and* population census data. Moreover the approach is built on the assumption that the household survey and census represent the same underlying population. When the survey corresponds to exactly the same time period as the census, this assumption is relatively innocuous. If some time span separates the survey and the census, however, the assumption becomes stronger. The assumption is likely to become untenable if the period separating the two data sources is characterized by major economic upheaval or some other dramatic event. Even where this assumption (and others that underpin the methodology) seems plausible, exploring opportunities to *validate* results from the poverty mapping exercise is advisable. It might be possible to identify case-study opportunities to compare predictions of poverty for a specific locality with actual observed measures from detailed microeconomic studies. Such validation activities must be conducted with care, but they could assist significantly in guiding interpretation of the poverty mapping results and how they can best be used.

Finally, it is important to bear in mind that poverty maps, as described in this chapter, are best seen as offering a snapshot of the geographic distribution of poverty, corresponding to the date of the population census. Policymakers are likely to be interested, as well, in tracing the evolution of this geographic profile of poverty over time. Short of waiting for the next census (there is usually a 10-year interval between censuses), it is not obvious how a poverty map can be updated over time. Current research is exploring methods to apply similar estimation techniques to predict changes in the poverty map, as a function of locational characteristics that can be tracked over time. Such methods appear to be promising but have not yet yielded any conclusive results.

Notes

1. Elbers, Lanjouw, and Lanjouw (2002, 2003) refine and extend considerably an approach first outlined in Hentschel and others (2000).

2. The explanatory variables are observed values and need to have the same degree of accuracy in addition to the same definitions across data sources.

3. Consider the following model: $\ln y_{ch} = E(\ln y_{ch} \mid x_{ch}^T + u_{ch} = x_{ch}^T\beta + \eta_c + \varepsilon_{ch}$, where η and ε are independent of each other and uncorrelated with observables. This specification allows for an intracluster correlation in the disturbances. One expects location to be related to household income and consumption, and it is certainly plausible that some of the effect of location might remain unexplained even with a rich set of regressors. For any given disturbance variance, σ_{ch}^2, the greater the fraction due to the common component η_c, the less one benefits from aggregating over more households. Welfare estimates become less precise. Further, failing to account for spatial correlation in the disturbances would result in underestimated standard errors on poverty estimates and possibly bias the inequality estimates.

4. If the target population includes sample survey households, then some disturbances are known. As a practical matter we do not use these few pieces of direct information on y.

5. Elbers and others (2002a) use a second survey in place of the census, which then also introduces sampling error.

6. Computation error has been set effectively to zero by means of a sufficiently large number of simulations.

7. The absence of a penalty in terms of statistical precision arises out of the fact that survey-based estimates are imprecise due to *sampling error*, while applying the poverty mapping methodology to project poverty estimates in the population census avoids sampling error but incurs *prediction error* (comprising the idiosyncratic, model, and computation errors described in the text).

8. Fofack (2000) applies a related method to combine two household surveys in Ghana for the purpose of estimating the incidence of poverty in one survey based on the welfare definition available in the second. His analysis is confined to the headcount measure of poverty and does not address the question of statistical precision. See also Bigman and Fofack (2000).

References

The word *processed* describes informally reproduced works that may not be commonly available through library systems.

Angrist, J., and A. Krueger. 1992. "The Effect of Age of School Entry on Educational Attainment: An Application of Instrumental Variables with Moments from Two Samples." *Journal of the American Statistical Association* 87: 328–36.

Arellano, M., and C. Meghir. 1992. "Female Labour Supply and on the Job Search: An Empirical Model Estimated Using Complementary Data Sets." *Review of Economic Studies* 59: 537–59.

Bardhan, P. 2002. "Decentralization of Governance and Development." *Journal of Economic Perspectives* 16(4): 185–205.

Bigman, D., and Hippolyte Fofack. 2000. "Geographical Targeting for Poverty Alleviation." World Bank: Regional and Sectoral Studies, Washington, D.C.

Demombynes, G., C. Elbers, J.O. Lanjouw, P. Lanjouw, J. A Mistiaen, and B. Özler. Forthcoming. "Producing an Improved Geographic Profile of Poverty: Methodology and Evidence from Three Developing Countries." In Rolph van der Hoeven and Anthony Shorrocks, eds., *Growth, Inequality and Poverty*. Oxford, U.K.: Oxford University Press.

Elbers, C., J.O. Lanjouw, and Peter Lanjouw. 2002. "Welfare in Villages and Towns: Micro-Level Estimation of Poverty and Inequality." Policy Research Working Paper 2911. World Bank, Development Economics Research Group, Washington, D.C. Processed.

———. 2003. "Micro-Level Estimation of Poverty and Inequality." *Econometrica* 71 (January): 355–64.

Elbers, C., J.O. Lanjouw, Peter Lanjouw, and P. G. Leite. 2002a. "Poverty and Inequality in Brazil: New Estimates from Combined PPV-PNAD Data." World Bank, Development Economics Research Group, Washington, D.C. Processed.

Elbers, C., Peter Lanjouw, J. A. Mistiaen, B. Özler, and K. Simler. 2002b. "Are Neighbours Equal? Estimating Local Inequality in Three Developing Countries." Paper presented at the conference on Spatial Distribution of Inequality, sponsored by the London School of Economics, Cornell University, and World Institute for Development Economics Research, London.

Ferreira, F., P. Lanjouw, and M. Neri. Forthcoming. "A New Poverty Profile for Brazil Using PPV, PNAD and Census Data." *Revista Brasileira de Economia*.

Fofack, H. 2000. "Combining Light Monitoring Surveys with Integrated Surveys to Improve Targeting for Poverty Reduction: The Case of Ghana." *World Bank Economic Review* 14 (January): 195–219.

Galasso, Emanuela. 2002. "The Geographical Dimension of Public Expenditures and Its Link to Poverty: The Case of Madagascar." Paper presented at the conference on Public Expenditures and Poverty Reduction: Issues and Tools, sponsored by the World Bank Poverty Reduction and Economic Management Network, Cape Town, South Africa. Processed.

Ghosh, M., and J.N.K. Rao. 1994. "Small Area Estimation: An Appraisal," *Statistical Science* 9(1): 55–93.

Hellerstein, J., and G. Imbens. 1999. "Imposing Moment Restrictions from Auxiliary Data by Weighting." *Review of Economics and Statistics* 81(1): 1–14.

Hentschel, J., J.O. Lanjouw, P. Lanjouw, and J. Poggi. 2000. "Combining Census and Survey Data to Trace the Spatial Dimensions of Poverty: A Case Study of Ecuador." *World Bank Economic Review* 14(1): 147–65.

Lusardi, A. 1996. "Permanent Income, Current Income and Consumption: Evidence from Two Panel Data Sets." *Journal of Business and Economic Statistics* 14(1): 81–90.

Malec, D., W. Davis, and X. Cao. 1999. "Model-based Small Area Estimates of Overweight Prevalence Using Sample Selection Adjustment." *Statistics in Medicine* 18: 3189–200.

Mansuri, G. and V. Rao. 2003. "Evaluating Community Driven Development: A Review of the Evidence." World Bank, Development Economics Research Group, Washington, D.C. Processed.

Mistiaen, J.A. 2002. "Small Area Estimates of Welfare Impacts: The Case of Food Price Changes in Madagascar." World Bank, Development Economics Research Group, Washington, D.C. Processed.

Mistiaen, J.A., B. Özler, T. Razafimanantena, and J. Razafindravonona. 2002. "Putting Welfare on the Map in Madagascar." World Bank, Development Economics Research Group, Washington, D.C. Processed.

Rao, J.N.K. 1999. "Some Recent Advances in Model-Based Small Area Estimation." *Survey Methodology* 25(2): 175–86.

5

Assessing the Poverty Impact of an Assigned Program

Martin Ravallion

Some public programs are assigned more or less exclusively to certain units that are observable. These may be people, households, villages, or larger geographic areas. The key point is that some units receive the program and some do not. This chapter reviews tools that can help assess the impacts of such a program, judged against its agreed objectives. The following are examples of the types of programs that can be assessed with the tools discussed in this chapter:

- A social fund asks for proposals from community organizations, with preference for proposals from poor areas. Some areas do not apply, and some do but are rejected.
- A workfare program entails extra earnings for participating workers and gains to the residents of the areas in which the work is done. Others receive nothing from the program.
- Infrastructure projects (road or water connections, for example) are targeted to areas that are both poor and poorly endowed in that infrastructure. Other areas do not participate.

Notice that in each of these examples, there may be some indirect (or second-round) effects on nonparticipants. A workfare program may lead to higher earnings for nonparticipants. Or a road improvement project in one area might improve accessibility elsewhere. Depending on how important these indirect effects are thought to be in the specific application, the "program" may need to be redefined to embrace the spillover effects. Or one might need to combine the type of evaluation discussed here with other tools, such as a model of the labor market, to pick up other benefits.

The following discussion assumes that the program is already in place, which makes this a case of ex post impact assessment.[1] That assessment includes the evaluation of a pilot project, as an input to the ex ante assessment of whether the project should be scaled up. However, doing ex post evaluations does not mean that the evaluation should start after the program finishes, or even after it begins. Indeed, the best ex post evaluations are designed ex ante—often side-by-side with the program itself. This early planning can greatly facilitate the evaluation, for example, by allowing pre-intervention data to be collected on probable participants and nonparticipants.

The indicators by which a program is to be assessed are taken to be given, as appropriate to the type of program. For direct anti-poverty programs, for example, one is usually concerned about the program's impacts on incomes of the participants and possibly also on other indicators such as school attendance. Knowing the impact is of obvious interest in its own right as a means of measuring the aggregate benefits from the program. However, when reducing poverty is the overall objective of the program, one also wants to know the *incidence* of the welfare gains. Incidence can be known only by knowing the welfare impact at given values of the pre-intervention welfare indicator. To know incidence, one must know impact.

Figure 5.1 is an example of the type of "impact–incidence" assessment that might be made for an assignable antipoverty program; in this example, it is Argentina's Trabajar program (a combination of workfare program and social fund). The figure gives the poverty incidence curves (PICs) showing how the headcount index of poverty (the percentage below the poverty line) varies across a wide range of possible poverty lines (when that range covers all incomes, it produces the standard cumulative distribution function). The vertical line is an indicative poverty line for Argentina. The figure also gives the estimated counterfactual PIC, after deducting the imputed income gains from the observed (postintervention) incomes of all the sampled participants. Thus we can see the gain at each percentile of the distribution (looking horizontally) or the impact on the incidence of poverty at any given poverty line (looking vertically).

This chapter demonstrates how figure 5.1 is estimated.[2] Along the way, the chapter also discusses other tools used for impact assessments of assignable programs. The methods share some common features related to their data requirements, as summarized in box 5.1.

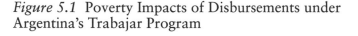

Figure 5.1 Poverty Impacts of Disbursements under Argentina's Trabajar Program

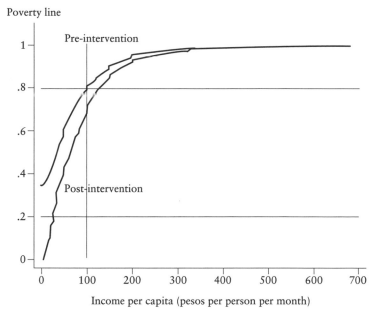

Source: Jalan and Ravallion (2003b).

Randomization

Clearly data are needed on an appropriate outcome indicator for the participants. However, to assess impact, one also has to have some way of inferring the counterfactual of what one expects the value of the outcome indicator would have been in the absence of the program. That calls for data on nonparticipants.

Even with good data on outcome measures for both participants and nonparticipants, retrieving a reliable estimate of the program's impact is far from easy. The main reason for the difficulty is that public programs are generally not assigned randomly across the population of units. So the observed differences in measured outcome indicators between units who receive the program and those who do not cannot be attributed to the program. The measured differences in the data could simply mean that the program participants were purposely selected. This is often called *selection bias.*

Selection bias is not a problem with randomized assignment (a genuine experiment), because everyone then has the same chance ex

Box 5.1 Data for Impact Evaluation

- Know the program well. It is risky to embark on an evaluation without knowing a lot about the administrative and institutional details of the program. Such information typically comes from the program administration.
- It helps a lot to have a firm grip on the relevant "stylized facts" about the setting. The relevant facts might include the poverty map, the way the labor market works, the major ethnic divisions, other relevant public programs, and the like.
- Be eclectic about data. Sources can embrace informal, unstructured, interviews with participants in the program as well as quantitative data from representative samples.
- However, it is extremely difficult to ask counterfactual questions in interviews or focus groups. Try asking someone who is currently participating in a public program: "what would you be doing now if this program did not exist?" Talking to program participants can be valuable, but it is unlikely to provide a credible evaluation on its own.
- You also need data on the outcome indicators and relevant explanatory variables. The latter are needed to deal with *heterogeneity* in outcomes conditional on program participation. Outcomes can differ depending on whether one is educated, say. It may not be possible to see the impact of the program unless one controls for that heterogeneity.
- You might also need data on variables that influence participation but do not influence outcomes given participation. Such instrumental variables can be valuable in sorting out the likely causal effects of nonrandom programs.
- The data on outcomes and other relevant explanatory variables can be either quantitative or qualitative. But it has to be possible to organize the data in some sort of systematic *data structure*. A simple and common example is values of various variables including one or more outcome indicators for various observation units (individuals, households, firms, communities).
- The variables you collect data on and the observation units you use are often chosen as part of the evaluation method. These choices should be anchored to prior knowledge about the program (its objectives, of course, but also how it is run) and the setting in which it is introduced.
- The specific data on outcomes and their determinants, including program participation, typically come from survey data of some sort. The observation unit could be the household, firm, or geographic area, depending on the type of program one is studying.
- Survey data can often be supplemented with other useful data on the program (including the project monitoring database) or setting (including geographic databases).

ante of receiving the program. The distributions of both observed and unobserved attributes before the program intervention are the same, whether or not a unit receives the program. In such cases the observed ex post differences in the outcome indicators are attributable to the program.

Randomization is the theoretical ideal and a natural benchmark for assessing nonexperimental (sometimes called quasi-experimental) methods. There are sometimes opportunities for randomizing the assignment of an antipoverty program, possibly on a pilot basis. A number of evaluations of active labor market programs have used randomized assignment. In the case of training programs, two examples are the U.S. Job Training Partnership Act (see, for example, Heckman, Ichimura, and Todd 1997) and the U.S. National Supported Work Demonstration (studied by Lalonde 1986 and Dehejia and Wahba 1999, among others). For wage subsidy programs, randomized evaluations have been done by Burtless (1985), Woodbury and Spiegelman (1987), and Dubin and Rivers (1993)—all for targeted wage subsidy schemes in the United States. A recent example for a World Bank–supported program can be found in Galasso, Ravallion, and Salvia (2001), who randomized a wage subsidy and training program to help workfare participants in Argentina find regular, private sector jobs. Besides labor market programs, randomization has also been used in assessing (inter alia) residential relocation programs (Katz, Kling, and Liebman 2001) and school voucher programs (Angrist and others 2001).

In practice, the chosen participants sometimes do not want to comply with the randomized assignment. That is to be expected in almost any social experiment. Most analyses want to know the impact of receiving the treatment, which clearly cannot be assumed to be exogenous when compliance is selective. Angrist, Imbens, and Rubin (1996) have shown how one can correct for selective compliance by using the randomized assignment as the instrumental variable for treatment in a regression for the outcome measure. Applications can be found in Galasso, Ravallion, and Salvia (2001) and Katz, Kling, and Liebman (2001).

Sometimes, however, randomization is not a feasible option. The government does not want to assign the program randomly, but rather to target it purposively to certain groups, such as the income poor or those with low current access to the facilities provided by the program. What can be done to assess impact when it is known that a program was not randomly placed? The rest of this chapter aims to provide an overview of the best methods currently available for addressing this question.

Propensity-Score Matching Methods

Along with randomization, matching is one of the oldest tools of evaluation. The idea is to find a comparison group that looks like the treatment group in all respects except one: the comparison group did not get the program. In practice, however, the problem was always how to define "looks like"; there are potentially many characteristics one might look for to match on, and it has not been clear whether a match has to be "identical" in all these characteristics, and (if not) how each characteristic should be weighted.

The method of propensity-score matching (PSM), devised by Rosenbaum and Rubin (1983), can justifiably claim to be the solution to this problem—and thus the observational analog of a randomized experiment. The method balances the *observed* covariates between the treatment group and a control group (sometimes called *comparison group* for nonrandom evaluations) based on similarity of their predicted probabilities of receiving the treatment (called their *propensity scores*). The difference between PSM and a pure experiment is that the latter also ensures that the treatment and comparison groups are identical in terms of the distribution of unobserved characteristics. Box 5.2 summarizes the steps in PSM.

The key to PSM is understanding and modeling the assignment mechanism for the program. Two groups are identified: those households that have the treatment (denoted $D_i = 1$ for household i) and those that do not ($D_i = 0$). Treated units are matched to nontreated units on the basis of the propensity score:

$$P(X_i) = \text{Prob}(D_i = 1 | X_i) \quad (0 < P(X_i) < 1)$$

where X_i is a vector of pre-exposure control variables. The choice of variables must be based on knowledge of the program and are often also informed by theories of the economic, social, or political factors influencing the assignment of a program. Clearly if the data do not include important determinants of participation, then the presence of these unobserved characteristics means that PSM will not be able to reproduce the results of a pure experiment.

PSM uses $P(X)$—or a monotone function of $P(X)$—to select controls for each of the subjects treated. It is known from Rosenbaum and Rubin (1983) that if the D_is are independent over all i and if outcomes are independent of participation given X_i, then outcomes are also independent of participation given $P(X_i)$, just as they would be if participation were assigned randomly.[3] Exact matching on $P(X)$ implies that the resulting matched control and treated subjects have the same distribution of the covariates. This is the sense in which PSM is the observational analog to an experiment; just like

Box 5.2 Propensity-Score Matching

The aim of matching is to find the comparison group from a sample of nonparticipants that is closest to the sample of program participants. "Closest" is measured in terms of observable characteristics. If there are only one or two such characteristics, then matching should be easy. But typically there are many potential characteristics. This is where propensity-score matching comes in. The main steps in matching based on propensity scores are as follows:

Step 1: You need a representative sample survey of eligible non-participants as well as one for the participants. The larger the sample of eligible nonparticipants the better, to facilitate good matching. If the two samples come from different surveys, then they should be highly comparable surveys (same questionnaire, same interviewers or interviewer training, same survey period, and so on).

Step 2: Pool the two samples and estimate a logit model of program participation as a function of all the variables in the data that are likely to determine participation.

Step 3: Create the predicted values of the probability of participation from the logit regression; these are called the *propensity scores*. You will have a propensity score for every sampled participant and nonparticipant.

Step 4: Some of the nonparticipants in the sample may have to be excluded at the outset because they have a propensity score that is outside the range (typically too low) found for the treatment sample. The range of propensity scores estimated for the treatment group should correspond closely to that for the retained subsample of nonparticipants. You may also want to restrict potential matches in other ways, depending on the setting. For example, you may want to allow matches only within the same geographic area to help ensure that the matches come from the same economic environment.

Step 5: For each individual in the treatment sample, you now want to find the observation in the nonparticipant sample that has the closest propensity score, as measured by the absolute difference in scores. This is called the *nearest neighbor*. You will get more precise estimates if you use the nearest five neighbors, say.

Step 6: Calculate the mean value of the outcome indicator (or each of the indicators if there is more than one) for the five nearest neighbors. The difference between that mean and the actual value for the treated observation is the estimate of the gain attributable to the program for that observation.

Step 7: Calculate the mean of these individual gains to obtain the average overall gain, which can be stratified by some variable of interest such as incomes in the nonparticipant sample.

an experiment, PSM equalizes the probability of participation across the population—the difference is that with PSM, probability is conditional, and it is conditional on the X variables.

Common practice uses the predicted values from standard logit or probit models to estimate the propensity score for each observation in the participant and the comparison group samples.[4] Using the estimated propensity scores, $\hat{P}(X)$, matched pairs are constructed on the basis of how close the scores are across the two samples. The "nearest neighbor" to the ith participant is defined as the nonparticipant that has the closest value of the propensity score among all participants. One can apply caliper bounds; for example, matches might be accepted only if the absolute difference in scores is less than, say, 0.01.

Letting ΔY_j denote the gain in a welfare indicator for the jth unit attributable to access to the program, the PSM estimator of mean impact is:

$$(5.1) \qquad \Delta \overline{Y} = \sum_{j=1}^{T} \omega_j \left(Y_{j1} - \sum_{i=1}^{C} W_{ij} Y_{ij0} \right)$$

where Y_{j1} is the postintervention outcome indicator, Y_{ij0} is the outcome indicator of the ith nontreated unit matched to the jth treated unit, T is the total number of treatments, C is the total number of nontreated households, ω_js are the sampling weights used to construct the mean impact estimator, and the W_{ij}s are the weights applied in calculating the average income of the matched nonparticipants.

Several weights can be used, ranging from nearest-neighbor weights to nonparametric weights based on kernel functions of the differences in scores (Heckman, Ichimura, and Todd 1997; Heckman and others 1998).[5] It is a good idea to use more than just the nearest neighbor; for example, one can use the mean for the nearest five neighbors, that is, one can take the average outcome measure of the closest five matched nonparticipants as the counterfactual for each participant.[6]

One can also use a regression-adjusted estimator. This assumes a conventional linear model for outcomes in the matched comparison group, $Y_0 = X\beta_0 + \mu_0$ in obvious notation. (The regression is only run for the matched comparison group, so it is not contaminated by the endogeneity of access to the program.) The impact estimator in this case is then defined as:

$$\Delta \overline{Y} = \sum_{j=1}^{T} \omega_j \left[(Y_{j1} - X_j \hat{\beta}_0) - \sum_{i=1}^{C} W_{ij} (Y_{ij0} - X_i \hat{\beta}_0) \right]$$

where $\hat{\beta}_0$ is the ordinary least squares (OLS) estimate for the comparison group sample.

Conditional mean impact estimators can be obtained by calculating equation 5.1 conditional on certain observed characteristics. For antipoverty programs one is interested in comparing the conditional mean impact across different pre-intervention income levels. For each sampled participant, the income gain from the program is estimated by comparing that participant's income with the income for matched nonparticipants. Subtracting the estimated gain from observed postintervention income, it is then possible to know where each participant would have been in the distribution of income without the program. Thus one can construct the empirical and counterfactual PICs, as in figure 5.1. (These PICs can be smoothed, by using locally weighted means for example.) Box 5.3 summarizes the steps for doing this and for interpreting the results to form a qualitative assessment of poverty impact. The same steps can all be repeated for multiple programs, which can then be compared with each other.

One can also construct a *concentration curve*, showing the cumulative share of benefits going to the poorest x percent of the population, ranked by household income per person, with x ranging from 1 to 100. Figure 5.2 gives the concentration curve for the earnings gains from the Trabajar program. Of course, the concentration curve does not give the impact on poverty; for that purpose one needs the PIC, as in figure 5.1.

Figure 5.2 Concentration Curve of Participation in Argentina's Trabajar Program

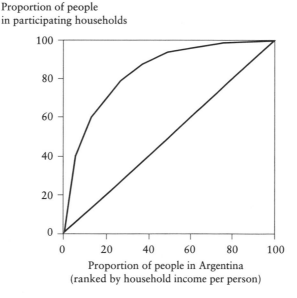

Proportion of people
in participating households

Proportion of people in Argentina
(ranked by household income per person)

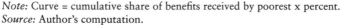

Note: Curve = cumulative share of benefits received by poorest x percent.
Source: Author's computation.

Box 5.3 Graphical Representation of Poverty Impact

The empirical and counterfactual poverty incidence curves (as in figure 5.1) are constructed as follows:

Step 1: You should already have the postintervention income (or other welfare indicator) for each household in the whole sample (comprising both participants and nonparticipants); this is data. You also know how many people are in each household. And, of course, you know the total number of people in the sample (N; or this might be the estimated population size, if inverse sampling rates have been used to "expend up" each sample observation).

Step 2: You can plot this information in the form of a poverty incidence curve (PIC). The curve gives (on the vertical axis) the percentage of the population living in households with an income less than or equal to that value on the horizontal axis. To make this graph, you can start with the poorest household, mark its income on the horizontal axis, and then count up on the vertical axis by 100 times the number of people in that household divided by N. The next point is the proportion living in the two poorest households, and so on. This gives the postintervention PIC.

Step 3: Now calculate the distribution of pre-intervention income. Do this by subtracting the estimated gain for each household from its postintervention income. You then have a list of pre-intervention incomes, one for each sampled household. Then repeat Step 2 to get the pre-intervention PIC.

How should these curves be interpreted? If one thinks of any given income level on the horizontal axis as a poverty line, then the difference between the two PICs at that point gives the impact on the headcount index for that poverty line. Alternatively, looking horizontally gives you the income gain at that percentile. If none of the gains are negative, then

---

How Does PSM Compare with Other Methods?

Probably the most common method used to assess the impact of an assigned program is comparison of average outcome indicators between units that have the program and those that do not. For example, past methods of assessing health gains from water and sanitation programs have often compared villages with piped water and those without. Similarly, assessments of the impacts of providing new rural roads often compare the incomes or other outcome indicators of villages with roads and those without. Clearly failure to control for differences in the pre-intervention characteristics of the participants and nonparticipants could severely bias such comparisons. Van de Walle (2002) gives an example for rural road eval-

the postintervention PIC must lie below the pre-intervention on. Poverty will have fallen no matter what poverty line is used. Indeed, this result also holds for a broad class of poverty measures; see Atkinson (1987). If some gains are negative, then the PICs will intersect. The poverty comparison is then ambiguous; the answer will depend on which poverty lines and which poverty measures are used. You might then use a priori restrictions on the range of admissible poverty lines. For example, you may be confident that the poverty line does not exceed some maximum value, and if the intersection occurs above that value, then the poverty comparison is unambiguous. If the intersection point (and there may be more than one) is below the maximum admissible poverty line, then a robust poverty comparison is possible only for a restricted set of poverty measures. To check how restricted the set needs to be, you can calculate the *poverty depth curves* (PDCs). These are obtained by simply forming the cumulative sum up to each point on the PIC, so the second point on the PDC is the first point on the PIC plus the second point, and so on.

If the PDCs do not intersect, then the direction of the program's impact on poverty is unambiguous as long as one restricts attention to the poverty gap index or any of the distribution-sensitive poverty measures, such as the Watts (1968) measure or the squared poverty gap index of Foster, Greer, and Thorbecke (1984). If the PDCs intersect then you can calculate the *poverty severity curves* with and without the program, by forming the cumulative sums under the PDCs. If these do not intersect over the range of admissible poverty lines, then the direction of impact on any of the distribution-sensitive poverty measures is unambiguous.

For further discussion, see Ravallion (1994).

uation in which a naïve comparison of the incomes of villages that get the program with those that do not indicates large income gains when in fact there are none.[7]

Another method found in the literature is a regression of the outcome indicator on a dummy variable for treatment or facility placement, allowing for the observable covariates entering as linear controls. The widely used OLS regression method requires the same conditional independence assumption as PSM, but it also imposes arbitrary functional form assumptions concerning the treatment effects and the control variables. By contrast PSM does not require a parametric model linking program participation to outcomes. Thus PSM allows estimation of mean impacts without arbitrary assumptions about functional forms and error distributions. As a result PSM can also facilitate testing for the presence of potentially complex interaction effects; see, for example, the analysis in Jalan and Ravallion (2003a) of the interaction effects between income and education in influencing the gains to child health from access to piped water.

A variation on this regression method uses an instrumental variables estimator (IVE), treating placement as endogenous. This method also makes an untestable conditional independence assumption: the exclusion restriction that the instrumental variable is independent of outcomes given participation. And again the validity of causal inferences rests on the ad hoc functional form assumptions required by standard (parametric) IVE. Under these assumptions, the IVE identifies the causal effect robustly to unobserved heterogeneity. The validity of the exclusion restriction required by IVE is particularly questionable with only a single cross-sectional data set. Although one can imagine many variables that are correlated with placement, such as geographic characteristics of an area, it is questionable on a priori grounds that those variables are uncorrelated with outcomes given placement.

PSM also differs from commonly used regression methods with respect to the sample used. In PSM attention is confined to the matched subsamples; unmatched comparison units are dropped. (In the terminology of the literature on PSM, matching is confined to the region of "common support," where "support" refers to the estimated propensity scores.) By contrast, the regression methods commonly found in the literature use the full sample. The simulations in Rubin and Thomas (2000) indicate that impact estimates based on full (unmatched) samples are generally more biased, and less robust to misspecification of the regression function, than those based on matched samples.

A further difference relates to the choice of control variables. In the standard regression method, one looks for predictors of the outcome measure, with preference given to variables that are thought to be exogenous to outcomes. In PSM one is looking instead for exogenous variables ("covariates") of participation, possibly including variables that are poor predictors of outcomes. (Notice that it is important that the variables are exogenous to participation.) Indeed, simulations indicate that variables with weak predictive ability for outcomes can still reduce bias in estimating causal effects using PSM (Rubin and Thomas 2000).

The possibility that some treatment units may have to be dropped for lack of sufficiently similar comparators points to the possibility of a tradeoff between two possible sources of bias in the resulting estimates of the mean impact. On the one hand, the need to ensure comparability of initial characteristics speaks to the importance of assuring common support. On the other hand, assuring common support can create a sampling bias in inferences about impact, to the extent that treatment units have to be dropped to achieve common support; this problem is well known in the evaluation literature.[8] Recognizing this tradeoff, it is wise to check robustness of the estimates to eliminating only nonparticipating units that are outside the propensity-score range found for treatment units, while retaining the original sample of treatment villages.[9]

There has been some recent work comparing PSM with other methods. A classic study by Lalonde (1986) found large biases in nonexperimental methods compared with a randomized evaluation of a U.S. training program. On the same data set, Dehejia and Wahba (1999) found that propensity-score matching achieved a good approximation—much better than the nonexperimental methods studied by Lalonde.[10]

Double Difference

A popular approach to nonexperimental evaluations in the literature is the double difference (or "difference-in-difference," or DD) method. This approach compares outcome changes over time for treatment and comparison groups to the outcomes observed for a pre-intervention baseline. DD allows for conditional dependence in the levels arising from additive, time-invariant, latent heterogeneity. Box 5.4 summarizes the steps in constructing a DD estimate of program impacts.

Since PSM optimally balances *observed* covariates between the treatment and comparison groups, it is the obvious method for selecting the comparison group in DD studies. The changes over time in the outcome indicator will no doubt contain heterogeneity in observables that would bias an unmatched DD.[11] PSM is the obvious method to clean this out before doing the differencing. If there is no observable heterogeneity in the differences (that is, if it has all been washed out by differencing), then there is no gain from matching on top of DD. Combining PSM for selecting the comparison group with DD can reduce (though probably not eliminate) the bias found in other evaluation methods, including single-difference matching.

Nonetheless, DD estimators have their limitations. In some circumstances it is implausible that the selection bias (attributable to unobserved heterogeneity) is time invariant. DD estimators have a potential bias when the changes over time are a function of initial conditions that also influence program placement. There is also the

---

Box 5.4 Double Difference

The double difference method entails comparing a treatment group with a comparison group (as might ideally be determined by the score-matching method described on the previous page) both before and after the intervention. The main steps are as follows:

Step 1: You need a baseline survey before the intervention is in place, and the survey must cover both nonparticipants and participants. If you do not know who will participate, you have to make an informed guess. Talk to the program administrators.

Step 2: You then need one or more follow-up surveys, after the program is put in place. These should be highly comparable to the baseline surveys (in terms of the questionnaire, the interviewing, and so forth). Ideally the follow-up surveys should be of the same sampled observations as the baseline survey. If this is not possible, then the surveys should be of the same geographic clusters or strata in terms of some other variable.

Step 3: Calculate the mean difference between the "before" and "after" values of the outcome indicator for each of the treatment and comparison groups.

Step 4: Calculate the difference between these two mean differences. That is your estimate of the impact of the program.

---

well-known bias for inferring long-term impacts that can arise when there is a preprogram earnings dip (known as *Ashenfelter's dip,* after Ashenfelter 1978).

For safety-net interventions, such as workfare programs, that have to be set up quickly in response to a macroeconomic or agroclimatic crisis, it is often unfeasible to delay the operation in order to do a baseline survey. Nor is randomization usually feasible in such settings. Suppose instead that samples of participants and nonparticipants are followed up over time, after intervention, and that some participants become nonparticipants. What can one then learn about the program's impacts?

The approach proposed by Ravallion and others (2001) is to examine what happens to participants' incomes (or other welfare indicator) when they leave the program, and to compare the findings with the incomes of continuing participants, after netting out economywide changes, as revealed by a matched comparison group of nonparticipants. The authors wanted to estimate the net income gain to participants, net of their forgone income from the work displaced by the program. The standard DD estimate of program impact is the difference in the income gains over time between a treatment group of program participants and the matched comparison group of non-participants. The *double-matched triple difference* estimator of Ravallion and others (2001) is the difference between the value of the double difference (between matched participants and nonparticipants) for the matched stayers and leavers. The difference between the program's benefit level and the triple-difference estimate of impact gives an estimate of the mean gain to participants.

Although this approach is feasible without a baseline survey, it brings its own problems. First, differencing over time can eliminate bias caused by latent (time-invariant) matching errors, but a potential bias remains due to any selective retrenchment from the program based on unobservables. Ravallion and others (2001) argue that the direction of bias can be determined under plausible assumptions. Second, there may well be a postprogram Ashenfelter's dip, namely, when earnings drop sharply at retrenchment but then recover. As in the preprogram dip, this is a potential source of bias in assessing the longer-term impact; as with the preprogram version, however, to the extent that the dip entails a welfare change, it can still be relevant to assessing the short-term impact of a safety-net intervention. And the postprogram dip is of interest in assessing the dynamics of recovery from retrenchment. To help address this issue, initial participants can be followed up over multiple survey rounds (Ravallion and others 2001).

Under certain conditions, this type of follow-up study of participants can identify the gains to current participants from a program. There are concerns about selection bias, and there is the problem that past participation may bring current gains to those who leave the program. Assuming these lagged gains are positive, the net loss from leaving the program will be less than the gain from participation relative to the counterfactual of never participating. Ravallion and others (2001) derive a test for the joint conditions needed to identify the mean gains to participants from this type of study, also exploiting further follow-up surveys of past participants.

The study also illustrates the potential pitfalls of PSM when data are weak. Compared with the study by Jalan and Ravallion (2003b) on the same program, Ravallion and others (2001) had no choice but to use a lighter survey instrument, with far fewer questions on relevant characteristics of participants and nonparticipants. This instrument did not deliver plausible single-difference estimates using PSM when compared with the Jalan and Ravallion estimates using single-difference PSM for the same program on richer data. The likely explanation is that using the lighter survey instrument meant that there were many unobservable differences; in other words the conditional independence assumption of PSM was not valid. It would appear, however, that Ravallion and others were able to address this problem satisfactorily by tracking households over time, even using the lighter survey instrument. The follow-up evaluation design apparently was able to difference out the mismatching errors. From the point of view of evaluation design, this finding points to the importance of tracking participants over time when there are thought to be important omitted variables in the cross-sectional data available for the purpose of single-difference matching.

On Behavioral Responses

Behavioral responses to a program can often be identified using the same methods discussed above, but substituting some intermediate indicator(s) of behavior as the "outcome" variable(s), rather than the actual outcome variable(s) relevant to the program's objective(s). For example, Chen and Ravallion (2003) were interested in the savings behavior of the participants in a World Bank–supported poor-area development program in China. They wanted to know how much of the income gains from the program the participants saved. It was agreed that the program's aim was to raise living standards of the poor, but there was also a concern about how well this outcome would be captured within the evaluation period. Identifying the savings response of participants provided a clue about the possible future welfare gains beyond the project's life span. Indeed, Chen and Ravallion found that the participants saved about half of the income gains from the program, as estimated using the matched double-difference method described above.

This example also illustrates a common concern in evaluation studies, given behavioral responses. The study period is rarely much longer than the period of the program's disbursements. However, a share of the impact on peoples' living standards may occur beyond the life of the project. This realization does not necessarily mean that credible evaluations need to track welfare impacts over much longer periods than is typically the case—raising concerns about feasibility. But it does suggest that evaluations need to look carefully at impacts on partial intermediate indicators of longer-term impacts—such as incomes in the Chen-Ravallion example—even when good measures of the welfare objective are available within the project cycle. The choice of such indicators needs to be informed by an understanding of participants' behavioral responses to the program.

Conclusions

No single evaluation tool can claim to be ideal in all circumstances. The art of good evaluation is to draw carefully from the full range of tools available to deal pragmatically with the problem at hand in its specific context. The best evaluations often combine multiple methods: randomizing some aspects and using econometric methods to deal with the nonrandom elements, for example; or combining score-matching methods with longitudinal observations to try to eliminate matching errors with imperfect data. Good evaluations also need to be designed early in the program cycle, both to ensure quality and to allow more rapid feedback into decisionmaking about the program.

Notes

1. For an example of an ex ante impact assessment of an antipoverty program, see Ravallion (1999).

2. This article does not attempt to review all of the tools that have been used for impact evaluation. The focus is on more recent developments that appear likely to have relevance to the assessment of antipoverty programs and active labor market and other "social protection" programs in developing country settings. More comprehensive discussions of the methods found in practice can be found in Moffitt (1991); Blundell and Costa Dias (2000); and Ravallion (2001).

3. The second assumption is sometimes referred to in the literature as the "conditional independence" assumption, and sometimes as "strong ignorability."

4. Dehejia and Wahba (1999) report that their PSM results are robust to alternative estimators and alternative specifications for the logit regression. However, this may not hold in other applications.

5. Jalan and Ravallion (2003b) discuss the choice further. They used a range of weighting schemes, including nearest neighbor, nearest five neighbors, and a kernel-based weighting scheme in which the weight is a function of the absolute difference in propensity scores. They found that their results for estimating income gains from an antipoverty program are reasonably robust to the choice. However, that may not be so in other applications.

6. Rubin and Thomas (2000) use simulations to compare the bias in using the nearest five neighbors to that in using just the nearest neighbor; no clear pattern emerges.

7. Van de Walle used simulation methods in which the data were constructed from a model in which the true benefits were known with certainty

and the roads were placed in part as a function of the average incomes of different villages.

8. Also see the discussion of the problem of "nonoverlapping support bias" in Heckman, Ichimura, and Todd (1997) and Heckman and others (1998).

9. For further discussion and an example, see Chen and Ravallion (2003).

10. Also see Heckman and others (1998) and Smith and Todd (2001), who question the robustness of the Dehejia and Wahba PSM estimates to the choices made in sample selection and model specification.

11. For example, Jalan and Ravallion (1998) show that this can seriously bias evaluations of poor-area development programs that are targeted on the basis of initial geographic characteristics that also influence the growth process.

References

The word *processed* describes informally reproduced works that may not be commonly available through library systems.

Angrist, Joshua, Eric Bettinger, Erik Bloom, Elizabeth King, and Michael Kremer. 2001. "Vouchers for Private Schooling in Colombia: Evidence from a Randomized Natural Experiment." NBER Working Paper 8343. Cambridge, Mass.: National Bureau of Economic Research.

Angrist, Joshua, Guido Imbens, and Donald Rubin. 1996. "Identification of Causal Effects Using Instrumental Variables." *Journal of the American Statistical Association* 91: 444–55.

Ashenfelter, Orley. 1978. "Estimating the Effect of Training Programs on Earnings." *Review of Economic Studies* 60: 47–57.

Atkinson, Anthony B. 1987. "On the Measurement of Poverty." *Econometrica* 55: 749–64.

Blundell, Richard, and Monica Costa Dias. 2000. "Evaluation Methods for Non-Experimental Data." *Fiscal Studies* 21(4): 427–68.

Burtless, Gary. 1985. "Are Targeted Wage Subsidies Harmful? Evidence from a Wage Voucher Experiment." *Industrial & Labor Relations Review* 39: 105–15.

Chen, Shaohua, and Martin Ravallion. 2003. "Hidden Impact? Ex-Post Evaluation of an Anti-Poverty Program." Policy Research Working Paper 3049. World Bank, Development Research Group, Washington, D.C. Processed.

Dehejia, R. H., and S. Wahba. 1999. "Causal Effects in Non-experimental Studies: Re-evaluating the Evaluation of Training Programs." *Journal of the American Statistical Association* 94: 1053–62.

Dubin, Jeffrey A., and Douglas Rivers. 1993. "Experimental Estimates of the Impact of Wage Subsidies." *Journal of Econometrics* 56(1–2): 219–42.

Foster, James E., Joel Greer, and Erik Thorbecke. 1984. "A Class of Decomposable Poverty Measures." *Econometrica* 52(3): 761–66.

Galasso, Emanuela, Martin Ravallion, and Agustin Salvia. 2001. "Assisting the Transition from Workfare to Work: A Randomized Experiment." Policy Research Working Paper 2738. World Bank, Washington, D.C. Processed.

Heckman, James, Hedehiko Ichimura, and Petra Todd. 1997. "Matching as an Econometric Evaluation Estimator: Evidence from Evaluating a Job Training Programme." *Review of Economic Studies* 64: 605–54.

Heckman, James, Hedehiko Ichimura, James Smith, and Petra Todd. 1998. "Characterizing Selection Bias Using Experimental Data." *Econometrica* 66: 1017–99.

Jalan, Jyotsna, and Martin Ravallion. 1998. "Are There Dynamic Gains from a Poor-Area Development Program?" *Journal of Public Economics* 67(1): 65–86.

———. 2003a. "Does Piped Water Reduce Diarrhea for Children in Rural India?" *Journal of Econometrics* 112: 153–73.

———. 2003b. "Estimating Benefit Incidence for an Anti-poverty Program Using Propensity Score Matching." *Journal of Business and Economic Statistics* 21(1): 19–30.

Katz, Lawrence F., Jeffrey R. Kling, and Jeffrey B. Liebman. 2001. "Moving to Opportunity in Boston: Early Results of a Randomized Mobility Experiment." *Quarterly Journal of Economics* 116(2): 607–54.

Lalonde, Robert. 1986. "Evaluating the Econometric Evaluations of Training Programs." *American Economic Review* 76: 604–20.

Moffitt, Robert. 1991. "Program Evaluation with Nonexperimental Data." *Evaluation Review* 15(3): 291–314.

Ravallion, Martin. 1994. *Poverty Comparisons, Fundamentals in Pure and Applied Economics* vol. 56. Chur, Switzerland: Harwood Academic Publishers.

———. 1999. "Appraising Workfare." *World Bank Research Observer* 14(1): 31–48.

———. 2001. "The Mystery of the Vanishing Benefits: An Introduction to Impact Evaluation." *World Bank Economic Review* 15(1): 115–40.

Ravallion, Martin, Emanuela Galasso, Teodoro Lazo, and Ernesto Philipp. 2001. "Do Workfare Participants Recover Quickly from Retrenchment?" Policy Research Working Paper 2672. World Bank, Washington, D.C. Processed.

Rosenbaum, Paul, and Donald Rubin. 1983. "The Central Role of the Propensity Score in Observational Studies for Causal Effects." *Biometrika* 70: 41–55.

————. 1985. "Constructing a Control Group using Multivariate Matched Sampling Methods that Incorporate the Propensity Score." *American Statistician* 39: 35–39.

Rubin, Donald B., and N. Thomas. 2000. "Combining Propensity Score Matching with Additional Adjustments for Prognostic Covariates." *Journal of the American Statistical Association* 95: 573–85.

Smith, Jeffrey, and Petra Todd. 2001. "Reconciling Conflicting Evidence on the Performance of Propensity-Score Matching Methods." *American Economic Review* 91(2): 112–18.

van de Walle, Dominique. 2002. "Choosing Rural Road Investments to Help Reduce Poverty." *World Development* 30(4): 575–89.

Watts, H. W. 1968. "An Economic Definition of Poverty." In Daniel Patrick Moynihan, ed., *On Understanding Poverty.* New York: Basic Books.

Woodbury, Stephen, and Robert Spiegelman. 1987. "Bonuses to Workers and Employers to Reduce Unemployment." *American Economic Review* 77: 513–30.

6

Ex Ante Evaluation
of Policy Reforms
Using Behavioral Models

*François Bourguignon and
Francisco H.G. Ferreira*

The tools for incidence analysis of taxation and public spending reviewed in the previous chapters are fundamentally ex post. Given some tax or public expenditure, these tools show (a) who pays the tax or receives the benefits provided through public spending; (b) how much everyone pays or receives, in accounting terms; (c) how much everyone receives when taking into account behavioral responses to taxes or the free delivery of public services; and (d) what the indirect effects of public programs are. This sort of ex post analysis sheds valuable light on the actual distribution of a tax or public expenditure and thus improves policymakers' ability to judge whether individual spending items are "worth their cost" or whether a reform of the instrument under analysis should be considered.

Ex post analyses have one significant limitation, however. Only existing taxes or public programs may be analyzed in this way. This chapter turns to techniques designed to shed light on the potential distributional impacts of policies or policy designs that *do not currently exist,* but that *might* exist in the future. Suppose ex post analysis of an existing program pointed to the necessity of reforming it. Suppose further that several alternative designs—rather than a single one—are suggested for the reform. The government might find it helpful to have some estimate of how much each alternative reform would cost and of which households would be affected, and by how much, under each alternative. If pure experimentation on actual live subjects (such as people or communities of people) of all possible reform designs is not possible or would take too much time, no actual data would be available to evaluate these hypothetical reforms directly. Some counterfactual must be generated, showing how each household in a sample survey would fare depending on the reform being undertaken and how much the reform would cost. Since households respond to policy changes by changing their own actions, this counterfactual must rely on some representation of household behavior.

Essentially, ex ante analysis is *what if* analysis. *What if* some features of the tax system or public spending were modified? How would the modification change the situation for individual households from their initial situation, or status quo? As the introduction to this part of the volume explained, ex ante analysis is *marginal* because it is meant to capture differences between the proposed reform(s) and the status quo. And it is almost necessarily *behavioral,* because of the need to generate counterfactuals that take agent responses into account.[1]

Like ex post analysis, ex ante policy evaluation that is concerned with distributional or poverty outcomes generally relies on household surveys. However, ex ante evaluation requires an additional and preliminary use of the household survey data. Whereas the secret of good ex post impact evaluation is to identify which actual samples should be compared, ex ante analysis requires the simulation of a counterfactual sample, which should represent the population characteristics of interest, *as they would be under the counterfactual policy in question.* To achieve that, some *model* is required that transforms the actual sample into the counterfactual one. At its simplest, this model may be a simple arithmetic representation of the incidence of a tax or benefit, without simulating any policy response by the agents (that is, assuming that all relevant elasticities are zero).

If a simple arithmetic representation seems inadequate because, say, one believes that the policy change may have important price or income effects on consumption or labor-supply behavior, then a *behavioral* model would be needed. Such a model may be obtained in one of two basic ways: through the estimation of a *structural econometric model* on the cross-section of households provided by the household survey; or through the calibration of a model with a given structure so as to make it consistent with what is observed in the survey.

The archetypal example of ex ante analysis of this kind is a tax-benefit model with labor-supply response, such as those commonly estimated for industrial countries. Changes in the tax-benefit system in these models have two general effects. First, tax or benefit changes modify the disposable income of households with an unchanged labor supply. Second, through this income effect as well as through the price effects induced by changes in the after-tax price of labor, they also modify labor-supply decisions. The quantitative extent of these effects—and their net impact—is determined through a behavioral model that is generally estimated econometrically across households observed in the status quo.

There are many models of this type in industrial countries.[2] By contrast, not much has been done along these lines in developing countries, except perhaps for a few examples of the pure accounting microsimulation approach. One reason may be that the cash element of the redistribution system is not usually important enough to modify labor supply significantly and to warrant this kind of analysis. It may also be that estimating structural econometric models of labor supply is made complex because of the informality of a large part of the labor market. Nevertheless, the growing importance of cash transfers and the increasing concern for distributional issues is generating greater need for this kind of analysis. In addition, there are dimensions of household behavior other than labor supply that matter from a welfare point of view and that may be affected by transfers and other public policies. Demand for schooling or health care are some examples.

In this chapter we first present the basic workhorse structural model used for ex ante evaluation of policy reforms: the tax-benefit model with labor-supply response. We use this model to illustrate the sequence of steps needed to build a model, generate the counterfactual distribution, and compare it with the actual in order to simulate and evaluate the reform. We then introduce discrete choice occupational or labor-supply models to show how a change in the model can be used to expand the set of policies that can be analyzed. This methodology is then applied to the simulation of a targeted conditional cash transfer in a developing country to illustrate the final steps of the ex ante evaluation approach. Extensions and limitations are considered in the last section of the chapter.

The Basic Model: Accounting for Labor-Supply Responses to Changes in Taxes

This section outlines the logical sequence a practitioner should follow when using ex ante evaluation tools to simulate alternative outcomes for a policy or program reform. To make the approach as concrete as possible, we base the discussion on a model of labor supply decisions that are made when the budget constraints facing individuals may be nonlinear because of taxes and transfers. The basic reference is the first model of this type, proposed by Hausman (1980). We break down the approach into five steps: definition of the problem; identification of the required data; specification of the model; model estimation; and policy simulation.

Step 1: Identify a well-defined, tractable policy reform question.

For example, determine the likely effect of an increase in income taxes or in benefits on the distribution of incomes, and on the government's budget. The simulation approach has often been used to address fiscal questions of this type because actual tax experiments (such as the application of different tax rates to comparable population subgroups) are generally difficult to justify politically. Additionally, a model that simulated such tax changes without taking agents' responses into account would be likely to generate wrong revenue predictions.

Step 2: Find a data set that contains reliable information on the variables that need to be included in the model.

In this case, one would need a household or labor force survey, with information on earnings and hours of work for a representative cross-section of the population of interest. Additionally, one would ideally need information on which taxes each individual pays, and at what rates. If the best available surveys do not contain this information, then one would need a clear description of the tax rules to make assumptions (such as 100 percent compliance) about how those rules apply over the sample.

Step 3: Write the simplest economic model that contains enough structure to capture the mechanisms that are likely to affect the agent responses to the policy under consideration.

In this case, the logical economic structure is that of the textbook utility-maximizing consumer. An economic agent with characteristics z chooses a volume of consumption, c, and a labor supply, L, so as to maximize the agent's preferences represented by the utility function $u(\ )$ under a budget constraint that incorporates the tax-benefit system. The important point is that the taxes under consideration enter explicitly into the budget constraint, so that any changes in the parameters of the tax system will affect the consumer's optimal choices. This model is written in a general form below, so that other tax or transfer changes can also be considered:

(6.1)   Max $u(c, L; z; \beta, \varepsilon)$ subject to
$$c \le y_0 + wL + NT(wL, L, y_0; z; \gamma), L \ge 0$$

In the budget constraint, y_0 stands for (exogenous) nonlabor income, w for the wage rate and $NT(\ )$ for the net transfer defined by the tax-benefit schedule. Taxes and benefits depend on the characteristics of the agent, his nonlabor income and his labor income, wL. Taxes and benefits may also depend directly on the quantity of labor being supplied, as in workfare programs. γ stands for the parameters of the tax-benefit system such as the various tax rates, means-testing of benefits, and the like. Likewise, β and ε are coefficients that parameterize preferences. The solution of that program yields the following labor-supply function:

$$L = F(w, y_0; z; \beta, \varepsilon; \gamma)$$

This function is nonlinear. In particular, it may be equal to zero for some subset of the space of its arguments. The set of restrictions on the vector γ that ensures that $L > 0$ is known as a participation condition.

Step 4: Estimate the model.

Suppose now that a sample of agents (indexed by i) are observed in some household survey containing reliable information on L, w, y_0, and z. The problem is now to estimate the function $F(\ )$ above or, equivalently, the preference parameters, β and ε, since all the other variables or tax-benefit parameters are actually observed. To do so, it is assumed that the set of coefficients β is common to all agents, whereas ε is idiosyncratic. It is not observed, but some assumptions can be made on its statistical distribution in the sample. This leads to the following econometric specification:

(6.2) $L_i = F(z_i, w_i, y_{0i}; \beta, \varepsilon_i; \gamma)$

where ε_i plays the usual role of the random term in standard regressions.

Estimation proceeds as in standard models, minimizing the role of the idiosyncratic preference term in explaining cross-sectional differences in labor supply. This leads to a set of estimates $\hat{\beta}$ for the common preference parameters and $\hat{\varepsilon}_i$ for the idiosyncratic preference terms. By definition of the latter, it is true for each observation in the sample that

$$L_i = F(z_i, w_i, y_{0i}; \hat{\beta}, \hat{\varepsilon}_i; \gamma)$$

While the estimation process just described is conceptually simple, its implementation in practice is generally not so straightforward.

That is because of the nonlinearity of the budget constraint and its possible nonconvexity due to the tax-benefit schedule, $NT(\ )$, and corner solutions at $L = 0$. Functional forms must be chosen for preferences, which may introduce some arbitrariness in the procedure. Finally, it may be feared that imposing full economic rationality and a functional form for preferences severely restricts the estimates that are obtained. There has been a debate on this point ever since this model first appeared in the literature.[3] We return to this estimation problem later, where we suggest a simple and robust alternative, the cost of which is discreteness.

Step 5: Simulate the policy reform using the empirical estimate of the model.

It is now possible to simulate alternative tax-benefit systems, which simply requires modifying the set of parameters γ.[4] *In the absence of general equilibrium effects,* the change in labor supply due to moving to the set of parameters γ^s is given by

$$L_i^s - L_i = F(z_i, w_i, y_{0i}; \hat{\beta}, \hat{\varepsilon}_i; \gamma^s) - F(z_i, w_i, y_{0i}; \hat{\beta}, \hat{\varepsilon}_i; \gamma)$$

The change in the disposable income may also be computed for every agent. It is given by

$$C_i^s - C_i = w_i(L_i^s - L_i) + NT(y_{0i}, w_iL_i^s, L_i^s, z_i; \gamma^s) - NT(y_{0i}, w_iL_i, L_i; z_i; \gamma)$$

At this point one may also derive changes in any measure of individual welfare, and construct from each of them a full counterfactual distribution over the sample.

Discrete Models of Labor Supply or Occupational Choice

We now return to the caveat made in the last paragraph of step 4, where we noted the main weakness of the approach outlined here so far. That is, despite its conceptual simplicity, estimation of the nonlinear (but piecewise continuous) labor-supply function is generally complex, often involving maximization of nontrivial likelihood functions and requiring the specification of possibly arbitrary utility functional forms.

It turns out that simpler and less restrictive specifications may be used that considerably reduce this problem. In particular, specifications used in recent work consider labor supply as a discrete variable that may take only a few alternative values; these specifications evaluate the utility of the agent for each of these values and the corresponding disposable income given by the budget constraint. If this discreteness is not seen as too costly in terms of the reliability of the policy simulation under consideration, it can buy a great deal of simplicity in estimation.

As before, the behavioral rule is simply that agents choose the value that leads to the highest level of utility. However, the utility function may now be specified in a very general way. In particular, its parameters may be allowed to vary with the various quantities of labor that may be supplied, with no restriction being imposed on these coefficients. Such a representation is therefore as close as possible to what is revealed by the data.

Formally, a specification that generalizes what is most often found in the recent tax and labor-supply literature is the following:

(6.3) $$L_i = D_j \text{ if } U_i^j = f(z_i; w_i; c_i^j; \beta^j, \varepsilon_i^j) \geq U_i^k$$
$$= f(z_i; w_i; c_i^k; \beta^k, \varepsilon_i^k) \text{ for all } k \neq j$$

where D_j is the duration of work in the jth alternative, U_i^j the utility associated with that alternative, and c_i^j the disposable income given by the following budget constraint:

$$c^j = y_0 + wL + NT(wD, D, y_0; z_i; \gamma)$$

When the function $f( )$ is linear with respect to its common preference parameters and when the idiosyncratic terms are assumed to be identically and independently distributed with a double exponential distribution, this model is the standard multinomial logit. It may also be noted that it encompasses the initial model 6.1. It is sufficient to make the following substitution:

$$f(z_i; w_i; c_i^j; \beta^j, \varepsilon_i^j) = u(c_i^j; D^j; z_i; \beta, \varepsilon_i^j)$$

This specification, which involves restrictions across the various labor-supply alternatives, is actually the one that is most often used.

Even under this more general form, one might be tempted to argue that the preceding specification is still too restrictive, because it relies on some utility-maximizing assumption. It turns out that ex ante incidence analysis or policy evaluation cannot dispense with such a basic assumption. *The ex ante nature of the analysis requires that some assumption be made about the way agents choose between different alternatives.* Given that, assuming that agents maximize some criterion defined in a different way for each alternative is not really that restrictive. It also should be clear that if no restriction is imposed across alternatives, then the utility-maximizing assumption is compatible with the most flexible representation of the way in which labor-supply choices observed in a survey are related to individual characteristics, including the wage rate and the disposable income defined by the tax-benefit system, $NT( )$.

The fact that model 6.3 can be interpreted as representing utility-maximizing behavior is to some extent secondary, although this interpretation permits implementing counterfactual simulations in a simple way. More important is that this model fits the data as closely as possible. Interestingly enough, the only restriction affecting that objective is the assumption that the income effect in each alternative—that is, the c_i^j argument in $f(\ )$—depends on disposable income as given by the budget constraint that incorporates the tax-benefit schedule, $NT(\ )$. The economic structure of this model thus lies essentially in the income effect. If it were not for that property, it would simply be a reduced-form model aimed at fitting the data as well as possible.

In effect, the restriction that the income effect must be proportional to disposable income seems to be a *minimal* assumption to ensure that this representation of cross-sectional differences in labor-supply behavior may at the same time represent a rational choice among various labor-supply alternatives. After all, within this framework, the simulated effect on individual labor supply of a reform of the tax-benefit system, $NT(\ )$, is estimated on the basis of the cross-sectional disposable income effect in the status quo.

The role of idiosyncratic terms, $\hat{\varepsilon}_i$ or $\hat{\varepsilon}_i^j$, in the whole approach should not be downplayed. They represent the unobserved heterogeneity of agents' labor-supply behavior. Thus, they are responsible for some of the heterogeneity in responses to a reform of taxes and benefits. It can be seen in equation 6.3 that agents who are otherwise identical might react differently to a change in disposable incomes, even though these changes are the same for all of them. It is enough that the idiosyncratic terms, $\hat{\varepsilon}_i^j$, be sufficiently different among them.

Estimates of the idiosyncratic terms result directly from the econometric estimation of the common preference parameters $\hat{\beta}$ or $\hat{\beta}^j$.[5] Note, however, that it is possible to use a "calibration" rather than an estimation approach. With the former, some of the coefficients $\hat{\beta}$ or $\hat{\beta}^j$ would not be estimated but given arbitrary values deemed reasonable by the analyst. Then, as in the standard estimation procedure, estimates of the idiosyncratic terms would be obtained by requiring that predicted choices, under the status quo, and actual choices coincide.

Before closing this section, it is important to emphasize that there is some ambiguity about who the "agents" behind the labor-supply model 6.1 should be. Traditionally, the literature considers individuals, even though the welfare implications of the analysis concern households. Extending the model to households requires considering simultaneously the labor-supply decision of all household members of working age, a factor that makes the analysis more complex.

Applications of the preceding model are numerous in industrial countries. Surveys are given in Blundell and MaCurdy (1999) and in Creedy and Duncan (2002). The discrete approach underlined above is best illustrated by Van Soest (1995), Hoynes (1996), or Keane and Moffitt (1998). A nice application of this approach for predicting the likely effect of the introduction of the Working Families Tax Credit in the United Kingdom is Blundell and others (2000).

A Developing Country Application: Cash Transfers, Demand for Schooling, and Labor Supply

The preceding framework has not very often been applied to developing countries, for a number of reasons. First, direct transfers to households, whether positive or negative, have usually been less important in developing countries. Second, the functioning of the labor market may make the concept of labor supply somewhat artificial or insufficient in several instances. In particular, the distinction between formal and informal employment is important, with the former often being rationed and the latter often leading to an imprecise observation of income and income effects. Both limitations apply more strongly to the poorest segment of society.

Nevertheless, the broad issue of agent response to policy changes—which motivated the preceding models—is becoming increasingly relevant in the developing world, as both tax and transfer systems develop. For instance, it was observed in South Africa that the payment of lump-sum pensions to elderly people without other resources was accompanied by changes in the labor supply of the households they belonged to (Bertrand, Mullainathan, and Miller 2002). As a result, the change in monetary income in poor households differed from what had been expected. The amplitude of this phenomenon might be measured either through ex post "differences in differences" techniques of the type discussed in chapter 5, or by ex ante models of the type shown here. Of course, the ex ante approach could be useful, say, in designing reforms to the existing minimum pension system.

Progresa in Mexico, *Bolsa Escola* in Brazil, and similar conditional cash transfer programs in several other countries offer a second example of the ex ante evaluation approach. This section provides a summary presentation of an ex ante evaluation of the effects of *Bolsa Escola* in Brazil and of potential changes in the format of that program. This evaluation may be seen as an extension or a variation of the framework discussed in the previous section. The discussion is based on Bourguignon, Ferreira, and Leite (2002), where the exercise is described and analyzed in greater detail.

The *Bolsa Escola* program consists of transfers to households whose incomes per capita are below R\$90—approximately US\$30—a month, provided that all children in the household ages 6 to 15 are enrolled in a public school, and that their individual attendance rates do not fall below 85 percent in any given month. The monthly transfer is equal to R\$15 per child going to school, up to a maximum of R\$45 per household. This program may be considered as a conditional cash transfer program because it combines cash transfers based on a means-test with some additional conditionality, that is, having children of school age actually attending school.

Because the main occupational alternative to school is work, evaluation of the *Bolsa Escola* program really is a labor-supply problem similar to the one analyzed above. The discrete approach is used for each child aged 10 to 15, with the following three labor-supply alternatives, indexed by k: $k = 1$ if the child has some market earnings and does not go to school; $k = 2$ if the child has some earnings and goes to school; and finally $k = 3$ if the child does not work in the market but does go to school. Following equation 6.3, the utility of the household to which child i belongs is specified

$$(6.4) \qquad\qquad U_i^k = z_i\beta^k + \alpha^k(Y_i + y_i^k) + \varepsilon_i^k$$

for $k = 1, 2, 3$. As before, z_i stands for characteristics of both the child and the household; Y_i is household income without the child's earnings; y_i^k is the income earned by the child in alternative k; and ε_i^k stands for idiosyncratic preferences.

The key variable for describing the conditional cash transfer program is clearly y_i^k, since transfers depend on income per capita in the household and on the schooling status of the child, which itself affects the child's earnings. Under the status quo—before the program was launched—and in the household survey being used for estimation, this variable is defined as follows. In alternative 1, y_i^k equals the observed market earnings of the child, w_i. In alternative 2, the child is assumed to work only a proportion M of the time available when not going to school. The child's observed earnings therefore are Mw_i on average. In the third alternative, the child does not bring home any market earnings. But that does not prevent the child from contributing to domestic production. Assume this contribution to be, on average, some fixed proportion of the earnings obtained from market work by children with the same observable characteristics. Let Λw_i be the corresponding amount. A difference with model 6.3 is that Λ is not observed.

Substituting the preceding values of y into equation 6.4 leads to

$$(6.5) \qquad\qquad U_i^k = z_i\beta^k + \alpha_k Y_i + \rho^k w_i + \varepsilon_i^k$$

where ρ^k is given by

$$(6.6) \qquad \rho^1 = \alpha_1, \ \rho^2 = \alpha_2 M, \ \rho^3 = \alpha_3 \Lambda$$

Expression 6.5 is comparable to the discrete choice labor-supply model 6.3. It can be estimated by a multinomial logit model. A potential problem might be that this model allows estimating the coefficients corresponding to some alternative only as a deviation from those of some other alternative, which is taken as a reference. In this application, since the child's earnings variable differs across alternatives, it is necessary to estimate all three α^k, $k = 1, 2, 3$. In this case that is achieved through the restrictions given by equation 6.6, which allow the identification of the three coefficients α^k and Λ.[6] It is those restrictions, and the fact that M can be estimated (as a coefficient on a dummy variable for school attendance in an earnings equation for children with positive earnings) that permits estimating the whole model. See Bourguignon, Ferreira, and Leite (2002) for details.

Estimates $\hat{\beta}^k$, $\hat{\alpha}_k$, and $\hat{\varepsilon}_i^k$ of the preferences may thus be obtained from the observation of adult and child incomes, various household and child attributes, and the demand for schooling and supply of child labor taken from a household survey conducted before the program began. Once these estimates have been obtained, the effect of *Bolsa Escola* on the decisions about children's occupations is easy to simulate. The alternative with the highest utility is chosen, with the utility of each alternative being now given by:

$$
\begin{aligned}
U_i^1 &= Z_i \hat{\beta}^1 + \hat{\alpha}^1 Y_i + \hat{\alpha}^1 w_i + \hat{\varepsilon}_i^1 \\
U_i^2 &= Z_i \hat{\beta}^2 + \hat{\alpha}^2 (Y_i + \gamma_1) + \hat{\alpha}^2 M w_i + \hat{\varepsilon}_i^2 & \text{if } Y_i + M w_i \leq \gamma_2 \\
(6.7) \quad U_i^2 &= Z_i \hat{\beta}^2 + \hat{\alpha}^2 Y_i + \hat{\alpha}^2 M w_i + \hat{\varepsilon}_i^2 & \text{if } Y_i + M w_i > \gamma_2 \\
U_i^3 &= Z_i \hat{\beta}^3 + \hat{\alpha}^3 (Y_i + \gamma_1) + \hat{\alpha}^3 \Lambda w_i + \hat{\varepsilon}_i^3 & \text{if } Y_i \leq \gamma_2 \\
U_i^3 &= Z_i \hat{\beta}^3 + \hat{\alpha}^3 Y_i + \hat{\alpha}^3 \Lambda w_i + \hat{\varepsilon}_i^3 & \text{if } Y_i > \gamma_2
\end{aligned}
$$

In this system, γ_1 and γ_2 stand for the parameters of the tax-benefit system being modeled. The former stands for the *Bolsa Escola* transfer for each child in school, and the latter is the means test. Together, these conditions incorporate the fact that *Bolsa Escola* can make the schooling alternatives 2 and 3 more attractive for poorer families. Moving from alternative 1 to 2 (respectively alternative 3) increases or reduces monetary income according to whether the transfer γ_1 is above or below $(1 - M) w_i$ (respectively w_i). In all cases, however, these moves potentially mean a higher future income for the child.

This model was estimated on all children ages 10 to 15 in the Brazilian household survey sample PNAD 1999. The number of children under age 10 involved in market activities and not enrolled in school was not sufficient to estimate the model. Results turned out to be quite consistent. In particular, the value of M derived from the comparison of earnings among those working children who do not go to school and those who do go was found to be around 70 percent. Likewise, the coefficient measuring the market equivalent of the domestic production of children going to school but not active in the labor market, Λ, was found to be 75 percent. Finally, it turned out that, as in several other studies of the demand for schooling, the income effect, as measured by differences $\alpha^2 - \alpha^1$ and $\alpha^3 - \alpha^1$, is rather weak.

After estimating all the coefficients of the model and the idiosyncratic preference terms, $\hat{\varepsilon}_i^k$, the *Bolsa Escola* program and alternative formats of that program were simulated on each of the households in the PNAD survey. Focusing on all children between ages 10 and 15 led to a sample of 42,000 persons. However, only 26 percent of them passed the means test in *Bolsa Escola* and were thus potentially directly affected by the program.

Table 6.1 shows the effect of the *Bolsa Escola* program on the schooling of children ages 10–15 living in poor households, as simulated with the model sketched above. [7] The table shows that the program is indeed quite effective in reducing the number of poor children who do not go to school. Their proportion in the population of poor children ages 10–15 falls from 8.9 percent without the program to 3.7 percent under the simulated program. Interestingly enough, the proportion of children who both go to school and have some activity in the labor market tends to increase, which suggests that the program has little effect on child labor when children are already going to school. Alternative specifications of the program scenarios have the expected effect on schooling. In particular, raising the amount of the transfer or making it age-progressive further reduces the proportion of children not going to school. However, making the program more generous by changing the level of the means test has very little effect. Another interesting finding is that the schooling conditionality is extremely important to achieving the objective of universal schooling. As shown by the last scenario, the income effect attributable to the cash transfer would have practically no effect on schooling without the conditionality of *Bolsa Escola*.

Table 6.2 shows the expected effect of the *Bolsa Escola* program on poverty, defined here for the whole population and on the basis of monetary income only. This effect turns out to be more muted. The poverty headcount goes down by only 1.3 percentage points, reflecting the moderate size of the program (shown in the last row of the table), the substantial inequality within the poor segment of

Table 6.1 Simulated Effect on Schooling and Working Status of Alternative Specifications of Conditional Cash Transfer Program

| All children ages 10–15 | Original | Bolsa Escola program | Poor Households | | | | |
			Scenario 1	Scenario 2	Scenario 3	Scenario 4	Scenario 5
Not going to school	8.9	3.7	1.9	0.6	1.8	3.6	8.9
Going to school and working	23.1	24.7	25.1	25.4	25.2	24.9	23.0
Going to school and not working	68.1	71.6	72.9	74.0	73.0	71.4	68.2
Total	100.0	100.0	100.0	100.0	100.0	100.0	100.0

Note: Scenario 1: Transfer equal R$30, maximum per household R$90 and means test R$90.
 Scenario 2: Transfer equal R$60, maximum per household R$180 and means test R$90.
 Scenario 3: Different values for each age, no household ceiling and means test R$90.
 Scenario 4: Transfer equal R$15, maximum per household R$45 and means test R$120.
 Scenario 5: *Bolsa Escola* without conditionality.

Sources: PNAD/IBGE 1999 and authors' calculation.

Table 6.2 Simulated Distributional Effect of Alternative Specifications of the Conditional Cash Transfer Program

Poverty measures	Original	Bolsa Escola program	Scenario 1	Scenario 2	Scenario 3	Scenario 4	Scenario 5
Poverty headcount	30.1	28.8	27.5	24.6	27.7	28.8	28.9
Poverty gap	13.2	11.9	10.8	8.8	10.9	11.9	12.0
Total square deviation from poverty line	7.9	6.8	5.9	4.6	6.0	6.8	6.8
Annual cost of the program (million Reals)	n.a.	2,076	4,201	8,487	3,905	2,549	2,009

Note: n.a. = Not applicable.

Scenario 1: Transfer equal R$30, maximum per household R$90 and means test R$90.

Scenario 2: Transfer equal R$60, maximum per household R$180 and means test R$90.

Scenario 3: Different values for each age, no household ceiling and means test R$90.

Scenario 4: Transfer equal R$15, maximum per household R$45 and means test R$120.

Scenario 5: *Bolsa Escola* without conditionality.

Sources: PNAD/IBGE 1999 and authors' calculation.

the population, and the negative (child) labor-supply effect of the program. The comparison of the *Bolsa Escola* simulation with the results obtained under scenario 5—no conditionality—suggests that this last effect is small, however. Indeed, there is almost no difference in the poverty measures reported under the two scenarios. Other scenarios have the expected effect on poverty, with increases in transfer amounts being once again more potent than hikes in the level of the means test.

A much more detailed analysis than the results shown in these two tables is of course possible. Some additional detail is provided in Bourguignon, Ferreira, and Leite (2002). Because the main purpose of this chapter is to present and discuss the methodology of ex ante evaluation approaches to public redistribution programs, we go no further here. The few results presented above are sufficient to illustrate both the principles and the potential usefulness of the approach.

Despite the appeal of this methodology, few applications are available for developing countries. In most cases, applying it requires only a structural model of some dimension of household behavior that permits simulating a change in one or many policy parameters. Thus, models of demand for schooling along the lines of Gertler and Glewwe (1990) could be used to simulate the impact of several policies in the field of education, such as reducing the direct cost of schooling, providing school lunches, or changing the quality of schooling. For example, Younger (2002) uses this kind of approach to analyze the consequences of uniformly reducing the distance to school in rural Peru.

Conclusions, Extensions, and Limitations

A reliance on the multinomial logit model of discrete occupational choice (or labor supply) considerably facilitates the estimation of this kind of structural model, which can then be used to simulate the impact of policy or program reforms taking behavioral responses into account. Yet it is still probably true that starting such an exercise from scratch is not the easiest tool in this toolkit. It is therefore worth considering pure accounting ex ante marginal incidence techniques, at least as an initial step. Even this (much simpler) approach is not yet of generalized use, and one can plausibly argue that in many cases the first-order approximation generated by such a non-behavioral simulation might be informative in its own right; it may also serve as a learning stage before attempting the behavioral part of the model. A pure accounting approach to the evaluation of the *Bolsa Escola* program, assuming 100 percent enrollment in the program, would have led to a poverty simulation that was a bit—but not massively—off the results obtained with the preceding simulation.

The most obvious field of application of the ex ante marginal incidence approach has to do with all the consequences of a change in the budget constraint faced by households, especially through all types of means-tested or conditional transfers. Behavioral features that are the most sensitive to income changes are the safest to study, because strong estimates for cross-sectional income effects are the most likely to translate into actual responses to a program that modifies the income of agents. Thus, labor supply and related behavior such as schooling at one end of the active life cycle and inactivity at the other end are the first candidates for behavioral analysis.

Ex ante simulations are less easy with other components of public finance because they generally involve price and quality dimensions that are very imperfectly observed. Public services financed through user fees are a case in point. If some health care facility is made available in a locality, then it is most likely that users will first be differentiated by income. If there is some cost recovery, then regular users will be those agents with an income above some threshold. Extending health care to poorer people could be done either by lowering cost recovery or by subsidizing low-income users on the basis of some permanent income criterion. Such systems are used in several countries—one example is the SISBEN system for health care in Colombia. Under the assumption of fixed price and quality, these systems could be studied with the same techniques discussed here. The problem is that quality and price are highly unlikely to stay fixed, and simulating the effects of variations in these two dimensions adds considerable complexity. Although some household surveys record visits to health centers, they do not record price and quality characteristics, or there may not be enough variation across households to estimate demand elasticities in any convincing way. The analysis may thus be only partial.[8]

Consumption responses to changes in prices through taxes or subsidies also face this problem of zero or unknown variation in prices within household surveys. From a welfare point of view, the demand response need not be known because, as a first approximation, the effect of a price change is simply the change in total expenditures that it causes at constant consumption behavior. Behavioral responses are important only to figure out the change in net tax receipts at the aggregate level. But then, aggregate demand analysis based on time series may be used for this.[9] The same applies to changes in the prices of goods that are produced by households, that is, the price of the output of self-employed households or simply the wage rate of those employed in the formal labor market. Overall, analysis of indirect taxes, including labor taxes, thus differs substantially from analysis of changes in direct taxes and transfers or in the supply of public services. The latter are more susceptible to ex ante evaluation—or marginal incidence analysis—than the former.

To conclude, we stress some of the limitations of the ex ante evaluation approach that have not been mentioned explicitly in this short presentation. First, this approach may be difficult to implement because it generally requires the estimation of an original behavioral model that fits the policy to be evaluated or designed, and of course the corresponding microeconomic data. It is thus unlikely that an analysis conducted in a given country for a particular policy can be applied without substantial modification to another country or another type of policy. The methodological investment behind this approach may thus be important. Therefore, preceding this approach with a pure accounting microsimulation based on simpler assumptions can be useful. Second, we emphasize the fact that the behavioral approach relies necessarily on a structural model that requires some minimal set of assumptions. In general, these assumptions are difficult to test. In the labor-supply model with a discrete choice representation, the basic assumption is that net disposable income, as given by the tax-benefit system, is what matters for occupational decisions. A reduced form model would say that the exogenous idiosyncratic determinants of the budget constraint are what matters. Econometrically, the difference may be tenuous, but the implications in terms of simulation are huge. For instance, the modeling of *Bolsa Escola* is based on the implicit assumption that income is pooled at the household level. That is not a given, and simulation results would be different if the model were specified otherwise.

Finally, the strongest hypothesis is that cross-sectional income effects, as estimated on the basis of a standard household survey, coincide with the income effects that will be produced by the program under study or reforms in it. In other words, income effects over time for a given agent should coincide with the effect of cross-sectional income differences. Here again, this is a hypothesis that is hard to test and yet rather essential for ex ante analysis. The only test we can think of would be to combine ex ante and ex post analysis. For instance, one could run some ex ante analysis on a Mexican household survey taken before the launching of *Progresa* and then compare those results with the results obtained for schooling and income in the ex post evaluations that have been made of that program. Combinations of ex ante and ex post evaluations—such as the studies undertaken by Todd and Wolpin (2002) and Attanasio, Meghir, and Santiago (2002)—are at the cutting edge of the applied microeconomics of development.

In the absence of such validation exercises, which are possible only in rather special circumstances, some uncertainty about the predictions generated by ex ante evaluations based on structural behavioral modeling is bound to remain. That being said, ex ante evaluation can be a valuable tool to visualize the distributional impact of alternative designs of policies that are likely to generate strong behavioral responses. A pure accounting approach to marginal incidence analysis is often a useful first step. But, because people do generally change their behavior when the policy environment around them changes, introducing behavior on an ex ante basis is ultimately desirable for simulating policy reform in most realms.

Notes

1. Pure accounting micro-simulation methods need not be totally discarded, at least as a first approximation. They may be useful to describe first-round effects on a sample of households, at least when previous evidence suggests that behavioral responses may be slow to come or have small effects. We return to this point in the last section of the chapter.

2. See Creedy and Duncan (2002).

3. See in particular MaCurdy, Green, and Paarsch (1990). For a survey of empirical strategies suitable for estimating a nonlinear labor-supply function such as 6.2, see Blundell and MaCurdy (1999).

4. Assuming indeed a structural specification of the $NT(\ )$ function general enough for all reforms to be represented by a change in parameters γ.

5. They would be standard residuals with specification 6.2 and most likely pseudo residuals in the discrete formulation 6.3.

6. This is not true of coefficients β^k, but it may be seen from 6.7 that only the knowledge of differences of these coefficients across alternatives matters when determining the utility-maximizing alternative.

7. Note that the definition of poverty used here does not coincide with the means-test in *Bolsa Escola*.

8. Note that this issue is present in the demand for schooling problem too. Although public schools in Brazil do not charge user fees, the analysis described above implicitly assumes that quality is maintained constant everywhere. Effects of quality variations in the country are simply summarized by the idiosyncratic preference terms.

9. See chapter 1 in this volume.

References

The word *processed* describes informally reproduced works that may not be commonly available through library systems.

Attanasio, O., C. Meghir, and A. Santiago. 2002. "Education Choices in Mexico: Using a Structural Model and a Randomized Experiment to Evaluate Progresa." University College, London. Processed.

Bertrand, M., S. Mullainathan, and D. Miller. 2002. "Public Policy and Extended Families: Evidence from South Africa." University of Chicago. Processed.

Blundell, R., and T. MaCurdy. 1999. "Labor Supply: A Review of Alternative Approaches." In O. Ashenfelter and D. Card, eds., *Handbook of Labor Economics, Vol. 3A*. Amsterdam: Elsevier.

Blundell, R., A. Duncan, J. McCrae, and C. Meghir. 2000. "Evaluating In-Work Benefit Reforms: The Working Families' Tax Credit in the UK." Discussion Paper, Institute for Fiscal Studies, London. Processed.

Bourguignon, François, Francisco H.G. Ferreira, and P. Leite. 2002. "Ex Ante Evaluation of Conditional Cash Transfer Programs: The Case of *Bolsa Escola*." Policy Research Working Paper 2916. World Bank, Policy Research Department, Washington, D.C.

Creedy, J., and A. Duncan. 2002. "Behavioral Micro-simulation with Labor Supply Responses." *Journal of Economic Surveys* 16(1): 1–39.

Gertler, P., and P. Glewwe. 1990. "The Willingness to Pay for Education in Developing Countries: Evidence from Rural Peru." *Journal of Public Economics* 42(3): 251–75.

Hausman, J. 1980. "The Effect of Wages, Taxes, and Fixed Costs on Women's Labor Force Participation." *Journal of Public Economics* 14: 161–94.

Hoynes, H. 1996. "Welfare Transfers in Two-Parent Families: Labor Supply and Welfare Participation under AFDC-UP." *Econometrica* 64(2): 295–332.

Keane, M. P., and R. Moffitt. 1998. "A Structural Model of Multiple Welfare Program Participation and Labor Supply." *International Economic Review* 39(3): 553–89.

MaCurdy, T., D. Green, and H. Paarsch. 1990. "Assessing Empirical Approaches for Analyzing Taxes and Labor Supply." *Journal of Human Resources* 25(3): 415–90.

Todd, Petra, and Kenneth I. Wolpin. 2002. "Using Experimental Data to Validate a Dynamic Behavioral Model of Child Schooling and Fertility: Assessing the Impact of a School Subsidy Program in Mexico." Department of Economics, University of Pennsylvania. Processed.

Van Soest, A. 1995. "A Structural Model of Family Labor Supply: A Discrete Choice Approach." *Journal of Human Resources* 30: 63–88.

Younger, S. 2002. "Benefits on the Margin: Observations on Marginal Benefit Incidence." Cornell University, Ithaca, N.Y. Processed.

7

Generating Relevant Household-Level Data: Multitopic Household Surveys

Kinnon Scott

As the other chapters in this volume demonstrate, the evaluation of the poverty impact of social and economic policy creates substantial needs for data from a variety of sources. Data needs range from those at the household level, to program and project specifics on inputs and outputs, to the administrative records maintained by line ministries, to national budget allocations and expenditures. Often it is the merger or combination of different data sources that leads to breakthroughs in analysts' ability to evaluate and design effective policy. Although the techniques outlined in this volume rely on various sources and types of data, a common thread running through them is the need for household-level data.

Understanding household behavior is a critical ingredient for moving from stated goals and objectives to policies that will lead to the attainment of such goals. One must be able to identify the constraints that households face and the factors affecting observed outcomes. Only household-level data allow one to measure the actual impact of policies and programs and to assess the distributional effects of public spending. To evaluate the poverty impact of policies, one needs to be able to measure welfare and its changes over time at the household level, identifying those households receiving benefits from public spending and policies (direct and indirect) and determining the actual impact of such policies. Household surveys have struggled to provide such data, but the reliance on single-topic or one-sector surveys has meant that information on households has typically been collected in a piecemeal fashion. This chapter summarizes the key sources of household data, their strengths, and their weaknesses, and argues for the need for multitopic surveys.

Household-Level Data in Developing Countries

Clearly for any country, there is no single method for collecting data at the household level. Censuses and surveys come in a variety of forms and have very specific goals and purposes. Each country needs a system of surveys to meet the data requirements of policymakers and analysts. The adequacy of each survey is a function of its quality, timeliness, and relevance as well as its contribution to filling the overall data needs of the country. Because surveys in any given country lack uniformity and are conducted relatively infrequently, a variety of sources of household data have been used for measuring welfare and the poverty impact of policies. Unfortunately many, otherwise excellent, surveys are woefully inadequate for this purpose. Household data that can be used must meet certain requirements. First they must allow for the measurement of household and individual welfare, preferably using a money-metric measure of welfare. Second, the data collected should allow the correlation between the welfare measure and other facets of welfare along with access and use of government services and the degree to which these affect the households' well-being.

The majority of the surveys available to analysts are of limited usefulness for the purposes of assessing the poverty impact of programs and policies either because they lack a decent measure of welfare or because they do not have the coverage of topics related to the use of government services. A brief summary of the most prevalent sources of household-level data in developing countries demonstrates this point.

Population and Housing Census

A census is designed to collect data from every household or person in a country with the goal of providing accurate measures of the demographic status of a country. Some countries have added additional questions to their censuses, such as the Eastern Caribbean countries, which collected quite extensive information on health, education, and labor activities in the 2003 census. The typical census, however, is restricted to basic demographics—age, sex, family and household composition, basic education levels—and housing questions—quality and infrastructure. Given the universal coverage, the census is a staggeringly expensive undertaking. Thus, it is conducted infrequently: international recommendations are once every ten years.

To minimize both costs and the logistical burden, the contents of a census, or the number of questions and topics covered, is minimal. The limited scope of the census, in terms of information collected, means that it is not useful for poverty measurement short of a basic-needs approach. Such a measure is of limited usefulness for several reasons. First, the indicators captured in a census change slowly and thus make monitoring poverty impacts difficult in the short or medium term. Second, the indicators typically used often reflect patterns of government investment more than household welfare. Third, the basic-needs index suffers from the problems inherent in the construction of an index based on subjective assessments of needs. And, finally, the infrequency of the census makes it impossible to measure or monitor poverty in the intercensal period. Recent work linking census data to household surveys has increased the usefulness of census data (see chapter 4), but, again, its value comes from the merger with household surveys that provide money-metric measures of welfare.

The crucial importance of a census for poverty monitoring and evaluation is that it generates the frame for carrying out appropriate and accurate sampling of households for all types of household surveys. Thus the census is an integral part of any effort to evaluate the poverty impact of policies, even if, by itself, it is not an adequate tool.

Labor Force Surveys

Labor force surveys (LFSs) are perhaps the most prevalent type of household survey done in many parts of the developing world.[1] An LFS is designed to provide precise estimates of key labor market variables such as labor force participation rates, unemployment rates, sectoral distribution of employment, and characteristics of the labor activities of the working age population. To obtain precise estimates of employment and unemployment rates, samples are large. Ideally the survey is carried out at various times throughout the year to capture seasonal differences. In many countries LFSs are the only surveys carried out systematically over time and thus have been used, in the absence of other data, to measure welfare and monitor poverty. However, these surveys are of limited or dubious use for such purposes for several reasons. First, to measure the welfare level of a household, a comprehensive measure of household income is needed that includes not just labor income, but also income from social assistance (public and private transfers), home production (particularly in agriculture), rents, gifts, and the use value or flow of services from housing and durable goods. Although most Labor Force Surveys collect income data related to labor activities, seldom are data collected concerning all sources of income. This lack leads to two problems. First, any measure of welfare constructed from LFS data will underestimate the absolute level of income (welfare) in the country. Second, and more problematic, is that the underestimation is not consistent—some types of incomes and the incomes of some types of households are likely to be underestimated more than others. This bias leads to the fatal problem of misranking of households by welfare level and misidentification of the poor.

Labor force surveys have a further problem that can seriously undermine efforts to use them for poverty measurement. This problem is related more to practical than conceptual or definitional issues and stems from the difficulties of accurately capturing income in a household survey, especially when the bulk of the population does not participate in the formal sector. Often households at the bottom of the income distribution are unable to provide any reasonable estimate of net income because their "accounts" of household and informal business activities cannot be disentangled. And those at the top of the income distribution are often prone to underreporting due to tax considerations or distrust of interviewers. Efforts to compare income aggregates from household surveys with national accounts estimates show that surveys underestimate income, often substantially. Moreover a study of 45 LFSs in Latin America in the 1990s (Feres 1998) showed that simple nonresponse (missing data) and the problems it creates were significant: on average more than 10 percent of the income data was missing; in several surveys, more than a quarter of all income data was missing.

Income and Expenditure Surveys

Most countries have implemented an Income and Expenditure Survey (IES), often called Family or Household Budget Surveys. In many of the transition economies, these are often the only surveys being done and are carried out on a continuous basis (data are collected throughout the year, every year). IESs are common in other regions of the world as well but are usually conducted only once every five or ten years. An IES is intended to provide inputs to national accounts on consumer expenditures, track changes in expenditures over time and in the relative share of different expenditures, and provide the weights for the consumer price index. Although often providing a more complete measure of income than a Labor Force Survey, IESs may suffer from the same underreporting of income that LFSs do.[2] The IESs offer the most complete measure of total consumption and from that perspective appear to be a potentially excellent source of data for poverty measurement.[3] However, some fundamental characteristics of IESs, based on their purposes, make them inappropriate for poverty measurement without specific changes.

The goal of an IES survey is not to measure household welfare, but to measure, with precision, mean expenditures on specific goods and services. As a result data collection methods are designed to enhance the latter goal, often at the expense of the former. That raises two issues that must be resolved before IES data can be used for evaluating the poverty impact of policy or even measuring poverty. The first is tied to the issue of reference periods. To minimize the amount of expenditures omitted, a very short reference period is used in an IES. This short reference period helps to capture accurate average expenditures at the national or regional level, but it makes the measurement of an individual household's expenditures, and thus welfare, problematic. Households make purchases at varying times, some items once a week, some only two or three times a year. Thus, depending on when the household is interviewed, its expenditures may appear quite high or quite low, regardless of what its actual annual consumption really is. Thus, for an IES survey to be useful for poverty measurement, longer reference periods for many items are required to avoid misranking of households and misidentifying the poor.

A second feature of the IES that creates problems for measuring poverty is that the survey is focused on expenditures, not consumption. This focus affects the usefulness, for poverty purposes, of the data on durable goods and housing. The IES typically captures information on purchases on durable goods. But durable goods are not consumed in one year, and thus the entire expenditure cannot be considered part of annual total consumption. To do so would overstate the welfare level of the household in a significant fashion. Instead, what is needed is a calculation of the use value or flow of services stemming from ownership of durable goods. Such a calculation requires two changes to the way data are collected in an IES. First, data need to be collected not only on goods purchased in the current year, but on all durable goods owned by the household; second, information is required on the age of the good and, at a minimum, the current value of the good in order to calculate the use value of each good. To impute the use value of housing, information is needed not only on monthly payments for owned housing, but also on housing characteristics.[4]

A third drawback of the Income and Expenditure Survey is that it is simply what its name implies and has little or no information on other key issues such as education, labor activities, social protection, and health. Often times, incorporating such topics into an IES is more difficult than the changes required to resolve the two previous problems outlined above. That is largely because these other topics are seen as unrelated to the purpose of the IES and threatening to the integrity of the survey. Clearly any effort to append such questions to an IES needs to respect the original purpose of the survey and not overburden respondents or interviewers. Making such changes must be seen as a long-term project, not a quick fix, as the changes need to be discussed, tested, and revised. The work of the Bangladesh Bureau of Statistics to revise and enhance its IES is one example of how this effort can be done successfully (World Bank 1999). The changes were made over a period of seven years (in fact, changes are still being made), and the survey now incorporates information on education, health, and social safety nets as well as allowing for poverty measurement. In other words, an IES can be made to work for poverty measurement and the evaluation of the poverty impact of programs and policies, but only with specific, and sometimes significant, revisions to the survey instruments.

Demographic and Health Surveys

Like Labor Force Surveys, Demographic and Health Surveys (DHSs) are focused primarily on one topic. These surveys are designed to look at specific factors affecting health outcomes and fertility patterns. Because of their focus on one topic, the DHS, like other one-topic surveys, are able to provide much greater depth of information on the subject of interest and allow a more thorough analysis than a multitopic survey would allow. To provide such in-depth coverage, the DHS (and others of its kind) limit the amount of information on other topics that might be of interest. Of particular concern for analysts interested in poverty is that no effort is made to measure welfare levels of households included in the survey. Instead it uses proxies of welfare, typically those requiring a minimum of questions and interviewing time to collect. The adequacy of this approach has been evaluated (Filmer and Pritchett 1998a, 1998b; Montgomery and others 2000) with mixed results. For poverty measurement itself, the proxies may not be adequate, although their use for hypothesis testing may well be sufficient. Thus, the use of a DHS or other single-topic survey may be limited. If the policy of concern is health or demographics, the use of proxy welfare measures may be enough to allow an assessment of welfare impacts, but the usefulness of the survey will need to be assessed on a case-by-case basis, depending on the analysis of interest. A final consideration is that DHS surveys are also done infrequently, and thus data may not be available for any analytical technique requiring before and after data or panel data.

Multitopic Household Surveys

Each of the surveys listed above is valuable in its own right, but even when taken together, they do not provide a comprehensive picture of the population and how it lives. Policymakers find themselves severely limited in their ability to understand the determinants of observed social and economic outcomes and hence their ability to design effective and efficient programs and policies.

Multitopic household surveys such as the National Socio-Economic Survey (SUSENAS) in Indonesia, the Integrated Surveys in many African countries, the Rand Family Life Surveys, and the Living Standards Measurement Study surveys (LSMS) attempt to fill this gap.[5] Specifically, these multitopic surveys have been designed to generate data for the analysis of welfare levels and distribution; the links between welfare and the characteristics of the population in poverty; the causes of observed social outcomes; the levels of access to, and use of, social services; and the impact of government programs.

Although designed to provide the data needed to measure welfare and assess the impact of policy on it, these surveys also suffer from some limitations. Given the complexity of the survey instruments, multitopic surveys tend to have small sample sizes, for both cost and quality considerations. That may limit their usefulness in assessing the impact of policies that affect only a very small group in the country or only one small geographic area. In such cases, oversampling in project areas or among specific subgroups of the population is needed. A second issue is that such surveys, with the exception of the SUSENAS in Indonesia, have, to date, been done only infrequently. Many of these surveys have been conducted only once or twice and are not an integral part of the statistics system. This lack of frequency is a problem when the analytic tool employed requires before and after data or panel data and is an issue that needs further attention.

Despite these flaws, multitopic surveys—either created as such or those stemming from substantial revision of an IES—are the best available data source for implementing most of the techniques discussed in this volume. The remainder of this chapter outlines in detail the necessary characteristics of such surveys and how they can be used to further the understanding of the links between policy and poverty reduction.

Main Elements of Multitopic Surveys

What makes a survey of particular use for measuring welfare and assessing the poverty impact of government policies and programs? In the broadest terms, it is a combination of the content of the survey—the data collected—and the methods used to collect the data and ensure its quality. This section outlines the important considerations related to the issues of content and quality.

To illustrate the points raised and to provide an example of what can and has been done, the experience with the Living Standards Measurement Study surveys is used. The LSMS is only one of the group of multitopic surveys available, but it provides a good point of departure for discussing the needs of analysts and policymakers regarding multitopic surveys. The LSMS survey was developed in the 1980s to fill the gaps in researchers' and policy analysts' knowledge of household behavior stemming from a lack of relevant data. Drawing on consultations with a wide range of researchers as well as reviews of existing surveys, the LSMS was designed to provide a comprehensive picture of household welfare and the factors that affect it. The first LSMS surveys were implemented in Côte d'Ivoire and Peru in the mid-1980s and demonstrated the feasibility of the approach. Since then, more than 60 such surveys have been carried out and the procedures used in the LSMS incorporated in many other surveys.

Content

For the content of a multitopic survey to meet poverty-related analytical needs, four elements need to be addressed. The first is simply that the survey provide an adequate measure of poverty or welfare at the household level. Regardless of whether one is concerned with absolute or relative measures of poverty, an accurate ranking of households from poorest to least poor is fundamental. Thus, the survey needs to collect data on total consumption or total income. The preference is for total consumption for both theoretical and practical reasons. It has been argued that consumption is a better measure of actual welfare, while income reflects potential welfare. Additionally, households are usually able to smooth consumption over a year's period. Thus measuring consumption is more likely to give a correct picture of a household's well-being, whereas income, because of its potential for large variations throughout a year, can lead to erroneous conclusions concerning individual households' welfare levels. Finally, as noted above in the discussion of Labor Force Surveys, total income is notoriously difficult to measure accurately (at both ends of the distribution): consumption presents fewer problems, although measuring consumption is not a simple task.

In the LSMS surveys, data on total consumption are collected in a variety of sections of the household questionnaire: in the housing module to obtain the expenditures on services and a measure of the use value of housing; in the education module to obtain accurate information on out-of-pocket payments for all education and training; in a special module on food and nonfood expenditures with varying reference periods to aid recall; and in agriculture and household business modules to capture home production. To enable the comparison of total consumption by households across the country, a price questionnaire is administered in each area where households are surveyed. This instrument provides the data needed for making spatial cost-of-living adjustments.

The second element is the subject coverage of the survey. A multitopic survey, as its name implies, is designed to collect data on a wide range of topics related to welfare and government programs and the linkages between them. These topics should include measures of human capital in terms of health and education, access to and use of government services and infrastructure, economic activities of the household, and other aspects of households and their members affected by government policies. The household survey instrument can be designed to capture all of the information from each household, or a "core and rotating" questionnaire can be designed where all households are asked the core questions and a subsample are asked more in-depth questions on a particular topic. It is important to remember that the real value of a multitopic survey is the ability to link a money-metric measure of welfare to other dimensions of welfare and the use of government programs and services. Thus, in the core and rotating model, care is needed to ensure that the core questionnaire has adequate coverage of all topics and that the rotating model is used only to explore a specific topic in detail.

There is no "ideal" questionnaire. The content of any multitopic survey will vary by country and even over time in a given country. Data needs change, new policies are implemented that need to be studied, new analytical techniques present additional data requirements, and the results of one survey should feed into changes in the next. Table 7.1 shows a list of the topics that have been covered in LSMS surveys over the past 17 years. Note that no one survey ever contained all these modules at once. The starred modules are the most common, some of the additional modules are less so, and some have been implemented only in one country. For example, in Bosnia and Herzegovina in 2001, the concern with the lingering impact of the war led to the incorporation of 14 depression-screening questions into the health module so as to be able both to measure the

Table 7.1 Modules Included in LSMS Surveys'
Household Questionnaire

Household demographics*	Agricultural activities*
Housing*	Nonfarm household businesses*
Education*	Food consumption (purchase, produce, gift)*
Health*	Nonfood consumption and durables*
Labor*	Other income (including public and private transfers)*
Migration*	Social capital
Fertility*	Shocks, vulnerability
Privatization	Time use
Credit	Subjective measures of welfare
Anthropometrics	

Note: Starred modules are those most often used.
Source: LSMS survey questionnaires.

incidence of this mental health condition and to identify the linkages between it and other aspects of welfare. Efforts to understand
the vulnerability of the population to economic shocks led to the
inclusion of a module on the topic in Peru in 1999 (among others).
And a concern with the effect of AIDS-related mortality on households led to significant changes in the Kagera (Tanzania) Survey in
1991–94. A final example is the inclusion in the LSMS of a module
on subjective welfare that allows this measure to be related to objective measures and other indicators.[6]

LSMS surveys have also collected data from the community in
which the household resides. A "community questionnaire" is
administered to collect complementary data on the environment in
which households function. These questionnaires have been most
often administered in rural areas, because the original assumption
was that all services and infrastructure existed in cities. Recent surveys have added urban instruments at the level of the "neighborhood" to address the problem of differential access to services
within a city.[7] Also, in a few cases, facility questionnaires have been
administered to local providers of health and education to gather
data on the types and quality of services available to households.
The community and facility instruments are used to capture policy
variables of interest to the analyst and allow these to be assessed in
relation to the households' characteristics and use of such services
and programs.

The third element in a successful multitopic survey is the relevance of the data collected and the ownership of results. Relevance

is the fundamental reason that there is no single ideal questionnaire that can be taken off the shelf and administered in any given setting. Developing appropriate survey instruments requires identifying the key policy issues and understanding the uses and limitations of household data to address them. Identifying the relevant issues requires a process of questionnaire design based on consultation with data users and policymakers. To do this, one needs to create a data users' group or steering committee with members from different line ministries, donors, and academics along with the national statistical office. This group should be responsible for identifying the appropriate data needed for evaluating or monitoring specific policies. In LSMS surveys the questionnaire design phase takes, on average, about eight months and involves a fairly large group. This rather lengthy process ensures that the right issues are covered. As important, it also serves to generate demand for, and ownership of, the resulting data. This, in turn, leads to a greater use of the data in policy than would otherwise occur.

Not all policy questions can or should be addressed using household data. A recent research project in the World Bank has led to publication of a new book outlining, by topic, the policy questions that can be addressed by LSMS data and providing guidance on questionnaire design for multitopic household surveys (Grosh and Glewwe 2000). This volume should be a basic reference guide in the questionnaire design process.

An additional input for the questionnaire design can come from qualitative studies. Such studies typically do not attempt to measure the incidence or occurrence of certain events but instead are designed to identify issues that might not be apparent from other sources. Insights gained from such studies can be used to improve the questionnaire and its content.[8] Such efforts can also serve to engage additional sectors of government or researchers in the country, furthering the relevance of the resulting data and the demand for it.

A final point that needs to be considered in determining the content of the questionnaire is comparability. This issue takes two forms: ensuring comparability over time, and ensuring comparability across countries. The former is critical. Small changes in the way in which welfare is measured can lead to large, spurious changes in the welfare levels over time. Thus questionnaire design and field work techniques need to be kept constant over time for all variables for which trend data are needed. The problem is easier dealt with when designing a new survey and planning for the future than trying to reconcile a new data set with a past one. There is often a strong temptation or pressure to look at trends in welfare over time. If the welfare measures are not the same, this tendency should be resisted because the results can be misleading at best and simply wrong at worst.

The second concern involves comparability across countries. Here the survey design team may be faced with having to make tradeoffs between having a questionnaire that meets all of its needs and having one that meets requirements at the international level for comparable data. In the simple case, no tradeoff is involved—both demands for data can be met. When that is not possible, the multitopic surveys have typically opted for the country-specific needs over the international comparison needs. This is a choice that must be addressed as it arises. But in the interests of providing country-relevant data and ownership of the data within the country and among its policymakers, meeting local needs is often likely to take precedence over international ones.

Quality

By its nature a multitopic household survey is complex. The household questionnaire is lengthy and intricate, and multiple instruments are needed (price, community) to ensure the accuracy and scope of the analysis. The focus on the relationship among variables, and not simply on measuring specific rates or averages, means that the completeness, consistency, and accuracy of the data collected within each household is imperative. To achieve these objectives, attention has to be given to the quality of the survey from the design to the analytical phase. Many of the procedures used in single-topic surveys may be inadequate for multitopic surveys. This section summarizes important features of quality control in multitopic surveys, focusing on sampling, field work, data entry, and data access.

Sample. In any survey two types of error are possible—sampling and nonsampling—and the two are inversely correlated. Nonsampling error, which consists of all errors that may occur during the survey implementation (interviewer errors, mistakes in data entry, and the like) are often hidden and can affect results in unknown ways. Thus minimizing such errors is critical. The LSMS and other multitopic surveys have focused on reducing this kind of error, and one result is that sample sizes are kept quite small. That, of course, increases sampling error, but unlike nonsampling error, there is a known degree of sampling error that can be taken into account in the analysis of the data. Samples in LSMS surveys are national probability samples of between 2,000 and 6,000 households. The sample is designed to allow results at the national, urban-rural, and regional levels. The sample sizes are too small, however, to provide data on more disaggregated levels. Analysis at more disaggregated levels requires a massively larger sample size that would have a significant negative impact on nonsampling errors and on data quality and reliability.

The small sample size presents some limitations in data analysis. But since the emphasis in multitopic surveys is on exploring the relationships among aspects of living standards, as opposed to measuring specific indicators or rates with great precision, the small sample size is less of a hindrance than it might be in other surveys. A Labor Force Survey, for example, needs to show very small changes in unemployment rates over time. That requires quite a large sample. In contrast, the goal of a multitopic survey is to understand the determinants of unemployment: that can be done with a much smaller sample but with wider coverage in the questionnaire design of the factors that are likely to influence unemployment. Additionally, recent work in linking LSMS survey data to population censuses also eliminates some of the restrictions that a small sample size may impose.[9]

Field Work: Data Collection. The standard survey method of highly centralized procedures used in single-topic surveys may be inadequate for a multitopic survey if quality is to be maintained. In a multitopic survey, interviewers and supervisors need to be extremely well trained and thus capable of decisionmaking as the work progresses. In LSMS surveys, for example, data are collected by mobile interview teams throughout the country. Each survey team incorporates a supervisor, two or three interviewers, a data entry operator, and computing equipment so that data can be entered concurrent to the interviews. Formally, each household is visited by an interviewer at least twice with a two-week period between visits. The first half of the questionnaire is completed in the first visit. Between visits, the data from the first visit is entered and checked for errors. The second visit is used to correct errors from the first visit and to administer the second half of the survey. Although two visits are formally scheduled, the use of direct informants for all sections of the questionnaire means that, in fact, interviewers visit each household as many times as are needed in order to interview all household members personally. Community and price questionnaires are administered by the team supervisors in the communities where the surveyed households live as are the facility questionnaires if these are included in the design.

Field Work: Data Entry.   Traditionally, data are collected through oral interviews with the completed questionnaires then passed to a central unit for data entry and cleaning. When errors, missing data, or inconsistencies are detected, complex batch cleaning procedures are employed to rectify the problems. This process creates internally consistent data sets, but not ones that best reflect each individual household's situation. The other drawback of this system is that lengthy gaps between data collection and the production of survey results often result.

To avoid these problems, a decentralized system of data entry is needed, where data entry takes place in the field and error correction is done by consulting the original informants. Computer-assisted personal interviewing techniques, such as that used by the U.S. Bureau of the Census for its Current Population Survey is the epitome of decentralized data entry. An alternative involves entering data in the field, concurrent to interviewing. Concurrent data entry entails using sophisticated data entry software in the field that checks for range errors, inter- and intrarecord inconsistencies and, when possible, checking data against external reference tables (anthropometrics, crop yield data, and prices, for example). Immediately after an interview is completed, the data from the questionnaire are entered, and a list of errors, inconsistencies, and missing information is produced. The interviewer returns to the household as needed to clarify any problems and to capture any missing information. This process avoids the lengthy gap between data collection and data production and creates a data set that better reflects each household's characteristics.

To take into account issues of seasonality, field work is typically done over a 12-month period, although many countries have opted for shorter periods. The concurrent data entry ensures that the lag between data collection and analysis is minimal. For surveys being done over a 12-month period, some countries have chosen to produce a mid-term analysis based on the first 6 months of data collection.

Open Access to Data.   One often-overlooked tool for improving data quality is the promotion of open access to the microeconomic data resulting from the survey. The complexity and richness of the multitopic household survey data sets is such that no one user, and certainly not the statistical office, will use all the resulting data. Obviously, ensuring the widespread use of the data sets by a range of researchers and policymakers increases the returns to the investment in the survey. But what is often forgotten is that the greater use of the survey also improves its quality because it leads to careful checking of the data set. And creating a feedback loop from data users to data producers is critical for increasing the quality (and relevance) of future surveys.

The open data access policy needs to be addressed in the very early stages of the survey. Statistical offices often resist opening access, because of issues of confidentiality and concern for misuse of the data. But confidentiality can be (must be) maintained by removing names and addresses from the disseminated data set. And misuse of data is something that is not restricted to users outside the government. The concern should be for transparency in analysis and improving the data users' analytical skills. The Rand Family Life Surveys are all public access data sets, and the majority of the LSMS surveys done to date have open data access policies.

General Issues of Quality.   In addition to the issues already discussed, there are a variety of survey techniques that are needed to ensure data quality. Many of these are standard, or should be, to all surveys; some are more relevant for a multitopic survey. The controls take a variety of forms, from the simplest—relying on verbatim questions, explicit skip patterns, questionnaires translated into the relevant languages in a country, using direct informants (not only the household head) to minimize informant fatigue and improve the accuracy of the data provided, and close-ended questions to minimize interviewer error—to the more complex one of concurrent data entry with immediate revisits to households to correct inconsistency errors or capture missing data. As an example, table 7.2 lists the key features of quality control incorporated into LSMS surveys.

Applications of Multitopic Household Surveys

Multitopic household survey data have been used to measure welfare levels, understand the determinants of observed social outcomes, carry out ex ante analysis of the impact of alternative policies, and evaluate the impact of government programs and policies. Many of the other chapters in this volume provide specific examples of how multitopic data can be, and have been, used to inform policymaking. Table 7.3 lists a few interesting examples of how such data have been used in recent years to improve policy. The reader is also referred to the overview of uses for household data done by Grosh (1997).

In addition to specific analyses of the data from one round of the survey, it is important to recognize other contexts in which the survey can be implemented and used. Collecting panel data, where households are reinterviewed at a later stage, provides information

Table 7.2 Quality Control Techniques

Area of quality control	Techniques
Questionnaire	• Explicit skip patterns • Limit number of open-ended questions
Format	• One physical questionnaire for all members of household • Verbatim questions • Direct informants (interview all individuals for individual-level data and then the best informed for household-level information) • Formally translate questionnaire into all relevant languages (use back translation to ensure accuracy); minimize use of field translations
Pilot test	• Formally pilot test the questionnaires and field work methodologies, including the concurrent data entry
Sample	• Small size to minimize nonsampling errors
Field work	• Intensive training (one month) of all field staff, both theoretical and practical • Decentralized field work with mobile teams incorporating supervisor, interviewers, data entry, and transportation • Two-round format to reduce informant fatigue, create bounded recall period for consumption, and allow for checking and correction in the field • Concurrent data entry to check for range and consistency errors, to allow for corrections in the household, and to minimize the lag between data collection and analysis • High supervision ratios: one supervisor for every two or three interviewers
Data access	• Agreement to ensure open access to the data by all users and to promote dissemination

Source: Scott, Steele, and Temesgten, forthcoming.

on how individuals and households move in and out of poverty (see chapter 3 and Glewwe and Nguyen 2002, for examples). In the case of Nicaragua, a small panel was used to measure the effect of a major shock to households. Shortly after the national LSMS had been done, Hurricane Mitch hit the country. Recognizing the importance of understanding the impact of this shock and the mechanisms

Table 7.3 Examples of Uses of Multitopic Household Surveys for Poverty-Related Purposes

Country	Policy analysis
Bangladesh, 2002	Evaluation of effectiveness of public social safety net programs
Bosnia and Herzegovina, 2003	Determinants of poverty
Jamaica, 1996	Evaluation of the targeting of a loan program for higher education
Kyrgyz Republic, 1999	Determinants of school dropout among the poor and nonpoor
Mexico, 1998–2001	Impact evaluation of the PROGRESA program of cash transfers for improving health and education outcomes
Nicaragua, 1999	Benefit incidence analysis of public spending on health and education
Tunisia, 1996	Assessment of the impact changing food subsidies would have on the caloric intake of the poor, comparison of two alternative revisions to food subsidies

Sources: Information on these analyses can be found in World Bank (2002) for Bangladesh; World Bank (2003) for Bosnia and Herzegovina; Blank and Williams (1998) for Jamaica; World Bank (2001a) for the Kyrgyz Republic; PROGRESA (1998), Skoufias and McClafferty (2001), Skoufias, Davis, and de la Vega (2001) for Mexico; World Bank (2001b) for Nicaragua; Tuck and Lindert (1996) for Tunisia.

households were using to cope, the statistical office reinterviewed all the households included in the original sample that were in the areas affected by Mitch. Although the sample did not allow an estimate of the national impact of the hurricane, it certainly provided quick insights into some of the major effects of the shock and the ability of households to maintain living standards.

A national LSMS can also be used to improve substantially the quality and power of other tools to evaluate government programs through the use of propensity-matching scores.[10] This technique allows one to create virtual control groups from the national LSMS that can be used to evaluate program impact. The evaluation of the Emergency Social Investment Fund, again in Nicaragua, is a good illustration of the important benefits of this (World Bank 2000).

Pressure from the international community has also generated new demands for LSMS data. The debt reduction processes for heavily indebted poor countries and the procedure for obtaining access to concessional lending from the International Development Association and the International Monetary Fund include a requirement for a government poverty reduction strategy. Such a strategy presupposes the ability to measure and monitor poverty as well as other social indicators. In countries such as Bolivia, Bosnia and Herzegovina, Kyrgyz Republic, and Vietnam, for example, the LSMS data are providing both the baseline data for measuring poverty and the tool to monitor the completion of the goals set out in the strategy.

The focus on the Millennium Development Goals (MDGs) have created another source of demand for timely, good quality, household-level data. Several of the MDGs can be measured using data from LSMS surveys: access to education by males and females, and poverty levels, for example. The small sample size does limit the ability of the LSMS to provide data for all the MDGs: mortality rates cannot be estimated from an LSMS survey as these rates require a substantially larger sample size. But the LSMS is a useful tool to help countries generate the needed information to monitor their progress in reaching the MDGs.

Capacity Building and Sustainability

There is often a discussion of the tradeoffs between short-term data needs and long-term capacity building. It is useful to recognize that in many cases, the lack of data availability in the short run is simply the result of previous planners not having invested in the long term. To avoid continuing this expensive focus on the short term, it is imperative to recognize the importance of capacity building when a multitopic household survey such as an LSMS is contemplated. The process of designing, implementing, and analyzing the data is key to creating a capacity for future quality survey work and analysis. It is a lengthy process, one often not suited to short project cycles, and it requires explicit attention in the planning and budgeting phases.

The ultimate goal is to create some level of sustainability: the ability of the country to produce and use policy relevant data over time. Creating the capacity in both survey techniques and analysis is a necessary, albeit not sufficient, condition for sustainability to occur. Experience with LSMS surveys (and others) has shown that sustainability is a long-term effort and cannot be obtained in the context of a single survey. Instead, a program that contemplates multiple rounds of an LSMS, in conjunction with other surveys needed by policymakers, is needed. Explicitly linking and involving data producers and users in both the design and the analysis of the data has also proved to be a key ingredient. Again, this process of learning to use microeconomic data is not achieved overnight. Pressures will always exist to generate data quickly, but it is important to maintain a long-term vision if the LSMS is truly to have an impact on government policy.

Conclusions

There is a strong need for increasing governments' use of empirical-based policymaking. Single-topic surveys are one tool, but they fail to provide governments and researchers with a comprehensive understanding of how households behave and the interaction of households with government social and economic policy. Multitopic household surveys, by explicitly linking the different factors affecting welfare, represent a potentially powerful tool for measuring how government policies affect households. By involving policymakers in the design and analysis phases of the survey, both the relevance and quality of the data can be improved, as well as the extent to which data is used in policymaking. Part of the process of carrying out any multitopic survey should be to build the overall capacity to design and implement the survey and to use the resulting data. Although that requires a substantial investment, the return in the form of increased effectiveness and efficiency of public spending and policies can be substantial.

Notes

1. One of the positive results of the United Nations' National Household Survey Capability Programme has been that of institutionalizing these surveys in many countries. In several countries in Latin America, for example, this survey may be the only household survey that has been done consistently.

2. An example from Uruguay (Grosskoff 1998) illustrates this point. A comparison of income estimates from a Labor Force Survey, an Income and Expenditure Survey, and the relevant section of the national accounts in Uruguay showed that although the IES did a better job of approximating the national accounts figures than the LFS, both surveys underestimated household income, relative to the national accounts.

3. A nice summary of the reasons why total consumption might be preferred as a measure of welfare over total income can be found in Deaton and Grosh (2000).

4. For a detailed discussion of the use value of durable goods and housing and the date required to estimate these, see Deaton and Zaidi (2002).

5. For detailed information on the Family Life Surveys, see the Rand Corporation Web site (www.rand.org); on Integrated Surveys, see World Bank (1992); for Living Standards Measurement Study Surveys, see Grosh and Munoz (1996) or the LSMS Web site (http://www.worldbank.org/lsms).

6. See Pradham and Ravallion (2000) and Ravallion and Lokshin (2001, 2002) for examples of the use of such measures.

7. About half of all LSMS surveys administered community question-naires.

8. See chapter 8.

9. See chapter 4.

10. See chapter 5.

References

The word *processed* describes informally reproduced works that may not be commonly available through library systems.

Blank, Lorraine, and Colin Williams. 1998. "Reanalysis of the First Impact Evaluation Study of 1996." Students Loan Bureau, Kingstown, Jamaica. Processed.

Deaton, Angus, and Margaret Grosh. 2000. "Consumption." In Grosh and Glewwe, eds., (2000).

Deaton, Angus, and Salman Zaidi. 2002. "Guidelines for Constructing Consumption Aggregates for Welfare Analysis." Living Standards Measurement Study Working Paper 135. World Bank, Development Economics Research Group, Washington, D.C. Processed.

Feres, Juan Carlos. 1998. "Falta de Respuesta a las Preguntas Sobre el ingreso. Su magnitud y efectos en las Encuestas de Hogares en América Latina." Programa para el Mejoramientos de las Encuestas y la Medición de las Condiciones de Vida en América Latina y el Caribe, 2° Taller Regional, Buenos Aires, Argentina, November 10-13, 1998.

Filmer, Deon, and Lant Pritchett. 1998a. "The Effect of Household Wealth on Educational Attainment around the World: Demographic and Health Survey Evidence." Policy Research Working Paper 1980. World Bank, Development Economics Research Group, Washington, D.C. Processed.

———. 1998b. "Estimating Wealth Effects without Expenditure Data—or Tears: An Application to Educational Enrollments in States of India." Policy Research Working Paper 1994. World Bank, Development Economics Research Department, Washington, D.C. Processed.

Glewwe, Paul, and Phong Nguyen. 2002. "Economic Mobility in Vietnam in the 1990s." Policy Research Working Paper 2838. World Bank, Development Economics Research Group, Washington, D.C. Processed.

Grosh, Margaret. 1997. "The Policymaking Uses of Multi-topic Household Survey Data: A Primer." *World Bank Research Observer* 12(2): 137–60.

Grosh, Margaret, and Paul Glewwe, eds. 2000. *Designing Household Survey Questionnaires for Developing Countries: Lessons from 15 Years of the Living Standards Measurement Study Surveys.* Washington, D.C.: World Bank.

Grosh, Margaret, and Juan Munoz. 1996. "A Manual for Planning and Implementing the Living Standards Measurement Study Survey." Living Standards Measurement Study Working Paper 126. World Bank, Development Economics Research Group, Washington, D.C. Processed.

Grosskoff, Rosa. 1998. "Comparación de las estadísticas de ingresos provenientes de encuestas de hogares con estimaciones externas." Programa para el Mejoramientos de las Encuestas y la Medición de las Condiciones de Vida en América Latina y el Caribe, 2° Taller Regional, Buenos Aires, Argentina, November 10-13, 1998.

Montgomery, Mark, Kathleen Burke, Edmundo Paredes, and Salman Zaidi. 2000. "Measuring Living Standards with Proxy Variables." *Demography* 37(2): 155–74.

Pradhan, Menno, and Martin Ravallion. 2000. "Measuring Poverty Using Qualitative Perceptions of Consumption Adequacy." *Review of Economics and Statistics* 82: 462–71.

PROGRESA. 1998. *Metodología para la Identificación de los Hogares Beneficiarios del PROGRESA.* Mexico City, Mexico.

Ravallion, Martin, and Michael Lokshin. 2001. "Identifying Welfare Effects Using Subjective Questions." *Economica* 68: 335–57.

———. 2002. "Self-Rated Economic Welfare in Russia." *European Economic Review* 46(8): 1453–73.

Scott, Kinnon, Diane Steele, and Tilahun Temesgten. Forthcoming. "Living Standards Measurement Study Surveys." In Ibrahim-Sorie Yansaneh, ed., *The Analysis of Operating Characteristics of Surveys in Developing Countries.* United Nations Technical Report, New York.

Skoufias, Emmanuel, and B. McClafferty. 2001. "Is PROGRESA Working? Summary of the Results of an Evaluation by IFPRI." FCND Discussion Paper 118. International Food Policy Research Institute, Washington, D.C. Processed.

Skoufias, Emmanuel, Benjamin Davis, and Sergio de la Vega. 2001. "Targeting the Poor in Mexico: An Evaluation of the Selection of Households into PROGRESA." *World Development* 29(10): 1769–84.

Tuck, Laura, and Kathy Lindert. 1996. "From Universal Food Subsidies to a Self-Targeted Program: A Case Study in Tunisian Reform." Discussion Paper 351. World Bank, Agricultural Operations Division, Middle East and North Africa Region, Washington, D.C. Processed.

World Bank. 1992. "The Social Dimensions of Adjustment Integrated Survey: A Survey to Measure Poverty and Understand the Effects of Policy

Change on Households." Social Dimensions of Adjustment in Sub-Saharan Africa Working Paper 14. Washington, D.C. Processed.

————. 1999. "Bangladesh: From Counting the Poor to Making the Poor Count." Country Study 19648. Washington, D.C. Processed.

————. 2000. "Nicaragua: Ex-Post Impact Evaluation of the Emergency Social Investment Fund (FISE)." Report 20400-NI. Washington, D.C. Processed.

————. 2001a. "Poverty in the 1990s in the Kyrgyz Republic." Report 21721-KG. Human Development Department, Country Department VIII, Europe and Central Asia Region, Washington, D.C. Processed.

————. 2001b. "Nicaragua Poverty Assessment Challenges and Opportunities for Poverty Reduction." Report 20488-NI. Poverty Reduction and Economic Management Sector Unit, Latin American and the Caribbean Region, Washington, D.C. Processed.

————. 2002. "Poverty in Bangladesh: Building on Progress." Report 24299-BO. Poverty Reduction and Economic Management Sector Unit, South Asia Region, Washington, D.C. Processed.

————. 2003. "Bosnia and Herzegovina: Poverty Assessment." Report 25343-BIH. Poverty Reduction and Economic Management Sector Unit, Europe and Central Asia, Washington, D.C. Processed.

8

Integrating Qualitative and Quantitative Approaches in Program Evaluation

Vijayendra Rao and Michael Woolcock

This chapter outlines some of the ways and means by which integrating qualitative and quantitative approaches in development research and program evaluation can help yield insights that neither approach would produce on its own. In assessing the impact of development programs and policies, it is important to recognize that the quantitative methods emphasized in this tool kit, while enormously useful, nonetheless have some important limitations and that some of these can be overcome by incorporating complementary qualitative approaches. An examination of the strengths and weakness of orthodox stand-alone quantitative (and qualitative) approaches is followed by a basic framework for integrating different approaches, based on distinguishing between data and the methods used to collect them. Some practical examples of "mixed-method" approaches to program evaluation are then given, and some conclusions drawn.

Mixed Methods and Program Evaluation

The advantages of quantitative approaches to program evaluation are well known. Conducted properly, they permit generalizations to be made about large populations on the basis of much smaller (representative) samples. Given a set of identifying conditions, they can help establish the causality of the impact of given variables on project outcomes. And (in principle) they allow other researchers to validate the original findings by independently replicating the analysis. By remaining several steps removed from the people from whom the data has been obtained, and by collecting and analyzing data in numerical form, quantitative researchers argue that they are upholding research standards that are at once empirically rigorous, impartial, and objective.

The Case for Integrating Different Approaches

In social science research, however, these same strengths can also be a weakness. Many of the most important issues facing the poor—their identities, perceptions, and beliefs, for example—cannot be meaningfully reduced to numbers or adequately understood without reference to the immediate context in which they live. Most surveys are designed far from the places where they will be administered and as such tend to reflect the preconceptions and biases of the researcher; there is little opportunity to be "surprised" by new discoveries or unexpected findings. Although good surveys undergo several rounds of rigorous pretesting, the questions themselves are usually not developed using systematically collected insights from the field. Thus, while pretesting can identify and correct questions that show themselves to be clearly ill suited to the task, these problems can be considerably mitigated by the judicious use of qualitative methods in the process of developing the questionnaire.

Qualitative methods can also help in circumstances where a quantitative survey may be difficult to administer. Certain marginalized communities, for example, are small in number (the disabled, widows) or difficult for outsiders to access (sex workers, victims of domestic abuse), rendering them unlikely subjects for study through a large representative survey. In many developing country settings, central governments (let alone local nongovernmental organizations or public service providers) may lack the skills and (especially) the resources needed to conduct a thorough quantitative evaluation. Moreover, external researchers with little or no familiarity with even the country (let alone region or municipality) in question often draw on data from context-specific household surveys to make broad "policy recommendations," yet rarely provide useful results to local program officials or the poor themselves. Scholars working from qualitative research traditions in development studies like to proclaim that their approaches rectify some of these concerns by providing more detailed attention to context, reaching out to members of minority groups, working with available information and resources, and engaging the poor as partners in the collection, analysis, and interpretation of data (in all its many forms).[1]

Furthermore, in conducting evaluations, quantitative methods are best suited to measuring levels and changes in impacts and to drawing inferences from observed statistical relations between those impacts and other covariates. They are less effective, however, in understanding *process*—that is, the mechanisms by which a particular intervention instigates a series of events that ultimately result in the observed impact. For example, consider a community-driven development (CDD) project that sets up a committee in a village and provides it with funds to build a primary school. Even if a perfect quantitative impact evaluation were set up, it would typically measure quantitative outcomes such as the causal impact of the CDD funds on increasing school enrollment or whether benefits were well targeted to the poor. With some carefully constructed questions, one could perhaps get at some more subtle issues, such as the heterogeneity in levels of participation in decisionmaking across different groups, or even more subjective outcomes, such as changes in levels of intergroup trust in the village. Nevertheless, the quantitative analysis would not be very effective at describing the local politics in the village that led to the formation of the committee or the details pertaining to deliberations within it: How were certain groups included and others excluded? How did some individuals come to dominate the process? These are called *process* issues, and they can be crucial to *understanding* impact, as opposed to simply *measuring* it. Qualitative methods are particularly effective in delving deep into issues of process; a judicious mix of qualitative and quantitative methods can therefore help provide a more comprehensive evaluation of an intervention.

Qualitative approaches on their own, of course, also suffer from a number of important drawbacks. First, the individuals or groups being studied are usually small in number or have not been randomly selected, making it highly problematic (though not impossible) to draw generalizations about the wider population. Second, because groups are often selected idiosyncratically (for example, on the basis of a judgment call by the lead investigator) or on the recommendation of other participants (as with "snowball" sampling procedures, in which one informant—say, a corrupt public official—agrees to provide access to the next one), it is difficult to replicate, and thus independently verify, the results. Third, the analysis of qualitative analysis often involves interpretative judgments on the part of the researcher, and two researchers looking at the same data may arrive at different interpretations. (Quantitative methods are relatively less prone to such subjectivities in interpretation, though not entirely free of them.) Fourth, because of an inability to "control" for other mitigating factors or to establish the counterfactual, it is hard (though again not impossible) to make compelling claims regarding causality.[2]

It should be apparent that the strengths of one approach potentially complement the weaknesses of the other, and vice versa. Unfortunately, however, research in development studies generally, and program evaluation in particular, tends to be heavily polarized along quantitative and qualitative methodological lines. That is largely because researchers are recruited, trained, socialized, evaluated, and rewarded by single disciplines (and their peers and superiors within them) that have clear preferences for one research tradition over another. This practice ensures intellectual coherence and "quality control" but comes at the expense of discouraging innovation and losing any potential gains that could be derived from integrating different approaches. We are hardly the first to recognize the limitations of different approaches or to call for more methodological pluralism in development research—indeed, notable individuals at least since Epstein (1962) have made pathbreaking empirical contributions by working across methodological lines.[3] What we are trying to do, however, is to take the strengths and weaknesses of each approach seriously and discern practical (if no less difficult) strategies for combining them on a more regular basis as part of the overall program evaluation exercise (see also Kanbur 2003 and Rao 2002).[4] What might this entail?

Distinguishing between Data and Methods in Program Evaluation

A possible point of departure for thinking more systematically about mixed-method approaches to program evaluation is to distinguish between forms of data and the methods used to collect them (Hentschel 1999). This distinction posits that data can be either quantitative (numbers) or qualitative (text), just as the methods used to collect that data can also be quantitative (for example, large representative surveys) or qualitative (such as interviews and observation), giving rise to a simple 2×2 table (figure 8.1). Most development research and program evaluation strategies call upon quantitative data and methods or qualitative data and methods (that is, the upper right or lower left quadrants), but it is instructive to note that qualitative methods can also be used to collect quantitative data—as is seen in the detailed household data reported in Bliss and Stern (1982) and Lanjouw and Stern (1998) from a single village in

Figure 8.1 Types of Data and Methods

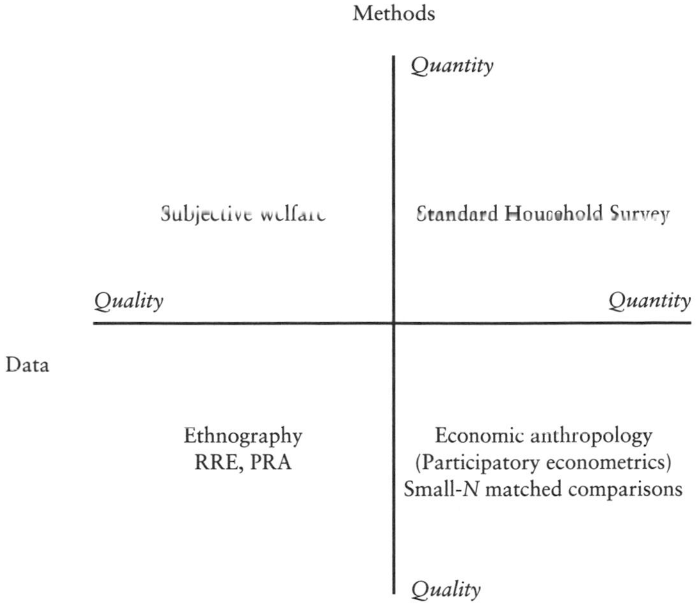

Methods

	Quantity
Subjective welfare	Standard Household Survey
Quality	*Quantity*

Data

Ethnography RRE, PRA	Economic anthropology (Participatory econometrics) Small-*N* matched comparisons
	Quality

Source: Adapted from Hentschel (1999).

India over several decades—and that quantitative methods can be used to collect qualitative data—as when open-ended or "subjective" response questions are included in large surveys (Ravallion and Pradhan 2000, for example), or when quantitative measures are derived from a large number of qualitative responses (Isham, Narayan, and Pritchett 1995, for example). Other examples from development that fall into this latter category include comparative case-study research, where the number of cases is necessarily small, but the units of analysis are large (such as the impact of the East Asian financial crisis on Korea, Thailand, and Indonesia).

Having made this distinction, it is instructive to consider in more detail the nature of some of the qualitative methods that are available to development researchers before exploring some of the ways in which they could be usefully incorporated into a more comprehensive mixed-method strategy for evaluating programs and projects. Three approaches are identified—participation, ethnography, and textual analysis. The particular focus of this chapter is on the use of qualitative methods to generate more and better quantitative data and to understand the process by which an intervention works, in addition to ascertaining its overall final impact.[5]

The first category of qualitative methods can be referred to as participatory approaches (Mikkelsen 1995; Narayan 1995; and Robb 2002). Introduced to scholars and practitioners largely through the work of Robert Chambers (see, most recently, Kumar and Chambers 2002), participatory techniques—such as Rapid Rural Appraisal (RRA) and Participatory Poverty Assessment (PPA)—seek to help outsiders learn about poverty and project impacts in cost-effective ways that reflect grounded experience. Since the Rapid Rural Appraisal is usually conducted with respondents who are illiterate, RRA researchers seek to learn about the lives of the poor using simple techniques such as wealth rankings, oral histories, role-playing, games, small group discussions, and village map drawings. These techniques permit respondents who are not trained in quantitative reasoning, or who are illiterate, to provide meaningful graphic representations of their lives in a manner that can give outside researchers a quick snapshot of an aspect of their living conditions. As such, RRA can be said to deploy *instrumental* participation research—novel techniques are being used to help the researcher better understand her subjects. A related approach is to use *transformative* participation techniques, such as Participatory Rural Appraisal (PRA), in which the goal is to facilitate a dialogue, rather than extract information, that helps the poor learn about themselves and thereby gain new insights that lead to social change ("empowerment").[6] In PRA exercises, a skilled facilitator helps villagers or slum dwellers generate tangible visual diagrams of the processes that lead to deprivation and illness, of the strategies that are used in times of crisis, and of the fluctuation of resource availability and prices across different seasons. Eliciting information in this format helps the poor to conceive of potentially more effective ways to respond (in ways that are not obvious ex ante) to the economic, political, and social challenges in their lives.

A crucial aspect of participatory methods is that they are conducted in groups. Therefore, it is essential that recruitment of participants be conducted so that representatives from each of the major subcommunities in the village are included. The idea is that if the group reaches a consensus on a particular issue after some discussion, then this consensus will be representative of views in the village because outlying views would have been set aside in the process of debate. For this technique to work, the discussion has to be extremely well moderated. The moderator must be dynamic enough to steer the discussion in a meaningful direction, deftly navigating his or her way around potential conflicts and, by the end, establishing a consensus. The moderator's role is therefore key to ensuring that high-quality data are gathered in a group discussion—a poor or inexperienced moderator can affect the quality of the data in a manner that is much more acute than an equivalently poor interviewer working with a structured quantitative questionnaire.

Other often-used qualitative techniques that can be classified as ethnographic face similar constraints. Focus-group discussions, for example, in which small intentionally diverse or homogenous groups meet to discuss a particular issue, are also guided by a moderator toward reaching consensus on key issues. Focus groups are thus similarly dependent on the quality of the moderator for the quality of the insights they yield. A focus group differs from a PRA in that it is primarily instrumental in its purpose and typically does not use the mapping and diagramming techniques that are characteristic of a PRA or RRA. Here, however, it should be noted that divergence from the consensus can also provide interesting insights, just as outliers in a regression can sometimes be quite revealing. Another important ethnographic technique that uses interview methods is the key-informant interview, which is an extended one-on-one exchange with someone who is a leader or unique in some way that is relevant to the study. Finally, the ethnographic investigator can engage in varying degrees of "participant observation," in which the researcher engages a community at a particular distance—as an actual member (for example, a biography of growing up in a slum), as a perceived actual member (a spy or police informant in a drug cartel, for example), as an invited long-term guest (such as an anthropologist), or as a more distant and detached short-term observer.[7]

A third qualitative approach is textual analysis. Historians, archaeologists, linguists, and scholars in cultural studies use such techniques to analyze various forms of media, ranging from archived legal documents, newspapers, artifacts, and government records to contemporary photographs, films, music, and television reports. (We provide an example below of the use of textual analysis in supplementing quantitative surveys in an evaluation of democratic decentralization in India.) Participatory, ethnographic, and textual research methods are too often seen as antithetical to or a poor substitute for quantitative approaches. In the examples that follow, we show how qualitative and quantitative methods have been usefully combined in development research and project evaluation, providing in unison what neither could ever do alone.

Mixed Methods Research and Project Evaluation: Pitfalls, Principles, and Examples

Having briefly outlined the *types* of qualitative methods available in our tool kit, we now sketch the different *methods of integration* between qualitative and quantitative techniques, providing examples for each method. The examples presented below are drawn from attempts to combine different methodological traditions in evaluation and policy research, but we stress from the outset that there are several good (as well as bad) reasons why mixed methods are not adopted more frequently. First, integrating different perspectives necessarily requires recruiting individuals with different skill sets, which makes such projects costly in terms of time, talent, and resources. Second, coordinating the large teams of people with diverse backgrounds that are often required for serious mixed-method projects generates coordination challenges above and beyond those normally associated with program evaluation. Third, these challenges, combined with institutional imperatives for quick turnaround and "straightforward" policy recommendations, mean that mixed-method research is often poorly done. Fourth, we simply lack an extensive body of evidence regarding how different methods can best be combined under what circumstances; more research experience is needed to help answer these questions and guide future efforts.

These concerns notwithstanding, it is nonetheless possible to discern a number of core principles and strategies for successfully mixing methods in project evaluation. The most important of these is to begin with an important, interesting, and researchable question and to then identify the most appropriate method (or combination of methods) that is likely to yield fruitful answers (Mills 1959). If taken seriously, this principle is actually remarkably difficult to live up to, since it is rare to find a good question that maps neatly and exclusively onto a single method. Three fields in which faithful efforts have been made, however, are comparative politics, anthropological demography, and anthropological economics. The first concerns itself primarily with questions that give rise to small sample sizes and large units of analysis—most commonly case studies of countries or large organizations studied historically—and is not discussed in detail here.[8] The second and third, however, are better suited to larger sample sizes and smaller units of analysis, and thus lessons from them are especially relevant to efforts to mix methods in poverty research and project evaluation.[9]

Methods of Integration

Qualitative and quantitative methods can be integrated in three different forms, which for convenience we call *parallel, sequential,* and *iterative.* In parallel approaches, the quantitative and qualitative research teams work separately but compare and combine findings during the analysis phase. This approach is best suited to very large projects, such as national level poverty assessments, where closer forms of integration are precluded by logistical and administrative realities. In "Poverty in Guatemala" (World Bank 2002), for example, two separate teams were responsible for collecting the qualitative and quantitative data. Previous survey material was used to help identify the appropriate sites for the qualitative work (five pairs of villages representing the five major ethnic groups in Guatemala), but the findings themselves were treated as an independent source of data and were integrated with the quantitative material only in the write-up phase of both the various background papers and the final report—that is, while useful in their own right, the qualitative data did not inform the design or construction of the quantitative survey, which was done separately. These different data sources were especially helpful in providing a more accurate map of the spatial and demographic diversity of the poor, as well as, crucially, a sense of the immediate context within which poverty was experienced by different ethnic groups, details of the local mechanisms that excluded them from participation in mainstream economic and civic activities, and the nature of the barriers they encountered in their efforts to advance their interests and aspirations. The final report also benefited from a concerted effort to place both the qualitative and quantitative findings in their broader historical and political context, a first for a World Bank poverty study.

Sequential and iterative approaches—which we call more specifically *participatory econometrics*—seek varying degrees of dialogue between the qualitative and quantitative traditions at all phases of the research cycle and are best suited to projects of more modest scale and scope.[10] Though the most technically complex and time consuming, these approaches are where the greatest gains are to be found from mixing methods in project and policy evaluation. Participatory econometrics works on the premise that

• The researcher should begin a project with some general hypotheses and questions, but an open mind regarding the results and even the possibility that the hypotheses and questions themselves may be in need of major revision.
• The researcher should both collect and analyze the data.
• A mix of qualitative and quantitative data is typically used to create an understanding of both measured impact and process.
• Respondents should be actively involved in the analysis and interpretation of findings.
• It is desirable to make broad generalizations and discern the nature of causality; consequently, relatively large sample sizes are likely to be needed (and thus the tools of econometrics employed on them).

This approach characterizes recent research on survival and mobility strategies in Delhi slums (Jha, Rao, and Woolcock 2002), in which extensive qualitative investigation in four different slum communities preceded the design of a survey that was then administered to 800 randomly selected households from all (officially listed) Delhi slums. The qualitative material not only helped design a better survey, but was also drawn upon in its own right to explore governance structures, migration histories, the nature and extent of property rights, and mechanisms underpinning the procurement of housing, employment, and public services.

The classical, or sequential, approach to participatory econometrics entails three key steps:

- Using PRA-type techniques, focus-group discussions, in-depth interviews, or all three to obtain a grounded understanding of issues.
- Constructing a survey instrument that integrates understandings from the field.
- Deriving hypotheses from qualitative work and testing with survey data. An intermediate step of constructing theoretical models to generate hypotheses may also be added (Rao 1997).

An example of the use of sequential mixed methods in project evaluation is a study of the impact of Social Investment Funds in Jamaica (Rao and Ibáñez 2003). The research team compiled case-study evidence from five matched pairs of communities in Kingston, in which one community in the pair had received funds from the Jamaica Social Investment Fund (JSIF) while the other had not—but had been selected to match the funded community as closely as possible in terms of its social and economic characteristics. The qualitative data revealed that the JSIF process was elite-driven, with decisionmaking processes dominated by a small group of motivated individuals, but that by the end of the project there was nonetheless broad-based satisfaction with the outcome. The quantitative data from 500 households mirrored these findings by showing that, ex ante, the social fund did not address the expressed needs of the majority of individuals in the majority of communities. By the end of the JSIF cycle, however, during which new facilities had been constructed, 80 percent of the community expressed satisfaction with the outcome. A quantitative analysis of the determinants of participation demonstrated that individuals who had higher levels of education and more extensive networks dominated the process. Propensity-score analysis revealed that the JSIF had a causal impact on improvements in trust and the capacity for collective action, but that these gains were greater for elites within the community.[11] This evidence suggests that both JSIF and non-JSIF communities are now more likely to make decisions that affect their lives—a positive finding indicative of widespread efforts to promote participatory development in the country—but that JSIF communities do not show higher levels of community-driven decisions than non-JSIF communities. A particular strength of this analysis is that here a development project that is by design both "qualitative" (participatory decisionmaking) and "quantitative" (allocating funds to build physical infrastructure) has been evaluated using corresponding methods.

The Bayesian, or iterative, approach to participatory economet rics is similar to the sequential approach, but it involves regularly returning to the field to clarify questions and resolve apparent anomalies. Here, qualitative findings can be regarded as a Bayesian Prior that is updated with quantitative investigation. One example comes from an initial study of marriage markets among potters in rural Karnataka, India, which led to work on domestic violence (Rao 1998, Bloch and Rao 2002); unit price differentials in everyday goods, that is, why the poor pay higher prices than the rich for the same good (Rao 2000); and public festivals (Rao 2001a, 2001b). An initial interest in marriage markets thus evolved in several different but unanticipated directions, uncovering understudied phenomena that were of signal importance in the lives of the people being studied. Moreover, the subjects of the research, with their participation in PRAs and PPAs, focus-group discussions, and in-depth interviews, played a significant role in shaping how research questions were defined, making an important contribution to the analysis and informing the subsequent econometric work, which tested the generalizability of the qualitative findings, measuring the magnitude of the effects and their causal determinants.

Iterative mixed-method approaches to project evaluation are most likely to be useful in situations where task managers are overseeing projects that have a diverse range of possible impacts (some of which may be unknown or unintended), and where some form of "participation" has been a central component of project design and implementation. Ideally an orthodox difference-in-difference strategy of collecting both baseline and follow-up data and identifying comparable program and nonprogram groups should be followed. But it is not always self-evident, a priori, how exactly one should go about selecting communities for intensive qualitative work or what precise questions should be included on a household survey.

Two evaluations of participatory (community-driven development) projects currently under way in Indonesia demonstrate the benefits of using iterative mixed-method approaches. The first is concerned with designing a methodology for identifying the extent of a range of impacts associated with a project in urban areas (known as the Urban Poverty Project 2, or UPP2); the second with assessing whether and how a similar project already operating for three years in rural areas (the Kecamatan Development Program, or KDP) helps to mediate local conflict.

UPP2 is a CDD project that provides money directly to communities to fund infrastructure projects and microcredit. To do this, the project organizes an elected committee called the BKM. In addition to poverty alleviation and improvements in service delivery, one of UPP2's goals is to create an accountable system of governance in poor urban communities. Here, again, both outcomes and process are of interest and therefore the evaluation is a prime candidate for a mixed-methods approach. The evaluation follows a difference-in-difference approach. A baseline survey is being conducted in a random sample of communities that will benefit from the intervention. These communities have been matched using a poverty score employed by the government to target UPP2 to poor communities. The "control" communities are those with low poverty scores in relatively rich districts, whereas the "experimental" communities are those with high poverty scores in relatively poor districts.

Two rounds of field work were conducted by an interdisciplinary team of economists, urban planners, and social anthropologists.[12] In the first round two to three days of field visits were conducted in each of eight communities that had benefited from a similar project (UPP1). The aim of this initial round of field work was to understand the UPP2 process, identify "surprises" that could be incorporated in the survey, and decide on a data collection methodology. Some of these unforeseen issues included the key role that facilitators played in the success or failure of a project at the local level, the inherent "competition" between BKMs and existing mechanisms for governance (such as the municipal officer, or *Pak Lurah*), and the crucial role that custom, tradition, and local religious institutions played in facilitating collective action. A quantitative survey methodology was developed that would give key informants such as the head of the BKM, the *Pak Lurah*, the community activist, and the local facilitator an in-depth structured questionnaire. In addition, a random sample of households within each community would receive a household questionnaire. When microcredit groups were formed in the experimental communities, they too would be given a household questionnaire.

To supplement this material, a qualitative baseline was also designed. The sample size of this baseline was limited by the high cost of conducting in-depth qualitative work in many communities. Therefore, it was decided to do a case-based comparative analysis: two "experimental communities" (one with a high degree of urbanization and the other with a low degree of urbanization) and two "control communities" (matched to the experimental communities using the poverty score) were chosen in each province. Since UPP2 is working in three provinces—Java, Kalimantan and Sulawesi—a total of 12 communities are in the sample. A team of field investigators will spend one week in each community conducting a series of focus-group discussions, in-depth interviews, and key-informant interviews in two groups. One group will snowball from the municipal office, focusing on the network of people who are centered around the for-mal government, while another group of investigators will snowball from the local mosque, church, or activist group to understand the role of informal networks and associations in the community.[13] The idea is that the qualitative work will provide in-depth insights into processes of decisionmaking, the role of custom (*adat*) and tradition in collective action, and the propensity for elite capture in the community. Hypotheses generated from the qualitative data will be tested for their generalizability with the quantitative data.

Finally, the whole process will be repeated three years after the initiation of the project to collect follow-up data. The follow-up will provide a difference across control and experimental groups, and a second difference across time to isolate the causal impact of UPP2 on the community and to examine the process by which communities changed because of the UPP2 intervention.

The Kecamatan Development Program in Indonesia—the model on which the UPP2 program is based—is one of the world's largest social development projects, and Indonesia itself is a country experiencing wrenching conflict in the aftermath of the Suharto era and the East Asian financial crisis. Although primarily intended as a more efficient and effective mechanism for getting targeted small-scale development assistance to poor rural communities, KDP requires villagers to submit proposals for funding to a committee of their peers, thereby establishing a new (and, by design, inclusive) community forum for decisionmaking on key issues (Wetterberg and Guggenheim 2003). Given the salience of conflict as a political and development issue in Indonesia, the question is whether these forums are able to complement existing local-level institutions for conflict resolution and in the process help villagers acquire a more diverse, peaceful, and effective set of civic skills for mediating local conflict. Such a question does not lend itself to an orthodox stand-alone quantitative or qualitative evaluation, but rather to an innovative mixed-method approach.

In this instance, the team decided to begin with qualitative work, since there was surprisingly little quantitative data on conflict in Indonesia and even less on the mechanisms (or local processes) by which conflict is initiated, intensified, or resolved.[14] Selecting a small number of appropriate sites from across Indonesia's 13,500 islands and 350 language groups was not an easy task, but the team decided that work should be done in two provinces that were very different (demographically), in regions within those provinces that (according to local experts) demonstrated both a "high" and "low" capacity for conflict resolution, and in villages within those regions that were otherwise comparable (as determined by propensity-score matching methods) but that either did or did not participate in KDP. Such a design enables researchers to be confident that any common themes emerging from across either the program or nonprogram sites are not wholly a product of idiosyncratic regional or institutional capacity factors. Thus quantitative methods were used to help select the appropriate sites for qualitative investigation, which then entailed three months of intensive fieldwork in each of the eight selected villages (two demographically different regions by two high/low capacity provinces by two program/nonprogram villages). The results from the qualitative work—useful in themselves for understanding process issues and the mechanisms by which local conflicts are created and addressed—will also feed into the design of a new quantitative survey instrument, which will be administered to a large sample of households from the two provinces and used to test the generality of the hypotheses and propositions emerging from the qualitative work.

A recent project evaluating the impact of "*panchayat* (village government) reform"—democratic decentralization in rural India—also combines qualitative and quantitative data with a "natural experiment" design.[15] In 1994 the Indian government passed the 73rd amendment to the Indian constitution to give more power to democratically elected village governments by mandating that more funds be transferred to their control and that regular elections be held, with one-third of the seats in the village council reserved for women and another third for "scheduled castes and tribes" (groups who have traditionally been targets of discrimination).

The four South Indian states of Karnataka, Kerala, Andhra Pradesh, and Tamil Nadu have implemented the 73rd amendment in different ways. Karnataka immediately began implementing the democratic reforms; Kerala emphasized greater financial autonomy, Tamil Nadu delayed elections by several years, and Andhra Pradesh emphasized alternative methods of village governance outside the *panchayat* system. Thus, contrasting the experiences of the four states could provide a nice test of the role of decentralization on the quality of governance. The problem, of course, is that any differences across the four states could be attributed to differences in the culture and history of the state (for instance, attributing Kerala's outcomes to the famous "Kerala model"). Things like culture and history are difficult to observe, so the evaluation design exploited the following natural experiment.

The four states were created in a manner that made then linguistically homogenous in 1955. Before 1955, however, significant portions of the four states belonged to the same political entity and were either ruled directly by the British or placed within a semi-autonomous "princely state." When the states were reorganized, "mistakes" were made along the border regions, with certain villages that originally belonged to the same original political entity and sharing the same culture and language finding themselves placed in different states. Such villages along the border can be matched and compared to construct a "first difference," which controls for the effects of historical path dependency and culture. Data on levels of economic development and other covariates that could affect differences across states are also being collected, as are data on several quantitative outcomes, such as objective measures of the level and quality of public services in the village and perceptions on public service delivery at the village level.

One challenge is to study the extent of participation in public village meetings (*gram sabhas*) held to discuss the problems faced by villagers with members of the governing committee. Increases in the quality of this form of village democracy would be a successful indicator of improvements in participation and accountability. Quantitative data, however, are very difficult to collect here because of the unreliability of people's memories about what may have transpired at a meeting they may have attended. To address this issue, the team decided to record and transcribe village meetings directly. This tactic provides textual information that can be analyzed to observe directly changes in participation. Another challenge was in collecting information on inequality at the village level. Some recent work has found that sample-based measures of inequality typically have standard errors that are too high to provide reliable estimates. PRAs were therefore held with one or two groups in the village to obtain measures of land distribution within the village. This approach proved to generate excellent measures of land inequality, and since these are primarily agrarian economies, measures of land inequality should be highly correlated with income inequality. Similar methods were used to collect data on the social heterogeneity of the village. All this PRA information has been quantitatively coded, thus demonstrating that qualitative tools can be used to collect quantitative data. In this example the fundamental impact assessment design was kept intact, and both qualitative and quantitative data were combined to provide insights into different aspects of interest in the evaluation of the intervention.

Using Mixed Methods in Time- and Resource-Constrained Settings

Some final examples demonstrating the utility of mixed-method approaches come from settings where formal data (such as a census) is limited or unavailable and where there are few skilled or experienced staff and little resources or time. Such situations are common throughout the developing world, where every day many small (and even not so small) organizations undertake good-faith efforts in desperate circumstances to make a difference in the lives of the poor. Are they having a positive impact? How might their efforts and finite resources be best expended? How might apparent failures be learned from, and successes be appropriately documented, and used to leverage additional resources from governments or donors? In these circumstances, calls for or requirements of extensive technical project evaluation may completely overwhelm existing budgets and personnel, multiplying already strong disincentives to engage in *any* form of evaluation (Pritchett 2002). The absence of formal data, skilled personnel, and long time horizons, however, should not mean that managers of such programs should ignore evaluation entirely. If nothing else, managers and their staff have detailed contextual knowledge of the settings in which they do and do not work, as do those people they are attempting to assist. From a basic commitment to "think quantitatively but act qualitatively" and to "start and work with what one has," local program staff have been able to design and implement a rudimentary evaluation procedure that is not a substitute for, but—we hope—a precursor to, a more thorough and comprehensive package (Woolcock 2001).

In St. Lucia, for example, the task manager preparing a social analysis had a budget to collect qualitative data from only 12 communities (from a sample size of 469) and wanted to ensure that those selected were as diverse as possible on seven key variables, namely, employment structure, poverty level, impact of a recent hurricane, access to basic services, proximity to roads, geography (regional variance, but with no two communities contiguous to one another), and exposure to the St. Lucia Social Development Program. How to choose these 12 communities so that they satisfied these criteria, with only a 10-year-old census to assist? The team decided to use the census data to make the first cuts in the selection process, using income data to identify the 200 poorest communities (on the assumption that over a 10-year period, the ordinal ranking of the income levels of the communities would not have changed significantly). The census also contained data on the number of households in each community receiving particular forms of water delivery and sewerage (public or private pipe, well, and so forth),

---

Box 8.1 Are Mixed-Methods Analyses Appropriate under Severe Budget or Time Constraints?

If the major objective of an evaluation is measuring the impact of the intervention, rather than understanding the processes by which the evaluation worked, then qualitative work may be unnecessary. Quantitative methods are not very effective at getting at process issues, however, so an exclusive dependence on them could give data that is incomplete for policy purposes. Mixed-methods evaluations can be conducted under a constrained budget—so long as there are enough funds to have a sample large enough to cover at least the primary heterogeneity in the population and in project impacts that are of interest. Be aware that the more time spent in the community, the better the quality of the qualitative data, so a brief visit of one or two days should not be expected to reveal anything more subtle than basic open-ended responses that could serve as a contextual accessory to quantitative findings. Participatory Rural Appraisal and Participatory Poverty Assessment methods can be especially useful under constrained circumstances because they can help the community encapsulate their points of view in a two-to-three hour group interview. The reliability of this information, however, is strongly affected by the quality of the moderator. Therefore, if the budget is severely constrained and skilled moderators are unavailable, it may not make sense to conduct qualitative work.

---

enabling a "quality of basic services" index to be constructed, and scored on a 1 (low) to 7 (high) scale. The 200 poorest communities could therefore be ranked according to their quality of basic services.

Finally, using geographical data, it was possible to measure the distance of all 200 communities from the main ring road that circumnavigates St. Lucia. Dividing the sample in half on the basis of their distance measure, those close to the road were labeled "urban," and those far from the road "rural." The team was thus able to construct a simple 2 × 2 matrix, with quality of basic services (high-low) on one axis, and rural-urban on the other. St Lucia's 200 poorest communities now fell neatly onto these axes, with 50 communities in each cell.

This procedure was followed up the next day by a four-hour session with field staff—all St. Lucia nationals—narrowing the field down to 16 communities. Twenty field staff gathered for this meeting, and after a brief presentation on the task at hand and the steps already taken with the census data, they were divided into four groups. Each group was given the names of 50 poor communities from one of the 2 × 2 cells above and was then asked to select five communities from this list that varied according to exposure to the recent hurricane, major forms of employment, and whether or not they had participated in the initial round of the St. Lucia Social Development Program. After two hours, the four groups reconvened with the names of their five communities, and over the final hour all field staff negotiated together to whittle the list of 20 names down to 16 to ensure that regional coverage was adequate and that no two communities were contiguous across regional boundaries. After an additional round of negotiation with senior program staff, the list was reduced to the final 12 communities, a group that maximized the variance according to the eight different criteria required by the task manager.

Reliance on quantitative or qualitative methods alone could never have achieved this result: formal data were limited and dated but nonetheless still useful; it was unrealistic and invalid to rely exclusively on local experts. Together, however, a superior outcome combining the best aspects of both methods enabled the selected sample to have maximum diversity, validity, *and* (importantly) full local ownership.

What Do Qualitative Methods Add to Quantitative Approaches?

There is clearly a large and important role for approaches to project evaluation that are grounded exclusively in sophisticated quantitative methods. This chapter has endeavored to show that these approaches nonetheless have many limitations, and that considerable value added can be gained by systematically and strategically including more qualitative approaches. By making a distinction between data and the methods used to collect them, we have shown that a range of innovative development research is currently under way in which qualitative data are examined using (or as part of) quantitative methods. The focus of this chapter, however, has been on the use of qualitative methods to improve, complement, and supplement quantitative data. By way of summary and conclusion, we outline six particular means by which qualitative methods demonstrate their usefulness in program evaluation.

By Generating Hypotheses Grounded in the Reality of the Poor

As the examples above demonstrate, when respondents are allowed to participate directly in the research process, the econometrician's work will avoid stereotypical depictions of their reality. The result could be unexpected findings that may prove to be important. Thus, the primary value of participatory econometrics is that hypotheses are generated from systematic fieldwork, rather than from secondary literatures, or flights of fancy. More specifically, the use of PRA-PPA, focus-group, and other methods allows respondents to inform researchers of their own understandings of poverty, which are then tested for generalizability by constructing appropriate survey instruments and administering them to representative samples of the population of interest.

By Helping Understand the Direction of Causality, Locating Identifying Instruments, and Exploiting Natural Experiments

Participatory econometrics can be of great value in improving econometrics beyond its obvious utility in generating new hypotheses. It can be very helpful in understanding the direction of causality, in locating identifying restrictions, and exploiting natural experiments (Ravallion 2001). For instance, in a recent study, researchers discovered that sex workers suffer economically when they use condoms, because of a client preference against condom use (Rao and others 2003). The econometric problem here is that identifying such compensating differentials is very difficult, because they tend to be plagued by problems of unobserved heterogeneity and endogeneity. Qualitative work in this case helped solve the problem by locating an instrument to correct for the problem. It turned out that an HIV-AIDS intervention that instructed sex workers on the dangers of unsafe sex was administered in a manner uncorrelated with income or wages, but yet had a great influence on the sex workers' propensity to use condoms. Using exposure to the intervention as an exclusion restriction in simultaneously estimating equations for condom use and wages enabled the researchers to demonstrate that sex workers suffered a 44 percent loss in wages by using condoms.

By Helping Understand the Nature of Bias and Measurement Error

In studying domestic violence, for example, a question in the survey instrument asked female respondents if their husbands had ever beaten them in the course of their marriage. Only 22 percent of the women responded positively, generating a domestic violence rate much lower than studies in Britain and the United States had shown. In probing the issue with in-depth interviews, researchers discovered that the women had interpreted the word *beating* to mean *extremely severe* beating—that is, when they had lost consciousness or were bleeding profusely and needed to be taken to the hospital. Hair pulling and ear twisting, which were thought to be more every-day occurrences, did not qualify as beating. (Responses to a broader version of the abuse question, comparable to the questions asked in the U.S. and U.K. surveys, elicited a 70 percent positive response.) Having tea with an outlier can be very effective in understanding *why* they are an outlier.

By Facilitating Cross-Checking and Replication

In participatory econometrics, the researcher has two sources of data, qualitative and quantitative, generated from the same popula-tion. That allows for immediate cross-checking and replication of results. If the qualitative and quantitative findings differ substan-tially, it could be indicative of methodological or data quality prob-lems in one or the other. In the Delhi slums project (Jha, Rao, and Woolcock 2002), for example, the focus-group discussions reveal several narratives of mobility, that is, of people leaving the slums, but this mobility is not reflected in the quantitative data because the sample does not include households who live outside slums. This finding indicates an important sample selection problem in the quan-titative data that limits its value in studying questions of mobility. At the same time, the qualitative data gave the impression that reli-gious institutions were an important source of credit and social sup-port for the urban poor. That this finding is not visible in the quan-titative data suggests that it may not be generalizable to all the residents of Delhi slums but is particular to the families participat-ing in focus-group discussions and in-depth interviews.

By Providing a Sense of Context and Helping Interpret Quantitative Findings While Using Quantitative Data to Establish the Generalizability of Those Findings

Participatory econometrics allows the researcher to interpret the quantitative findings in context. The more narrative, personalized information provided by open-ended focus-group discussions and in-depth interviews, the better the researcher can understand and interpret a quantitative result. In the work on domestic violence, for instance, a strong positive correlation was found between female sterilization and risk of violence. This finding would have been very difficult to explain without the qualitative data, which revealed that women who were sterilized tended to lose interest in sex with their husbands. At the same time their husbands tended to suspect their fidelity, fearing (unjustly) that the women would be unfaithful

Box 8.2 Ten Principles of Conducting Good
Mixed-Methods Evaluations

1. Use "participatory econometrics," an iterative approach where qualitative work informs the construction of a quantitative questionnaire. Allow for findings from the field to broaden your set of outcome or explanatory variables. This broadening will improve the analysis of possible externalities to the intervention as well as reduce the number of unobservables.

2. Unlike quantitative questionnaires, qualitative questions should be open-ended to allow respondents to give relatively unconstrained responses. The question should be an opportunity to have an extended discussion.

3. The data analyst should be closely tied to the data collection process.

4. Qualitative work should follow principles of evaluation design similar to those for quantitative work; even when exclusively qualitative methods are used, the evaluator should "think quantitatively, but act qualitatively."

5. The qualitative sample should be large enough to reflect the major elements of heterogeneity in the population.

6. Spend enough time in the community to allow an in-depth examination. This may sometimes mean anything from a week to several weeks depending upon the size and heterogeneity of the community.

7. Hypotheses derived from the qualitative work should be tested for their generalizability with the more representative quantitative data.

8. Use the qualitative information to interpret and contextualize quantitative findings.

9. A poor and inexperienced qualitative team can have a much larger adverse impact on the collection of good quality qualitative information than on quantitative data.

10. Qualitative methods should be thought of not as an inexpensive alternative to large surveys, but as tools to collect information that is difficult to gather and analyze quantitatively.

because they were now able to have sex without getting pregnant. This caused sterilized women to be at much greater risk for violent conflicts within the home. The strong correlation between sterilization and abuse observed in the quantitative data did not necessarily "prove" that the qualitative finding was generalizable, but, by demonstrating that the average sterilized woman in the population was in a more conflictual relationship, the quantitative findings were consistent with the quantitative.

By Identifying Externalities to an Intervention, Improving
the Measurement of Outcomes, and Finding Ways of
Measuring "Unobservables"

In recent work looking at the relationship between prices and
poverty, qualitative work found that the poor were paying much
higher unit prices for the same goods because the rich were able to
obtain quantity discounts (Rao 2000). This finding led to the collection of a household-level consumer price index that corrected for
the purchasing power of households affected by the variation in
household-specific prices. The improved "real" income measures of
inequality were found to be 17–23 percent higher than conventional
inequality measures.

In the UPP2 evaluation in Indonesia, qualitative work helped
emphasize the crucial role that project facilitators played in the
effectiveness of CDD projects at the community level. This recognition led to a special quantitative questionnaire being administered
to facilitators that would allow the team to examine the role of
"street-level workers" in project effectiveness. "Unobservables" can
also be made observable through field investigations. In the *panchayat* project, focus-group discussions proved to be effective at
uncovering villages that were oligarchic and ruled by a small group
of intermarrying families. This ability to see unobservables can be
potentially very important in determining the effectiveness of democratic decentralization initiatives at the village level.

Notes

The authors of chapter 8 are grateful to Pierre-Richard Agénor, Benu Bidani,
Hippolyte Fofack, and several other reviewers for their valuable comments
and suggestions.

1. On the specific role of qualitative methods in program evaluation, see
Patton (1987).

2. On the variety of approaches to establishing "causality," see Salmon
(1997); Mahoney (2000); and Gerring (2001).

3. See, for example, Tashakkori and Teddlie (1998); Bamberger (2000);
and Gacitua-Mario and Wodon (2001).

4. King, Keohane, and Verba (1993) and Collier and Adcock (2001)
provide a more academic treatment of potential commonalities among
quantitative and qualitative approaches.

5. For an extended discussion of the rationale for social analysis in policy, see World Bank (2002a). More details on the qualitative tools and techniques described in their application to project impact are available in
World Bank (2002b).

6. The Self-Employed Women's Association (SEWA) in India has used a related approach with great success, helping poor slum dwellers to compile basic data on themselves that they can then present to municipal governments for the purpose of extracting resources to which they are legally entitled. On the potential abuse of participatory approaches, however, see Cooke and Kothari (2001) and Brock and McGee (2002).

7. See, for example, the exemplary anthropological research of Berry (1993) and Singerman (1996).

8. For a more extensive treatment of methodological issues in comparative politics, see Ragin (1987) and the collection of articles in Ragin and Becker (1992).

9. For more on methodological issues in anthropological demography, see Obermeyer and others (1997).

10. See Rao (2002) for more on participatory econometrics.

11. See chapter 5.

12. The manager of UPP2 is Aniruddha Dasgupta, and the evaluation team includes Vivi Alatas, Victoria Beard, Menno Pradhan, and Vijayendra Rao.

13. This refers to a snowball sample, where new respondents are contacted on the basis of information collected from previous respondents. This method of sampling is useful in studying network interactions.

14. The task manager for KDP is Scott Guggenheim, and the evaluation team includes Patrick Barron, David Madden, Claire Smith, and Michael Woolcock.

15. This project is a collaboration among Tim Besley, Rohini Pande, and Vijayendra Rao.

References

The word *processed* describes informally reproduced works that may not be commonly available through library systems.

Bamberger, Michael. 2000. *Integrating Qualitative and Quantitative Research in Development Projects.* Washington, D.C.: World Bank.

Berry, Sara. 1993. *No Condition Is Permanent: The Social Dynamics of Agrarian Change in Sub-Saharan Africa.* Madison: University of Wisconsin Press.

Bliss, Christopher, and Nicholas Stern. 1982. *Palanpur: The Economy of an Indian Village.* New York: Oxford University Press.

Bloch, Francis, and Vijayendra Rao. 2002. "Terror as a Bargaining Instrument: A Case Study of Dowry Violence in Rural India." *American Economic Review* 92(4): 1029–43.

Brock, Karen, and Rosemary McGee. 2002. *Knowing Poverty: Critical Reflections on Participatory Research and Policy.* London: Earthscan Publications.

Collier, David, and Robert Adcock. 2001. "Measurement Validity: A Shared Standard for Qualitative and Quantitative Research." *American Political Science Review* 95(3): 529–46.

Cooke, Bill, and Uma Kothari. 2001. *Participation: The New Tyranny?* London: Zed Books.

Epstein, Scarlet. 1962. *Economic Development and Social Change in South India*. Manchester, U.K.: University of Manchester Press.

Gacitua-Mario, Estanislao, and Quentin Wodon, eds. 2001. "Measurement and Meaning: Combining Quantitative and Qualitative Methods for the Analysis of Poverty and Social Exclusion in Latin America." Technical Paper 518. World Bank, Washington, D.C. Processed.

Gerring, John. 2001. *Social Science Methodology: A Criterial Framework*. New York: Cambridge University Press.

Hentschel, Jesko. 1999. "Contextuality and Data Collection Methods: A Framework and Application to Health Service Utilization." *Journal of Development Studies* 35(4): 64–94.

Isham, Jonathan, Deepa Narayan, and Lant Pritchett. 1995. "Does Participation Improve Performance? Establishing Causality with Subjective Data." *World Bank Economic Review* 9(2): 175–200.

Jha, Saumitra, Vijayendra Rao, and Michael Woolcock. 2002. "Governance in the Gullies: A Mixed-Methods Analysis of Survival and Mobility Strategies in Delhi Slums." World Bank, Development Research Group, Washington, D.C. Processed.

Kanbur, Ravi, ed. 2003. *Q-Squared: Qualitative and Quantitative Methods of Poverty Appraisal*. New Delhi: Permanent Black Publishers.

King, Gary, Robert Keohane, and Sidney Verba. 1993. *Designing Social Inquiry: Scientific Inference in Qualitative Research*. Princeton, N.J.: Princeton University Press.

Kumar, Somesh, and Robert Chambers. 2002. *Methods for Community Participation*. London: Intermediate Technology Publications.

Lanjouw, Peter, and Nicholas Stern. 1998. *Economic Development in Palanpur over Five Decades*. New York: Oxford University Press.

Mahoney, James. 2000. "Strategies of Causal Inference in Small-N Analysis." *Sociological Methods and Research* 28(4): 387–424.

Mikkelsen, Britha. 1995. *Methods for Development Work and Research: A Guide for Practitioners*. New Delhi: Sage Publications.

Mills, C. Wright. 1959. *The Sociological Imagination*. New York: Oxford University Press.

Narayan, Deepa. 1995. *Toward Participatory Research*. Washington, D.C.: World Bank.

Obermeyer, Carla Makhlouf, Susan Greenhalgh, Tom Fricke, Vijayendra Rao, David I. Kertzer, and John Knodel. 1997. "Qualitative Methods in Population Studies: A Symposium." *Population and Development Review* 23(4): 813–53.

Patton, Michael. 1987. *How to Use Qualitative Methods in Evaluation.* Newbury Park, Calif.: Sage Publications.

Pritchett, Lant. 2002. "It Pays to Be Ignorant: A Simple Political Economy of Program Evaluation." Harvard University, Kennedy School of Government, Cambridge, Mass. Processed.

Ragin, Charles. 1987. *The Comparative Method: Moving Beyond Qualitative and Quantitative Strategies.* Berkeley: University of California Press.

Ragin, Charles, and Howard Becker, eds. 1992. *What Is a Case? Exploring the Foundations of Social Inquiry.* New York: Cambridge University Press.

Rao, Vijayendra. 1997. "Can Economics Mediate the Link between Anthropology and Demography?" *Population and Development Review* 23(4): 833–38.

———. 1998. "Wife-Abuse, Its Causes and Its Impact on Intra-Household Resource Allocation in Rural Karnataka: A 'Participatory' Econometric Analysis." In Maithreyi Krishnaraj, Ratna Sudarshan, and Abusaleh Shariff, eds., *Gender, Population, and Development.* Oxford, U.K.: Oxford University Press.

———. 2000. "Price Heterogeneity and Real Inequality: A Case-Study of Poverty and Prices in Rural South India." *Review of Income and Wealth* 46(2): 201–12.

———. 2001a. "Poverty and Public Celebrations in Rural India." *Annals of the American Academy of Political and Social Science* 573: 85–104.

———. 2001b. "Celebrations as Social Investments: Festival Expenditures, Unit Price Variation and Social Status in Rural India." *Journal of Development Studies* 37(1): 71–97.

———. 2002. "Experiments in 'Participatory Econometrics': Improving the Connection Between Economic Analysis and the Real World." *Economic and Political Weekly* (May 18): 1887–91.

Rao, Vijayendra, and Ana María Ibáñez. 2003. "The Social Impact of Social Funds in Jamaica: A Mixed-Methods Analysis of Participation, Targeting and Collective Action in Community-Driven Development." Policy Research Working Paper 2970. World Bank, Development Research Group, Washington, D.C. Processed. Available at http://econ.worldbank.org/files/24159_wps2970.pdf.

Rao, Vijayendra, Indrani Gupta, Michael Lokshin, and Smarajit Jana. Forthcoming. "Sex Workers and the Cost of Safe Sex: The Compensating Differential for Condom Use in Calcutta." *Journal of Development Economics.*

Ravallion, Martin. 2001. "The Mystery of the Vanishing Benefits: An Introduction to Evaluation." *World Bank Economic Review* 15: 115–40.

Ravallion, Martin, and Menno Pradhan. 2000. "Measuring Poverty Using Qualitative Perceptions of Consumption Adequacy." *Review of Economics and Statistics* 82(3): 462–71.

Robb, Caroline. 2002. *Can the Poor Influence Policy? Participatory Poverty Assessments in the Developing World.* Rev. ed. Washington, D.C.: International Monetary Fund.

Salmon, Wesley. 1997. *Causality and Explanation.* New York: Oxford University Press.

Singerman, Diane. 1996. *Avenues of Participation.* Princeton, N.J.: Princeton University Press.

Tashakkori, Abbas, and Charles Teddlie. 1998. *Mixed Methodology: Combining Qualitative and Quantitative Approaches.* Thousand Oaks, Calif.: Sage Publications.

Wetterberg, Anna, and Scott Guggenheim. 2003. "Capitalizing on Local Capacity: Institutional Change in the Kecamatan Development Program, Indonesia." World Bank, East Asia Department, Jakarta, Indonesia. Processed.

White, Howard. 2002. "Combining Quantitative and Qualitative Approaches in Poverty Analysis." *World Development* 30(3): 511–22.

Woolcock, Michael. 2001. "Social Assessments and Program Evaluation with Limited Formal Data: Thinking Quantitatively, Acting Qualitatively." Social Development Briefing Note 68. World Bank, Social Development Department, Washington, D.C. Processed.

World Bank. 2002a. "Social Analysis Sourcebook: Incorporating Social Dimensions into Bank-Supported Projects." World Bank, Social Development Department, Washington, D.C. Processed. Available at http://www.worldbank.org/socialanalysissourcebook/Social%20Analysis SourcebookAug6.pdf.

———. 2002b. "User's Guide to Poverty and Social Impact Analysis of Policy Reform." World Bank, Poverty Reduction Group and Social Development Department, Washington, D.C. Processed. Available at http://www.worldbank.org/poverty/psia/draftguide.pdf.

———. 2003. "Poverty in Guatemala." Report 24221-GU. World Bank, Washington, D.C. Available at http://wbln0018.worldbank.org/LAC/LACInfoClient.nsf/Date/By+Author_Country/EEBA795E0F22768D852 56CE700772165?OpenDocument.

Survey Tools for Assessing Performance in Service Delivery

Jan Dehn, Ritva Reinikka, and Jakob Svensson

It has become increasingly clear that budget allocations, when used as indicators of the supply of public services, are poor predictors of the actual quantity and quality of public services, especially in countries with poor accountability and weak institutions. At least four breaks in the chain can be distinguished between spending—meant to address efficiency and equity concerns—and its transformation into services (Devarajan and Reinikka 2002). First, governments may spend on the wrong goods or the wrong people. A large portion of public spending on health and education is devoted to private goods, where government spending is likely to crowd out private spending (Hammer, Nabi, and Cercone 1995). Furthermore, most studies of the incidence of public spending in health and education show that benefits accrue largely to the rich and middle-class; the share going to the poorest 20 percent is almost always less than 20 percent (Castro-Leal and others 1999). The first three chapters in this volume discuss benefit incidence analysis.

Second, even when governments spend on the right goods or the right people, the money may fail to reach the frontline service provider. A study of Uganda in the mid-1990s, using a Public Expenditure Tracking Survey (PETS)—the topic of this chapter—showed that only 13 percent of nonwage recurrent expenditures for primary education actually reached the primary school (Reinikka 2001). The considerable variation in grants received across schools was determined more by the political economy than by efficiency and

Box 9.1 Public-Sector Agencies, Measurability, PETS, and QSDS

The organizational structure of public sector agencies involves multiple tiers of management and frontline workers. Multiplicity is also a key aspect of the tasks they perform and the stakeholders they serve. For example, primary education teaches young children to read and write, and it also teaches social skills, instills citizenship, and so forth. The different tasks and interests at each tier may compete with each other for limited resources in a finite time period. Moreover, the output of public service agencies is often difficult to measure, and systematic information on specific inputs and outputs is rarely available in developing countries. In many cases management information systems are unreliable in the absence of adequate incentives to maintain them. On closer observation, the characteristics of public service agencies and the nature of their tasks explain why traditional tools for public expenditure analysis alone may not be adequate for evaluating performance. Because the Public Expenditure Tracking Survey (PETS) and Quantitative Service Delivery Survey (QSDS) can bring together data on inputs, outputs, user charges, quality, and other characteristics directly from the service-providing unit, more can be learned about the linkages, leakage, and the way spending is transformed into services.

Over and above the problem of vague output measures, the existence of multiple principals reduces the agent's incentives, because activities often desired by the principals to realize their respective

equity considerations. Larger schools and schools with wealthier parents received a larger share of the intended funds (per student), while schools with a higher share of unqualified teachers received less (Reinikka and Svensson 2002).

Third, even when the money reaches the primary school or health clinic, the incentives to provide the service may be weak. Service providers in the public sector may be poorly paid, hardly ever monitored, and given few incentives from the central government bureaucracy, which is mostly concerned with inputs rather than outputs. The result can be a high absenteeism rate among frontline workers. The Quantitative Service Delivery Survey (QSDS)—the other instrument featured in this chapter—is a useful tool for getting at these issues. A survey in Bangladesh, described later, showed that the absenteeism rate was 74 percent for doctors in primary health care centers (Chaudhury and Hammer 2003).

goals are substitutes for each other. Similarly, when some task outcomes are verifiable and others are not, it may not be optimal to provide explicit incentives for any tasks, as the agent would otherwise divert all effort from unverifiable to verifiable tasks. In education, for example, exam results would be disproportionately emphasized over aspects that lend themselves less easily to monitoring and measurement. Incentive schemes are most suitable when outcomes are clearly defined, observable, and unambiguous, and become weak when neither outcomes nor actions are observable, such as in a typical government ministry. Public service providers also often lack competitors. Although the introduction of competition does not in itself guarantee better performance, it places greater emphasis on other management devices.

PETS and QSDS can increase the observability of both outputs and actions and thereby provide new information about the complex transformation from public budgets to services. Tailored to the specific circumstances, these tools can help identify incentives and shed light on the interactions to which these incentives give rise, such as collusion and bribery. They can also illuminate the political economy, such as the effect of interest groups. The novelty of the PETS-QSDS approach lies not so much in the development of new methods of analysis per se, but in the application of known and proven methods (microsurveys) to service providers.

Sources: Bernheim and Whinston (1986); Dixit (1996, 1997, 2000).

Fourth, even if the services are effectively provided, households may not take advantage of them. For economic and other reasons, parents pull their children out of school or fail to take them to the clinic. These demand-side failures often interact with the supply-side failures to generate a low level of public services and human development outcomes among the poor.

This chapter argues that microeconomic-level survey tools are useful not only at the household or enterprise level but also at the service provider level to assess the efficiency of public spending and the quality and quantity of services. The two microlevel surveys discussed here, the PETS and the QSDS, both obtain policy-relevant information on the *agent* (say, a district education office) and the *principal* (say, the ministry of finance or a parent-teacher association) (box 9.1). Similarly, repeat PETSs or QSDSs can be used as tools to evaluate the impact of policy changes.

Key Features of PETS and QSDS

Government resources earmarked for particular uses flow within legally defined institutional frameworks, often passing through several layers of government bureaucracy (and the banking system) down to service facilities, which are charged with the responsibility of exercising the spending. But information on *actual* public spending at the frontline level is seldom available in developing countries. A PETS—frequently carried out as part of a public expenditure review—tracks the flow of resources through these strata to determine how much of the originally allocated resources reaches each level. It is therefore useful as a device for locating and quantifying political and bureaucratic capture, leakage of funds, and problems in the deployment of human and in-kind resources, such as staff, textbooks, and drugs. It can also be used to evaluate impediments to the reverse flow of information to account for actual expenditures.

The primary aim of a QSDS is to examine the efficiency of public spending and incentives and various dimensions of service delivery in provider organizations, especially on the frontline. The QSDS can be applied to government as well as to private for-profit and not-for-profit providers. It collects data on inputs, outputs, quality, pricing, oversight, and so forth. The facility or frontline service provider is typically the main unit of observation in a QSDS in much the same way as the firm is in enterprise surveys and the household is in household surveys. A QSDS requires considerable effort, cost, and time compared to some of its alternatives—surveys of perceptions, in particular (box 9.2). As the example of Uganda, discussed later, demonstrates, the benefits of quantitative data can easily offset the cost.

Both tools explicitly recognize that an agent may have a strong incentive to misreport (or not report) key data. This incentive derives from the fact that information provided, for example, by a health facility partly determines its entitlement to public support. In cases where resources (including staff time) are used for other purposes, such as shirking or corruption, the agent involved in the activity will most likely not report it truthfully. Likewise, official charges may only partly capture what the survey intends to measure (such as the user's cost of service). The PETS and QSDS deal with these data issues by using a multiangular data collection strategy—that is, a combination of information from different sources—and by carefully considering which sources and respondents have incentives to misreport and identifying data sources that are the least contaminated by these incentives. The triangulation strategy of data collection serves as a means of cross-validating the information obtained separately from each source.

Box 9.2 PETS, QSDS, and Other Tools to Assess
Service Delivery

The Public Expenditure Tracking Survey (PETS) and Quantitative Service Delivery Survey (QSDS) are distinct from other existing survey approaches, such as facility modules in household surveys or empirical studies to estimate hospital cost functions. Living Standards Measurement Study household surveys have included health facility modules on an ad hoc basis (Alderman and Lavy 1996). A number of the Demographic and Health Surveys carried out in more than 50 developing countries have also included a service provider component. Similarly, the Family Life Surveys implemented by RAND have combined health provider surveys with those of households. The rationale for including a facility module in a household survey is to characterize the link between access to and quality of public services and key household welfare indicators. Because the perspective in these surveys is that of the household, they pay little attention to the question of why quality and access are the way they are. In most cases facility information collected as a part of community questionnaires relies on the knowledge of one or more informed individuals (Frankenberg 2000). Information supplied by informants is therefore heavily dependent on the perception of a few individuals and not detailed enough to form a basis for analysis of service delivery parameters, such as operational efficiency, effort, or other performance indicators. To the extent that the information is based on perceptions, there may be additional problems attributable to the subjective nature of the data and its sensitivity to respondents' expectations. By contrast, the PETS-QSDS approach emphasizes and quantitatively measures provider incentives and behavior.

Unlike household surveys, the hospital cost function literature has a clear facility focus analogous to that applied to private firms in enterprise surveys. This literature typically looks at cost efficiency—mostly in hospitals in the United Kingdom and the United States—although work on hospital performance has also been conducted in developing countries (Wagstaff 1989; Wagstaff and Barnum 1992; and Barnum and Kutzin 1993). Perhaps more relevant, though, is the budding literature on cost efficiency and other performance indicators in clinics and primary health facilities in developing countries (McPake and others 1999; Somanathan and others 2000). In the PETS-QSDS approach, the main departure from the cost function literature is the explicit recognition of the close link between the public-sector service provider and the rest of the public sector. Providers of public services typically rely on the wider government structure for resources, guidance about what services to provide, and how to provide them. This dependence makes them sensitive to systemwide problems in transfer of resources, the institutional framework, and the incentive system, which private providers do not face.

Source: Lindelöw and Wagstaff (2003).

PETS and QSDS can also complement each other. Their combination allows for the evaluation of wider institutional and resource-flow problems on the performance of frontline service providers. With more precise (quantitative) measures, it will be easier for policymakers in developing countries to design effective policies and institutional reforms.

Design and Implementation

Like other microlevel surveys, PETS and QSDS require careful design and implementation. At least some members of the study team should have prior experience with surveys. The intuitive appeal of PETS and QSDS can belie the complexity involved in their planning and implementing.[1] This section outlines the steps involved in successful design and implementation of PETS and QSDS in light of the experience to date. Most steps are common to both surveys, given that PETS typically includes a facility component and that QSDS needs to relate government facilities to the public sector hierarchy.

Consultations and Scope of the Study

During the initial phase, the survey team needs to consult with in-country stakeholders, including government agencies (ministry of finance, sector ministries, and local governments), donors, and civil society organizations. Broad-based consultations are useful for:

- reaching agreement on the purpose and objectives of the study; and choosing the sector(s) for the study
- identifying key service delivery issues and problems (research questions) in the chosen sector(s)
- determining the structure of government's resource flow, rules for resource allocation to frontline facilities, and the accountability system
- obtaining a good understanding of the institutional setting of government and of private for-profit and not-for-profit providers
- checking data availability at various tiers of government or other provider organizations and at the facility level
- assessing available local capacity to carry out the survey and to engage in data analysis and research
- choosing the appropriate survey tool

A survey requires considerable effort, so it is advisable to limit the number of sectors to one or two. Until now, PETS and QSDS have mostly been carried out in the "transaction-intensive" health and education sectors with clearly defined frontline service delivery points (clinics and schools), but there is no reason to limit the use of these tools to health and education.

Rapid Data Assessment

A rapid data assessment may be needed to determine the availability of records at various layers of the government—as well as in the private sector—particularly at the facility level. Some studies have failed because the availability of records in local governments and facilities was not assessed beforehand. It is important to verify the availability of records early on, even if it means a delay and some extra up-front costs.

The consultations at the design stage often take place in the capital city, so it is easy to visit facilities in its vicinity to check on records, with the proviso that they may not be representative of facilities in remote locations. It may be important to assess data availability in more than one location. A simple questionnaire is usually sufficient for a rapid data assessment.

Questionnaire Design

It is important to ensure that recorded data collected at one level in the system can be cross-checked against the same information from other sources. A PETS or QSDS typically consists of questionnaires for interviewing facility managers (and staff) as well as separate data sheets to collect quantitative data from facility records. It also collects data from local, regional, and national provider organizations in three ownership categories: government, private for-profit providers, and private not-for-profit organizations. The combination of questionnaires and datasheets is usually flexible enough to evaluate most of the problems under study. A beneficiary survey can also be added.

As mentioned earlier, a crucial component of PETS-QSDS is the explicit recognition that respondents may have strong incentives to misreport (or not report at all) certain information. As a general guideline, information should be collected as close as possible to the original source. Data are thus typically collected from records kept by the facility for its own use (for example, patient numbers can be obtained from daily patient records kept by staff for medical use, drug use can be derived from stock cards, and funding to schools can be recorded from check receipts). It is also important to keep in mind that some information (for instance on corruption) is almost impossible to collect directly (especially from those benefiting from it). Instead, different sources of information have to be combined.[2]

To be comparable a core set of questions must remain unchanged across waves of surveys, across sectors, and across countries. Six core elements for all facility questionnaires have been identified:

- *Characteristics of the facility.* Record the size; ownership; years of operation; hours of operation; catchment population; competition from other service providers; access to infrastructure, utilities and other services; and range of services provided. Information about income levels and other features of the population living in the vicinity of the facility may also be useful.

- *Inputs.* Because service providers typically have a large number of inputs, it may not be feasible to collect data on all of them. Some inputs are typically more important than others. For example, labor and drugs account for 80–90 percent of costs in a typical primary health care facility. In addition, there may be important capital investments. The key point in the measurement of inputs is that they need to be valued in monetary terms. Where monetary values are not readily available, this requires that quantities be recorded carefully and consistently and price information (for example, wages and allowances for labor) be assembled for each key input.

- *Outputs.* Examples of measurable outputs include numbers of inpatient and outpatients treated, enrollment rates, and numbers of pupils completing final exams. Unlike inputs, outputs rarely convert to monetary values (public services are often free or considerably subsidized). Efficiency studies frequently use hybrid input-output measures, such as cost per patient.

- *Quality.* Quality is multidimensional, and an effort should be made to capture this multidimensionality by collecting information on different aspects of quality. Examples of these aspects of quality include observed practice, staff behavior and composition, availability of crucial inputs, and provision of certain services such as laboratory testing. Information collected from users can also capture aspects of quality.

- *Financing.* Information should be collected on sources of finance (government, donor, user charges), amounts, and type (in-kind versus financial support).

- *Institutional mechanisms and accountability.* Public facilities do not face the same competitive pressures as private facilities. Instead, they are subject to supervision and monitoring by central, regional, or local government institutions, civil society, political leaders, and the press. That means collecting information on supervision visits, management structures, reporting and record-keeping practices, parent or patient involvement, and audits.

Variations to this basic template can include modules to test specific hypotheses. Box 9.3 discusses sampling issues for PETS and QSDS.

Box 9.3 Sample Frame, Sample Size, and Stratification

Many developing countries have no reliable census on service facilities. An alternative is to create a sample frame from other sources (administrative records of some kind). A list of public facilities is often available from the central government or donors active in the sector. However, creating a reliable list of private providers may be a considerable undertaking or may simply not be feasible. An alternative is to mimic the two-stage design that is typically used in household surveys. In other words information on the private facilities is, at the first stage, gathered from randomly drawn sampling units (for example, a district or the catchment population of a government facility). At the second stage, the required number of private facilities is drawn from a list of facilities in the sampling unit.

When determining sample size, a number of issues must be considered. First, the sample should be sufficiently large and diverse enough to represent the number and range of facilities in the specified categories. Second, subgroups of particular interest (for example, rural and private facilities) may need to be more intensively sampled than others. Third, the optimal sample size is a tradeoff between minimizing sampling errors and minimizing nonsampling errors (the former typically decrease and the latter increase with the sample size). Arguably, in a Public Expenditure Tracking Survey (PETS) or Quantitative Service Delivery Survey (QSDS), nonsampling error (caused by poor survey implementation) is more of a concern than sampling error, as the data are often in a highly disaggregated form and hence labor-intensive to collect. Enumerator training and field testing of the instrument are therefore critical in obtaining high-quality data. Finally, these objectives must be achieved within a given budget constraint.

The above considerations often lead to a choice of a stratified random sample. Stratification entails dividing the survey population into subpopulations and then sampling these subpopulations independently as if they were individual populations. Stratification reduces sampling variance (increases sampling efficiency) and ensures a sufficient number of observations for separate analysis of different subpopulations. Stratification is an opportunity for the surveyor to use prior information about the population to improve the efficiency of the statistical inference about quantities that are unknown.

Sampling issues become more complicated when PETS and QSDS are combined. In PETS one may want to sample a relatively large number of local government administrations. But sampling a large number of districts reduces the number of facilities that can be sampled within each district for a given budget. From the perspective of QSDS, it is desirable to have more facilities within fewer districts in order to characterize the intradistrict variation among facilities.

Sources: Alreck and Settle (1995); Grosh and Glewwe (2000); Rossi and Wright (1983).

Training, Field Testing, and Implementation

Once the survey instruments (questionnaires and data sheets) are drafted according to the specific needs of the study, the next steps are piloting the questionnaire and then training the enumerators and their supervisors. Experience has shown that training is a crucial component and a significant amount of time has to be allocated for it. After completion of the training, survey instruments should be field tested. Supervision of enumerators is critical during implementation of the survey. It is also good practice to prepare a detailed implementation manual for the survey personnel. Using local consultants to conduct the PETS or QSDS is likely to be more cost-effective as well as beneficial for capacity building. In-country consultants are likely to have a comparative advantage over their international counterparts regarding knowledge of local institutions.

All instruments should be field tested on each type of provider in the sample (government, nongovernmental organization, and private), because different providers may have different practices of record-keeping. In case the field test leads to major modifications in the questionnaire, the modified questionnaire should be retested before finalization. The field-testing procedure takes between two weeks and one month to complete. More time is required if the final questionnaire is in more than one language, because changes made in one language need to be translated to the other.

Data Entry and Verification

Cost may limit the study team's ability to monitor the data collection process continuously. In this case the team should do spot checks during the early stages of data collection to discover possible problems and make the necessary adjustments in time. The team will also need to scrutinize the completed questionnaires and the data files, and, where necessary, request return visits to facilities or to various levels of the government. The output from this stage is the complete data set. It is also important to prepare comprehensive documentation of the survey soon after its completion.

Analysis, Report, and Dissemination

The analysis is typically done either by the study team or by the survey consultant in collaboration with the team. The reports and analysis should be widely disseminated to encourage debate and discussion to facilitate the alleviation of the problems highlighted in the survey.

Findings from PETS

Several countries have implemented public expenditure tracking surveys, including, Ghana, Honduras, Papua New Guinea, Peru, Rwanda, Tanzania, Uganda, and Zambia. This section summarizes findings from these studies, focusing on the Uganda and Zambia PETS in education, and a health and education PETS in Honduras. In the first two, leakage of public funds—defined as the share of resources intended for but not received by the frontline service facility—is the main issue. That was the main issue for the other PETSs carried out in Africa as well. The Honduras study diagnoses incentives that negatively affect staff performance, as manifested in ghost workers, absenteeism, and job migration.

Capture of Public Funds

Uganda, in 1996, was the first country to do a PETS. The study was motivated by the observation that despite a substantial increase in public spending on education, the official reports showed no increase in primary school enrollment. The hypothesis of the study was that actual service delivery, proxied by primary enrollment, was worse than budgetary allocations implied because public funds were subject to capture (by local government officials) and did not reach the intended facilities (schools). To test this hypothesis, a PETS was conducted to compare budget allocations to actual spending through various tiers of government, including frontline service delivery points in primary schools (Ablo and Reinikka 1998; Reinikka 2001).

Adequate public accounts were not available to report on actual spending, so a survey collected a five-year panel data set on provider characteristics, spending (including in-kind transfers), and outputs in 250 government primary schools. Initially, the objective of the PETS was purely diagnostic, that is, to provide a reality check on public spending. Subsequently, it became apparent that a quantitative tool like the PETS can provide useful microeconomic data for analyses of service provider behavior and incentives.

As mentioned earlier, the Ugandan school survey provides a stark picture of public funding on the frontlines. On average, only 13 percent of the annual capitation (per student) grant from the central government reached the schools in 1991–95. Eighty-seven percent either disappeared for private gain or was captured by district officials for purposes unrelated to education. Most schools (roughly 70 percent) received very little or nothing. The picture looks slightly better when constraining the sample to the last year of the survey period. Still, only 20 percent of the total capitation grant from the central government reached the schools in 1995 (Reinikka and Svensson 2002). About 20 percent of teacher salaries were paid to ghost teachers—teachers who never appeared in the classroom. Subsequent PETSs in Tanzania and Ghana showed similar problems of capture in health care and education, although of a somewhat smaller magnitude (Government of Tanzania 1999, 2001; Xiao and Canagarajah 2002).

Following publication of the findings, the central government made a swift attempt to remedy the situation. It began publishing the monthly intergovernmental transfers of public funds in the main newspapers, broadcasting information about them on radio, and requiring primary schools to post information on inflows of funds for all to see. This tactic not only made information available to parent-teacher associations, but also signaled to local governments that the center had resumed its oversight function. An evaluation of the information campaign (using a repeat PETS) reveals a large improvement. Although schools are still not receiving the entire grant (and there are delays), capture was reduced from an average of 80 percent in 1995 to 20 percent in 2001 (Reinikka and Svensson, 2003a).[3] A before-and-after assessment, comparing outcomes for the same schools in 1995 and 2001—and controlling for a broad range of school-specific factors, such as household income, teacher education, school size, and degree of supervision—suggests that the information campaign can explain two-thirds of this massive improvement (Reinikka and Svensson 2003a). This finding is likely to be an upper bound on the effect, since the effect of the information campaign cannot be distinguished from other policy actions or changes that simultaneously influenced all schools' ability to claim their entitlement.

A key component in the information campaign was the newspaper publication of monthly transfers of public funds to the districts. Thus schools with access to newspapers have been more extensively exposed to the information campaign. Interestingly, in 1995 schools with access to newspapers and those with no newspaper coverage suffered just as much from local capture. From 1995 to 2001, both groups experienced a large drop in leakage, which is consistent with the before-and-after findings. However, the reduction in capture is significantly higher for the schools with newspapers. On average these schools increased their funding by 12 percentage points more than the schools that lacked newspaper coverage. The results hold also when controlling for differences in income, school size, staff qualifications, and the incidence of supervision across the two groups.

With a relatively inexpensive policy action—provision of mass information—Uganda has managed dramatically to reduce capture of a public program aimed at increasing primary education. Being less able to claim their entitlement from the district officials before the campaign, poor schools benefited most from the information campaign.

According to a recent PETS in primary education in Zambia—unlike in Uganda in the mid-1990s—rule-based allocations seem to be reaching the intended beneficiaries well: more than 90 percent of all schools received their rule-based nonwage allocations, and 95 percent of teachers received their salaries (Das and others 2002). But rule-based funding accounts for only 30 percent of all funding. In discretionary allocations (70 percent of the total), the positive results no longer hold: fewer than 20 percent of schools receive *any* funding at all from discretionary sources. The rest is spent at the provincial and district level. Similarly, in the case of overtime allowances (which must be filed every term) or other discretionary allowances, 50 percent were overdue by six months or more.

In conclusion, the PETS carried out in Africa found leakage of nonwage funds on a massive scale. Salaries and allowances also suffer from leakage but to a much lesser extent. Given that availability of books and other instructional materials are key to improving the quality of schooling, the fact that between 87 percent (Uganda) and 60 percent (Zambia) of the funding for these inputs never reach the schools makes leakage a major policy concern in the education sector. Furthermore, there is clearly scope for better targeting of interventions to improve public sector performance. Instead of instituting more general public sector reforms, the PETS in Uganda shows that it may be more efficient to target reforms and interventions at specific problem spots within the public hierarchy. For example, the PETS pointed to the fact that nonwage expenditures are more prone to leakage than salary expenditures. The PETS also demonstrated that leakage occurred at specific tiers within the government. This knowledge can be exploited to effect more efficient interventions.

Ghost Workers, Absenteeism, and Job Migration

Honduras used the PETS to diagnose moral hazard with respect to frontline health and education staff (World Bank 2001). The study demonstrated that issues of staff behavior and incentives in public service can have adverse effects on service delivery, such as ghost workers, absenteeism, and job capture by employees, even when salaries and other resources reach frontline providers. One hypothesis was that the central payroll office had no means of ensuring that public employees really exist (ghost workers). Another concern was that employees were not putting in full hours of work (absenteeism). Yet another question was whether workers were working where they were supposed to be working (migration of posts). Migration of posts was considered to pose a major problem, because the Honduran system of staffing does not assign posts to individual facilities but rather to the central ministry. Given that the central ministry has discretion over the geographic distribution of posts, the system provides an incentive to frontline staff to lobby the ministry to have their posts transferred to more attractive locations, most often to urban areas. The implication is that posts migrate from rural areas and primary health care and primary school jobs toward cities and higher levels of health care and schooling. Such migration is neither efficient nor equitable.

The PETS set out to quantify the incongruity between budgetary and real assignments of staff and to determine the degree of attendance at work. The PETS used central government information sources and a nationally representative sample of frontline facilities in health and education. Central government payroll data indicated each employee's place of work. The unit of observation was not the facility but the staff member, both operational and administrative, and at all levels of the two sectors from the ministry down to the service facility level.[4]

In health, the study found that 2.4 percent of staff did not exist (ghost workers). For general practitioners (GPs) and specialists, 8.3 percent and 5.1 percent of staff, respectively, were ghost workers. Second, absenteeism was generic, with an average attendance rate of 73 percent across all categories of staff in the five days before the survey date. Thirty-nine percent of absences were without justifiable reason (such as sick leave, vacations, and compensation for extra hours worked). That amounts to 10 percent of total staff work time. Third, many health care providers, especially GPs and specialists, held multiple jobs. Fifty-four percent of specialist physicians had two or more jobs, of which 60 percent were in a related field. Fourth, 5.2 percent of sampled staff members had migrated to posts other than the one to which they were assigned in the central database, while 40 percent had moved since their first assignment. The highest proportions of migrators were found among GPs. Migration was typically from a lower-level to a higher-level institution, although there was also some lateral migration. Job migration was found to reflect a combination of employee capture and budget inflexibility.

In education, 3 percent of staff members on the payroll were found to be ghosts, while 5 percent of primary school teachers were unknown in their place of work. Staff migration was highest among nonteaching staff and secondary teachers. Absenteeism was less of a problem than in the health sector, with an average attendance rate of 86 percent across all categories of staff. Fifteen percent of all absences were unaccounted for. Multiple jobs in education were twice as prevalent as in health, with 23 percent of all teachers doing two or more jobs. Finally, 40 percent of all education sector workers had administrative jobs, suggesting perhaps a preference for nonfrontline service employment or deliberate employment creation on the part of the government.

In conclusion, the Honduras study illustrates well that efforts to improve public sector service delivery must consider not just resource flows, but also incentives the staff has to perform.

PETS and QSDS as Research Tools

For a careful policy evaluation, it is important to design the PETS and QSDS instruments in such a way that the data have enough observations (say, facilities) for robust statistical analyses.[5] Unless the policy change affects a subset of facilities, it is generally not possible to evaluate its effectiveness using only cross-sectional data. Hence, a panel data set is required. The first round of baseline QSDSs includes health care in Bangladesh, Chad, Madagascar, Mozambique, Nigeria, and Uganda.

The time dimension of the rounds of surveys depends on the speed at which policy changes translate into outcomes, that is, the time it takes for the policy change to be reflected in actual changes in spending, the speed at which the spending changes affect actual service delivery, and the time it takes the changes in service delivery to produce changes in outcomes. Several years of data may be needed, either by returning to the facility each year or, in the case of ex post policy evaluations, by collecting data on several time periods at once during the same visit. For example, five years of data was collected from schools in the Uganda PETS during one survey (Ablo and Reinikka 1998; Reinikka 2001).

The not-for-profit sector plays an important role in provision of social services in many developing countries. In the health sector, religious organizations are particularly prevalent. One of the purposes of the Uganda QSDS (box 9.4) was to examine the effect of not-for-profit providers on the quantity and quality of primary health care. To find this effect, one needs to know how the not-for-profit actors are motivated as service providers: are they altruistic or are they maximizing perks (Reinikka and Svensson 2003b)? The Uganda QSDS provides data that can be used for such an evaluation, since the survey collected data from government, private for-profit providers, and private not-for-profit (religious) providers.

Box 9.4 QSDS of Dispensaries in Uganda

A Quantitative Service Delivery Survey (QSDS) of dispensaries (with and without maternity units) was carried out in Uganda in 2000. A total of 155 dispensaries were surveyed, of which 81 were government facilities, 30 were private for-profit, and 44 were operated on a nonprofit basis. The survey collected data at the level of the district administration, the health facility, and the beneficiary to capture the links between these three levels. Comparisons of data from different levels permitted cross-validation (triangulation) of information. At the district level, a *district health team questionnaire* was administered to the district director of health services that included data on health infrastructure, staff training, supervision arrangements, and sources of financing for one fiscal year. A *district health facility data sheet* was also used to collect detailed information on the 155 health units, including staffing, salaries, the supply of vaccines and drugs to the facilities, and the monthly statistics from each facility on the number of outpatients, inpatients, immunizations, and deliveries.

At the facility level, a *health facility questionnaire* gathered a broad range of information relating to the facility and its activities. Each facility questionnaire was supplemented with a *facility data sheet* to obtain data from the health unit records on staffing, salaries, daily patient records, type of patients using the facility, immunization, and drug supply and use. These data were obtained directly from the records kept by facilities for their own use (medical records), rather than administrative records submitted to local government. Finally, also at the facility level, an *exit poll* was used to interview around 10 patients per facility on cost of treatment, drugs received, perceived quality of services, and reasons for preference for this unit instead of alternative sources of health care.

Source: Lindelöw, Reinikka, and Svensson (2003).

In the cross-section, religious not-for-profit facilities were found to hire qualified workers below the market wage. Moreover, these facilities are more likely to provide pro-poor services and services with a public good element and to charge strictly lower prices for services than do for-profit units. Religious not-for-profit and for-profit facilities both provide a better quality of care than their government counterparts, although government facilities are better equipped. These findings are consistent with there being a religious premium in working in a religious, nonprofit facility (that is, staff in such facilities are prepared to work for a salary below the market rate) and with religious nonprofits being driven (partly) by altruistic or religious concerns.

Detailed knowledge of the institutional environment not only is important for identifying the right questions to ask, but can also assist in identifying causal effects in the data. The Uganda QSDS is an example. The year of the survey, the government of Uganda initiated a program stipulating that each not-for-profit unit was to receive a fixed grant for the fiscal year. However, because this was a new, and partly unanticipated, program and because communications in general were poor, some not-for-profit facilities did not receive their first grant entitlement until the following fiscal year. This de facto phasing of the grant program provides a near natural policy experiment of public financial aid. Analysis of the QSDS data reveals that financial aid leads to more testing of suspected malaria and intestinal worm cases—an indication of quality—and lower prices, but only in religious not-for-profit facilities. The estimated effects are substantial.

Another interesting pattern in the data is related to prescription antibiotics. Preliminary analysis shows that antibiotic prescriptions are generally very high. In fact, almost half of the patients report receiving some antibiotic. In some cases, patients receive several types at the same time. Government facilities are significantly more likely to provide antibiotics than private providers, and the effect is particularly strong in government facilities without qualified (medical) staff. Work is under way to distinguish between three (complementary) explanations for these patterns: the provision of antibiotics is a substitute for effort; the provision of antibiotics is higher in government units because the opportunity cost of providing antibiotics is lower; and patients demand antibiotics when treated and when the provider has a weak (bargaining) position, it (over)provides antibiotics.

A QSDS-type survey was conducted in Bangladesh, where unannounced visits were made to health clinics with the intention of discovering what fraction of medical professionals were present at their assigned post (Chaudhury and Hammer 2003). The survey quantified the extent of this problem on a nationally representative scale. The first notable result is that, nationwide, the average number of unfilled vacancies for all types of providers is large (26 percent). Regionally, vacancy rates are generally higher in the poorer parts of the country. Absentee rates for medical providers in general are quite high (35 percent), and these rates are particularly high for doctors (40 percent; at lower levels of health facilities, the absentee rate for doctors increases to 74 percent). When exploring determinants of staff absenteeism, the authors find that whether the medical provider lives near the health facility, has access to a road, and has electricity are important.

Linkages to Other Tools

Facility-level analysis can be linked upstream to the public administration and political processes through public official surveys and
downstream to households through household surveys and thereby
can combine supply of and demand for services. Linking the PETS-
QSDS with the household surveys would include the demand for
services or outcomes, and linking it with public official surveys
would include political economy and administrative aspects. Taken
together, such data would allow a much more comprehensive analysis of service delivery performance and its determinants. The PETSs
in Zambia and Laos (the latter is currently in the field) include a
household survey, while the ongoing QSDS in Nigeria incorporates
a survey of local officials. Reports on these studies will become
available during 2003.

Benefit incidence analysis, common in many developing countries,
combines household data on consumption of public goods with
information on public expenditures. A unit subsidy per person is
determined, and household usage of the service is then aggregated
across key social groups to impute the pattern and distribution of
service provision. A methodological problem in incidence analysis,
however, is the practice of using budgeted costs as proxies for service
benefits—see chapter 2 in this volume. The PETS approach permits a
better measurement of these benefits by relaxing the assumption that
budgeted resources are automatically translated into actual services.
Specifically, a PETS or QSDS can provide a "filter coefficient" for
public expenditures, which can be used to deflate budget allocations.
For example, such a coefficient in primary education in Uganda was
0.2 for nonsalary spending and 0.8 for spending on teacher salaries
in the mid-1990s (Reinikka 2001). In Zambia this coefficient was
around 0.4 for nonwage public spending (average for rule-based and
discretionary spending) in 2002. For salaries it was 0.95, apart from
allowances for which the coefficient ranged between 0.85 and 0.5
(Das and others 2002). These examples are national averages. They
can be further refined, because evidence from the PETS indicates that
poorer schools tend to receive less funding (per student)—indeed
sometimes no nonwage funding at all—than better-off and larger
schools (Reinikka and Svensson 2002).

As mentioned above, the Zambia PETS includes a separate household survey. In addition to PETS providing filter coefficients for
benefit incidence analysis, the combination of the household survey
and PETS allows an innovative analysis of funding equity: gauging
the extent to which public funding can be regarded as progressive or

regressive. The Zambia study finds, for example, that rule-based nonwage spending is progressive, while discretionary nonwage spending is regressive in rural areas and progressive in urban areas. Salary spending is regressive (Das and others 2002).

Conclusions

In countries with weak accountability systems, budget allocations are a poor proxy for services actually reaching the intended beneficiaries. PETS and QSDS are new tools for measuring the efficiency of public spending and analyzing incentives for and the performance of frontline providers in government and the private sector. Together these tools can provide a better understanding of behavior of frontline providers and, by linking them to other surveys, the relationship between providers, policymakers, and users of services can be studied.

Studies carried out so far point to ways to improve public sector performance. First, interventions can be targeted far better at vulnerable types of expenditures, such as nonwage recurrent spending, and at weak tiers in the public sector hierarchy. This ensures more accurate interventions and a more efficient use of resources. Second, efforts to improve service delivery must consider not just resource flows, but also the institutional framework and incentives. Adequate resources are not sufficient to guarantee performance if, as in Honduras, these resources migrate away from where they were intended to be used. Third, information dissemination, both to vulnerable tiers in the public hierarchy and to end-users, as done in Uganda, can be a potent way to mitigate problems arising from the information asymmetries that characterize most public sectors.

Notes

The authors thank Magnus Lindelöw and Aminur Rahman for their comments and contributions.

1. Information on survey design, sampling, implementation, and costs as well as sample questionnaires are available at www.publicspending.org.

2. Another approach is to observe providers over a longer period of time on the assumption that the agent's behavior will revert to normal due to economic necessity. But this can be expensive, limiting the sample size. The study by McPake and others (1999), which used this approach, included only 20 health facilities.

3. Similar improvements are reported in Republic of Uganda in 2000 and 2001.

4. The health sample frame consists of 14,495 staff members in 873 workplaces. The education sample frame had 43,702 staff members in 9,159 workplaces. The total sample is 1,465 staff nationwide with 805 staff members from health and 660 staff members from education. These are clustered within 35 health establishments and 44 education establishments. The samples were stratified by type of facility and by type of employee. Population weighting was used to determine how many of each type of employee to draw from each type of facility. Two questionnaires were used for each institution from which individual staff members were sampled. One questionnaire was for the institution's manager and one was for each individual employee working in the sampled institution on the day of the visit. If the individual was not there, close colleagues filled in the required information about the employee.

5. In some cases, diagnostic PETSs have been carried out with, say, 20–40 facilities (Government of Tanzania 1999, 2001), which is not enough for statistical analysis.

References

The word *processed* describes informally reproduced works that may not be commonly available through library systems.

Ablo, Emmanuel, and Ritva Reinikka. 1998. "Do Budgets Really Matter? Evidence from Public Spending on Education and Health in Uganda." Policy Research Working Paper 1926. World Bank, Development Research Group, Washington, D.C.

Alderman, Harold, and Victor Lavy. 1996. "Household Responses to Public Health Services: Cost and Quality Tradeoffs." *World Bank Research Observer* 11(1): 3–22.

Alreck, Pamela L., and Robert B. Settle. 1995. *The Survey Research Handbook,* 2nd ed. Chicago: Irwin.

Barnum, Howard, and Joseph Kutzin. 1993. *Public Hospitals in Developing Countries: Resource Use, Cost, Financing.* Baltimore: Johns Hopkins University Press.

Bernheim, B. Douglas, and Michael D. Whinston. 1986. "Common Agency." *Econometrica* 54(4): 923–42.

Castro-Leal, Florencia, Julia Dayton, Lionel Demery, and Kalpana Mehra. 1999. "Public Spending in Africa: Do the Poor Benefit?" *World Bank Research Observer* 14(1): 49–72.

Chaudhury, Nazmul, and Jeffrey S. Hammer. 2003. "Ghost Doctors: Absenteeism in Bangladeshi Health Facilities." Policy Research Working Paper 3065. World Bank, Development Research Group, Washington, D.C.

Das, Jishnu, Stefan Dercon, James Habyarimana, and Pramila Krishnan. 2002. "Rules vs. Discretion: Public and Private Funding in Zambian Basic Education. Part I: Funding Equity." World Bank, Development Research Group, Washington, D.C. Processed.

Devarajan, Shantanayan, and Ritva Reinikka. 2002. "Making Services Work for Poor People." Paper presented at the African Economic Research Consortium, Nairobi, May. Processed.

Dixit, Avinash. 1996. *The Making of Economic Policy: A Transaction-Cost Politics Perspective*. Cambridge, Mass.: MIT Press.

———. 1997. "Power of Incentives in Public Versus Private Organizations." *American Economic Review Papers and Proceedings* 87(2): 378–82.

———. 2000. "Incentives and Organizations in the Public Sector: An Interpretative Review." Revised version of paper presented at the Conference on Devising Incentives to Promote Human Capital. National Academy of Sciences, Irvine, Calif., December 17–18. Processed.

Frankenberg, Elizabeth. 2000. "Community and Price Data." In Margaret E. Grosh and Paul Glewwe (2000).

Government of Tanzania. 1999. "Tanzania Public Expenditure Review: Health and Education Financial Tracking Study. Final Report, Vol. III." Report by Price Waterhouse Coopers, Dar es Salaam. Processed.

———. 2001. "ProPoor Expenditure Tracking." Report by Research on Poverty Alleviation and Economic (REPOA) and Social Research Foundation to Tanzania PER Working Group. March. Dar es Salaam. Processed.

Grosh, Margaret E., and Paul Glewwe. 2000. *Designing Household Survey Questionnaires for Developing Countries: Lessons from 15 Years of the Living Standards Measurement Study*. Washington, D.C.: World Bank.

Hammer, Jeffrey, Ijaz Nabi, and James Cercone. 1995. "Distributional Effects of Social Sector Expenditures in Malaysia, 1974 to 1989." In Dominique van de Walle and Kimberly Nead, eds., *Public Spending and the Poor: Theory and Evidence*. Baltimore, Md.: Johns Hopkins University Press.

Lindelöw, Magnus, and Adam Wagstaff. 2003. "Health Facility Surveys: An Introduction." Policy Research Working Paper 2953. World Bank, Development Research Group, Washington, D.C.

Lindelöw, Magnus, Ritva Reinikka, and Jakob Svensson. 2003. "Health Care on the Frontline: Survey Evidence on Public and Private Providers in Uganda." Africa Region Human Development Working Paper 38. World Bank, Washington, D.C.

McPake, Barbara, Delius Asiimwe, Francis Mwesigye, Mathias Ofumbi, Lisbeth Ortenblad, Pieter Streefland, and Asaph Turinde. 1999. "Informal Economic Activities of Public Health Workers in Uganda: Implications for Quality and Accessibility of Care." *Social Science and Medicine* 49(7): 849–67.

Reinikka, Ritva. 2001. "Recovery in Service Delivery: Evidence from Schools and Health Centers." In Ritva Reinikka and Paul Collier, eds.,

Uganda's Recovery: The Role of Farms, Firms, and Government. World Bank Regional and Sectoral Studies. Washington, D.C.: World Bank.

Reinikka, Ritva, and Jakob Svensson. 2002. "Explaining Leakage of Public Funds." CEPR Discussion Paper 3227. Centre for Economic Policy Research, London, U.K.

————. 2003a. "The Power of Information: Evidence from an Information Campaign to Reduce Capture." World Bank, Development Research Group, Washington, D.C. Processed.

————. 2003b. "Working for God? Evaluating Service Delivery of Religious Not-for-Profit Health Care Providers in Uganda." Policy Research Working Paper 3058. World Bank, Development Research Group, Washington, D.C.

Republic of Uganda. 2000. "Tracking the Flow of and Accountability for UPE Funds." Ministry of Education and Sports. Report by International Development Consultants, Ltd., Kampala.

————. 2001. "Study to Track Use of and Accountability of UPE Capitation Grants." Ministry of Education and Sports. Report by International Development Consultants, Ltd., Kampala, October.

Rossi, Peter H., and J. D. Wright, eds. 1983. *Handbook of Survey Research, Quantitative Studies in Social Relations.* New York: Wiley.

Somanathan, A., K. Hanson, B. A. Dorabawila, and B. Perera. 2000. "Operating Efficiency in Public Sector Health Facilities in Sri Lanka: Measurement and Institutional Determinants of Performance." Sri Lankan Health Reform Project (USAID). Processed.

Wagstaff, Adam. 1989. "Econometric Studies in Health Economics: A Survey of the British Literature." *Journal of Health Economics* 8: 1–51.

Wagstaff, Adam, and Howard Barnum. 1992. "Hospital Cost Functions for Developing Countries." Policy Research Working Paper 1044. World Bank, Development Research Group, Washington, D.C.

World Bank. 2001. "Honduras: Public Expenditure Management for Poverty Reduction and Fiscal Sustainability." Report 22070. Poverty Reduction and Economic Sector Management Unit, Latin America and the Caribbean Region. Washington, D.C.

Xiao, Ye, and Sudharshan Canagarajah. 2002. "Efficiency of Public Expenditure Distribution and Beyond: A Report on Ghana's 2000 Public Expenditure Tracking Survey in the Sectors of Primary Health and Education." Africa Region Working Paper Series 31. World Bank, Washington, D.C.

PART II

Macroeconomic Techniques

10

Predicting the Effect
of Aggregate Growth on Poverty

*Gaurav Datt, Krishnan Ramadas,
Dominique van der Mensbrugghe,
Thomas Walker, and Quentin Wodon*

This chapter explains the functioning of two simple tools linking poverty analysis with the simplest, most aggregated, representation of economic growth. In short, both tools can be considered the "ground floor" for evaluating the poverty and distribution effects of macroeconomic policies. The insight upon which both tools are built is that the change in poverty can be decomposed into two parts: a component related to the uniform growth of income, and a component due to changes in relative incomes. The consequences for poverty of a policy affecting aggregate output growth can be predicted using this insight, under the assumption that the policy under scrutiny will be distribution neutral, or conversely assuming a specific quantifiable form for the distributional change.

The basic principle of this decomposition is illustrated in figure 10.1, taken from Bourguignon (2002). Income levels measured in dollars per day (logarithmic scale) are ordered along the bottom axis, from lowest to highest. The vertical axis measures the share of population at each income level. The figure decomposes the two aforementioned components of poverty change under a log-normal income distribution. The "growth effect" represents income growth without changes in distribution, and shifts the log-income distribution to the right while leaving its shape unchanged. The share of the

Figure 10.1 Decomposition of Change in Poverty into Growth and Distribution Effects

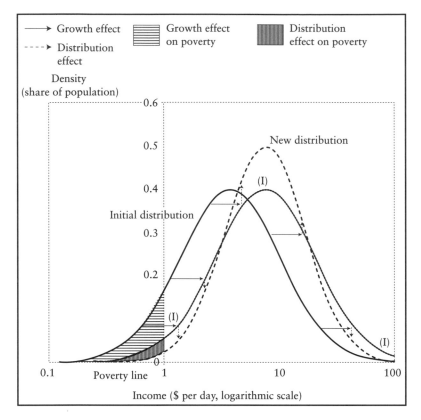

Source: Bourguignon (2002).

population below the poverty line (normalized at 1) decreases as a result of the shift. The "distribution effect," meanwhile, represents changes in income distribution. The taller curve defines a new income distribution with less dispersion around the mean, resulting in lower inequality. The distribution effect contributes to the poverty reduction by narrowing the dispersion of incomes, while holding overall mean income constant.

The two tools described below use the key idea of this decomposition to simulate the poverty effect of macroeconomic policies. Both develop this idea further to incorporate differential growth rates across major economic sectors. The two tools share similarities, and both are supported by the same software (Excel).

The first tool is the Poverty Module of the Simulations for Social Indicators and Poverty (SimSIP) provided by Wodon, Ramadas, and van der Mensbrugghe (2003). This module is part of a broader family of user-friendly Excel-based simulators that facilitate the analysis of issues related to social indicators in general and poverty in particular. [1] The SimSIP Poverty Module is a spreadsheet Excel-based software program that was recently built and made available to exploit the idea outlined above. The simulator can be useful to analysts who do not have access to the unit-level records of household surveys, but do have information by income level, as often provided, for example, in published reports from national statistical offices. The simulator can of course also be used for poverty estimations, decompositions, and simulations when access to the unit-level records from the household survey is feasible. In this case, the user would first estimate the mean consumption or income by, say, decile, and use that information for the simulations. However, a typically small error of approximation will then occur when using the simulator with the group data, as opposed to using the unit-level data directly.

The second tool, PovStat, relies on a similar procedure (see Datt and Walker 2002). PovStat generates poverty projections using household survey data and a set of user-supplied projection parameters for the country under analysis. The program's methodology assumes that the rate and sectoral pattern of growth determine how poverty measures evolve over time. PovStat offers a wide variety of options in specifying projection parameters, along with an output datasheet capability.

SimSIP Poverty

SimSIP Poverty uses group data, that is, it breaks down the total population originally observed in the survey data into ten or five groups (these can be deciles or quintiles, for examples). The user must provide information on population shares and on mean income or consumption in the various groups. The information can be provided nationally and by sector (such as urban and rural, or agriculture, manufacturing, and services). Using a parameterization of the Lorenz curve, the simulator then computes poverty and inequality measures nationally and within each of the sectors. Two ways of parameterizing the Lorenz curve are available (GQ Lorenz curve and Beta Lorenz curve).

The simulator builds on previous work at the World Bank using group data for the estimation of poverty and inequality, namely, the POVCAL program, which was created by Datt and Ravallion (1992) and written in DOS-Basic. One advantage of SimSIP Poverty over POVCAL is that it is Excel-based and thus easier to use. Additionally, the simulator provides interesting functions apart from the basic comparisons of poverty and inequality between sectors and over time. For example, the simulator provides various curves, including poverty dominance and Lorenz curves for robust comparisons of poverty and inequality among sectors or over time. Currently, the simulator reports only the most commonly used measures of poverty and inequality, namely the headcount index ($P0$), the poverty gap ($P1$), the squared poverty gap ($P2$) index for poverty (Foster, Greer, and Thorbecke 1984), and the Gini index for inequality (nationally and within the defined groups). For poverty, the user may specify two different poverty lines, to measure extreme poverty and overall poverty (the sum of extreme and moderate poverty).

Apart from providing sectoral and national measures of poverty, inequality, and social welfare, the simulator provides decompositions of the change in poverty over time. The decompositions are based on the additive property of the Foster-Greer-Thorbecke (FGT) class of poverty measures. This property ensures that any FGT poverty measure for a group is equal to the sum of the poverty measures for its subgroups when these subgroup poverty measures are weighted by the population shares of the subgroups. Denoting the poverty measures and population shares of the subgroups by P_i and w_i, we have $P = \Sigma_i\, w_i\, P_i$. Two poverty decompositions based on this property have been used to describe the dynamics of poverty in a country. The first decomposition is sectoral (Ravallion and Huppi 1991). It looks at the contributions of the urban and rural sectors to changes in the national poverty rate, P^t, between two dates t_1 and t_2. Denote by P_i^t the poverty measure for sector i ($i = u, r$) in year t, and by w_i^t the population share of sector i in t. This gives:

$$P^{t2} - P^{t1} = w_u^{t1}(P_u^{t2} - P_u^{t1}) + w_r^{t1}(P_r^{t2} - P_r^{t1})$$
$$+ \Sigma_i^{u,\,r}(w_i^{t2} - w_i^{t1})P_i^{t1} + \Sigma_i^{u,\,r}(w_i^{t2} - w_i^{t1})(P_i^{t2} - P_i^{t1})$$

The first term in this equation captures the intrasectoral changes in poverty between the two years. The second term captures the effect of intersectoral population shifts. The third term is a covariance measure of the interaction between the intrasectoral and intersectoral effects. The population shift component is often negative as the migration from rural to urban areas where poverty is lower tends to decrease the national poverty rate (at least in the way migration is captured in the decomposition).

The second decomposition consists of analyzing the contribution of growth and inequality to changes in poverty measures nationally or within the urban and rural sectors, along the lines of figure 10.1. Following Datt and Ravallion (1992), write the poverty measures as a function of the mean consumption and the Lorenz curve, so that $P^t = P(\mu^t, L^t)$, where μ^t denotes the mean consumption of households at time t, and L^t denotes the Lorenz curve of their consumption. Then define the growth component of a change in poverty between two dates as the change attributable to a change in mean consumption holding the Lorenz curve constant. The redistribution component is the change resulting from a change in the Lorenz curve, holding mean consumption constant. With R as residual, we have:

$$P(\mu^{t2}, L^{t2}) - P(\mu^{t1}, L^{t1}) = [P(\mu^{t2}, L^{t1}) - P(\mu^{t1}, L^{t1})]$$
$$+ [P(\mu^{t1}, L^{t2}) - P(\mu^{t1}, L^{t1})] + R$$

The simulator also performs standard dominance analysis, following Atkinson (1987). The objective is to assess the sensitivity of poverty comparisons to the choice of alternative poverty lines (and alternative poverty measures). For example, poverty incidence curves may plot on the vertical axis the headcount indices of poverty in two sectors or for two periods of time as functions, on the horizontal axis, of the poverty line (these are essentially cumulative density functions). For a given range of poverty lines, one sector (or time period) will be said to have first-order dominance over the other if its poverty incidence curve lies everywhere below that of the other sector (time period). First-order dominance implies not only that the headcount index of poverty, but also that a number of other poverty measures, including those of the Foster-Greer-Thorbecke class, will be lower in the first sector (time period) than in the other sector (time period). If first-order dominance does not obtain, one can easily check for higher orders of dominance. Lorenz curves for testing dominance in terms of inequality comparisons are also provided.

The simulator can also be used to assess the impact on poverty and inequality of alternative growth patterns, with these patterns defined using changes in income, distribution, and population in various subsectors of the economy (say, urban and rural sectors, or agriculture, industry, and services). The overall impact on poverty of growth can then be measured and compared with, for example, a pattern of growth identical in all sectors.

Finally, a new feature enables the user to test whether past patterns of growth or simulations for future growth can be deemed to be pro-poor using alternative potential definitions of what pro-poor growth actually is or should be, following Duclos and Wodon (2003). Additional features are progressively introduced as the simulator is developed further.

PovStat

PovStat is an Excel-based program designed to simulate poverty measures under alternative growth scenarios and to forecast or project poverty measures over a future projection horizon (or, more generally, beyond the current household survey period). The need for such projections naturally arises when assessing the poverty implications of expected growth scenarios. But the need also arises from another source. Poverty estimates are typically based on living standards data taken from national household surveys, which are generally available only on an infrequent basis. Even in countries with a well-established household survey tradition, it is not uncommon to find that these surveys are conducted only every two to five years. For more up-to-date poverty monitoring, therefore, poverty levels often need to be projected beyond the most recent available national household survey data.

Poverty projections are generated using country-specific (unit-record) household survey data and a set of user-supplied projection parameters for that country.[2] The survey data provide the distribution of household living standards in the country at a point in time, and the projection parameters characterize a particular projection scenario. PovStat is designed to process data at the country level, but it can also be used at higher and lower levels of aggregation. The program incorporates a wide variety of options, allowing flexibility in data specification. Once the program and data are loaded, the user can change the projection settings and options and generate an immediate update of the calculated statistics. Since PovStat is Excel-based, it allows the user to format, print, or save results as desired—making it a flexible simulation device for evaluating the poverty implications of alternative growth scenarios.

Methodology

PovStat uses per capita consumption as the measure of welfare for poverty calculations. The basic methodology underlying PovStat is that the rate and sectoral pattern of growth determine how poverty measures evolve over time. It distinguishes three major sectors, namely, agriculture, industry, and services. PovStat starts with the initial assumption that household per capita consumption grows at the same rate as that of per capita output in the sector of employment of the household head.[3] This assumption implies constant relative inequalities within sectors. The assumption can be relaxed at the user's discretion, however, by specifying a rate of increase or decrease in inequality within any sector over the projection horizon.

PovStat also allows poverty projections to be further conditioned by a number of projection parameters optionally supplied by the user. These additional projection parameters relate to employment shifts across sectors, changing terms of trade reflecting differential prices faced by consumers and producers, changes in the relative price of food that is a prominent part of the poor's consumption bundle, changes in inequality within sectors, changes in the average consumption-income ratio, and statistical drift in consumption growth between the national accounts and the surveys. By allowing these adjustments to be built in, PovStat offers a flexible approach to poverty projection that could help avoid the biases typically associated with the simple back-of-the-envelope forecasts relying only on per capita gross domestic product (GDP) growth and an empirical elasticity of poverty measures with respect to growth. Thus, PovStat can produce forecasts at varying levels of complexity depending upon the availability of reliable data for the postsurvey period and the extent to which various factors influencing poverty levels are incorporated. Further details on the specification of these projection parameters and their implementation within PovStat can be found in Datt and Walker (2002).

How PovStat Works

PovStat uses Excel's Visual Basic macro language to compute various poverty and inequality measures over a user-specified projection horizon (of up to 10 years), using two main inputs: unit-record survey data on household consumption from an input data file; and user-supplied projection parameters (as discussed above), either provided interactively by the user or taken from a settings file.

Once this information is loaded in, PovStat then calculates the poverty measures and other indexes and displays these on screen. The user can change the projection settings as desired, and rerun the calculations, or save the output and settings to a new Excel file for further manipulation.

Data Requirements for SimSIP Poverty

One of the advantages of SimSIP Poverty is that the data requirement is light. With at least one poverty line, the average income level of various groups in the economy, and their weight as a share of the population, SimSIP Poverty can calculate the poverty and inequality indicators. In addition, with two sets of observations, the program can compare over time the changes in poverty and inequality and run basic sectoral and growth-inequality decompositions to explain changes in poverty over time.

The typical data required for using all the features of the simulator are illustrated in table 10.1 with the case of Paraguay. The table provides population shares by group (in this case, 10 different groups corresponding to national deciles were used, so that within sectors, the share of the population in each group need not be equal to 10 percent) and mean income per capita. The user can then compute poverty for any set of two different poverty lines supposed to capture extreme poverty and total poverty, and all the decompositions and graphs will be provided automatically.

For simulations on the impact of future sectoral patterns of growth, the user needs in addition to specify the total rate of growth in each sector or nationally. For example, to simulate the impact of a growth rate of 1 percent in the per capita income or consumption for households occupied in agriculture over 10 years, the user would specify a total growth rate for that sector of 10.46 percent in the simulator, because $(1.01)^{10} = 1.1046$, and poverty and inequality measures would be computed again assuming that the mean income in each group (say, each decile) in the agriculture sector has been multiplied by 1.1046. Under such a scenario, inequality would remain unchanged within the agricultural sector. But if various growth rates are applied to various sectors, then apart from changes in poverty, there will also implicitly be changes in inequality at the national level. The same is true if the population shares in the various sectors are changing over time. In any case, to simulate future growth patterns, only one initial set of data (that is, population shares and mean income or consumption for one year in each group) are needed as a baseline. If data at the sectoral level are not available, the simulator can still estimate poverty and inequality where the data are provided (say, nationally).

When testing whether growth has been pro-poor or not, or whether a given expected sectoral growth pattern is likely to be pro-poor or not, the user must provide additional parameters that reflect the normative judgments made as to how pro-poor growth should be defined. Following Duclos and Wodon (2003), both relative and absolute pro-poor standards can be defined. Modified stochastic dominance curves then enable the user to provide a robust evaluation (for various classes of poverty measures and a range of poverty lines) as to whether growth can indeed be said to be pro-poor or not.

SimSIP Poverty also provides estimates of the elasticity of poverty to growth and to changes in inequality nationally and in the various sectors. One of the additional features that will soon be integrated in the simulator consists of analyzing the relationships between the levels of poverty, inequality, and growth on the one hand, and the

Table 10.1 Typical Data for SimSIP Poverty: Population Shares and Per Capita Income by Decile, Sector, and Nationally, Paraguay

	Urban areas		Rural areas		Agriculture		Industry		Services		National	
Decile	1997–98	2000–01	1997–98	2000–01	1997–98	2000–01	1997–98	2000–01	1997–98	2000–01	1997–98	2000–01
Population shares (%)												
1	4.2	5.3	16.8	15.5	21.2	20.2	3.9	5.0	3.8	4.3	10.0	10.0
2	7.0	8.0	13.5	12.4	16.8	15.0	7.2	6.0	5.6	8.1	10.0	10.0
3	9.8	10.5	10.3	9.4	12.1	12.8	10.9	10.3	7.9	7.5	10.0	10.0
4	10.0	11.4	10.0	8.3	11.2	8.9	9.9	13.3	9.0	9.1	10.0	10.0
5	11.9	10.1	7.8	10.0	8.4	9.2	10.7	13.2	11.1	9.0	10.0	10.0
6	11.2	10.9	8.6	8.9	8.1	8.3	13.4	11.7	9.9	10.5	10.0	10.0
7	11.2	10.8	8.6	9.1	6.6	6.9	12.1	10.7	11.8	12.3	10.0	10.0
8	11.0	11.0	8.9	8.7	6.3	6.5	11.4	10.0	12.4	12.9	10.0	10.0
9	12.1	10.3	7.6	9.8	4.9	5.4	11.9	11.2	13.3	13.3	10.0	10.0
10	11.7	11.7	8.0	7.9	4.4	6.9	8.6	8.8	15.5	13.2	10.0	9.9
Mean per capita income (Paraguayan guaranis)												
1	53,656	105,296	45,354	56,875	44,899	73,152	56,910	76,337	53,055	75,722	47,217	73,991
2	112,368	199,398	110,512	113,805	110,062	150,309	112,056	150,361	113,564	152202	111,208	150,956
3	167,764	257,891	166,065	169,360	164,667	217,732	170,586	219,701	167,381	223,853	166,960	220,132
4	223,450	309,650	223,548	231,906	222,748	281,709	222,959	272,289	224,586	281,683	223,495	278770
5	286,824	376,107	286,177	308,177	286,125	342,981	286,989	342,653	286,691	338,435	286,590	341,180
6	369,796	469,111	367,553	382,076	366,904	425,985	366,830	429,341	371,712	426,085	368,901	426,946
7	472,701	582,079	469,738	490,590	470,586	536,797	474,108	534,657	470,604	539,889	471,519	537,842
8	612,306	744,486	611,999	638,470	610,144	698,137	619,975	689,089	609,406	693,496	612,181	693,510
9	851,704	1,048,397	842,560	865,519	848,408	958,671	832,688	926,985	855,711	971,235	848,496	957,380
10	2,001,452	2,569,163	1,782,926	2,308,767	1,995,678	3,127,525	1,832,562	2,086,894	1,927,719	2,321,997	1,920,747	2,467,151

Sources: Robles, Siaens, and Wodon (2003). Estimation using 1997–98 and 2000–01 household surveys from Dirección General de Estadística, Encuestas y Censos. Mean per capita incomes have been normalized to take regional poverty lines into account.

elasticities between any two of these three variables on the other hand (holding the third variable constant.) It is well known that a higher level of initial inequality reduces the elasticity of poverty to growth. But other similar relationships are at work, which may be important for policy judgments. For example, one can show that in poorer countries (such as many of the countries in Africa), everything else being equal, growth is more important than redistribution for reducing poverty.

Data Requirements for PovStat

Two sets of data are needed to run PovStat. The first is household survey data, which can be set up as a user-specified text data file. This file has actual household-level survey data for a particular country and year. For instance, for the Philippines the file may have household-level data on selected variables from the 1997 Family Income and Expenditure Survey. While PovStat uses unit-record data from household surveys, only a limited number of variables from the survey are needed. The data file to be input into the program contains such variables as household identifier, per capita consumption in local currency units, sampling weight, an urban dummy variable, household size, and the sector of employment of household head.

Projection parameter settings are the second set of required data. The following set of projection parameters need to be specified for a PovStat run:

- Forecast horizon (up to 20 years beyond the survey year)
- Poverty line (national or international poverty lines, based on purchasing power parity, or PPP)
- Survey year and base year for PPP (if relevant)
- Survey year population
- If using an international poverty line, the country's PPP exchange rate, and base and survey year consumer price indexes (CPIs)
- Output growth rates by sector for each projection year
- Population growth rates and employment growth rates by sector for each projection year
- Survey-year sectoral GDP and employment shares

In addition, the user can optionally incorporate further factors into poverty projections by specifying the following:

- If using the income-consumption terms of trade option, the GDP deflator and CPI for each projection year.

- If using the food price option, changes in the relative price of food by year, and the shares of food in the poverty line consumption bundle and CPI.
- If using the average propensity to consume option, changes in the ratio of private consumption to GDP.
- If relaxing distribution neutrality, the percentage change in Gini within each sector for each projection year.
- Drift between surveys and national accounts, allowing for correction of any unaccounted discrepancy between survey-based and national accounts–based growth in private consumption.

Illustrations and Case Studies for SimSIP Poverty

How good are the estimates provided by SimSIP Poverty? As mentioned earlier, SimSIP Poverty uses group data, rather than the unit-level data available in the household surveys. This implies that poverty and inequality estimates are only approximations of the "true" values. Table 10.2 presents a comparison of the estimates of poverty obtained with the data presented in table 10.1 with the "true" measures estimated with the unit-level data. The parameterizations used are the GQ and the Beta Lorenz curves (there is a separate simulator for each parameterization). The estimates of the FGT poverty measures using SimSIP Poverty tend to be close to the actual values, but some differences are apparent. Overall, in most tests for various countries, we did not find major issues with the estimates obtained with the group data, as opposed to the unit-level data. In some cases, however, the estimations based on the GQ or the Beta parameterizations of the Lorenz curve may not respect some conditions or may not converge. In those cases, the user will be signaled because the estimates of poverty or inequality may then be somewhat off.

Table 10.3 presents the results of another exercise taking into account different sectoral growth patterns using 1997–98 data for Paraguay as a baseline. For example, holding inequality constant, a 2 percent annual growth in per capita income in every sector (that is, nationally) would lead to a headcount of 28.95 percent at the end of a five-year period (see column 2 of the table, second scenario), compared with 32.13 percent initially. The same result is obtained (with a small approximation error) when the same growth rate is applied to the various sectors and national poverty is obtained by summing poverty across sectors (see the headcount of 28.97 percent in column 3, and 28.92 percent in column 4). By contrast, if the growth rate in industry and services were higher,

Table 10.2 SimSIP Poverty: Comparing the FGT Poverty Measures Obtained with Unit and Grouped Data, Paraguay

Poverty measures	Urban areas		Rural areas		Agriculture		Industry		Services		National	
	1997–98	2000–01	1997–98	2000–01	1997–98	2000–01	1997–98	2000–01	1997–98	2000–01	1997–98	2000–01
Estimates with unit level data (1)												
Headcount of poverty	23.1	27.6	42.5	41.2	52.8	50.8	24.1	28.2	18.7	22.9	32.1	33.8
Poverty gap	8.1	9.2	21.4	18.8	26.9	23.9	8.0	8.5	6.8	8.0	14.3	13.6
Squared poverty gap	4.2	4.7	13.8	11.4	17.4	14.5	4.0	4.3	3.6	4.1	8.6	7.8
Estimates with data by per capita income decile—using GQ Lorenz curve (2)												
Headcount	23.8	28.7	42.0	40.6	52.4	51.1	23.5	28.2	20.0	23.8	32.1	34.2
Poverty gap	8.3	9.7	21.4	18.8	26.9	24.1	8.2	9.0	6.9	8.2	14.4	13.9
Squared poverty gap	3.8	4.3	13.9	11.4	17.4	14.3	3.9	3.9	3.2	3.8	8.5	7.5
Estimates with data by per capita income decile—using Beta Lorenz curve (3)												
Headcount	23.21	27.81	42.15	40.87	52.13	51.08	23.31	27.32	19.40	23.30	32.13	33.95
Poverty gap	8.42	9.79	21.76	18.73	27.24	24.03	8.17	9.15	7.04	8.19	14.54	13.92
Squared poverty gap	4.32	4.90	13.96	11.33	17.59	14.52	4.08	4.50	3.67	4.16	8.75	7.85
Difference in estimates (1) – (2)												
Headcount	-0.7	-1.1	0.5	0.6	0.4	-0.3	0.6	0.0	-1.3	-0.9	0.0	-0.4
Poverty gap	-0.2	-0.5	0.0	0.0	0.0	-0.2	-0.2	-0.5	-0.1	-0.2	-0.1	-0.3
Squared poverty gap	0.4	0.4	-0.1	0.0	0.0	0.2	0.1	0.4	0.4	0.3	0.1	0.3
Difference in estimates (1) – (3)												
Headcount	-0.1	-0.2	0.4	0.3	0.7	-0.3	0.8	0.9	-0.7	-0.4	0.0	-0.2
Poverty gap	-0.3	-0.6	-0.4	0.1	-0.3	-0.1	-0.2	-0.6	-0.2	-0.2	-0.2	-0.3
Squared poverty gap	-0.1	-0.2	-0.2	0.1	-0.2	0.0	-0.1	-0.2	-0.1	-0.1	-0.1	-0.1

Sources: Robles, Siaens, and Wodon (2003). Estimations using 1997–98 and 2000–01 household surveys from Dirección General de Estadística, Encuestas y Censos.

Table 10.3 Simulations for the Impact of Growth Patterns on Poverty in Paraguay Using SimSIP Poverty: Some Examples (percent)

		National poverty headcount		
	Period 1	*Period 2 National simulation*	*Period 2 National as weighted average of urban/rural sectors*	*Period 2 National as weighted average of employment sectors*
3% per sector, for 5 years	32.13	27.46	27.48	27.42
2% per sector, for 5 years	32.13	28.95	28.97	28.92
1% per sector, for 5 years	32.13	30.51	30.53	30.49
2% in agriculture, rural sectors; 3% elsewhere for 5 years	32.13	—	28.15	27.94
1% in agriculture, rural sectors; 3% elsewhere for 5 years	32.13	—	28.82	28.46
3% in agriculture, rural sectors; 1% elsewhere for 5 years	32.13	—	29.06	29.34

— Not applicable.
Source: Robles, Siaens, and Wodon (2003).

let's say at 3 percent, compared with 2 percent for the agricultural sector, the headcount of poverty computed as the weighted average of the predicted headcounts in each of the three sectors would decrease further to 27.94 percent (see the last column and the fourth simulation). More generally, the user can easily compare how different growth patterns add up for poverty reduction and compare these to the poverty reduction obtained with one aggregate equivalent rate of growth for the economy as a whole. Also, because poverty is higher in rural areas and in agriculture, any population shift away from those sectors is likely to decrease poverty. Although not shown in the table, this type of simulation can easily be conducted on top of the sectoral growth scenarios.

Illustrations and Case Studies for PovStat

Although PovStat was designed primarily as a poverty forecasting tool over the short-to-medium term, it can also be used to project poverty over a historical period, where actual economic variables (as opposed to forecasts) are available as input. This situation occurs frequently where up-to-date survey data are not available for a country, and a past survey is used. The benefit of hindsight, so to speak, is that the full range of PovStat's options can be used, whereas the inputs for these options—CPI and the GDP deflator, food prices, and so on—are hard to forecast for future years and therefore are typically unavailable.

To illustrate the way PovStat works, we look at poverty projections for the Philippines, for which household survey information from the Family Income and Expenditure Surveys is available for 1997 and 2000. We use the 1997 survey to obtain poverty projections up to 2003, with historical inputs for the period 1997–2001 and forecasts thereafter. The 2000 survey is used to obtain forecasts to 2003 using forecast economic variables only. We also comment on the comparison of the two sets of forecasts.

As noted earlier, PovStat requires several parameters to be input before projections can be made. These input data for each of the two runs can be found in table 10.4. The poverty lines used for the forecasts are $1 a person a day and $2 a person a day, equivalent to monthly values of $32.74 and $65.48 respectively (in 1993 PPP U.S. dollars). Population figures are required for the survey year to calculate the number of poor in each scenario. The PPP exchange rate, at 10.958 pesos to the dollar, is taken from the Penn World Tables. Output and employment growth rates up to 2001 are taken from national data sources, and from the World Bank Unified Survey thereafter. PovStat uses sectorally disaggregated data, if available, to incorporate differential growth rates and population shifts across sectors. For the Philippines, growth rates were used for three sectors: agriculture, industry, and services.

Five options are available in PovStat: adjustment for changes in income-consumption terms of trade; changes in the relative price of food; changes in the average propensity to consume; relaxation of distribution neutrality within sectors; and drift between national accounts and survey growth rates. Given the available data, the first three are used here for the historical period.

For the terms-of-trade adjustment, it is the ratio of the CPI to the GDP deflator that is important for projection purposes in PovStat. The data on the GDP deflator and the CPI are taken from national statistical sources for the historical period, and the relative terms

Table 10.4 Input Settings for PovStat Runs, 1997 and 2000

Input settings	1997	2000
PPP rate (1993 LCU / US$)	10.958	10.958
Survey year population (thousands)	73,527	78,231
Base year CPI (1997=100)	73.44	61.40
Food weight in poverty line	0.73	0.73
Food weight in CPI	0.55	0.55
Survey year sectoral labor shares		
Agricultural sector	40.4	38.8
Industry sector	16.7	16.8
Services sector	42.9	44.4

Output	1998	1999	2000	2001	2002	2003
Annual output growth (percent)						
Agricultural sector	-6.6	6.9	3.5	3.9	2.5	2.7
Industry sector	-1.8	0.6	3.9	1.9	3.8	5.5
Services sector	3.5	4.0	4.4	4.3	4.8	4.6
GDP growth	-0.5	3.3	4.0	3.4	4.0	4.5
Annual employment growth (percent)						
Agricultural sector	1.4	1.4	1.4	1.4	1.4	1.4
Industry sector	3.0	3.0	3.0	3.0	3.0	3.0
Services sector	4.0	4.0	4.0	4.0	4.0	4.0
Population growth	2.2	2.1	2.1	2.1	2.0	2.0
CPI (1997=100)	109.7	117.0	122.0	128.2	128.2	128.2
GDP deflator (1997=100)	111.2	119.6	127.6	136.1	136.1	136.1
Change in relative price of food (percent)	-2.1	-1.3	-2.3	-1.9	0.0	0.0
Change in C/Y ratio (percent)	1.5	-2.4	-2.6	0.0	0.0	0.0
Drift between national accounts and survey growth rates (percentage points)	0.0	0.0	0.0	0.0	0.0	0.0

Source: As discussed in text.

of trade are held constant beyond 2001. The relative price of food option requires the percentage change in the relative food price index (that is, the ratio of the food price index to the overall CPI) to be specified, along with the share of food in both the CPI and the poverty line consumption bundle. The average propensity to consume option adjusts for the specification of income growth rates rather than consumption growth rates and requires the user to provide the percentage change in the ratio of nominal GDP to nominal consumption in each year.

PovStat requires the user to specify the input data file (which contains the household-level survey data) and the settings file (containing the projection settings discussed above). The user sets the projection horizon (which was six years for the 1997 case, and three years for the 2000 case) and verifies the settings. PovStat calculates the poverty and inequality indexes, which are presented on the program's main worksheet. The user can choose to save these settings and results to a new file for further manipulation.

The results of both runs, at the poverty lines of $1 a day and $2 a day, are presented in table 10.5. Starting with the projections based on the 1997 survey, note that these show an increase in headcount index for both poverty lines in 1998, reflecting the negative growth rates associated with the Asian financial crisis (see table 10.4). Economic recovery since 1998 is then reflected in declining poverty levels.

However, a comparison of the results shows that the link-up between the 1997 and 2000 survey-based projections is not perfect. Thus, for instance, based on the 1997 survey, the predicted headcount for $1 a day ($2 a day) is 11.0 (43.6) percent against the actual 2000 estimate of 13.2 (46.8) percent. This discrepancy seems to be mainly on account of an overestimation of the mean consumption for 2000 when national accounts–based growth rates are applied to the 1997 survey mean consumption. Once we control for this drift between national accounts growth rates and survey growth rates, the predicted headcount indexes for 2000 are 13.0 and 46.4 percent respectively at $1-a-day and $2-a-day poverty lines. The difference between predicted and actual poverty levels is almost fully accounted for. Beyond 2000 the projections (both those based on the 1997 survey as well as those based on the 2000 survey) suggest continued reductions in poverty levels toward 2003.

Table 10.5 Results from PovStat Runs, Philippines

Survey	1997	1998	1999	2000	2001	2002	2003
1997							
Headcount ($1/day)	12.5	13.3	12.2	11.0	9.3	8.7	7.9
Headcount ($2/day)	45.9	46.0	45.0	43.6	41.2	40.2	38.9
Mean per capita consumption (1993 US PPP $/month)	108.6	110.2	111.0	113.9	118.6	121.1	124.0
Gini coefficient	0.460	0.467	0.462	0.460	0.458	0.458	0.458
Number of poor, millions ($1/day)	9.2	10.0	9.3	8.7	7.5	7.1	6.6
Number of poor, millions ($2/day)	33.8	34.5	34.6	34.1	33.0	32.8	32.3
2000							
Headcount ($1/day)				13.2	11.5	10.8	10.0
Headcount ($2/day)				46.8	44.7	43.6	42.3
Mean per capita consumption (1993 US PPP $/month)				107.7	112.1	114.5	117.2
Gini coefficient				0.462	0.460	0.460	0.459
Number of poor, millions ($1/day)				10.3	9.2	8.8	8.3
Number of poor, millions ($2/day)				36.6	35.7	35.5	35.2

Source: Authors' calculations based on PovStat runs.

Conclusions

PovStat and SimSIP are two simple tools for projecting the poverty effects of aggregate growth that exploit the idea that changes in poverty measures depend on changes in mean incomes across sectors and changes in relative inequalities. These tools are relatively easy to use and have modest data requirements. Although the tools are similar in nature, there are some differences in their application. PovStat is better geared to household-level data on income or consumption distribution, while SimSIP is better suited to grouped data.

Both tools impose minimal structure on the relationship between economic growth and poverty. This is their strength as well as their weakness. For analyzing the poverty impact of a broad range of specific macroeconomic policies, more complex tools would be needed that can link relevant policy variables with average incomes and relative inequalities through factor and product market channels. But greater complexity comes at a price, with heavier data requirements, a relative loss of transparency, and the need to make possibly less realistic assumptions.

Notes

1. Other SimSIP modules deal with, among other things, the evaluation of the impact of programs and policies on poverty and inequality, the cost of reaching development targets (for example, in the education sector), debt projections and fiscal sustainability analysis, and the impact of tax reforms on poverty and inequality. Originally, the various simulators were designed to help governments preparing Poverty Reduction Strategies, but they can be used for other purposes as well. Most simulators are "generic," hence they can be used for any country. Two simulators are regional, meaning that their applicability is restricted to the countries of a given region. Technical explanations on the methodology underlying the various simulators are available in each simulator's manual available on the SimSIP Web site, at http://www.worldbank.org/simsip.

2. The program can be adapted for grouped data. That is done by first fitting a parametric Lorenz curve to the grouped data and then generating, say, 100 or 1,000 points on the Lorenz curve, which are then used as synthetic household survey data for PovStat.

3. The current version of PovStat does not capture heterogeneity within households with multiple income earners in different sectors, primarily because of the nature of data available. Many countries do not provide information on the occupation of all (working age) household members. If such data were available, PovStat could easily be run with individual, rather than household-level, data.

References

The word *processed* describes informally reproduced works that may not be commonly available through library systems.

Atkinson, Anthony. 1987. "On the Measurement of Poverty." *Econometrica* 55: 749–64.

Bourguignon, François. 2003. "The Growth Elasticity of Poverty Reduction: Explaining Heterogeneity across Countries and Time Periods." In T. Eicher and S. Turnovsky, eds., *Inequality and Growth*. Cambridge, Mass.: MIT Press.

Datt, Gaurav, and Martin Ravallion. 1992. "Growth and Redistribution Components of Changes in Poverty Measures: A Decomposition with Applications to Brazil and India in the 1980s." *Journal of Development Economics* 38(2): 275–95.

Datt, Gaurav, and Thomas Walker. 2002. "PovStat 2.12: A Poverty Projection Toolkit, User's Manual." World Bank, East Asia Poverty Reduction and Economic Management Unit, Washington, D.C. Processed.

Duclos, Jean-Yves, and Quentin Wodon. 2003. "Pro-poor Growth." World Bank, Africa Poverty Reduction and Economic Management Department, Washington, D.C. Processed.

Foster, James, Joel Greer, and Erik Thorbecke. 1984. "A Class of Decomposable Poverty Measures." *Econometrica* 52(3): 761–66.

Ravallion, Martin, and Monika Huppi. 1991. "Measuring Changes in Poverty: A Methodological Case Study of Indonesia during an Adjustment Period." *World Bank Economic Review* 5(1): 57–82.

Robles, Marcos, Corinne Siaens, and Quentin Wodon. Forthcoming. "Poverty, Inequality and Growth in Paraguay: Simulations Using SimSIP Poverty." *Economía & Sociedad*.

Wodon, Quentin, Krishnan Ramadas, and Dominique van der Mensbrugghe. 2003. "SimSIP Poverty Module," available at www.worldbank.org/simsip.

11

Linking Aggregate Macroconsistency Models to Household Surveys: A Poverty Analysis Macroeconomic Simulator, or PAMS

Luiz A. Pereira da Silva, B. Essama-Nssah, and Issouf Samaké

This chapter presents a simple technique, the Poverty Analysis Macroeconomic Simulator, or PAMS, for linking household surveys (described in chapter 7) and average benefit or tax incidence analysis (described in chapters 1 and 2) to simple aggregate macroeconomic models of various types. The key feature of PAMS is the possibility to infer changes in levels of disposable income for specific categories of workers from expected changes in aggregate variables such as gross domestic product (GDP) by sector. The only requirement concerning the aggregate variables is that they be consistent, as in national accounts. Such a link allows one to project ex ante national accounts and to conduct poverty and distributional analysis in a way that makes income growth, transfers, employment, poverty, and inequality estimates consistent with the macroeconomic framework. The basic idea in linking the macroeconomic framework to the household sector is to multiply the incomes or expenditures of each household of a specific group by the relevant growth rate based on changes in disposable income of that specific group induced by changes in aggregate variables.[1]

PAMS has three recursive layers, as depicted in figure 11.1. The first, or macro, layer features an aggregate macroeconomic framework that can be taken from any macroconsistency model (such as Financial Programming, RMSM-X, or the simple 1-2-3 CGE [computable general equilibrium] model described in chapter 13 with an additional "growth" story).[2] The objective of this top layer is to project GDP, national accounts, the national budget, balance-of-payments, aggregate price level, and so forth in consistent flow-of-funds accounts.

The second, or meso, layer is a simplified labor and earnings market model that calculates disposable income across representative groups of households. Individuals and family units from the household survey are grouped in several (country-specific) representative groups of households defined by the labor category of the head of the household. Each of the representative household groups matches one—and only one—economic productive sector. The sum of the production of all economic sectors is consistent with total output of the macroeconomic framework. Within each representative group, the disposable income of a typical household can be decomposed into labor income, nonlabor income, average taxes, and average transfers. Labor demand in each economic sector depends on sectoral output and real unit labor cost. Labor income in each economic sector can thus be determined by equilibrium on the labor market. In addition, each representative group has exogenous average nonlabor income. Finally, policy-based general tax rates and different levels of budgetary transfers across representative groups can be added to labor and nonlabor income. All these components of household income determine an average level of disposable income for each unit inside a representative group. Overall, a growth rate of disposable income can be calculated for each specific representative household group.

The third, or micro, layer is a poverty and distribution simulator. The simulator follows the basic approach of incidence analysis of public spending or taxation (see chapters 1 and 2) where changes in taxes or transfers can be transmitted into each household's income or expenditure according to some pre-defined characteristics (such as income level). Here, what matters is the household's representative group. PAMS uses the calculated average growth rate of disposable income for each representative group, determined in layer 2, to simulate the income growth for each individual or family unit inside its own representative group. The key assumption is that the change in the disposable income for each individual or family unit in one

Figure 11.1 The Functioning of PAMS

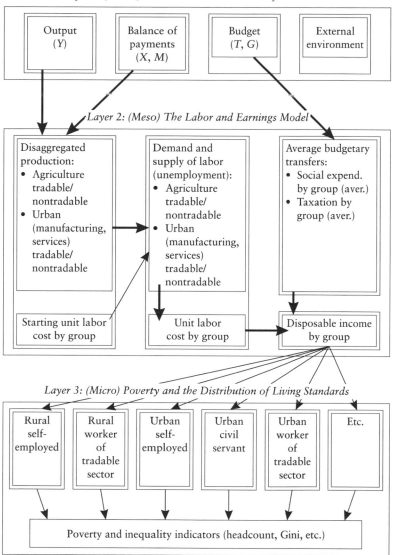

Layer 1: (Macro) Macroeconomic Consistency Framework

| Output (*Y*) | Balance of payments (*X, M*) | Budget (*T, G*) | External environment |

Layer 2: (Meso) The Labor and Earnings Model

Disaggregated production:
- Agriculture tradable/nontradable
- Urban (manufacturing, services) tradable/nontradable

Demand and supply of labor (unemployment):
- Agriculture tradable/nontradable
- Urban (manufacturing, services) tradable/nontradable

Average budgetary transfers:
- Social expend. by group (aver.)
- Taxation by group (aver.)

Starting unit labor cost by group

Unit labor cost by group

Disposable income by group

Layer 3: (Micro) Poverty and the Distribution of Living Standards

| Rural self-employed | Rural worker of tradable sector | Urban self-employed | Urban civil servant | Urban worker of tradable sector | Etc. |

Poverty and inequality indicators (headcount, Gini, etc.)

group will be the same as the change for the group itself. Hence the income distribution within each of the representative household groups remains constant. Therefore, the income of each individual or family unit of the household survey can be projected using the group-specific rate of income growth and the average tax and budgetary transfer accruing to the group. It is assumed that there are no "leakages" in public spending (in contrast to the assumption described in chapter 9). After projecting individual incomes, PAMS calculates the incidence of poverty and intergroup inequality.

Naturally, the third layer of PAMS can be used independently as a stand-alone tool of incidence analysis. For each representative group, one can set exogenously (that is, without using a macroeconomic framework) the uniform growth of labor income and changes in other sources of income. Then the third, micro layer of PAMS can use this information in the country-specific household survey to project individual incomes and calculate the incidence of poverty and intergroup inequality as before.

A few important features and caveats need to be well understood and kept in mind when using PAMS. First, to construct a linkage between a macroeconomically consistent framework and the household survey, it is necessary to select a few appropriate "linkage aggregate variables," or LAVs, from the macroeconomic model (by disaggregating its projected output level into different economic sectors) and to inject this information into the household survey data (rearranged by representative household groups). The LAVs used by PAMS are GDP, GDP and employment by economic sectors, the general price level, the overall tax revenue, the overall budgetary transfers to households, and the noninterest public expenditure level. Data in the household survey also need to be extracted in a specific format (that is, income and expenditure and the occupation of the head of the household). The number of representative groups corresponds to a breakdown by economic sectors that reflects the structure of the economy being analyzed.

Second, PAMS works in a mechanical top-down fashion. The decomposition of GDP into its sectoral components and the accuracy with which it depicts—at the top—the functioning of the economy is key to determining the accuracy—at the bottom—of its poverty and distributional analysis.

Third, if the macroeconomic framework running on top of PAMS does not take into account some degree of substitution between factors of production caused by relative price changes, PAMS will not capture any change that affects both sectoral output and relative factor prices, resulting in a substitution between factors of production.[3] Most of the action in PAMS happens through changes in sectoral output levels. This analysis can explore the extent to which different sectoral growth patterns are "pro-poor," that is, which sectoral growth patterns will affect economic sectors and representative household groups that employ relatively more poor people. However, the different sectoral output levels are projected to be simply consistent in terms of national accounting.

Fourth, and finally, the labor market in the second layer of PAMS, which is key to transforming macroeconomic variables into factor prices, is kept very simple. For instance, each sector of activity uses one category of workers only; there is no mobility of workers between sectors; the unit labor cost level for workers is determined by historical trend or government intervention; and the rental price of land and capital is obtained as a residual, without consideration given to the demand for these factors of production. Although these features have the advantage of keeping the model simple, they also constitute its limitations. These limitations are particularly relevant to the analysis of second-round effects of reforms that involve sub-stitution of production factors. Traditional CGE models (such as those discussed in chapter 15) tend to have a richer factor demand module, involving imperfect elasticity of substitution between cate-gories of workers, and factors of production more generally, at the sectoral level.

Structure of the PAMS Framework

As explained above and portrayed in figure 11.1, PAMS has three layers:

• a top, macroeconomic layer where a macroeconomic frame-work imposes overall consistency;
• an intermediate, mesoeconomic layer describing both the func-tional distribution of income and various redistributive mechanisms linked to the budgetary policies; and
• a bottom, microeconomic or household layer that reflects the most recent size distribution of income and is used to predict the distributional and poverty impact of events taking place in the top two layers of the economy.

Layer 1 (Macro): The Macroeconomic Framework

The macroeconomic framework is described by equations 11.1 through 11.4 in box 11.1. It provides consistency in national accounts and predicts, at an aggregate level, the changes in key macroeconomic variables such as the production of goods and ser-vices, or gross domestic product (Y), public expenditure (G), overall taxes (T), private consumption (C), savings and investment (I), the balance of payments (exports, X, and imports, IM) and the aggregate price level (p) that is used to project the poverty line (z). The fiscal deficit ($T–G$) has to be financed by some sort of increase in domes-tic financial liabilities (here a full monetization, ΔM). The current account deficit $(X-M)$ has to be financed by some sort of an increase in external financial liabilities (here a change in reserves, ΔR). The aggregate price level can be calculated in a variety of ways: in most macroeconomic frameworks usually correlated to changes in aggregate demand (such as gross domestic product, ΔY) and some measure of the money supply (ΔM).

Layer 2 (Meso): The Labor and Earnings Model

The meso, or second, layer is summarized by equations 11.5 through 11.10 in box 11.1. This layer models the labor demand and earnings that simulate the functioning of a simplified labor market (this may be modeled and calibrated econometrically with country-specific time-series or using parameters estimated in cross-section; see Fallon and Verry 1988). The meso framework disaggregates Y into

• m adequate sectoral real components (y_k) (equation 11.5), used in modeling labor demand (L_k);
• m components (G_k) of average nominal public spending (equation 11.6), accruing to each of the m representative groups;
• m components (T_k) of average nominal taxes (equation 11.7), paid by each of the households in each of the m representative groups.

PAMS features taxes, transfers, and social expenditures (consistent with the macroeconomic model and the government's budget constraint in the macroeconomic framework). Each household in its representative group pays general taxes (on consumption, income, and so forth). Each household in its representative group also receives lump sum budgetary transfers from the government's budget. The government is not capable of targeting the transfers and therefore simply provides them on a per capita basis. For each of the country's m representative groups (along the lines of a macroconsistent incidence analysis, for example), the user of PAMS can establish the average transfers or average taxation of that specific group using a country-specific average tax or average transfer rate. These instruments determine the disposable income of each of the m representative groups.

A classic procedure (see Agénor, Izquierdo, and Fofack 2001) at the meso level is to decompose Y into rural and urban GDPs; within each component, the formal sector is then distinguished from the informal sector; and within each one of these sectors, tradable goods are distinguished from nontradable goods. The economic relevance of the breakdown is key in linking each economic sector of the production side of PAMS to a specific segment of the labor market. In

Box 11.1 Key Equations of the Three Layers of the PAMS Framework

Layer 1 (Macro): The Macroeconomic Framework (NA, BOP, fiscal, general price level)

11.1 $\quad Y_t = C_t + I_t + G_t + \left(X_t - IM_t\right)$

11.2 $\quad \left(X_t - IM_t\right) = \Delta R_t$

11.3 $\quad \left(T_t - G_t\right) = \Delta M_t$

11.4 $\quad p_t = f\left(\overline{p_t}, \Delta Y_t, \Delta M_t \text{ etc.}\right)$

Layer 2 (Meso): The Labor and Earnings Model

11.5 $\quad Y_t = p_t \sum_k y_{k,t}$

11.6a $\quad G_t = \sum_k G_{k,t}$

11.6b $\quad G_{k,t} = L^s_{k,t}\left(G_t / L^s_t\right)$

11.7a $\quad T_t = \sum_k T_{k,t}$

11.7b $\quad T_{k,t} = L^s_{k,t}\left(T_t / L^s_t\right)$

11.8a $\quad DINC_{k,t} = \left(p_t w_{k,t}\right)L^d_{k,t} - T_{k,t} + G_{k,t} + \overline{OINC_{k,t}}$

11.8b $\quad \sum_k DINC_{k,t} = Y_t - T_t$

11.9a $\quad L^d_{k,t} = \kappa^d_k y^\alpha_{k,t} w^{-\beta}_{k,t}$

11.9b $\quad L^s_{k,t} = L^s_{k,t-1}\left(1+n\right) - \overline{MIGR_{k,t}}$

11.9c $\quad L^s_t = \theta_t\left(POP_t\right) = \sum_k L^s_{k,t}$

11.10 $\quad w_{k,t} = \eta_k \overline{w_k}^{-\varepsilon}\left(\dfrac{L^d_{k,t}}{L^s_{k,t}}\right)^{-\delta}_{k,t}$

Layer 3 (Micro): Poverty and the Distribution of Living Standards

11.11 $\quad P0_t = f\left(POP_t, L^d_{k,t}, dinc_{k,t}, \overline{z_t}\right)$

11.12 $\quad GINI_t = f\left(L^d_{k,t}, dinc_{k,t}\right)$

11.13 $\quad \overline{z_t} = \overline{z_{t-1}}\left(1+p_t\right)$

the modeling of the production side of PAMS, national account identities ensure cross-sectoral consistency with the aggregate gross domestic product (Y) that is determined at the macro level. In other words, it is simply necessary to determine residually the production of one subsector (for example, the urban informal sector, or the rural subsistence sector). The simplest way to determine the tradable portion of the formal rural and urban sectors is to look at the export data (manufacturing and basic commodities, for example) at the aggregate level. The projected level of activity for each tradable sector usually depends on foreign demand and the real exchange rate as determined by the aggregate domestic and foreign price levels. Then a simple way to model the rest of the urban and rural economy would need to be found and set in the model (for example, simple elasticities of output to factors of production can be used).

Labor demand (equation 11.9a) is broken down by k sectoral components. Even though each sector may employ both skilled and unskilled labor, PAMS assumes that each sector employs only one kind of labor. Thus, there is no substitution between types of labor in the production process except for the exogenous migration described earlier.[4] Demand for labor in the kth sector (L_k) depends on the level of activity in the kth sector (y_k) and on the kth sector's real unit labor cost (w_k). The labor supply for each group k (in equation 11.9b) is driven by demographic considerations (an exogenous growth rate for each group that relates to total labor supply) and exogenous migrations of labor from one representative group into another.[5] Total labor supply (equation 11.9c) depends on a participation rate θ. As a result the unemployed workers (the difference between supply and demand of labor in each sector) implicitly remain in their sector of origin. Since PAMS does not model occupational choices inside each representative group, the unemployed cannot be identified at the household level. However, PAMS determines the total labor income in each group that accrues only to active workers. Accordingly it corrects the group's labor income by weighting the disposable income of households in each representative group by the relative size of the active workers in the group. In each period, this weight is recalculated, meaning that the unemployed in each period are reposted in the sector's labor market.

PAMS (equation 11.8a) determines the level of disposable income in the kth sector ($DINC_k$) as the sum of labor income, average per capita taxes (T_k/L_k), per capita transfers (G_k/L_k), and other, exogenous, average sector-specific nonlabor income ($OINC_k$). To account for the changes in the relative share of each representative group in the total labor force caused by changes in employment levels across the groups, PAMS reweights the individual labor income in each of the k sectors by the number of employed individuals in the sector divided by total labor supply of that sector (equation 11.9b). As a result the labor income of the unemployed is implicitly assumed not to grow.

The real labor income (equation 11.10) in each of the k sectors (w_k) is determined by a sector-specific general trend $\bar{w}_k$ and by the level of unemployment in the *same* sector. This general trend should be such that the level of unemployment in each sector remains approximately constant. There is, however, a "scale" in trend labor income levels across sectors, starting from a low bottom in the rural nontradable sectors moving up to the top urban tradable sector and the civil service, that corresponds to a sector-specific return.

The excess of total disposable income $(Y-T)$ generated in the economy over total labor income represents profits that are included in other incomes. In other words, the difference between income taken from the national accounts and income calculated from household survey data is assigned to a class of rentiers (equation 11.8b). PAMS does not track down financial assets and their returns. However, the interest revenue from the macroeconomic framework can conceivably be redistributed to various socioeconomic groups according to some rule. Because the inequality indicator in PAMS is an intergroup Gini coefficient, the level and growth rate of profits is important.[6]

Layer 3 (Micro): Poverty and the Distribution of Living Standards

Knowing the disposable income received by each representative group allows the projection of income of each household or individual in the household survey. One needs to assume—as explained above—that the income or expenditure of each individual shifts in exactly the same proportion as it does for the representative group to which the individual belongs.

Prices are an important linkage variable from the macroeconomic to the microeconomic layers of PAMS. The aggregate price level, p, of the macroeconomic framework applies to the calculation of nominal disposable incomes in equation 11.5 and to the determination of how the poverty line, z, shifts in equation 11.13 (although p is not specifically a consumption price).

The poverty headcount P_0 can be calculated (equation 11.11) once PAMS has established both the disposable income ($DINC$) of each individual in the household survey and the poverty line z. The number of poor is computed from the projected disposable incomes compared with the projected poverty line. In parallel, the intergroup inequality (a Gini coefficient) is computed using the disposable incomes of each of the representative groups of the PAMS (equation 11.12). However, to account for structural changes in the economy, coming from changes in the sectoral composition of the labor force (by representative group), its allocation across sectors (sectoral labor demand), and the relative shifts in the structure of production, PAMS reweights the number of households belonging to each group from the original household survey to reflect the sectoral structure of production and employment in the simulated scenario.

Building and Running PAMS

Six steps must be followed to use PAMS.

Step 1: Data Requirement and Processing

PAMS is conceived as a shell that can host data from any typical developing country. The minimum data requirement consists of the data necessary to construct a macroconsistency framework (such as national accounts broken down into m economic sectors), employment data (by the same m economic sectors), and a household survey.

The minimum data at the macroeconomic level can come from any typical national accounts consistency framework: aggregate GDP decomposed by the relevant m sectors mentioned before (including an exogenous public sector and balance-of-payments data on exports of agricultural and manufacturing goods); aggregate public expenditure G decomposed by the relevant m representative group beneficiaries mentioned earlier, possibly simply proportionally to their population or income size; and aggregate taxes T decomposed by the relevant m group taxpayers, as mentioned earlier.

PAMS is constructed to accommodate various degrees of complexity in modeling the functioning of the macroeconomy. One can decide to keep the simplicity of macroeconomic consistency frameworks used in many public and private agencies (such as the RMSM-Xs of the World Bank, the Financial Programming frameworks of the International Monetary Fund, or other typical macroconsistency models).

PAMS also requires a "good" household survey that includes information about household expenditure and income, as well as the employment status and the sector of occupation for the head of the household (which allows one to allocate the household into a specific production sector, see box 11.2). There is an alternative to the method currently used by PAMS, in which changes in labor forces net incomes are transformed into changes in poverty.[7] PAMS requires "mining" household data sets.

Box 11.2 Mining a Household Data Set for PAMS Categories

This box describes the basic steps involved in organizing the available information from a household survey to fit the PAMS framework. Given the emphasis on earnings, it is important that the household survey have a labor module as well, with sufficiently detailed (and reliable) information on the employment status of individuals, the economic sector (such as agriculture, industry, services) and the institutional sector (public, private, formal, informal) of employment, earnings, and benefits. This information is then combined with that from other modules of the survey such as geodemographic data (area of residence, age, gender, and so forth), education, and expenditures.

In principle the data may be processed either at the individual or household level. The real constraint is that some modules of the household survey provide household-level data (such as expenditures), while others provide information at the individual level. Because the household is generally chosen as the unit of analysis, individual level information must be aggregated up to the household level, and socioeconomic groups created on the basis of the characteristics of the head of household. Clearly this approach leads to coarser results than the one based on relevant individual-level information.

After the necessary data have been pulled into a master file, one can then create basic binary variables along the dimensions of interest. These might include, for example, working versus not working, rural versus urban, public versus private, formal versus informal, tradable versus nontradable, and skilled versus unskilled. PAMS categories are subsets of the cross-product (in the sense of Cartesian product) of these elemental variables. To conduct the analysis at the individual level, household-level variables must be converted by dividing them by the household size. The extraction technique is supported by an EViews program that exports the data to Excel.

In its current version, PAMS' proposed method for mining data sets involves the following steps. First, data on each household are analyzed to determine the household characteristics needed for the creation of socioeconomic groups. Second, a variable is computed that measures the disposable income or consumption of each of the households whose head belongs to the same category of workers. Third, this variable is adjusted by the change in the income of the corresponding representative group category. Fourth, all households are pooled together again, and poverty indicators are computed based on the adjusted income or consumption variable.

With the same basic information, and a comparable mining effort, the following strategy could be considered. First, the income of each household is decomposed into its main sources, according to the factor prices considered in the PAMS (such as labor by sector, land, and capital). This decomposition should take into account the labor earnings of other family members apart from the household head as well as earnings resulting from any household business or farm. Second, the income from each of the sources is adjusted to reflect the change in the corresponding factors of production, resulting from the PAMS. Third, the income or consumption of the household is adjusted in the same proportion as its total income, as computed in the previous step. And fourth, poverty and inequality indicators are computed based on the adjusted consumption variable.

The household survey needs to be the most recent one so as to match the most recent macroeconomic data. Alternatively, one can update an old data set—using available information on prices and income and expenditure growth by representative group—to match the latest set of national accounts. The steps described in box 11.2 should be followed. The household survey data are carefully analyzed, and individuals and households are regrouped into representative groups. These groups may be constructed on the basis of the socioeconomic characteristics of the head of the household (other bases for regrouping are also possible). The result of the process needs to be stored in a specific data set.

Step 2: Selecting or Constructing a Simple Macroeconomic Framework

PAMS can use various types of macroeconomic frameworks for its first layer. If none is available, the construction of a simple macroeconomic framework, such as the RMSM-X, involves three key steps. The first is the construction of an accounting framework that imposes consistency on real and financial transactions of agents (flow-of-funds consistency). The second is the specification of behavioral equations and projection rules for the variables (the most famous—and most criticized—one being the usage of a fixed linear relationship to project GDP growth from the ratio of past investment to GDP). The last step entails the choice of residual variables used to satisfy underlying budget and macroeconomic constraints. Such constraints usually take the form of accounting identities.

Step 3: Establishing the Meso Layer: the Labor and Earnings Model

The first task in this third step involves the disaggregation of aggregate production into subsectors (such as rural or urban production, tradable or nontradable goods, and formal or informal activities) to match the labor categories of the representative groups created from the household survey. One of the subsectors has to be modeled as a residual, to ensure consistency with the macroeconomic model.

Once production is disaggregated and projections of sectoral growth are completed for each subsector (minus the residual), one can model the functioning of a segmented labor market. There is only "exogenous" mobility between labor categories (for example, from rural to urban areas) and each sector employs only one specific type of labor (for example, the rural sectors employ only unskilled labor). Sectoral output growth and its sector-specific real unit labor cost—cost that is sensitive to the sector-specific level of unemployment, as in a wage curve specification (following Blanchflower and Oswald 1994)—drive the demand for that sector-specific category of labor. The supply of that specific category of labor is given by demographic and exogenous variables that can mimic policies (for example, migration can be set to mimic expected income differentials as in the Harris-Todaro model). The resulting unemployment levels by category of labor lowers unit labor costs and thus increases the demand for that category of labor. Finally, the relevant elasticities used in the projections can be estimated econometrically outside the model (using, for example, either time-series when available for the country being studied, or a cross-section estimate; see Hamermesh 1993).

Step 4: Establishing a Baseline Scenario

A PAMS user must first construct a macroeconomic scenario using the first layer macroconsistency model. This scenario would comprise, at a minimum, aggregate GDP growth (such as that associated with a program involving policy shifts, and a combination of inflation, fiscal balances, and current account balances; disaggregated sectoral growth combining different paths for growth rates for agricultural or industrial, tradable or nontradable goods sectors within a given aggregate GDP growth rate; rates of general taxation by representative group (within the macroconsistent budget constraint); and different levels of social (budgetary) transfers to different representative groups (within the macroconsistent budget constraint).

PAMS then transmits the macroeconomic baseline scenario to the intermediate layer model to derive the corresponding labor demands and earnings by sectors. The procedure captures the effect of average tax and transfers for households in each of the representative groups. This meso layer produces the disposable income for each group, adding to wage and other nonwage income, the different (average) general tax rates and different (average) budgetary transfers across each of the representative group categories, all consistent with the overall budget.

Finally, running the microeconomic layer, PAMS calculates disposable income growth rates for each representative group category and uses the average, group-specific growth rate to multiply the income of each unit of the household survey belonging to the same group. Each household in its specific category will see its income grow by the average growth rate of its own category. PAMS takes these new levels of income for each household and, using the new poverty line z adjusted by the new price level p, simulates the new poverty headcount and the new level of inequality. It should be noted that the procedure "projects" the new poverty headcounts and the income distribution based on the "old" household survey, reweighted according to the new structure of the economy and its labor market. The pattern of income distribution within a representative group from the most recent household survey is assumed to hold throughout the simulation period. Thus, the simulation process projects the mean income of each of the representative groups in the economy, assuming that there are no changes in the intragroup distribution of income or expenditure.

Step 5: Establishing a Comparison Scenario

Step 4 can be conducted by making marginal changes to any of the following instruments: aggregate GDP growth (caused by a domestic or external shock, for example, or a change in policies); disaggregated sectoral growth (again, caused by a shock or a change in sectoral policies); changes in the rates of general taxation by representative group (within the macroconsistent budget constraint); changes in the levels of social (budgetary) transfers to different representative groups (within the macroconsistent budget constraint); changes in the unit labor cost level in each economic sector; changes in migration of labor between sectors; or changes in the poverty line. Once the new scenario is run, one can compare the results of this scenario with the baseline scenario.

Step 6: Establishing a Target Scenario

One can use the third layer to establish a combination of economic growth rates for representative groups that will attain the country's poverty reduction goal. Then, working backward, one can calculate the required sectoral and overall GDP growth that needs to be achieved to reach the target. Finally, given the country's macroeconomic constraints and the overall macro framework, one could use PAMS to calculate the overall financing required.

An Application to Burkina Faso

Burkina Faso is a poor landlocked country in Sub-Saharan Africa with a limited resource base, high vulnerability to external shocks, and very low human development. Since 1991 the country has embarked upon a comprehensive reform program and has made some headway in its transition toward a market-oriented economy and a more appropriate role for the state. Despite the good progress achieved, the country remains one of the poorest in the world. Real gross national product per capita was estimated at US$230 in 2001.

Poverty Profile and Social Indicators for Burkina Faso

In 1996 and 2000 the government of Burkina Faso issued poverty profiles based on the results of priority surveys conducted in 1994 and 1998. Over this period poverty incidence remained broadly stable (moving from 44.5 percent in 1994 to 45.3 percent in 1998). Rural poverty predominates in Burkina Faso, accounting for 94.5 percent of national poverty, and the incidence of poverty is markedly higher in rural areas (estimated at 45.3 percent in 2002) than in urban areas (28.9 percent). But the incidence of urban poverty increased from 10 percent to 16 percent between 1994 and 1998 and was accompanied by an increase in urban inequality. The analysis of poverty among socioeconomic groups (based on source of income) shows that between 1994 and 1998 the incidence of poverty increased for all groups except cash crop farmers. It is highest among food crop farmers, who account for most of the population living in poverty.

Burkina Faso's Poverty Reduction Strategy Paper (PRSP) sets an ambitious target for the reduction of poverty incidence. [8] The proportion of people below the poverty line is supposed to decline from about 45 percent to 30 percent between 2000 and 2015. In light of recent exogenous cotton price shocks and the continued vulnerability of the Burkinabè economy to other export shocks, this ambitious target may not be attained unless significant efforts are taken to ensure that growth is both sustained and pro-poor. To do that, the government must find an appropriate mix of fiscal, monetary, and public investment policies that can bring the economy to a higher and stable growth path while maintaining an adequate level of consumption, and it must find a sectoral growth composition that provides greater benefits for the poorest representative household groups in the economy (in other words, a composition that is pro-poor in the sense that the income of the poor grows faster than income for other groups (Ravallion 2001).

Although final figures were not available when this chapter was written, real GDP growth was expected to reach an estimated

5.7 percent in 2002. Assuming a normal cereal crop, the primary sector was expected to grow by 3.2 percent. Growth was expected to pick up in the secondary and tertiary sectors (6.6 percent and 7 percent, respectively) as a result of stronger demand linked to the economic recovery. Inflation was forecast to decline to some 2 percent. The current account deficit, excluding current official transfers, was projected to improve to 14.1 percent of GDP, as a result of substantial increases in the volume of cotton harvested in late 2001 but exported in 2002.

The overriding fiscal objective for 2002 and the medium term is to consolidate Burkina Faso's budgetary position. Reaching this objective entails significant efforts to increase fiscal revenues, improve budgetary management, and introduce greater efficiency in public spending to support the government's poverty reduction program. For 2002 fiscal revenue was projected to rebound to 13.8 percent of GDP. Expenditure was forecast to continue to be contained at levels compatible with revenue performance, while social expenditure would continue to increase in 2002. For the medium term, assuming no exogenous shocks and the maintenance of sound economic policies, growth could remain at around 5.5 percent.

Using PAMS in the Construction of a Baseline Scenario for Burkina Faso

PAMS is first used to provide a set of projections for some of the important macroeconomic and (some microeconomic) policy objectives stated in the PRSP, which is supported by an IMF program (PRGF, or Poverty Reduction and Growth Facility) and a series of World Bank credits (three Poverty Reduction Strategy Credits). Are the poverty reduction objectives achievable in the time frame that is contemplated and with the stated policy mix? To illustrate our earlier explanation of PAMS, we use the technique to calibrate a baseline scenario on the macroeconomic assumptions of the PRSP.[9] The main "engine" for poverty reduction in this baseline scenario would be the relatively high levels of growth projected under the macroeconomic framework behind the PRSP (an average of 5.5 percent over the next decade). The poverty line shifts with the overall price level.

Table 11.1 provides medium-term (up to 2010) projections of poverty and social indicators and shows that there could be some progress in the reduction of the poverty headcount over the next decade. Only a relatively minor reduction in the poverty headcount P_0 of 4–5 percent is projected in the first two years, 2002 and 2003, compared with 2000.[10] But then the poverty headcount falls to 37.9 percent in 2004 and to 35.1 percent in 2010, only slightly short of the 30 percent level targeted for 2015. Graphical results of the simulation are given in figure 11.2a, b, and c. The high average

Table 11.1 Poverty Line and Income Distribution, Burkina Faso, 2002–2010

Scenario with: Expenditure–Weighted	2002	2003	2004	2005	2006	2007	2008	2009	2010
Country:									
Poverty line (in LCU/day)	330	334	339	345	355	365	376	387	398
Poverty line (in LCU/year)	79,313	80,190	81,448	82,875	85,209	87,699	90,263	92,904	95,622
Poverty line (in current US$/year)	112	116	118	121	122	124	126	128	129
Total population*	11,593,626	11,923,095	12,261,513	12,608,879	12,966,088	13,331,400	13,705,679	14,089,102	14,483,255
Total labor force	6,555,898	6,742,384	6,933,938	7,130,559	7,332,755	7,539,539	7,751,400	7,968,439	8,191,555
Poor population*	4,991,270	4,852,755	4,646,164	4,534,156	4,590,408	4,716,309	4,838,967	4,960,182	5,086,595
P0 (headcount index) (%)	43.1	40.7	37.9	36.0	35.4	35.4	35.3	35.2	35.1
P1 (poverty gap) (%)	13.0	12.2	10.9	10.2	10.0	9.9	9.9	9.9	9.8
P2 (%)	6.1	5.8	5.3	5.1	5.1	5.2	5.4	5.5	5.6
Gini	0.382	0.392	0.400	0.409	0.417	0.427	0.435	0.444	0.452
Theil	0.246	0.258	0.269	0.281	0.292	0.306	0.319	0.332	0.346
Rural Areas:									
Rural population*	10,023,187	10,329,100	10,643,607	10,966,705	11,299,282	11,639,592	11,988,493	12,346,158	12,714,167
Poor population*	4,537,055	4,424,865	4,237,061	4,132,420	4,198,300	4,337,013	4,469,510	4,601,779	4,737,308
P0 (headcount index) (%)	45.3	42.8	39.8	37.7	37.2	37.3	37.3	37.3	37.3
Gini	0.360	0.357	0.352	0.349	0.345	0.342	0.339	0.336	0.333
Urban Areas:									
Urban population (millions)*	1,570,439	1,593,995	1,617,905	1,642,174	1,666,807	1,691,809	1,717,186	1,742,944	1,769,088
Urban labor force	867,170	907,660	949,472	992,655	1,037,247	1,083,292	1,130,822	1,179,879	1,230,505
Poor population*	454,215	427,890	409,103	401,736	392,108	379,296	369,457	358,403	349,287
P0 (headcount index) (%)	28.9	26.8	25.3	24.5	23.5	22.4	21.5	20.6	19.7
Gini	0.200	0.207	0.213	0.220	0.226	0.233	0.239	0.245	0.251

Note: * Weighted calculations show population (in millions) at the national level. Unweighted calculations show population at the sample level (in units).

Figure 11.2 PAMS Baseline Projections on Poverty in
Burkina Faso, 2002–2010

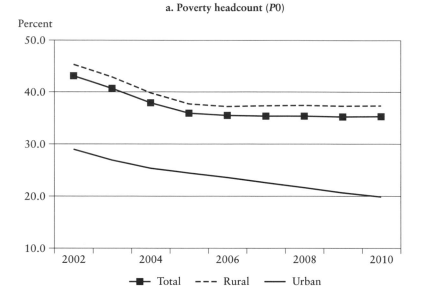

a. Poverty headcount (P0)

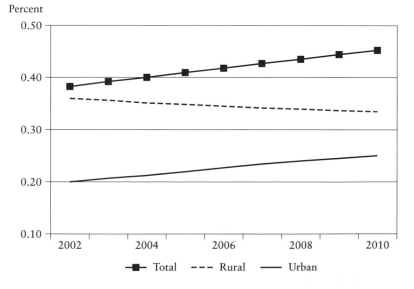

b. Intergroup Gini

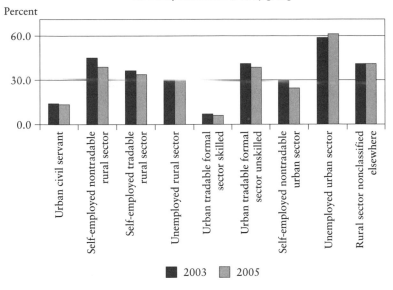

c. Poverty headcount (*P0*) by group

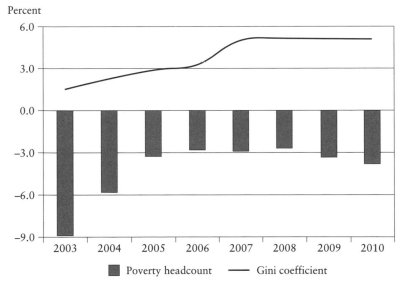

d. Difference baseline minus shock scenario (Côte d'Ivoire crisis) output growth planned in the PRSP during the simulation period (up to 2010) boosts average nominal income from about Franc CFA 100,000 to more than CFA 140,000, contributing to the fall in the poverty headcount.

The rise in average income and the fall in poverty is accompanied by some less positive signs. The baseline scenario projects an increase in urban inequality measured by the Gini, which increases from about 0.20 to 0.25 in 2010. That explains the overall increase in the projected national intergroup Gini for both the rural and urban areas, which rises from 0.39 in 2003 to 0.45 in 2010. Therefore, what this simulation shows is that if sectoral growth and income distribution follows the current projected baseline scenario, income poverty in Burkina Faso will decline—although not enough to meet the 2015 target—at the expense of a significant increase in inequality.

Finally, the projected baseline scenario in PAMS shows that poverty varies across socioeconomic groups (table 11.2). Although predominantly a rural phenomenon, poverty can reach very high levels (over 60 percent) among the unemployed in urban areas. Hence the projection demonstrates the need for additional thinking about complementary policies that could help achieve the PRSP objectives and lower poverty in specific areas and among specific groups.

Construction of a Sensitivity Analysis Scenario for Burkina Faso with PAMS

Another important question is how realistic the GDP growth projections in the baseline scenario are. Given the past volatility of GDP growth in Burkina Faso (in particular, the volatility of cotton prices, its main export product), reliance on strong output growth to achieve the PRSP objectives is risky. For example, figure 11.2d shows the increase in poverty and inequality caused by a negative output shock of –3.2 percent in 2003, –1.7 percent in 2004, and –0.7 percent in 2005 as a consequence of the 2002–03 political crisis in neighboring Côte d'Ivoire. The shock also entails a 5 percent decline in external demand for the country's exports. We assume that both shocks are sustained (that is, there is no subsequent recovery compared with the base case). Even if the only socioeconomic effects of what appears to be a serious regional crisis are the ones mentioned above, the attainment of the poverty reduction objective becomes quite problematic. By the end of 2005, the poverty headcount would still hover around 39 percent overall, instead of 36 percent as in the base scenario, and reach a high of 41 percent in rural areas.

This type of analysis illustrates the fragility of social progress in a country such as Burkina Faso. Unfortunately, the likelihood of

Table 11.2 Occupational Categories, Representative Groups

HHS categories: Calculated with: Expenditure–Weighted	Urban Civil Servant	Self-Employed Nontradable Rural Sector	Self-Employed Tradable Rural Sector	Unemployed Rural Sector	Urban Tradable Formal Sector Skilled	Urban Tradable Formal Sector Unskilled	Self-Employed Nontradable Urban Sector	Unemployed Urban Sector	Rural sector Non-Classified Elsewhere
	UG-2	RP-5	RP-6	RPX-7	UP-8	UP-9	UP-12	UPX-16	RN-17
2003									
Poverty line (in LCU/day)	550	301	301	301	550	550	550	550	301
Poverty line (in LCU/year)	132,010	72,193	72,193	72,193	132,010	132,010	132,010	132,010	72,193
Avg exp/inc of group	675	68	65	340	967	662	478	276	194
Income gap of group	35.5%	29.8%	28.4%	18.5%	20.1%	30.9%	31.9%	43.0%	29.5%
Population, total	480,883	7,824,417	2,009,000	68,114	112,501	224,734	648,350	127,828	427,569
Population of poor	65,926	3,507,928	723,798	19,985	7,281	91,368	188,737	74,578	173,153
P0 (head count index)	13.7%	44.8%	36.0%	29.3%	6.5%	40.7%	29.1%	58.3%	40.5%
P1	4.9%	13.3%	10.2%	5.4%	1.3%	12.6%	9.3%	25.1%	11.9%
P2	2.6%	6.4%	4.8%	1.8%	0.4%	6.0%	4.4%	14.5%	5.7%
2004									
Poverty line (in LCU/day)	559	306	306	306	559	559	559	559	306
Poverty line (in LCU/year)	134,255	73,421	73,421	73,421	134,255	134,255	134,255	134,255	73,421
Avg exp/inc of group	688	71	66	339	1,030	686	507	274	191
Income gap of group	35.3%	28.7%	27.3%	17.8%	18.5%	30.4%	30.9%	43.4%	29.5%
Population, total	488,096	8,062,660	2,070,171	70,188	114,188	228,105	657,771	129,746	440,588
Population of poor	65,361	3,320,425	717,617	20,593	6,303	87,121	174,622	75,697	178,425
P0 (head count index)	13.4%	41.2%	34.7%	29.3%	5.5%	38.2%	26.5%	58.3%	40.5%
P1	4.7%	11.8%	9.5%	5.2%	1.0%	11.6%	8.2%	25.3%	11.9%
P2	2.5%	5.7%	4.5%	1.7%	0.3%	5.5%	3.8%	14.9%	5.8%

continued

255

Table 11.2 Occupational Categories, Representative Groups (Continued)

HHS categories: Calculated with Expenditure–Weighted	Urban Civil Servant UG-2	Self-Employed Nontradable Rural Sector RP-5	Self-Employed Tradable Rural Sector RP-6	Unemployed Rural Sector RPX-7	Urban Tradable Formal Sector Skilled UP-8	Urban Tradable Formal Sector Unskilled UP-9	Self-Employed Nontradable Urban Sector UP-12	Unemployed Urban Sector UPX-16	Rural sector Non-Classified Elsewhere RN-17
2005									
Poverty line (in LCU/day)	570	312	312	312	570	570	570	570	312
Poverty line (in LCU/year)	136,782	74,803	74,803	74,803	136,782	136,782	136,782	136,782	74,803
Avg exp/inc of group	701	73	66	335	1,096	713	537	272	189
Income gap of group	34.7%	28.2%	27.0%	17.6%	13.6%	28.2%	29.6%	42.3%	29.5%
Population, total	495,418	8,307,410	2,133,013	72,319	115,901	231,526	667,637	131,692	453,962
Population of poor	65,536	3,213,114	714,246	21,219	6,397	87,557	162,385	79,861	183,842
P0 (head count index)	13.2%	38.7%	33.5%	29.3%	5.5%	37.8%	24.3%	60.6%	40.5%
P1	4.6%	10.9%	9.0%	5.2%	0.8%	10.7%	7.2%	25.7%	11.9%
P2	2.5%	5.4%	4.5%	1.8%	0.2%	5.1%	3.3%	15.4%	6.0%

events such as the one in 2002 affecting Côte d'Ivoire is not low, whether it is produced by political crisis, negative terms-of-trade shocks, foreign demand shocks, or all of the above. The current crisis in Côte d'Ivoire can produce in 2003-04 an increase in the poverty headcount in Burkina Faso of 6-9 percent and an increase in inequality, as measured by the Gini coefficient, of 2 to 3 percentage points.

Construction of a "Flat" Scenario for Burkina Faso with PAMS

The baseline scenario—projecting an average GDP growth of 5 percent over the next decade or so—can be considered optimistic. It is therefore useful to use the PAMS framework to check the room for maneuvering around this growth rate. Is there a way out? We define in this section a new base case with 0 percent GDP and income growth for all agents throughout the simulation period. Poverty and inequality also remain identical to their 2000 values (43.1 percent for P_0 and 38.2 percent for the intergroup Gini). We want to find adjustments and policy instruments that will reduce poverty while at the same time controlling the rise of inequality. PAMS has two instruments to do this (we assume that these instruments can be implemented within the existing sociopolitical context, that is, that lump-sum changes in taxes and transfers could be achieved with few transaction costs assuming some participation from all parties in civil society through some sort of a social compact).

We choose to use lump-sum transfers, and we construct a hypothetical sensitivity scenario for the new base (with zero GDP and income growth) along the following lines. We project an increase in social spending by reducing, say, military expenditures or general and nonassignable expenditures by 1 percent every year and allocating the resulting savings to a targeted transfer (say, a social fund) to the poorest groups in Burkina-Faso: the self-employed in the rural nontradable sector. As an example, in 2003, the transfer amount (a 1 percent savings from all current public expenditures other than wages) represents about 1,789 million LCUs (local currency units). Each of the 7,368,145 individuals of this group (recall that these are lump-sum average transfers that can reach only one representative household group at a time) would receive 243 LCUs a year or about 0.66 LCUs a day. That means each individual, including the 3,624,908 who are counted as poor in this group, will have the average daily income of 67 LCUs increase by about 1 percent.

PAMS simulates this new counterfactual scenario. Given the characteristics of this representative group in Burkina Faso (that is, with roughly three-fourths of the country's 4.9 million poor in this group), we get the expected reduction in poverty despite the untargeted nature of this kind of lump-sum transfer. The overall poverty headcount declines by 1 percent a year. Overall, by 2010, about half a million people are lifted out of poverty. This kind of exercise can be replicated with various representative groups and combinations of lump-sum tax and budgetary transfers.

Conclusion and Some Limitations of the PAMS Approach

Three caveats about the PAMS approach must be mentioned. First, PAMS is constrained by the macroeconomic framework implied by the macroeconomic model chosen for the first layer. In that sense, it inherits the strengths and weaknesses of the particular model selected. If the model is a simple macroeconomic accounting (RMSM-X) type of framework, it will have inherent limitations such as the absence of relative price effects on the production side of the economy. Thus the simulation of alternative sectoral growth stories will only be as good as the macroeconomic sectoral framework that is used.

The second caveat comes from the assumption used to determine income (wages, transfers) for each socioeconomic group. The simulations assume that the mean income growth of each representative group affects homogeneously all households in that particular group (that is, there are no changes in the intragroup distribution of income) and moreover that there are no changes in the composition of the population of each group. For example, there is no endogenous shift between workers from one representative group to another for those households that could migrate from one to another given their characteristics and the incentives provided by relative income growth rates.

Third, the framework assumes simple labor demand functions that are sector- and skill-specific. It is equivalent to assuming a homogeneous labor factor with different, sector-specific remuneration.

In conclusion, PAMS can be viewed as a first-order approximation in linking alternative growth and labor-demand scenarios to household survey data. The framework shows that the results that can be obtained from cross-section regressions—where aggregate growth "by definition reduces poverty" (by the sign of the estimated elasticity of growth to P_0)—can sometimes hide contrasting situations in terms of where (rural-urban) poverty is reduced, and whether growth is accompanied by an increase or a decrease of inequality. Although the simulations shown here are simple, they illustrate well the usefulness of the model in policy dialogue and in the design and evaluation of economic policies.

Notes

1. When the group is the entire population, we have the general aggregate analysis shown in Bourguignon (2002).

2. For the typical "work horse" models used by the International Monetary Fund and the World Bank to conduct macroeconomic projections, see World Bank (1994).

3. For example, land reform would produce, supposedly, an increase in agricultural output, and this is the way PAMS would capture it. With a given elasticity of labor demand in the rural sector, the output increase could yield an increase in the demand for labor and, for a given supply, an increase in the corresponding wage level. This would be the simple story considered by the PAMS, but the true story could be more complex. The redistribution of land increases productivity by changing incentives. It also yields a positive land rent, accruing to the farmers. The increase in productivity could be translated into an increase in output. But the emergence of a new factor price, and the transfer of the usage of this factor to farmers, could have an effect on the demand for other factors of production that would be neglected by PAMS.

4. Precluding any substitution between skilled and unskilled labor within sectors can be interpreted as using one (homogeneous) labor input, whose return differs depending on the sector of occupation.

5. The migration movements, however, could be made compatible with a rationale à la Harris-Todaro (depending upon expected wage differentials across sectors).

6. Reconciling disposable income is a well-known difficulty when one compares income data from national accounts and household surveys. PAMS implicitly assumes that the discrepancy accrues to rentiers and capitalists only.

7. Suggested by Martin Rama. Problems might arise if the information at the individual household level does not break down income by sources other than wage.

8. Poverty Reduction Strategy Papers (PRSPs) are the new general policy documents elaborated by the governments of developing countries that want to access concessional resources from the International Monetary Fund and the World Bank. The PRSPs replaced in 1999-2000 the Policy Framework Papers written by the staff of the IMF and the World Bank in consultation with governments.

9. For more details, see Pereira da Silva, Essama-Nssah, and Samaké (2002).

10. Note that the departure 2000 number for the poverty headcount is a projection from the 1998 actual number (from the 1998 household survey). There could be a *difference* between the projected and actual poverty headcount in 2002, which will only be known when the 2002-03 household survey results become available. The 2000 number (45 percent) used by PAMS as the initial poverty headcount is the current best estimate and matches official projections. There are also other minor differences between the way the government projects its own poverty line over the simulation period, and PAMS' indexation of its two poverty lines to the RMSM-X inflation rate measured by the consumer price index.

References

The word *processed* describes informally reproduced works that may not be commonly available through library systems.

Agénor, Pierre-Richard, Alejandro Izquierdo, and Hippolyte Fofack. 2000. "IMMPA: A Quantitative Macroeconomic Framework for the Analysis of Poverty Reduction Strategies." World Bank Institute, Washington, D.C. Processed. (www.worldbank.org/wbi/macroeconomics/modeling/immpa.htm)

Blanchflower, D., and A. Oswald. 1994. *The Wage Curve*. Cambridge, Mass.: MIT Press.

Bourguignon, François. 2003. "The Growth Elasticity of Poverty Reduction: Explaining Heterogeneity across Countries and Time Periods." In T. Eicher and S. Turnovsky, eds., *Inequality and Growth*. Cambridge, Mass.: MIT Press.

Fallon Peter R., and D. Verry. 1988. *The Economics of Labor Markets*. Oxford, U.K.: Philip Allan.

Hamermesh, Daniel S. 1993. *Labor Demand*. Princeton, N.J.: Princeton University Press.

Pereira da Silva, Luiz, B. Essama-Nssah, and Issouf Samaké. 2002. "A Poverty Analysis Macroeconomic Simulator (PAMS): Linking Household Surveys with Macro-models." Working Paper 2888. World Bank, DEC-PREM (Poverty Reduction and Economic Management Network), Washington, D.C. Processed.

Ravallion, Martin. 2001. "Growth, Inequality and Poverty: Looking Beyond Averages." Policy Research Working Paper 2558. World Bank, Development Research Group, Washington, D.C. Processed.

World Bank. 1994. *User's Guide, World Bank RMSM-X*. Washington, D.C.

12

Partial Equilibrium
Multimarket Analysis

Jehan Arulpragasam and Patrick Conway

This chapter presents a technique that links household incomes and expenditures to changes in a limited number of markets in an economy. Hence it uses partial equilibrium analysis of changes in prices and quantities in markets affected by a change in economic policies.

Analysts charged with providing ex ante estimates of the impact of policy reform on the incidence and depth of poverty know that the phrase *ceteris paribus,* or all else being equal, can be an especially worrisome part of the analysis. The reason is simple: each policy reform has both direct effects and indirect effects on wages, prices, and private income. These indirect effects alter the incidence and depth of changes in poverty attributable to the policy reform. If the analyst reports estimates of policy effects that are derived for unchanging wages, prices, and private income, the estimates will be biased in unknown directions.

There have been two dominant responses to this conundrum in the policy analysis literature, and each is well-represented in this volume. One response has been to create sophisticated computable general equilibrium (CGE) models of the economies in question, with goods and factor markets modeled explicitly and wages, prices, and private income determined endogenously (see chapters 13 and 15). Although these models meet the *ceteris paribus* critique head-on, they have large data requirements and are quite involved to develop. The second response has been to assume away the indirect effects through benefit incidence studies of the direct effect in isolation—to take *all else being equal* literally. This response has the advantages of simplicity and relatively small data demands, but it retains the disadvantage of assuming away potentially large indirect effects.

Multimarket models are intermediate responses to this conundrum. Whether they are called *limited general equilibrium* as in Mosley (1999) or *multimarket partial equilibrium* as in Arulpragasam and del Ninno (1996) these models focus the analysis on the combination of direct and indirect effects through price and quantity changes in a small group of commodities or factors with strong interlinked supply and demand. They are most appropriate for the evaluation of policies that change the relative price of a specific good—for example, the removal of a subsidy or the elimination of a tariff or quota. The indirect effects explicitly modeled are those attributable to relative price responsiveness of demand and supply in markets for substitute goods.

These models are improvements over the benefit incidence studies: the indirect effects of the policy reform on poverty are explicitly traced through the supply and demand responses for substitute and complement goods. By endogenizing prices through the equating of supply and demand in key markets, this approach goes a step beyond standard benefit incidence analysis that sets elasticities to zero. Multimarket models fall short of the general equilibrium models: the impacts of policy reform on government budgets and on prices and quantities outside the group explicitly considered are treated as unchanged. In short, the *ceteris paribus* restriction is relaxed, but not eliminated, in the analysis. This class of models is most useful in analysis when the policy reform under consideration is targeted to one commodity or factor for which there is a well-defined set of close substitutes or complements.

The Technique

The use of multimarket models in the economic development context can probably be traced to the estimation of agricultural household models in the 1980s. These were integrated models of production and consumption of multiple crops by agricultural households and were estimated econometrically on agricultural sector surveys. The multimarket models of the 1980s, such as those used in the World Bank–sponsored research of Braverman and Hammer (1986, and succeeding papers with various co-authors), expanded this basis to include nonagricultural demands for these crops and a definition of market equilibrium for each crop. Although the treatment of the nonagricultural actors in the economy was rudimentary at first, the growing availability of Living Standards Measurement Study Surveys has made accurate modeling possible in both agricultural and nonagricultural sectors. Sadoulet and de Janvry (1995) provide an introduction to this technique. They also compare the data requirements and computational difficulty of multimarket models to both agricultural household and CGE models.

Multimarket models have grown markedly in detail and sophistication since those early efforts. The early analyses focused on the substitution effects among a small number of agricultural products in household demand in response to relative price changes, using demand and supply elasticities culled from others' work. The more recent analyses, such as Dorosh, del Ninno, and Sahn (1995) and Minot and Goletti (1998), have introduced market-clearing conditions in a greater number of goods, sophisticated econometric estimation of demand and supply parameters, and an explicit consideration of the link between policy reform and poverty. These more recent analyses have also gone beyond reform of a price-based policy to consider quantity restrictions in markets, technological improvements, and internal trading restrictions. The spatial multimarket analysis of Minot and Goletti (1998) extends the concept of markets to include arbitrage conditions in individual goods across geographic regions, thus admitting the possibility of partially integrated markets in a single commodity.

With a multimarket model, the analyst expands traditional benefit incidence analysis to capture the induced substitution effects across selected goods in response to policy reform. The procedure has four steps:

- First, the analyst begins with the policy reform to be evaluated. She identifies the market (or markets) in which this policy reform will have its direct effect. She also identifies (through data examination, survey of experts, or other prior knowledge) those markets strongly interlinked in demand or supply with the markets in which the direct effect is measured.
- Second, household survey information is used to derive estimates of income and own-price and cross-price elasticities of demand for the entire set of interlinked markets. Producer survey information is used to derive estimates of own-price and cross-price elasticities of supply for the set of interlinked markets. These estimates are combined to create a system of demand and supply functions.
- Third, market closure (either price- or quantity-clearing) is imposed for each good in the system of equations. This closure is made consistent with the observed macroeconomic outcomes

through requiring the resulting equilibrium to duplicate international relative prices and trade flows in each good and other national statistics for the base year chosen. The impact of the policy reform in this system of equations is then calculated by introducing the desired policy change. Relative prices and quantities produced and consumed domestically are derived for this new equilibrium.

• Fourth, the derived relative prices and quantities are combined with household survey information, in which households can be consumers and producers, to determine the marginal impact of the policy reform on the incidence and depth of poverty.

Data Requirements for the Technique

The data requirements for a multimarket analysis of the impact of policy reform can be thought of as an extension of the data requirement for standard incidence analysis. The following are needed:

• A defined poverty line and a disaggregated set of data on income or consumption distribution across households to measure the incidence and depth of poverty. These are common to all policy evaluation measures in this volume.

• Complete parameterization for supply and demand functions in the market directly affected by policy reform. Supply and demand functions for goods in which strong interlinkages to the "direct" market are conjectured or known to exist are also required, as are the relative prices of the goods and the quantities imported and exported at any relative price. These prices may be exogenous (as for some prices of tradable goods) or endogenously determined (as for the prices of nontraded goods or labor).

• A determination of the closures of the markets being modeled. For example, are they traded or nontraded goods? Is rationing a feature of equilibrium? This determination, used to build market equilibrium conditions from the supply and demand functions, requires aggregated data for the relevant factors and commodities.

• Software to solve a system of potentially nonlinear equations for the endogenous prices and quantities.

• A quantitative mapping of these endogenous variables into the income and consumption of households.

It is rare to find all these data requirements in place for the country and policy reform under study. In most cases, the researcher must devote time to the development of these components. The critical difference in practice between this approach and other approaches is the complete specification of the supply and demand behavior and the characteristics of market equilibrium for all the goods or factors closely interlinked with the market in which reform occurs. Those researchers with interest in an illustrative calibration of such interlinkages could construct the supply and demand functions using parameters found in research on similar countries: for these, the entire exercise could require less than a week's effort. For those researchers with an interest in more precise quantitative measurement, analysis of supply and demand behavior will require a detailed data set on prices, quantities produced and consumed, and inputs into production for each of the interlinked goods. These data can then be analyzed through systems estimation to derive the appropriate supply and demand functions. This procedure typically requires months of research effort. The "best-practice" case studies by Dorosh, del Ninno, and Sahn (1995) and Minot and Goletti (1998) illustrate the application of this more accurate approach. The greater time commitment leads to greater confidence in the results of the study, but as Sadoulet and de Janvry (1995) note, even the most rudimentary multimarket analysis performs a consistency check that is not available from other partial-equilibrium models.

There is no theoretical limit on the number of interlinked goods or factors that can be considered in a multimarket model. However, the practical data requirements for accurate supply and demand conditions for each interlinked good place an upper bound on the number of simultaneously estimated functions. Analyses of agricultural market reforms have introduced the largest multimarket models, and these have typically included no more than ten closely substitutable foodstuffs. As institutional complexities (such as regionally distinct markets) are introduced, researchers have generally narrowed the number of interlinked goods or factors considered. Ultimately, a tradeoff must be recognized between a more comprehensive and complex system of equations with more interlinked markets and expositional simplicity focused on capturing the main indirect effects of most relevant interlinked markets. Indeed one of the strengths of multimarket models is their potential simplicity as expositional tools upon which to base policy dialogue.[1]

The advantages and disadvantages of multimarket analysis, examined in more detail below, are evident from the simple example in box 12.1. This example simulates the impact on income distribution of the removal of a food subsidy. It then provides a summary of the proportion of the policy impact that will be captured by single-market analysis, multimarket analysis, and full system analysis. The key advantage of multimarket analysis is the ability to include the interlinked nature of markets in policy evaluation: here, recognition that meat and bread are substitute goods corrects a bias

Box 12.1 A Simple Application of the
Multimarket Model

Critical components in a multimarket model's application to the incidence of policy reform on poverty are a description of the current
income distribution, a description of the supply characteristics for the
goods produced in the interlinked markets, a description of the preferences for those represented in the income distribution, definition of
market-clearing conditions, and a proposed policy reform. To illustrate the technique, consider the following simple economy.

• *Consumption characteristics.* There are three goods produced and
consumed: meat (M), bread (B), and housing (H). The prices of the
three goods are defined as P_M, P_B, and P_H. All individuals k in the economy are assumed to have identical preferences over the three goods.
These are summarized in the Almost Ideal Demand System of Deaton
and Muellbauer (1980) as shares (W_i) of total expenditure. X_k is the
real wealth of individual k. P is the appropriate consumption-weighted
price index of the three consumer goods. Appropriate cross-equation
restrictions on the α_i, β_i, and γ_{ji} are imposed.

• $W_{ik} = \alpha_i + \Sigma_j \gamma_{ji} \ln(P_j) + \beta_i \ln(X_k)$ for $i, j = M, B, H$

• *Current income distribution.* There are 100 individuals in the
economy, and they have integer values of real income ranging from 11
to 110 real pesos. The poverty line is defined in consumption terms:
an individual falls below the poverty line if $(M^{.2}B^{.4}H^{.4}) < 15$.

• *Production characteristics.* Bread is produced domestically and
is also imported. Meat and housing are produced domestically and
are nontraded goods. Each producer is assumed to have a nonzero
supply elasticity σ_i (for $i = M, B, H$). The exchange rate is set equal to
one as a normalization, and there is a value added subsidy (s) to bread
consumption, so that $P_B = (1 - s)P_B^*$. Scaling factors are chosen to
calibrate the model:

$M^s = 1{,}247\ P_M^{\sigma}$
$B^s = 572\ P_B^{\sigma}$
$H^s = 1{,}213\ P_H^{\sigma}$

• The markets for these three goods are governed by market-
clearing conditions.

$M^s = \Sigma_k W_{Mk} X_k P / P_M$
$B^s = \Sigma_k W_{Bk} X_k P / P_B + IM_B$
$H^s = \Sigma_k W_{hk} X_k P / P_H$

with imports of bread (IM_B) clearing the market of this traded good,
and price adjusting in the other two markets. In addition to the income
distribution and poverty line, then, the analyst will need estimates of

σ_i, α_i, β_i, and γ_{ji}. The last three equations are solved for P_M, P_H, and IM_B as functions of s.

- The policy reform in this example will be to shift the consumption subsidy s from 0.125 to zero.

The table below summarizes the results of this exercise for one set of parameters characterized by rather large own- and cross-elasticities in price between bread and the other two goods. The parameter values chosen are $\alpha_M = 0.2$, $\alpha_B = 0.4$, $\alpha_H = 0.4$, $\beta_M = 0.05$, $\beta_H = 0$, $\beta_B = -0.05$, $\gamma_{MM} = \gamma_{HH} = -0.2$, $\gamma_{BB} = -0.28$, $\gamma_{MB} = \gamma_{BM} = 0.14$, $\gamma_{MH} = \gamma_{HM} = 0.06$, $\gamma_{BH} = \gamma_{HB} = 0.14$. $\Sigma_i = 0.3$ for $i = M, B, H$. These values are consistent with a bread own-price elasticity of demand of -1.14, and cross-price elasticities of demand of 0.34 (with M) and 0.35 (with H).

Table Box 12.1 Simulation Results

	Initial equilibrium	Single-market analysis	Multi-market analysis	Full-system analysis
P_B	7	8	8	8
P_M	7.54	7.54	8.03	8.38
P_H	7.54	7.54	7.535	8.38
X_M	2,286	2,286	2,330	2,360
X_B	1,026	1,086	1,086	1,086
X_H	2,223	2,223	2,223	2,295
IM_B	358	−100	−23	232
Number below poverty line	37	41	39	38

Note: The initial equilibrium is characterized by a 12.5 percent subsidy in bread, with endogenous values given in the first column. Bread is imported in that equilibrium. Meat and housing prices adjust to clear their respective markets. Of the 100 people in the economy, 37 cannot afford consumption bundles above the poverty line. If the bread subsidy is removed but other prices are assumed unchanging, the results of the single-market analysis of column two are derived. Bread is exported, and 41 of the population fall below the poverty line. A multimarket analysis can be represented by a modeling exercise that investigates the impact of removing the subsidy while allowing the price of meat to clear its market—but ignoring the market-clearing condition for housing. As is evident in the third column, the impact on poverty is smaller: the spillover effect of bread price increases in the meat market leads to higher P_M and a supply response in that market as well. Of the population, 39 fall below the poverty line in this exercise. In the final column the results are reported if both meat and housing markets are required to clear. Note that all non-wage prices rise in this case relative to the initial equilibrium, and all production rises as well.

in attributing poverty increases to removal of the subsidy. The disadvantage of multimarket analysis is the exclusion of the remaining markets. In this case, the price in the housing market P_H is treated as unchanging in the multimarket analysis. The full-system analysis endogenizes P_H, and it is in this case quite responsive to the policy reform. Holding P_H constant leaves biases in policy evaluation, although these biases are less pronounced as price elasticities of demand approach zero.[2] Also ignored in this example are the impact of removal of the subsidy on the government budget and on the external account of the economy.

Three Examples of the Use of Multimarket Modeling

The three studies described below illustrate not only good-practice application of multimarket analysis, but also the evolution of the use of this technique in the literature. The basic concept has not changed: consistency conditions in interlinked markets always determine endogenously relative prices and quantities. The change over time has come in the focus of analysis—for example, from government expenditure to the incidence of poverty—in the growing sophistication of estimation techniques for the parameters of the model, and in the increasing complexity of the market-closure conditions imposed.

Braverman, Hammer, and Gron (1987) note that in Cyprus in 1985 the government sold barley as a feedstock for the livestock sector. The sales price to the livestock sector was 49 percent of the price on world markets for barley. The government justified this subsidy by noting its indirect effect in reducing consumer prices of foodstuffs. The authors consider the impact of removing this subsidy to barley on Cypriot welfare.

The authors construct equilibrium conditions for markets in beef, fresh lamb, frozen lamb, milk, pork, poultry, wheat, barley, and hay. They obtain estimates of own-price and cross-price elasticities of demand from agricultural sector surveys, and infer estimates of supply elasticities from studies for neighboring countries. By equating supply and demand, they calculate the percentage change in relative prices in the agricultural sector and the supply responses predicted for a 1 percent reduction in the barley subsidy.

The authors do not examine the incidence of poverty. They examine the budgetary saving associated with a reduction in the barley subsidy. The authors conclude that if the analysis is limited to the market for barley, then there will be budgetary savings of 1.21 percent for every 1 percent reduction in per unit subsidy. However, once the interlinked markets are considered, the budgetary savings shrink to 1.02 percent for every 1 percent reduction. Although still sizeable, the quantitative impact is greatly altered by the consideration of interlinked markets.

Dorosh, del Ninno, and Sahn (1995) examine the impact of food aid on the incidence of poverty in Mozambique. The proposed policy reform is to increase the sale of donated foreign yellow maize at below-world price in the markets of the capital, Maputo. Such sales are anticipated to have a direct positive effect in reducing poverty because of the expected reduction to urban residents in the cost of purchasing the poverty-line bundle of commodities and services. The authors also anticipate that the policy could have negative consequences through impoverishing the rural smallholders producing agricultural substitutes for the yellow maize.

The key indirect effects of the policy work through the channels of consumer substitution among foodstuffs and supply responsiveness of domestic farmers. The authors thus build a multimarket model of the food sector of Mozambique. Demand functions for yellow maize, white maize, rice, wheat, meat, and vegetables are derived from a theoretically consistent preference ordering. The parameters of the demand system are estimated using data from a survey of households in Maputo. These estimated demand functions are equated to supply functions to determine endogenously the quantities produced domestically and the quantity imported and exported (for traded goods) or the quantities produced domestically and the market price (for nontraded goods). These effects, both direct and indirect, are then incorporated in a simulation study to determine the impact of the yellow maize distribution on the incidence and depth of poverty.

The multimarket structure of the study provides important information about the ex ante evaluation of the food-aid policy. Most critical is the finding that yellow maize is not a close substitute in demand for any of the other foodstuffs, and that it is an inferior good for more affluent urban residents, while a normal good with small income elasticity for the poor. These features of the Maputo consumer ensure that the negative indirect effects of the food-aid program are minimal. The authors find that a 15 percent increase in food-aid sales in Maputo will raise the real incomes of the urban poor by 3.6 percent. The incomes of the urban nonpoor rise only slightly, while the incomes of rural residents fall slightly. Using a caloric-intake poverty line, the authors find that the number of households below the poverty lines falls from 34 percent to 23 percent.

This study illustrates both the advantages (relative to incidence analysis) and drawbacks (relative to general equilibrium modeling) of the multimarket approach. The striking advantage is the explicit attention to the potential for poverty effects through interlinked markets. An incidence analysis would simply assume that there are no substitute foodstuffs for yellow maize, whereas this study investigated the possibility systematically. The striking drawback is the lack of attention to alternative uses of scarce government funds or foreign aid. A general equilibrium model would consider those resources as fungible, so that the benefits from the food-aid program could be weighed against the opportunity cost of the scarce aid resources.

Minot and Goletti (1998) note that a binding export quota on rice in Vietnam in the mid-1990s had the effect of subsidizing domestic consumption of rice. They estimate that the quota led to roughly a 30 percent subsidy to consumers, and their study addresses the impact of removing such a subsidy on the incidence of poverty in Vietnam. They consider a multimarket analysis with four commodities (rice, maize, sweet potatoes, and cassava) modeled explicitly. They also introduce an important innovation—they allow regional disparities in prices through explicit modeling of transport costs for the foodstuffs. The demand interlinkages among markets are represented by the cross-price elasticities of the Almost Ideal Demand System of Deaton and Muellbauer (1980), with parameters of the demand system estimated using household survey data. The supply decision for each region for each foodstuff is assumed to respond to both own-price and cross-price effects, and the parameters of the supply functions are derived from separate analysis by Khiem and Pingali (1995). Welfare is measured through use of a net-benefit metric, as in Deaton (1989b), with disaggregation by household category (urban-rural or quintile of the income distribution) and by region of the country.

Minot and Goletti (1998) begin with the presumption that an increase in the rice price will make those households with net sales of rice (that is, production by the household exceeds the consumption of the household) better-off, while those with net purchases will be disadvantaged. They reach a paradoxical conclusion: "less than a third of the households in Vietnam have net sales of rice, and yet the rice price increases associated with export liberalization tend to reduce (slightly) the incidence and depth of poverty." (Minot and Goletti, 1998, p. 745.) One reason is straightforward: those households with net sales of rice are disproportionately found among the poor. The second reason relies upon the interlinkages captured in the multimarket model: the ability to substitute demand away from the higher-priced rice to less-expensive foodstuffs provides households with the opportunity to avoid poverty.

The advantage of the multimarket modeling approach is evident in the second effect: the demand substitution effect will not be measured if a multimarket analysis is not done. The disadvantage can only be inferred: there is no attention given to the impact of the policy on decisions in labor or credit markets, for example, nor is there consideration of the impact of the policy on the government budget or external balances.

Operational Hints for Using the Technique

While the papers cited in the preceding section illustrate the conceptual advances in multimarket models, there are more practical concerns to keep in mind as the technique is implemented. Consider a simple example, expanding upon the description of demand for foodstuffs in Côte d'Ivoire from Deaton (1989a). Suppose that the government provides a subsidy to rice consumption: it buys rice at the world market price and then provides it to consumers at a lower price. It absorbs the difference into its budget deficit. Domestic producers provide some of the rice, but the remainder is imported. Through the subsidy, some of those otherwise below the poverty line are raised above that line.

Removal of the rice subsidy would certainly affect the depth and incidence of poverty. There are clear direct effects on those above the poverty line who must pay more for rice: these will, all else being equal, drop into poverty. Those already below the poverty line would sink further, increasing the depth of poverty.

This calculation would be an overstatement of the negative policy impact, however, if agricultural commodity markets are interlinked. Removal of the subsidy would raise the consumer price of rice and would thus encourage substitution of yams or cassava in the diet. The demand substitution would lessen the welfare impact of the rice price increase, while the resulting increase in prices of substitute goods would induce a supply response among farmers producing these substitute foodstuffs. The consumer's ability to remain above the poverty line would be enhanced by this substitution, while the increased prices of substitute foodstuffs would raise incomes of farmers and perhaps reduce poverty in that cohort.

The analyst in this instance runs through four steps.

• First, the policy reform will have its direct impact in the domestic market for rice. However, since rice consumption is potentially substitutable for yams, cassava, and other starches, modeling the indirect impacts of policy reform in those markets is important as well. The analyst can determine whether many markets are important to the analysis through estimation of a system of demand equations from household survey data. If cross-elasticities of demand or supply are significant, then the added complexity will be worthwhile.

• Second, the analyst builds a model of these interlinked agricultural markets through a series of market equilibrium conditions. There is one for each good included: here the goods include rice, yams, and cassava. The estimates from systems estimation of demand and supply behavior can be used, or the analyst can use her own judgment or evidence from other countries to proxy for the unknown behavioral parameters. Although it is common to model these as neoclassical flexible-price markets, other techniques are also available for handling multimarket disequilibrium models.

• Third, the rice subsidy is a parameter in this system of equations. The analyst then removes the subsidy (that is, changes it to zero) and resolves the system of interlinked equations. The resulting solution provides estimates of the relative prices of rice, yams, and cassava as well as the quantities supplied and demanded in equilibrium. These equilibrium values reflect both the direct and indirect effects of the policy reform.

• Fourth, the analyst already has a definition of the poverty line and a representative sample of households for which the incidence and depth of poverty can be calculated. She introduces this new set of equilibrium values into the sample and recalculates the poverty line and the distribution of households relative to that poverty line based upon the new equilibrium values. The substitution away from rice in this example could indeed fall on non-foodstuffs. If so, and if the analyst has defined the poverty line in caloric terms, then the cost of the market basket that satisfies the poverty line could well rise with the reform.

The change in the number of households falling below the poverty line and the changed depth of poverty for those below is the ex ante forecast of the marginal impact of removing the rice subsidy.

Evaluation and Conclusion

Multimarket analysis as applied in the literature has been an effective tool for ex ante analysis of policy reforms that involve changing the relative price of a good in the economy. It is preferred to incidence analysis or to single-market analysis in cases when the good directly affected by the reform is a close substitute or complement, on either the demand or supply side, with other goods. The transmission of the effects of the policy through these other markets is then an important component of policy evaluation.

The most impressive examples of the technique are currently found in analyzing policy reforms to agricultural pricing or consumer subsidies. This is a natural application of the technique, as agricultural goods are substitutes both in household consumption and in farm land allocation. Poverty lines are also sensitive to prices of agricultural products, with some poverty lines defined explicitly in term of calories consumed. Policy choices that result in changing food prices, whether through elimination of consumer subsidies or provision of food aid, will be naturally modeled in this framework.

The technique can be compared either to ex ante incidence analysis or to CGE modeling. Relative to incidence analysis, multimarket modeling offers the greater precision of accounting for interlinked markets. It also permits analyzing situations where price changes are nonmarginal and the first-order approximation used in tax-incidence analysis (chapter 1) is highly unsatisfactory. But multimarket modeling has the additional data cost of requiring knowledge of supply and demand functions in the interlinked markets. Relative to CGE modeling, multimarket modeling is more transparent in application and has less-demanding data requirements, but it neglects the interlinkages from the highlighted markets to all others, both through cross-price substitution and through budget and external account balances.

Although the technique has been most carefully developed in agricultural sector models, its potential application is much wider. One application is suggested by Mosley (1999) in his analysis of the impact of financial liberalization on formal and informal credit markets. He discusses the interlinked nature of the formal and informal credit markets and the participation in each by the poor. If he were to model explicitly the supply and demand for credit in each market, he could then provide an analysis similar to those cited earlier. The policy reform in this instance is the change in the real interest rate on formal-sector credit. As has been evident since Buffie (1984) and van Wijnbergen (1983), the interaction of the formal-sector credit rate with the rate in informal credit markets is central to the effect of the policy reform on real incomes. Explicit consideration of this interlinkage would improve the standard incidence analysis of financial liberalization reforms. Another application could be to evaluate the effect of removing a formal-sector minimum wage in the presence of a large informal labor market. The interlinked nature of these markets implies that evaluation of policy reform should model the spillovers explicitly.

To have confidence in the results of multimarket modeling, two sets of parameters must be estimated with precision:

- The parameters of the demand and supply functions for the goods explicitly modeled
- The parameters of the mapping from relative prices of these goods to the consumption or real income index to be compared to the poverty line

The greatest confidence would of course come from econometric estimation on household and producer surveys for the country under consideration. Estimation can be either parametric or nonparametric and can be based on either linear or nonlinear supply and demand functions. If the data are not available for such econometric work, or if an initial analysis needs to be completed under severe time pressure, it is also possible (although with less confidence) to use parameters derived for supply and demand in other countries. Clearly, such a short-cut would circumvent the microeconomic-level data and analysis requirements otherwise necessary to undertake this approach. The sole requirement is that the estimation, modeling, or borrowing yields an explicit quantitative prediction for quantities demanded and supplied that can be used in imposing a market-clearing closure. The resulting relative prices are then used with the consumption index to derive the incidence and depth of poverty.

It is also prudent for the analyst to conduct a sensitivity analysis of the results for different values of these parameters. Estimation defines confidence bounds of the coefficients, and these bounds can be used to define alternate values for sensitivity analysis. If there is no estimation to guide the analyst, substantial changes to parameters should be introduced. The goal is to observe whether the policy evaluation is sensitive to the specific parameters estimated (or chosen).

Notes

1. Arulpragasam, Ajwad, and others are working on a generic multimarket template that can be reparameterized quickly for analysis on various countries. This template promises to capture some of the economies of scale for future users and may reduce the time commitment to such a study to a matter of weeks.

2. It appears from the change in the poverty measure from multimarket analysis to full-system analysis that the bias is minimal. In fact, this is an artifact of the calculation of the consumption basket for each individual.

Given the P_H assumed in the multimarket analysis, X_H = 2,283 and aggregate demand as given by equation 12.4 is C_H = 2,684. There will be excess demand for the nontraded housing good at that price.

References

The word *processed* describes informally reproduced works that may not be commonly available through library systems.

Arulpragasam, Jehan, and Carlo del Ninno. 1996. "Do Cheap Imports Harm the Poor? Rural-Urban Tradeoffs in Guinea." In David Sahn, ed., *Economic Reform and the Poor in Africa*. Oxford, U.K.: Oxford University Press.

Braverman, Avishay, and Jeffrey Hammer. 1986. "Multimarket Analysis of Agricultural Pricing Policies in Senegal." In Inderjit Singh, Lyn Squire, and John Strauss, eds., *Agricultural Household Models: Extensions, Applications and Policy*. Baltimore: Johns Hopkins University Press.

Braverman, Avishay, Jeffrey Hammer, and Anne Gron. 1987. "Multimarket Analysis of Agricultural Price Policies in an Operational Context: The Case of Cyprus." *World Bank Economic Review* 1(2): 337–56.

Buffie, Edward. 1984. "Financial Repression, the New Structuralists, and Stabilization Policy in Semi-Industrialized Countries." *Journal of Development Economics* 14(3): 305–22.

Deaton, Angus 1989a. "Household Survey Data and Pricing Policies in Developing Countries." *World Bank Economic Review* 3(2): 183–210.

———. 1989b. "Rice Prices and Income Distribution in Thailand: A Non-Parametric Analysis." *Economic Journal* 99: 1–37.

Deaton, Angus, and J. Muellbauer. 1980. "An Almost Ideal Demand System." *American Economic Review* 70(3): 312–26.

Dorosh, Paul, Carlo del Ninno, and David Sahn. 1995. "Poverty Alleviation in Mozambique: A Multimarket Analysis of the Role of Food Aid." *Agricultural Economics* 13: 89–99.

Khiem, N., and P. Pingali. 1995. "Supply Response of Rice and Three Foodcrops in Vietnam." In G. Denning and V. Xuan, eds., *Vietnam and IRRI: A Partnership in Rice Research*. Manila: International Rice Research Institute.

Minot, N., and Francesci Goletti. 1998. "Export Liberalization and Household Welfare: The Case of Rice in Vietnam." *American Journal of Agricultural Economics* 80(4): 738–49.

Mosley, Paul. 1999. "Micro-Macro Linkages in Financial Markets: The Impact of Financial Liberalization on Access to Rural Credit in Four

African Countries." Finance and Development Research Programme Working Paper 4. University of Manchester, Manchester, U.K. Processed.

Sadoulet, Elisabeth, and Alain de Janvry. 1995. *Quantitative Development Policy Analysis*. Baltimore: Johns Hopkins University Press.

van Wijnbergen, Sweder. 1983. "Credit Policy, Inflation and Growth in a Financially Repressed Economy." *Journal of Development Economics* 13(1): 45–65.

13

The 123PRSP Model

Shantayanan Devarajan and Delfin S. Go

This chapter describes a quantitative framework to evaluate some of the macroeconomic aspects of Poverty Reduction Strategy Papers (PRSPs) and illustrates it with an application to Zambia.[1] Such a framework is necessary for at least two reasons. Existing macroeconomic models used in country economic work, such as the International Monetary Fund's Financial Programming Model (FPM) or the World Bank's RMSM-X, take economic growth and relative prices as exogenous. The two most important determinants of poverty—growth and income distribution—are outside these models. Second, the links between macroeconomic policies and poverty are complex—and likely to be contentious.[2] Fiscal sustainability may dictate that a country cut its public expenditures, whereas poverty concerns may require that these same expenditures be increased. A quantitative framework that identifies the critical relationships on which the outcome depends can make a useful contribution to the preparation of PRSPs.

Given that we need such a framework, what are some of its desirable characteristics? First, as indicated above, the framework should be capable of identifying some of the critical tradeoffs in poverty-reducing macroeconomic policies. For example, how do the costs (in terms of poverty) of higher spending (and higher fiscal deficits) compare with the benefits of targeting that spending on the poor? Second, the framework should be consistent with economic theory on the one hand, and with basic data, such as national accounts and household income and expenditure surveys, on the other. Otherwise, the framework will not be able to foster a dialogue between conflicting parties on these issues. Third, the framework should be simple enough that operational economists can use it on their desktops. This means it should not make undue demands on data; it should be based on readily available software, such as Microsoft Excel; and, most important, it should permit ready interpretation of model results.

In developing a framework with these characteristics, we make some strategic simplifications. Instead of building a full-blown, multisector, multihousehold, dynamic general equilibrium model, we opt for a modular approach.[3] Specifically, the framework links together several existing models. One advantage of this approach is that the individual component models already exist. Another is that, if a particular component model is not available for data or other reasons, the rest of the framework can be implemented without it. The cost of adopting this approach is that the causal chain from macroeconomic policies to poverty is in one direction only: we do not capture the feedback effect of changes in the composition of demand (due to shifts in the distribution of income) on macroeconomic balances. We emphasize that the modular approach means that different models (based on different views about how the economy functions) can be incorporated as alternative subcomponents of the framework.

Figure 13.1 is a schematic representation of our macroeconomic framework for PRSPs. Specifically, we link macroeconomic policies to poverty (households) through two channels. First, we examine the distributional consequences of policies, holding growth fixed. For instance, we look at the effect of an increase in government spending on distribution (through its effect on relative prices and wages), assuming the aggregate level of output remains unchanged. Next, we look at the growth consequences of the same policies, holding distribution fixed. Thus, we would calculate the impact of the increase in government spending on output, assuming no change in relative prices and wages. The overall effect on poverty would then be the sum of these two impacts.

We turn now to a description of the individual modules of the macroeconomic framework for PRSPs, which we call the 123PRSP Model (figure 13.2). We begin with a static, aggregate, macroeconomic consistency framework, such as the IMF's Financial Programming Model. This model has the advantage of having a consistent set of national accounts, linked with fiscal, balance of payments, and monetary accounts. Most of the macroeconomic policies, such as the level of government spending, taxation, and the composition of deficit financing, will be contained (as exogenous variables) in this module. Since the FPM is an accounting framework, with few behavioral assumptions, there are no real alternatives to this part of the framework. However, unlike the standard practice with the FPM, the economy's growth rate and its real exchange rate are not

Figure 13.1 A Schematic Representation of the Framework

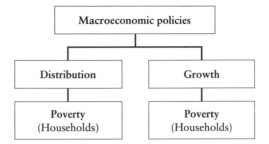

Source: Authors' depiction.

Figure 13.2 The 123PRSP Model

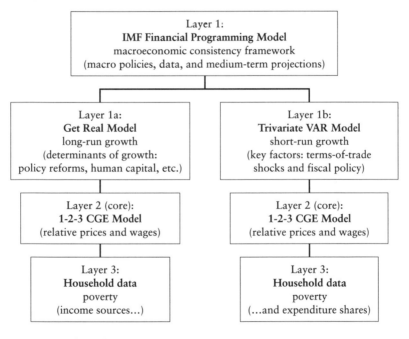

Source: Authors' depiction.

taken as given (or as targets), but rather they are explicitly derived in the models that follow.

The information, such as the reference medium-term economic projections, in the financial programming module (layer 1), is then read into each of the following models: the two growth models, the "Get Real" model (layer 1a), which is a long-run growth model, and a Trivariate VAR model (layer 1b) that captures short-run growth effects; and the "1-2-3 Model," a static, multisector, general equilibrium model, which is the core of the framework (layer 2). The 1-2-3 Model assumes aggregate output is fixed, but it captures the effect of macroeconomic policies and shocks on relative prices and wages (as well as on the composition of output). Conversely, the two growth models capture the effects of policies on growth, assuming that relative prices, wages, and the composition of output are unchanged. The link with poverty analysis (layer 3) is made when the models' projected changes in prices, wages, profits, and growth are plugged into household data on wages, profits, and commodity demands of representative groups (or segments of the distribution, say, deciles). In principle, the model can calculate the impact on each household in the sample so as to capture the effect on the entire distribution of income or on the poverty rate. In sum, the 123PRSP framework allows for a forecast of household welfare measures and poverty outcomes consistent with a set of macroeconomic policies and shocks within the limited time and resources usually available for the PRSP process.

The Layers in the 123PRSP Framework

In this section we describe the two sets of models in detail, as well as the process of linking them with household survey data. Note that in layer 1 the medium-term projections are taken as given and the underlying macroeconomic consistency framework is not described here.[4]

Starting at the Core Layer with the 1-2-3 Model

The 1-2-3 Model is one of the fiscal tools developed at the World Bank (Devarajan, Lewis, and Robinson 1990, 1993; Devarajan and others 1997). Despite (or perhaps because of) its simplicity, the 1-2-3 Model has been applied to a variety of policy problems, including the pre-1994 overvaluation of the CFA franc (Devarajan 1997, 1999), and regional integration (Addison 2000). The model has been extended to incorporate rational-expectations dynamics (Devarajan and Go 1998) and export externalities (de Melo and Robinson 1992). Finally, Devarajan, Go, and Li (1999) provide empirical estimates of the two critical parameters, the elasticities of substitution and transformation between foreign and domestic goods, σ and Ω, respectively, for 60 countries. Since the model is now well documented, we provide only a thumbnail sketch here.

The key equations of the 1-2-3 Model are presented in table 13.1. The model takes the aggregate information from the FPM but then

Table 13.1 Basic Equations in the Core Layer:
The 1-2-3 Model

Real Flows	*Prices*
(1) $\overline{X} = G(E,D^S;\Omega)$	(10) $P^m = (1 + t^m)\cdot R\cdot pw^m$
(2) $Q^S = F(M,D^D;\sigma)$	(11) $P^e = (1 + t^e)\cdot R\cdot pw^e$
(3) $Q^D = C + Z + \overline{G}$	(12) $P^t = (1 + t^s)\cdot P^q$
(4) $E/D^S = g_2(P^e,P^d)$	(13) $P^x = g_1(P^e,P^d)$
(5) $M/D^D = f_2(P^m,P^d)$	(14) $P^q = f_1(P^m,P^d)$
	(15) $R = 1$

Nominal Flows	*Equilibrium Conditions*
(6) $T = t^m\cdot R\cdot pw^m\cdot M$	(16) $D^D - D^S = 0$
$\qquad + t^s\cdot P^q\cdot Q^D$	(17) $Q^D - Q^S = 0$
$\qquad + t^y\cdot Y$	(18) $pw^m\cdot M - pw^e\cdot E - ft - re = \overline{B}$
$\qquad - t^e\cdot R\cdot pw^e\cdot E$	(19) $P^t\cdot Z - S = 0$
(7) $Y = P^x\cdot\overline{X} + tr\cdot P^q + re\cdot R$	(20) $T - P^t\cdot G - tr\cdot P^q - ft\cdot R - S^g = 0$
(8) $S = \overline{s}\cdot Y + R\cdot\overline{B} + S^g$	
(9) $C\cdot P^t = (1 - \overline{s} - t^y)\cdot Y$	

Accounting Identities
(i) $P^x\cdot \equiv P^e\cdot E + P^d\cdot D^S$
(ii) $P^q\cdot Q^S \equiv P^m\cdot M + P^t\cdot D^D$

Endogenous Variables:	*Exogenous Variables:*
E: Export good	pw^m: World price of import good
M: Import good	pw^e: World price of export good
D^S: Supply of domestic good	t^m: Tariff rate
D^D: Demand for domestic good	t^e: Export subsidy rate
Q^S: Supply of composite good	t^s: sales/excise/value-added tax rate
Q^D: Demand for composite good	t^y: direct tax rate
P^e: Domestic price of export good	tr: government transfers
P^m: Domestic price of import good	ft: foreign transfers to government
P^d: Producer price of domestic good	re: foreign remittances to
P^t: Sales price of composite good	$\quad$ private sector
P^x: Price of aggregate output	s: Average savings rate
P^q: Price of composite good	X: Aggregate output
R: Exchange rate	G: Real government demand
T: Tax revenue	B: Balance of trade
S^g: Government savings	Ω: Export transformation elasticity
Y: Total income	σ: Import substitution elasticity
C: Aggregate consumption	
S: Aggregate savings	
Z: Aggregate real investment	

Figure 13.3 A Diagrammatic Exposition of the 1-2-3 Model

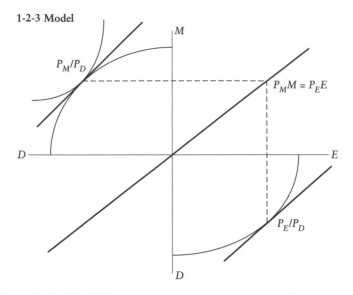

Source: Authors' depiction.

divides the economy into two sectors: exports (E) and all other final goods produced, called domestic goods (D). Thus, gross domestic product, which is real $GDP(X)$ multiplied by the GDP deflator (P_X) can be expressed as

$$P_X X = P_E E + P_D D$$

where P_E and P_D are the prices (in local currency) of exports and domestic goods, respectively

The model makes the assumption that there is a constant elasticity of transformation function linking output in the two sectors, with the level of output determined by the point where the function is tangent to the relative price of exports to domestic goods (see the lower right quadrant in figure 13.3). The price of exports is exogenous (small country assumption).

In symbols,

$$P_E = RP_E^*$$

where R is the nominal exchange rate and P_E^* the world price of exports; and

$$E/D = k(P_E/P_D)^{\Omega}$$

where Ω is the (constant) elasticity of transformation.

There is one other good in the economy, which is imports (M)—hence the name, "one country, two sectors, three commodities." Consumers have a constant elasticity of substitution utility function in D and M, and the level of demand is determined by the highest indifference curve that is tangent to the consumer's budget line. The price of imports is also exogenous. That is,

$$P_M = RP_M^*$$

where P_M^* is the world price of imports; and

$$M/D = K(P_D/P_M)^\sigma$$

where σ is the (constant) elasticity of substitution. The price of D is determined by that price that equilibrates supply and demand for D. Inasmuch as D is a domestic good that is neither exported nor imported, the relative price of D to E or M is a real exchange rate. The salient aspect of the 1-2-3 Model, therefore, is that it captures the effects of macroeconomic policies on a critical relative price, namely, the real exchange rate.

The transformation frontier between E and D is based on the allocation of factors between the two sectors. Thus behind this function is a market for labor and capital. For simplicity, we assume that there is only one labor market in the economy and that it is a competitive one. We further assume there is full employment. Finally, we assume that capital is fixed and sector-specific in this static model. All these assumptions can be relaxed if there are data on different labor categories and information on how the factor markets operate. In this simple model, the assumptions imply that associated with the equilibrium price of D is also an equilibrium wage rate. Profits in each sector are then the residual of output after the wage bill. To summarize, starting with a set of national accounts for a given set of macroeconomic policies, the 1-2-3 Model generates a set of wages, sector-specific profits, and relative prices (of D, M, and E) that are mutually consistent. The 1-2-3 Model is but one way of eliciting the relative-price implications of a set of macroeconomic policies. The particular sectors chosen—exports and domestic goods—highlight one critical relative price, the real exchange rate. Other approaches would be consistent with this framework. Data permitting and where structural details of the economy are important, a full-blown, multisector general equilibrium model could be inserted into the framework at this stage (Devarajan, Lewis, and Robinson 1990). The multisector version would capture the effects of these macroeconomic policies and shocks on several agricultural and manufacturing sectors, say. Some of these models also have a more complex treatment of labor markets, including the informal labor market, rural-urban migration, and labor unions (Agénor and Aizenman 1999; Devarajan, Ghanem, and Theirfelder 1999). Other applications looking at the impact of trade reform have incorporated several occupational labor groups and detailed household information (Devarajan and van der Mensbrugghe 2000 for South Africa) or several fiscal instruments and a complex import quota and rationing system (Go and Mitra 1999 for India). The additional cost of these complexities is, of course, the use of a more specialized programming language.

Layer 1a: The Get Real Model

As mentioned earlier, the 1-2-3 Model is a static model. For a given growth rate of the economy, it calculates the wages, profits, and relative prices that are consistent with that rate. Also as mentioned earlier, this "given growth rate" is normally a forecast or a target in most macroeconomic models used by country economists. Yet, there is reason to believe that the macroeconomic policies in question may have an impact on the economy's long-run growth rate. Presumably that is why policies such as trade liberalization, infrastructure development, and monetary and fiscal stability are advocated. The Get Real Model (Easterly 2001) presents a parsimonious set of cross-country growth regressions that capture the long-run growth effect of these policies. The coefficients of an extended version that includes long-term trade and debt factors are given in table 13.2. Note, for example, that the long-run growth effects of increases in secondary-school enrollment and in infrastructure stocks (telephone lines) are captured by this model.

Again, we emphasize that the Get Real Model is one alternative for capturing the long-run growth effects of macroeconomic policies. It is a reduced-form model, and since it is based on cross-country regressions, the coefficients are the same for all countries.[5] Another alternative would be to estimate a country-specific model. The problem here is that there is not enough intertemporal variation in policies to obtain significant coefficients. Nevertheless, if the analyst has an alternative model of long-run growth determination, there is nothing stopping him or her from inserting it in place of the Get Real Model at this stage in the framework.

Layer 1b: Trivariate VAR Model

The Get Real Model captures the long-run effects of macroeconomic policies—approximately five years after the policies have been enacted. What about the first five years? One option is to use the consensus forecast for growth in those five years. However, this

Table 13.2 Growth Coefficients of the Get Real Model
(Layer 1a)

Variable	Coefficient	t statistic
Policy determinants		
Black market premium	−0.0153	(−4.02)
M2/GDP	0.0004	(3.31)
Inflation	−0.0014	(−0.21)
Real exchange rate	−0.0087	(−2.36)
Secondary enrollment	0.0003	(2.40)
Telephone lines/1,000	0.0054	(2.13)
Shocks		
Terms of trade as % of GDP	0.2125	(2.45)
Interest on external debt as % of GDP	−0.0029	(−3.28)
OECD trading partner growth	0.0210	(3.56)
Initial conditions		
Initial income	−0.0105	(−2.33)
Intercept	0.0236	(0.71)
Shifts 1980s	−0.0021	(−0.41)
Shifts 1990s	0.0046	(0.60)
Zambia's economic growth		
Actual, 1990s	−1.5%	
Estimated	−2.1%	

Source: Easterly (2001).

forecast would not show the short-run growth impact of, say, a terms-of-trade shock or an increase in government expenditure. To capture these impacts, we estimate a trivariate vector autoregression (VAR), where the three variables are the exogenous shock or policy (terms of trade or government expenditure), the real exchange rate, and growth. For Zambia, for example, the short-run growth elasticity of the trivariate VAR (from the impulse response) for a terms-of-trade shock (the price of copper) is 0.053 in the first year and 0.024 in the second year; for government spending, it is 0.038 in the first year and −0.033 in the second year.

Since the 1-2-3 and Get Real (or Trivariate VAR) models render endogenous relative prices and growth (respectively), the resulting projections may not match those generated by the IMF's Financial Programming Model that takes these variables as exogenous. For instance, the projections on tax collections may be different from those obtained by projecting an exogenous growth rate. The discrepancy can only be reconciled by examining the assumptions underlying the models that endogenize these variables and comparing them with the (implicit) assumptions behind the IMF's exogenous forecasts.

Finally, the division between short- and long-term growth is necessarily arbitrary and depends on what works best—for example, the long-term growth may be applied right after the medium-term projections. Ideally, what is needed is a dynamic or intertemporal transition from the short-term adjustment to the long-term steady state, as has been incorporated in Devarajan and Go (1998). Such dynamic extension, however, would require specialized implementation beyond a spreadsheet program.

Layer 3: Household Data

So far, we have not mentioned poverty, and yet this framework is supposed to capture the effects of macroeconomic policies on poverty. We turn therefore to the final (and most important) module, which is labeled "household data" in figure 13.2. Consider each of the households in the household survey. If each household maximizes its utility (over labor supply and consumption), the indirect utility function, v, is a function of wages, w, profits, π, and prices, p: $v = v(w, \pi, p)$.

To look at the impact of small changes in prices on this utility, we differentiate v and apply Shephard's lemma:

$$dv/\lambda = wL(dw/w) + d\pi -pC(dp/p)$$

where $\lambda = \partial v/\partial \pi$, the marginal utility of income, L is net labor supply, and C is net commodity demand.

Each of the variables on the right-hand side is portrayed by the results of the combined 1-2-3 and Get Real/Trivariate VAR models. Thus, with the information on changes in wages, profits, and the prices of the three goods given by the models, and with the initial levels of labor income and commodity consumption given by the household surveys, we can calculate the impact of macroeconomic policies on household welfare.

Table 13.4 shows the information on wages, profits, and commodity demands for the ten deciles in Zambia. An examination of table 13.3 reveals several interesting features of the distribution of income and expenditures in Zambia. First, note that the poor spend more of their income on domestic goods, whereas the rich spend more on imported goods. A policy that leads to an appreciation of the real exchange rate (increased government spending on nontradables, for instance) would favor the rich over the poor. On the income side, the poor get more of their nonwage income from the domestic sector, so a real depreciation would hurt the poor.

In principle, we can calculate the impact on each household in the sample so as to capture the effect on the entire distribution of income. Of course, for a given poverty line, the effect on different poverty measures can also be reported. In short, the framework

Table 13.3 Distribution of Income and Expenditure by Household Groups, Zambia (Layer 3)

Deciles	Share of income			Share of expenditure	
	W	Π_D	Π_E	ExpM	ExpD
1 (poorest)	0.00	0.98	0.02	0.23	0.77
2	0.01	0.92	0.07	0.24	0.76
3	0.06	0.82	0.13	0.26	0.74
4	0.33	0.52	0.15	0.28	0.72
5	0.55	0.34	0.11	0.28	0.72
6	0.83	0.14	0.04	0.29	0.71
7	0.88	0.09	0.02	0.30	0.70
8	0.89	0.09	0.02	0.30	0.70
9	0.90	0.09	0.02	0.31	0.69
10 (richest)	0.64	0.13	0.23	0.30	0.70
Average	0.71	0.14	0.16	0.30	0.70

Note: W = wage income, Π_D = profit income from nontradable good supply, Π_E = profit income from export good supply, *ExpM* = import good, *ExpD* = domestic good.
Source: Zambia Household Survey.

described so far allows for a forecast of welfare measures and poverty outcomes consistent with a set of macroeconomic policies. Since the model is quite flexible, it will eventually permit the analysis of poverty across different regions in a country, when the data allow for such a level of disaggregation.

Application of the Technique: Zambia

Zambia represents an extraordinary case of an undiversified and land-locked economy, exhibiting a very high dependence on mineral resources and exports, subject to external price shocks as well as transport problems throughout its history. With a per capita income of US$300, Zambia is among the poorest countries in Africa.[6] It is also one of the most heavily indebted and recently qualified for debt relief under the Heavily Indebted Poor Countries (HIPC) Initiative. Not surprisingly, Zambia's poverty has remained high; poverty incidence is over 70 percent measured by the national poverty line and near 64 percent based on $1 a day (purchasing power parity). Its population, about 10 million in 2000, is highly urbanized, and large parts of the country are thinly populated. Population is concentrated along the "Line of Rail" that links the Copperbelt with Lusaka, the capital, and with the border town of Livingstone. Apart from South Africa, Zambia is the most urbanized country in Southern Africa. At 20 percent, it also has one of the highest prevalence rates of HIV/AIDS.

Figure 13.4 Copper Price and Zambia's Per Capita Income

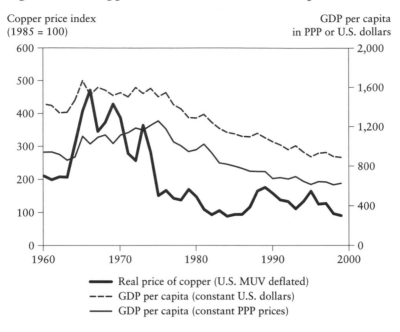

Copper price index
(1985 = 100)

GDP per capita
in PPP or U.S. dollars

—— Real price of copper (U.S. MUV deflated)
--- GDP per capita (constant U.S. dollars)
—— GDP per capita (constant PPP prices)

Zambia's lack of per capita growth is not a recent problem and is widely documented.[7] The long-term economic decline is closely associated with the deterioration of copper fortunes (figure 13.4). It has brought about painful contractions to a predominantly urban-based wage economy, which was once relatively rich in the region. It has also made unaffordable previously high levels of public expenditure, public employment, and social assistance. Outside of copper dependence and the long-term decline in the price of copper, key constraints to Zambia's growth include transportation problems and disruptions arising from regional circumstances, ineffective public expenditure by a dominant but inefficient public sector, and the debt overhang. This anemic growth has continued despite significant liberalization in the 1990s. The large quasi-fiscal deficit stemming from losses of large parastatals and the delays in the privatization of the largest state-owned enterprise, Zambia Consolidated Copper Mines Limited (ZCCM), until the late 1990s were key factors.

Zambia's Medium-Term Macroeconomic Framework

Zambia's economic outlook continues to depend on the supply response of the copper mines to the recent privatization of ZCCM, better copper prices, and the debt relief brought about by HIPC. Moreover, much remains to be done to ensure that the government continues with economic reforms, including governance reforms. Key aspects of the consensus forecast include the following points (table 13.4):

- GDP growth is projected to rise to a modest 5.5 percent in 2003. Inflation is expected to go down to about 10 percent in 2003. The overall fiscal deficit (cash basis), about 7.3 percent of GDP in 2000, is expected to fall to about 4.5 percent by 2003.
- Public revenue and expenditure as a percent of GDP will remain relatively stable at about 18 and 30 percent, respectively.
- Extrabudgetary headroom is created, however, with HIPC debt relief, amounting to about 2.7 percent of GDP in 2001 and rising to 3.2 percent in 2003. The government has identified about US$86 million (about 2.7 percent of GDP) in poverty-related activities that will be funded by HIPC resources.

The consensus forecast is contingent on the realization of key reform measures identified in the credits and should therefore be interpreted as policy target.

The two main risk factors to the consensus forecast in the short and medium-term are weakening of copper prices because of a possible slowdown in world demand, and expenditure pressures from the presidential election in late 2001.

Over the long run, failure to implement the structural and policy reform measures are key risks. Additionally, the benefits of reforms may not be realized quickly or within the time horizon of the medium-term framework. We explore the factors that may elevate the long-term growth of Zambia by considering the lessons and determinants of growth compiled from many countries and their implications to the composition of public expenditure and policy reform.

Deviations from the Medium-Term Projections

The main short-run risk factors are expenditure pressures and a copper price shock.[8]

Shocks in Public Expenditure. The growth elasticities from the Trivariate VAR analysis indicate that increases in government consumption do not have much short-term beneficial impact on growth—the slight positive effect in the first year is offset by the second year. In fact, the cyclical behavior between GDP and shocks to government consumption was broken in 1987, when macroeconomic balances deteriorated rapidly. Before 1987 the connection was more positive and significant; after 1987 it began to move in opposite directions when large swings in government expenditure occurred, particularly between 1987 and 1992.

Table 13.4 Consensus Forecast: Medium-Term
Macroeconomic Framework, Zambia (IMF Financial
Programming/Bank RSMS-X) (percent change unless otherwise specified)

Category	1999	2000	2001	2002	2003
Real GDP	2.4	3.6	5.0	5.0	5.5
Inflation–end year CPI	20.6	30.1	17.5	12.0	10.0
Inflation–average annual CPI	26.8	26.1	22.5	13.7	10.8
GDP deflator	21.7	27.9	24.9	17.2	13.2
Term of trade	−5.7	1.9	3.1	3.5	2.4
Copper price (US$/lb)	0.70	0.83	0.87	0.91	0.92
End-period exchange rate (kwacha/US$)	2630	4160	—	—	—
Average exchange rate (kwacha/US11$)	2380	3110	—	—	—
Current account balance (percent of GDP)	−15.2	−18.5	−19.9	−21.1	−19.3
Broad money	29.2	67.5	17.1	—	—
Net foreign assets	−14.7	63.9	16.3	—	—
Net domestic assets	43.9	1.6	0.8	—	—
Net claims on government	10.2	12.4	−4.2	—	—
Claims on public enterprises	12.0	3.6	−4.4	—	—
Revenue and grants (percent of GDP)	25.5	25.4	26.7	23.5	23.4
Revenue (percent of GDP)	17.6	19.6	17.3	17.7	18.1
Expenditure (percent of GDP)	29.2	31.2	31.3	29.7	28.2
Overall balance (cash basis–percent of GDP)	-4.0	−7.1	−5.0	−6.6	−5.2
Overall balance w/o grants (cash basis–percent of GDP)	−11.9	−12.9	−14.5	−12.4	−10.5
Domestic balance (cash basis–percent of GDP)	0.4	−3.4	−3.3	−2.2	−1.2

— Not available.

Note: The figures and ratios to GDP may differ from PRGF/FSC numbers for a number of reasons—the assumptions of the consensus forecast are run through to the 123PRSP model to derive the reference run numbers; the tax rates are smoothed out if the implied taxes from the revenue to GDP ratios suggest wide variations in the tax rates.

Source: Authors' calculations.

Shocks in Copper Prices. Changes in Zambia's GDP can be traced almost completely to changes in the world price of copper (except for a brief period between 1970 and 1974). The response of GDP to changes in copper prices persists for two to three years, but the response has been tighter since the balance-of-payments situation deteriorated in the late 1980s.

The results of two simulations are shown in table 13.5. The first simulation is the expenditure shock.

• Using the consensus forecast as a reference run, election pressures raise expenditure (government consumption) by 15 percent in the first year and by 10 percent in the next year. The mode of adjustment to the shocks assumed is to keep foreign borrowing as a percent of GDP constant relative to the reference run (that is, a constraint); investment adjusts to available savings.

• Relative to the consensus forecast, the small Keynesian effect of additional expenditure on GDP, a percentage point deviation of 0.6 in the first year, is largely dissipated by the second year.

• Even without the availability of additional foreign financing, the overall fiscal deficit of the central government deteriorates to 6.0 percent of GDP in 2001, 7.8 percent in 2002, and 6.3 percent in 2003, raising issues of sustainability.

• With no room to expand the current account deficit (by assumption), macroeconomic adjustment falls heavily on investment, crowding out private investment in particular. Investment falls from the reference run by about 4 to 5 percent in general.

• The effects in the external sector are very small in terms of the real exchange rate or relative price of exports and imports and the volume of exports and imports.

Consumption and household incomes increase slightly relative to the reference run, but nowhere near the magnitude of the expenditure increase. In fact, if fiscal or tax adjustment is needed to reduce the fiscal deficit, the small gains will be reversed.[9]

The findings confirm the arguments about expenditure policy in Zambia—the benefits are few, but the risks of fiscal deficit and the crowding of investment are high. We return later to the issues about the links between public expenditure, growth and poverty.

In the second simulation, a terms-of-trade shock is added to the above:

• Over the first simulation, the copper price also deviates from the medium-term framework by –20 percent in the first year, –15 percent in the second year, and –10 percent in the third year. For

Table 13.5 Impact of Shocks in Government Expenditures
and Copper Price (percent deviation from the reference run unless otherwise stated)

Indicator	2001	2002	2003
Real GDP (percentage point +/–)			
Expenditure shock	0.6	–0.1	0.1
Expenditure + TOT shock	–0.5	–1.4	–1.3
Overall fiscal balance (cash basis–% of GDP)			
Reference run	–5.0	–6.6	–5.2
Expenditure shock	–6.0	–7.8	–6.3
Expenditure + TOT shock	–7.3	–9.8	–8.6
Real exchange rate of imports (depreciation >0)			
Expenditure shock	0.0	0.0	0.0
Expenditure + TOT shock	21.8	35.9	35.8
Real exchange rate of exports (depreciation>0)			
Expenditure shock	0.0	0.0	0.0
Expenditure + TOT shock	7.9	12.7	13.6
Imports (real)			
Expenditure shock	0.5	0.4	0.6
Expenditure + TOT shock	–12.8	–20.1	–21.2
Exports (real)			
Expenditure shock	0.6	0.4	0.6
Expenditure + TOT shock	2.7	3.2	2.2
Investment (real)			
Expenditure shock	–4.3	–4.9	–4.5
Expenditure + TOT shock	–14.6	–25.3	–25.1
Consumption (real)			
Expenditure shock	0.6	0.4	0.6
Expenditure + TOT shock	–7.6	–11.6	–13.0
Household income in real terms			
Expenditure shock			
Decile 1 (poorest)	0.5	0.4	0.6
Decile 2	0.6	0.6	0.7
Decile 3	0.6	0.6	0.7
Decile 4	0.6	0.5	0.7
Decile 5	0.6	0.5	0.7
Decile 6	0.6	0.5	0.7
Decile 7	0.6	0.5	0.7
Decile 8	0.6	0.5	0.7
Decile 9	0.6	0.5	0.7
Decile 10	0.6	0.5	0.7
Total	0.6	0.5	0.7
Expenditure + TOT shock			
Decile 1 (poorest)	–4.6	–8.0	–9.8
Decile 2	–4.2	–7.4	–9.2
Decile 3	–4.0	–7.0	–8.8
Decile 4	–3.6	–6.4	–8.2
Decile 5	–3.4	–6.1	–7.8
Decile 6	–2.6	–5.0	–6.6
Decile 7	–2.4	–4.7	–6.3
Decile 8	–2.7	–5.1	–6.7
Decile 9	–2.5	–4.8	–6.4
Decile 10	–1.7	–3.7	–5.3
Total	–2.1	–4.4	–5.8

TOT—terms of trade.
Source: Authors' calculations.

comparison, the average volatility of the spot price of copper is about 23 percent; during 1997–99 copper prices fell by more than 45 percent from peak to trough.

• The adverse effects of such a copper price shock will be devastating in Zambia. GDP growth will fall by –0.5 percentage point immediately, –1.4 percentage points in the second year, and a further –1.3 percentage points in the third year.

• The loss of tax base means that the fiscal deficit will rise to 7.3 percent of GDP immediately and to about 10 percent eventually.

• Triggered by the need for the economy to adjust to this sharp drop in terms of trade, the depreciation of the real exchange rate or relative price of foreign goods will be high, particularly for imports. Imports will be much more expensive relative to domestic goods by 22 percent in the second year and by more than 35 percent in the third year. The relative price of exports over nontraded goods also rises by about 8–13 percent.

• As a consequence, expenditure and production switching will take place. Imports fall strongly relative to the reference run, by about 13 percent in the first year and by more than 20 percent the next two years. As the economy contracts but the real exchange rates of exports rise, exports will rise slightly in real terms, by about 2–3 percent despite the general fall in their dollar prices.

• The contraction in aggregate demand is strongest in investment, which deviates from the reference run by 15–25 percent. Aggregate consumption falls by 8–13 percent.

• As a consequence, household welfare generally declines. Relative to the reference run, household incomes in general will fall by 2 percent immediately, accumulating to about 6 percent in the third year. The impact on each income decile is shown in table 13.6. The results generally confirm that such a terms-of-trade shock will be hard on all household groups, particularly the poorest. They also show how a "macro shock," even if it is accommodated by a real exchange rate depreciation, can have severe distributional consequences.

Deviations from the Long-Term Growth Path

Is it possible for the government of Zambia to undertake further reforms and reallocate public expenditure in order to raise long-term aggregate growth? We turn to that important question next and examine possible deviations from the long-term growth or historical trends.

Get Real Model. To derive alternative long-term growth in Zambia, we employ an extended version of the Get Real Model (see table 13.2), which presents a parsimonious set of cross-country growth regressions and captures the long-run growth impact of key economic policies and factors. Determinants generally fit in four broad groups—physical capital, human capital, policy, and shocks.

Alternative Long-Term Growth Rate. Strictly speaking, there is no long-term growth rate in the consensus forecast, a medium-term framework covering the next three years from 2001 to 2003. The GDP growth rate of 5.5 percent in 2003 is therefore assumed to continue and is taken as the implied long-term growth rate in the consensus forecast. It should be noted further that initial conditions and inertia are significant factors in the Get Real Model, and substantial reforms are necessary to attain such a growth rate. Starting from the realities of the 1990s, a 5.5 percent GDP growth would require, for example, the following: no economic distortions (zero black market premium and zero overvaluation of the real exchange rate); HIPC debt relief that reduced the interest payment as a ratio to GDP by more than half; an inflation rate of less than 10 percent;[10] a very favorable export environment; and substantial increases (over 30 percent) in the school enrollment rate and investment in infrastructure.

Two alternative long-term growth paths are examined (counting the two VAR simulations, simulation 3 is the starting point):

• Simulation 3: A 10 percent improvement across the board on all the underlying variables in the Get Real Model (except initial income). The net effect is to add 0.9 percentage point to the economic growth of Zambia. Household income in all deciles increases by about 1 percent relative to the reference run.

• Simulation 4: As a policy target, the consensus forecast is generally higher and more optimistic than the historical trends or what the Get Real Model would suggest.[11] In Zambia's case, the Get Real Model would imply a lower long-term GDP growth of less than 2 percent a year and a negative growth for GDP per capita. If progress is not made and all growth determinants remain the same as in the 1990s, a −4.6 percentage point reduction in GDP growth from the reference long-term growth is projected (that is, 0.9 percent GDP growth). The negative deviations of household incomes from the reference run are generally of the same magnitude for all household groups (table 13.6), and they measure the income forgone from a reform program that is seriously off track.

Table 13.6 Alternative Long-Term Growth
(percent deviation from the reference run)

	Sim 3	Sim 4
Real GDP (percentage point +/−)	0.9	−4.6
Household income in real terms (by decile)		
1 (poorest)	1.1	−4.7
2	1.0	−4.7
3	1.0	−4.6
4	1.0	−4.6
5	1.0	−4.6
6	1.0	−4.6
7	1.0	−4.5
8	1.0	−4.5
9	1.0	−4.5
10	0.9	−4.5
Total	0.9	−4.5

Source: Authors' calculations.

Concluding Remarks

As we said in the introduction, the PRSP process emphasizes country ownership, consultation, and a poverty focus for all policies. In particular, the poverty focus of macroeconomic policies calls for a new framework that can capture some of the tradeoffs and distributional implications of traditional macroeconomic policies and shocks. The framework presented here, the 123PRSP Model, attempts to portray some of these effects. For instance, in an application to Zambia, the model showed that a terms-of-trade shock (a fall in the price of copper) could have adverse distributional consequences, harming the poor more than the rich, even if the shock were fully accommodated by macroeconomic policies. This outcome was caused by differences in the sectoral composition of income sources in Zambia between the poor and the rich. Similarly, the model showed that in the case of Zambia at least, greater fiscal flexibility may not be so desirable. The first-round Keynesian multiplier effects of an increase in government spending (financed domestically) are offset by the crowding-out effects of higher fiscal deficits in the near term. That this model could be put together in a relatively short time, in a country with limited data, and that policy-relevant results could be generated and used by policymakers in their PRSP, is evidence that the first objective of the PRSP, country ownership, could also be reinforced with the current exercise.

To be sure, the framework presented here, while tractable, is a patchwork of models with different philosophies. For instance, the neoclassical structure of the 1-2-3 Model is based on a different philosophy from the reduced-form Get Real Model. Future work will aim to better integrate the various pieces. For example, a more satisfactory description of the labor market—keeping in mind the requirement that the model be applicable in countries with poor data—is a high priority. A second task is to develop some two-way interactions between at least some of the model's building blocks, so that eventually a fully simultaneous system can be developed.

Nevertheless, the model fulfills many of the criteria for a macroeconomic framework for PRSPs: it is capable of identifying some of the salient tradeoffs; it is based on solid economic foundations; it can be estimated with data from low-income countries; and—perhaps more important—it is simple enough that model results are easy to interpret. Alternative frameworks will have to ensure they do not sacrifice these desirable characteristics.

Notes

The authors thank Florence M. Charlier, Leonid Koryukin, Andrew Dabalen, William R. Easterly, Hippolyte Fofack, and Alejandro Izquierdo for their contributions; and are grateful to Pierre-Richard Agénor, Jeffrey Lewis, Luiz Pereira da Silva, Christian Petersen, Kaspar Richter, and Luis Servén for their comments and suggestions.

1. In October 1999, the executive boards of the World Bank and International Monetary Fund decided to base future assistance to low-income countries on the country's Poverty Reduction Strategy Paper (PRSP). This decision represented a shift in policy along several dimensions. First, unlike its predecessor (the Policy Framework Paper), which was a tripartite document, the PRSP has to be prepared by the country (country ownership). Second, the PRSP has to be the result of a consultative process, involving not just the government, but also the private sector and civil society. Finally, the PRSP has to show the implications for poverty reduction of all aspects of the government's program. In particular, it has to gauge the impact on poverty of macroeconomic policies. To date, the model has been developed and used by teams from low-income countries, such as Cameroon, Mauritania, Senegal, and Zambia, in their PRSP process and policy analysis.

2. See, for example, World Bank (2000); Dollar and Kraay (2000).

3. Examples of the full-blown approach include Adelman and Robinson (1978); Lysy and Taylor (1979); Sahn (1996); Benjamin (1996); Devarajan

and van der Mensbrugghe (2000); and Agénor, Izquierdo, and Fofack (2001). The approach adopted here is closer to the tradition of microsimulation models (Bourguignon, Robinson, and Robillard 2002).

4. See Khan, Montiel, and Haque (1990) for a description and comparison between the analytical approaches of the IMF and the World Bank.

5. Although the coefficients are the same for all countries, the long-run growth rates will be different since the levels of the explanatory variables will be different. Other growth regressions or models that account for different sets of determinants or factors such as HIV/AIDS may also be used, see, for example, Barro (1997); Bonnel (2000); and other works listed in the references.

6. 2000 GDP per capita converted to U.S. dollars using the World Bank Atlas method.

7. See, for example, World Bank (2001) and Go (2003).

8. A third possible risk is shock in the agriculture sector. Random weather changes such as drought continue to be important factors in agricultural production and its impact to GDP. However, we generally did not find that agricultural value added was a good predictor of the underlying shocks to agricultural production and GDP. Nevertheless, the responsiveness of GDP growth to changes to the value added in agriculture has been stronger since the late 1980s.

9. A fiscal adjustment simulation (not shown) confirms the results.

10. Note that the coefficient for inflation is not significant. The variable may be multicolinear with other determinants. The growth effects of inflation may also cancel out over the cycle of inflation crises.

11. In many countries, there is a tendency for overestimation with regard to the execution of reforms and the impact of future investments on growth. See, for example, Easterly (1998).

References

The word *processed* describes informally reproduced works that may not be commonly available through library systems.

Addison, Douglas. 2000. "A Preliminary Investigation of the Impact of UEMOA Tariffs on the Fiscal Revenues of Burkina Faso." In Shantayanan Devarajan, Lyn Squire, and F. Halsey Rogers, eds., *World Bank Economists Forum*. Washington, D.C.: World Bank.

Adelman, Irma, and Sherman Robinson. 1978. *Income Distribution Policy in Developing Countries: A Case Study of Korea*. Stanford: Stanford University Press and Oxford University Press.

Agénor, Pierre-Richard, and Joshua Aizenman. 1999. "Macroeconomic Adjustment with Segmented Labor Markets." *Journal of Development Economics* 58 (April): 277–96.

Agénor, Pierre-Richard, Alejandro Izquierdo, and Hippolyte Fofack. 2001. "IMMPA: A Quantitative Framework for Poverty Reduction Strategies." World Bank Institute, Washington, D.C. (www.worldbank.org/wbi/macroeconomics/modeling/immpa.htm).

Barro, Robert J. 1997. *Determinants of Economic Growth—A Cross-Country Empirical Study.* Cambridge: MIT Press.

Benjamin, Nancy. 1996. "Adjustment and Income Distribution in an Agricultural Economy: A General Equilibrium Analysis of Cameroon." *World Development* 24(6): 1003–13.

Bonnel, René. 2000. "HIV/AIDS and Economic Growth: A Global Perspective." *South African Journal of Economics* 68(5): 820–35.

Bourguignon, François, Anne-Sophie Robillard, and Sherman Robinson. 2002. "Representative vs. Real Households in the Macroeconomic Modeling of Inequality." International Food Policy Research Institute, Washington, D.C. Processed.

de Melo, Jaime, and Sherman Robinson. 1992. "Productivity and Externalities: Models of Export-Led Growth." *Journal of International Trade and Economic Development* 1:41–68.

Devarajan, Shantayanan. 1997. "Real Exchange Rate Misalignment in the CFA Zone." *Journal of African Economies* 6(10): 35–53.

———. 1999. "Estimates of Real Exchange Rate Misalignment with a Simple General-Equilibrium Model." In Lawrence E. Hinkle and Peter J. Montiel, *Exchange Rate Misalignment: Concepts and Measurement for Developing Countries.* Washington, D.C.: World Bank and Oxford University Press.

Devarajan, Shantayanan, and Delfin S. Go. 1998. "The Simplest Dynamic General Equilibrium Model of an Open Economy." *Journal of Policy Modeling* 29(6): 677–714.

Devarajan, Shantayanan, and Dominique van der Mensbrugghe. 2000. "Trade Reform in South Africa: Impact on Households." World Bank, Development Research Group, Washington, D.C. Processed.

Devarajan, Shantayanan, Hafez Ghanem, and Karen Theirfelder. 1997. "Economic Reform and Labor Unions: A General Equilibrium Analysis Applied to Bangladesh and Indonesia." *World Bank Economic Review* 11(1): 145–70.

———. 1999. "Labor Market Regulations, Trade Liberalization, and the Distribution of Income in Bangladesh." *Journal of Policy Reform* 3(1): 1–28.

Devarajan, Shantayanan, Delfin S. Go, and Hongyi Li. 1999. "Quantifying the Fiscal Effect of Trade Reform: A General Equilibrium Model Estimated for 60 Countries." Policy Research Working Paper 2162. World Bank, Development Research Group, Washington, D.C.

Devarajan, Shantayanan, Jeffrey D. Lewis, and Sherman Robinson. 1990. "Policy Lessons from Trade-focused, Two-sector Models." *Journal of Policy Modeling* 12(4): 625–57.

———. 1993. "External Shocks, Purchasing Power Parity, and the Equilibrium Real Exchange Rate." *World Bank Economic Review* 7(1): 45–63.

Devarajan, Shantayanan, Delfin S. Go, Jeffrey D. Lewis, Sherman Robinson, and Pekka Sinko. 1997. "Simple General Equilibrium Modeling." In Joseph F. Francois and Kenneth A. Reinert, eds., *Applied Methods for Trade Policy Analysis: A Handbook*. Cambridge. Cambridge University Press.

Devarajan, Shantayanan, Sherman Robinson, A. Yúnez-Naude, Raúl Hinojosa-Ojeda, and Jeffrey D. Lewis. 1999. "From Stylized to Applied Models: Building Multisector CGE Models for Policy." *North American Journal of Economics and Finance* 10 (1999): 5–38.

Dollar, David, and Aart Kraay. 2000. "Growth Is Good for the Poor." Policy Research Working Paper 2587. World Bank, Development Research Group, Washington, D.C. Processed.

Easterly, William R. 1998. "The Ghost of Financing Gap: Testing the Growth Model Used in the International Financial Institutions." *International Monetary Fund Seminar Series* 1998-2:1-29.

———. 2001. "The Lost Decades: Developing Countries' Stagnation in Spite of Policy Reform 1980–1998." *Journal of Economic Growth* 6(2):135-57.

Go, Delfin S. Forthcoming. "Public Expenditure, Growth, and Poverty in Zambia."

Go, Delfin S., and Pradeep Mitra. 1999. "Trade Liberalization, Fiscal Adjustment, and Exchange Rate Policy in India." In G. Ranis and L. Raut, eds., *Trade, Growth, and Development (Essays in Honor of Professor T.N. Srinivasan)*. New York: North-Holland.

Khan, Mohsin S., Peter Montiel, and Nadeem U. Haque. 1990. "Adjustment with Growth: Relating the Analytical Approaches of the IMF and the World Bank." *Journal of Development Economics* 32: 155–79.

Lysy, Frank J., and Lance Taylor. 1979. "Vanishing Income Redistributions: Keynesian Clues About Model Surprises in the Short Run." *Journal of Development Economics* 6: 11–29.

Sahn, David E., ed. 1996. *Economic Reform and the Poor in Africa*. Oxford: Clarendon Press.

World Bank. 2000. *World Development Report: Attacking Poverty*. Washington, D.C.

———. 2001. *Zambia Public Expenditure Review: Public Expenditure, Growth and Poverty*. Report 22543-ZA. Washington, D.C. Processed.

14

Social Accounting Matrices and SAM-Based Multiplier Analysis

Jeffery Round

This chapter sets out the framework of a social accounting matrix (SAM) and shows how it can be used to construct SAM-based multipliers to analyze the effects of macroeconomic policies on distribution and poverty. Estimates provided by a social accounting matrix can be useful—even essential—for calibrating a much broader class of models having to do with monitoring poverty and income distribution. But this chapter is limited to a review of the way SAMs are used to develop simple economywide multipliers for poverty and income distribution analysis.

What is a SAM? A SAM is a particular representation of the macroeconomic and mesoeconomic accounts of a socioeconomic system, which capture the transactions and transfers between all economic agents in the system (Pyatt and Round 1985; Reinert and Roland-Holst 1997). In common with other economic accounting systems, a SAM records transactions taking place during an accounting period, usually one year. The main features of a SAM are threefold. First, the accounts are represented as a *square matrix*, where the incomings and outgoings for each account are shown as a corresponding row and column of the matrix. The transactions are shown in the cells, so the matrix displays the interconnections between agents in an explicit way. Second, it is *comprehensive*, in the sense that it portrays all the economic activities of the system (consumption, production, accumulation, and distribution), although not necessarily in equivalent detail. Third, the SAM is *flexible*, in that, although it is usually set up in a standard, basic framework, there is a large measure of flexibility both in the degree of disaggregation and in the emphasis placed on different parts of the economic system. Because it is an accounting framework, not only the SAM square, but also the corresponding row and column totals must be equal. Clearly, at one extreme, any set of macroeconomic aggregates can be set out in a matrix format. But it would not be a "social" accounting matrix in the sense in which the term is usually used. An overriding feature of a SAM is that households and household groups are at the heart of the framework; only if some detail exists on the distributional features of the household sector can the framework truly earn the label *social* accounting matrix. Also a SAM typically shows much more detail about the circular flow of income, including transactions between different institutions (including different household groups) and between production activities. In particular it records the interactions between both these sets of agents through the factor and product markets.

The origins of matrix accounting go back a long way, but SAMs are generally attributed to Sir Richard Stone, who did his initial and pioneering work for the United Kingdom and some other industrialized countries. Pyatt, Thorbecke, and others (Pyatt and Thorbecke 1976; Pyatt and Round 1977) further developed these ideas and used them to help address poverty and income distribution issues in developing countries from the early 1970s onward. A large number of SAM-based multiplier studies have since followed, some of the earliest being for Sri Lanka (Pyatt and Round 1979), Malaysia (Chander and others 1980), Botswana (Hayden and Round 1982), Republic of Korea (Defourny and Thorbecke 1984), Indonesia (Thorbecke and others 1992), and more recently, for Ghana (Powell and Round 1998, 2000) and Vietnam (Tarp, Roland-Holst, and Rand 2002). In all of these studies the aim has been to examine the nature of the multiplier effects of an income injection in one part of an economic system on the functional and institutional distribution in general and on the incomes of socioeconomic groups of households in particular. It should be noted that some similar multiplier analyses that aimed to close the input-output model with respect to households by incorporating a (Keynesian-type) income-expenditure loop within an input-output framework were proposed by Miyazawa (1976) and others also in the early 1970s (see Pyatt 2001 for a discussion of this earlier history).

Three principal motivations underlie the development of SAMs. First, the *construction* of a SAM helps to bring together data from many disparate sources that describe the structural characteristics of an economy. A SAM can also be used to good effect in helping to improve the range and quality of estimates by highlighting data needs and identifying key gaps. Second, SAMs are a very good way of *displaying* information; the structural interdependence in an economy at both the macroeconomic and mesoeconomic levels are shown in a SAM in a simple and illuminating way. A SAM shows clearly the linkage between income distribution and economic structure, which is, of course, especially important in the context of this volume. Third, SAMs represent a useful analytical framework for *modeling*; that is, they provide a direct input into a range of models, including fixed-price multiplier models, and are also an integral part of the benchmark data set required to calibrate computable general equilibrium (CGE) models (Pyatt 1988).

In summary, a suitably designed and disaggregated SAM shows a great deal about the structural features and interdependencies of an economy. It represents a snapshot of the transactions (flows) taking place in a given year. The SAM is a mesoeconomic framework: it serves as a useful bridge between a macroeconomic framework and a more detailed description of markets and institutions. Of course the detail in the SAM might not be limited to the real economy, and there are some notable examples of SAMs and SAM-based models that incorporate the financial sectors and the flow of funds (see Sadoulet and de Janvry 1995). Clearly the economic structure of the SAM may change just as the economy changes and responds to shocks. A more formal modeling approach should therefore include structural or behavioral specifications for the various groups of transactions. This is especially true, for example, if the structure changes as a result of changes in relative prices.

Often as a first-cut ex ante analysis, however, a SAM is frequently used to examine the partial equilibrium consequences of real shocks, using a multiplier model that treats the circular flow of income endogenously. The circular flow captures the generation of income by activities in producing commodities, the mapping of these income payments to factors of production of various kinds, the distribution of factor and nonfactor income to households, and the subsequent spending of income by households on commodities. These patterns of payments are manifested in the structure of the SAM and are modeled analogously to the input structure of activities in an input-output model based only on interindustry transactions. However, it is important to stress that the results differ from input-output by virtue of the fact that input-output multipliers are augmented by additional multiplier effects induced by the circular flow of income among activities, factors, and households. A main outcome of the SAM-based multiplier analysis is an examination of the effects of real economic shocks on the distribution of income across socioeconomic groups of households. One other important feature of SAM-based multiplier analysis is that it lends itself easily to decomposition, thereby adding an extra degree of transparency in understanding the nature of linkage in an economy and the effects of exogenous shocks on distribution and poverty.

SAM-Based Techniques

A simple, stylized SAM framework is shown in table 14.1. It is a square matrix that represents the transactions taking place in an economy during an accounting period, usually one year. Table 14.1 shows a matrix of order 8 by 8. Without further detail the table represents a macroeconomic framework of an economy with three institutions: households, corporate enterprises, and government. Each account is represented twice; once as a row (showing receipts) and once as a column (showing payments). The SAM records the transactions between the accounts in the cells of the matrix (T_{ij}). So a payment from the jth account to the ith account is shown in cell T_{ij} according to the standard accounting convention in an input-output table. The ordering of the rows and columns is not crucial, although the rows are always ordered in the same way as the columns. In many SAMs and SAM-based analyses, the leading accounts are chosen to reflect a primary interest in living standards and distributional issues, so that institutions (households) or factors of production are ordered first. In table 14.1 the ordering begins with production, as it does in an input-output table, although this order does not affect the data structure or the modeling techniques in any other way.

Viewed as a macroeconomic SAM, table 14.1 shows clearly the three basic forms of economic activity—production (accounts 1, 2, and 3), consumption (accounts 4, 5, and 6), and accumulation (account 7)—plus the transactions with the rest of the world (account 8). It is a simple and comprehensive framework corresponding directly to a flow chart of the same transactions shown in figure 14.1. The main economic aggregates can be ascertained directly from the macroeconomic SAM. Thus, the generation of value added by domestic activities of production, which constitutes gross domestic product (GDP), is found in cell 32; final consumption expenditure by households is shown in cell 14, and so on. It has been conventional for quite some time to distinguish production activities from the commodities that they produce. That means that the underlying input-output tables come with two components: a matrix of "uses" of commodities, and a matrix of commodity "supplies"

Table 14.1 A Basic Social Accounting Matrix (SAM)

Account	(1)	(2)	(3)	(4)	(5)	(6)	(7)	(8)	*Totals*
Production									
Commodities (1)		Intermediate consumption		Household consumption		Government consumption	Fixed capital formation and change in stocks	Exports	Demand for products
Activities (2)	Domestic sales								Sales of commodities
Factors of production (3)		Gross value added payments to factors						*Net* factor income from RoW	Factor income receipts
Institutions (current accounts)									
Households (4)			Labor and mixed income	Inter-household transfers	Distributed profits to households	Current transfers to households		*Net* current transfers from RoW	Current household receipts
Corporate enterprises (5)			Operating surplus			Current transfers to enterprises		*Net* current transfers from RoW	Current enterprise receipts
Government (&NPISH) (6)	*Net* taxes on products			Direct taxes	Direct taxes		Capital transfers	*Net* current transfers from RoW	Current government receipts
Combined capital accounts (7)				Household savings	Enterprise savings	Government savings		*Net* capital transfers from RoW	Capital receipts
Rest of world (RoW) (combined account) (8)	Imports						Current external balance		Aggregate receipts from RoW
TOTALS	Supply of products	Costs of production activities	Factor income payments	Current household outlays	Current enterprise outlays	Current government outlays	Capital outlays	Aggregate outlays to RoW	

Note: NPISH: Nonprofit institutions serving households.
Source: Round (2003).

Figure 14.1 The Economywide Circular Flow of Income

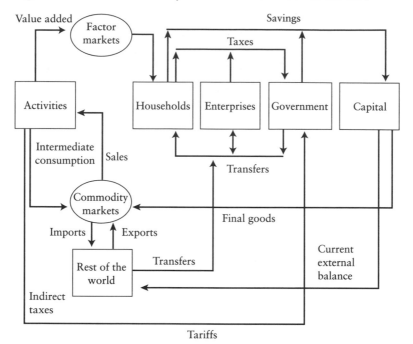

Note: The arrows show direction of payments.
Source: Adapted from Chung-I Li (2002).

(that is, supply-use tables). Overall, therefore, there is a clear relationship between a SAM and the national accounts; the latter can be directly ascertained from the former (box 14.1).

The main interest in compiling and using a SAM is to engage in further disaggregation of certain accounts in the macroeconomic system and to estimate the transactions in more detail. Thus the macroeconomic SAM evolves into a mesoeconomic SAM. It records consistent and sometimes quite detailed sets of transactions and transfers between different kinds of agents often interacting through different markets, especially the commodity and factor markets. In principle, there is no limitation on the extent to which accounts may be disaggregated. However, for the purpose of tracing the process of income generation, its distribution and redistribution across households, and the structure of production in multiplier models, the accounts that have typically been subject to most disaggregation are the production accounts (activities and commodities), factor accounts, and household and other institution accounts. Extended modeling and analysis may require further disaggregation of the tax

---

Box 14.1 Relationship between SAMs and the National Accounts

It is highly desirable that a SAM should be consistent with the national accounts, and an aggregate SAM is a particular way of representing the national accounts within a matrix framework. This is sometimes referred to as a macroeconomic SAM, although it has few of the socioeconomic details and features of a true mesoeconomic SAM.

The System of National Accounts (SNA 1993) is an international system that is now in the process of being implemented by many developing countries. It is based around a set of Integrated Economic Accounts (IEA) defined by transactor (that is, institutional sector). There are sets of current accounts, accumulation accounts, and balance sheets. In common with current national accounting practice, most of the detailed estimates are compiled for the current accounts, including summary accumulation accounts, that is the summary flow accounts for capital transactions. As yet, the balance sheets, recording the changes in the values of stocks of assets and liabilities held by institutions, are rarely estimated for countries. Each flow account in the system tracks a particular kind of economic activity such as production, or the generation, distribution, redistribution, and use of income. In each account individual kinds of transactions are recorded by transactor of origin (resource) or destination (use), or both, and a balancing item carries forward from one account in the sequence to the next. Thus, "value added" is the balancing item in the production account, which is carried forward to the generation of income account; and "disposable income" is carried forward from the (re)distribution of income account to the use of income account. It can be viewed as a system whereby income "cascades" from one account to another. In this respect, although the SNA is not explicitly organized into a matrix format, there are features that can be helpful in deriving a SAM from it. But not all transactions are identifiable by origin and by destination, so additional work has to be done in deriving a full SAM, even confining it to the broad institutional level.

Preparing a more detailed SAM, highlighting detailed household groups and factor accounts, that is consistent with the national accounts is even more problematic (see box 14.2). National accounting handbooks, now being prepared and becoming available, are very helpful in providing a bridge between the national accounts and SAMs (Leadership Group on Social Accounting Matrices 2003).

---

and government accounts (say, to distinguish taxes for tax incidence analysis), capital accounts (to identify the flow of funds and to depict different kinds of financial and asset markets), and external accounts (to show more detail of external transactions for trade analysis).

More disaggregation and increased detail in the SAM does not come without a cost. The SAM has a voracious appetite for data, although it must be said that much can be (and has been) achieved with small data sets, a careful choice of classifications, and few simplifying assumptions. The single-entry system means that with more transactors (such as households or production activities), there is a need to identify the origins and destinations of a much greater set of transactions in the system. This requirement is often nontrivial. The compilation process requires detailed information from production surveys and household and labor force surveys (such as Living Standards Measurement Studies or Integrated Household Surveys) alongside the national accounts, balance of payments statistics, and a supply-use table. (See box 14.2 for an illustration of some compilation issues.) Some basic guiding principles for choosing the classifications for the household and factor disaggregations have evolved and suggest the following:

Households. These are usually represented by socioeconomic group, classified according to characteristics of either the household head or the principal earner (gender, employment status), often by locations (rural-urban, for example), and sometimes other characteristics including assets or main income source (such as farm-nonfarm). Income level is usually avoided as a criterion because individual households may be mobile between income groups, thus creating difficulties in targeting specific households or any analysis of changes in poverty or distribution (Pyatt and Thorbecke 1976). Nevertheless it is possible to disaggregate the socioeconomic groups further, according to their income distribution, and therefore to show the within-group characteristics of poverty and inequality. Based on real observations over time, this level of disaggregation would give some comparative measure of changes in poverty and inequality within groups.[1]

Factors. These accounts record the income generated by production activities in employing various kinds of factors of production. Income is mapped to those households and other institutions that supply these factor services in accordance with their factor endowments and their access to factor markets. Apart from broad functional distinctions between labor, capital, and land, the labor accounts are usually disaggregated (by gender, skill, education level, location, and the like) relatively more than are the capital accounts (by domestic and foreign capital, for example). The main aim is usually to focus on any labor market segmentation that might have structural consequences, especially in determining impacts on different groups of households.

Box 14.2 Constructing a SAM

The construction of a SAM with any significant degree of disaggregation of the principal accounts (activities, commodities, factors, and households) requires the availability of some key data sets. Principally, these include:

- supply and use tables (input-output tables), or the necessary primary survey data to compile them.
- a household survey incorporating a labor force survey (a multipurpose, integrated household survey).
- government budget accounts, trade statistics, and balance of payments statistics.
- national accounts.

If any components of these key data sets are not available, then a fully comprehensive SAM cannot be constructed. Not all surveys are necessarily available for the same year, but if they are, or are available for a proximate year, then that usually provides sufficient usable information.

Many compilers begin by assembling a macroeconomic SAM from the national accounts. The macroeconomic SAM defines a set of control totals for the subsequent disaggregations and means that the SAM is consistent with any macroeconomic analysis. Often macroeconomic SAMs are available for a more recent year than are the detailed data sets, such as input-output tables and household surveys. Therefore the latter essentially provide shares to recalibrate and fit to the macroeconomic aggregates.

In contrast, Pyatt and Round (1984) have pointed out that compiling detailed SAMs can be part of a process to improve the national accounts estimates. Many countries now rebase their national accounts periodically in accordance with a set of commodity balances (input-output table). Otherwise household survey data are not always fully utilized in estimating the national accounts (for example, consumer expenditure is obtained as a residual in the commodity balances), so there might be a case for adjusting the macroeconomic SAM in some circumstances. One particular area concerns the coverage of subsistence and informal sector activities. Household surveys provide a unique source of information on this household sector activity. Nevertheless there are some continuing well-known problems in deriving estimates at the individual household, or even at the household group level, such as the tendency for respondents to underreport incomes and transfer income (Round 2003).

Estimates from primary or disparate secondary sources are often inconsistent, and several alternative matrix balancing methods are available to adjust the initial estimates for consistency (Byron 1978; Robinson, Cattaneo, and El-Said 2001; Round 2003). A good example of constructing a SAM is described in Chung-I Li (2002). Several similar examples can be found on the International Food Policy Research Institute Web site http://www.ifpri.org/ and Powell and Round (1998).

SAM-Based Multiplier Models

The SAM is not, in itself, a model. It is simply a representation of a set of macro- and mesoeconomic data for an economy. However, suitably designed and supported by survey data and other information, it does suggest some important and useful features about socioeconomic structure in general, and the relationship between the structure of production and the distribution of income in particular. The basic approach to SAM-based multiplier models is to compute column shares (column coefficients) from a SAM to represent structure and, analogous to an input-output model, to compute matrix multipliers. In doing so, one or more of the accounts must be designated as being exogenous; otherwise the matrix is not invertible, and there are no multipliers to be had. Therefore, in developing a simple multiplier model, the first step is to decide which accounts should be exogenous and which are to be endogenous. It has been customary to regard transactions in the government account, the capital account, and the rest-of-the-world account to be exogenous. That is because government outlays are essentially policy-determined, the external sector is outside domestic control, and because the model has no dynamic features, investment is exogenously determined. The corporate enterprise outlays (such as distributed profits and property incomes) are variously treated as being either exogenously or endogenously determined. The endogenous accounts are therefore usually limited to those of production (activities and commodities), factors, and households. Defining the endogenous transactions in this way helps to focus on the interaction between two sets of agents (production activities and households) interacting through two sets of markets (factors and commodities). For simplicity the exogenous accounts may be aggregated into a single account, which records an aggregate set of injections into the system and the leakages from it (table 14.2).

Like an input-output model, the matrix of endogenous transactions, which are represented in summary form by the matrix T, can be used to define a matrix A of column shares by dividing elements in each column of T by the column total: $T = Ay$, where T and, correspondingly, A, have the partitioned structure shown in table 14.2. The component submatrices of A show, for example, that A_{32} is the matrix of value added shares of factor incomes generated by activities, A_{43} is the shares of factor incomes distributed across households, and A_{14} shows the pattern of expenditures by each household group. Several submatrices show no transactions in the SAM, and these are recorded as zeros. Similarly x and y are, respectively, the vectors of exogenous injections and account totals, where, for exam-

Table 14.2 SAM: Endogenous and Exogenous Accounts

Account		Endogenous				Exogenous	Total
		(1)	(2)	(3)	(4)	(5)	
Commodities	(1)		Intermediate consumption T_{12}		Household consumption expenditures T_{14}	Other final demands x_1	Total demands for products y_1
Activities	(2)	Domestic supplies T_{21}					Total activity outputs y_2
Factors	(3)		Value added T_{32}			Factor income from abroad x_3	Total factor income receipts y_3
Households	(4)			Factor income to households T_{43}	Interhousehold transfers T_{44}	Nonfactor income receipts x_4	Total household incomes y_4
Other accounts (exogenous)	(5)	Imports, indirect taxes l_1	Indirect taxes l_2	Other factor payments l_3	Savings, etc. l_4		Total exogenous receipts Σ_l
TOTAL		Total supply of products y_1	Total activity outputs y_2	Total factor income payments y_3	Total household outlays y_4	Total exogenous payments Σ_x	

Source: Adapted from Pyatt and Round (1979; table 2).

ple, x_1 is the vector of all purchases of final goods and services other than those by households and y_1 is the total demand for products. The endogenous row accounts in table 14.1 can then be written as a series of linear identities, and the system can be solved to give

(14.1) $$y = Ay + x = (I - A)^{-1} = M_A x$$

where M_A is the SAM multiplier matrix. More precisely, it is a matrix of "accounting" multipliers. If A represents the pattern of outlays (that is, expenditure and distribution coefficients) and is assumed to be fixed, then M_A is fixed, and equation 14.1 determines the equilibrium total outputs and incomes y consistent with any set of injections x. To illustrate its use, suppose we examine the possible effects of a reduction of government expenditure, including a reduction in wage and salary payments to government employees. Government expenditure is part of the exogenous accounts so, assuming the same endogenous *patterns* of expenditures and income payments hold elsewhere in the economy, equation 14.1 computes the simple multiplier effects (which would be reductions in this case) on outputs of activities of production and, importantly, on incomes of household groups. In more detail, the reductions in government expenditures reduce the activity levels and household incomes not only directly but also indirectly (the multiplier effects) in that value added is reduced, lowering factor incomes and reducing household incomes according to the combination of factors each household owns. The latter translates into changes in the total income of each group, or equivalently, in the mean household group income. This example is illustrative of the focus of SAM multipliers in determining the total income effects on different household groups that arise from an exogenous (policy-determined or external) shock. Input-output multipliers capture only the interindustry effects, even though these propagate some income effects insofar as changes in outputs directly and indirectly affect incomes. However, SAM-based multipliers account not only for the direct and indirect effects but also for the induced effects on factor and household incomes and activity outputs due to the (Keynesian) income-expenditure multipliers (Robinson 1989; Adelman and Robinson 1989).

"Fixed-price" multipliers, based on marginal responses, are distinguished from "accounting" multipliers, based on average patterns, although both sets of multipliers are derived in constant prices and are therefore fixed price in a formal sense. The distinction simply recognizes that the marginal responses in the system, even in a fixed-price world, may be different from what they are on average. Thus

$$dy = (I - C)^{-1} dx = M_C \, dx$$

where C is the matrix of marginal propensities and M_C is now the multiplier matrix. C is computed from A as follows: $C_{ij} = \eta_{ij}A_{ij}$ where η_{ij} is the elasticity of i with respect to j. Pyatt and Round (1979) computed both kinds of multipliers in a study for Sri Lanka, by using data on income elasticities for one part of the SAM, namely household expenditures on commodities. All other elasticities were effectively set at unity, so the numerical differences between the two sets of multipliers were very small, but conceptually this helps to break away from relying on the outlay patterns portrayed by the SAM per se. In most studies accounting multipliers are used as though they are fixed-price multipliers, and equivalently the income elasticities are set at one.

SAM-based multipliers rely on some strong assumptions; so, rather like the data side, simplicity and transparency do not come without cost either. First, using the model to explore the distributional consequences of positive shocks (that is, expansion of export demand, or increases in either government spending or investment), the implicit assumption is that there is excess capacity in all sectors and unemployed (or underemployed) factors of production. In this case the multipliers work through to the equilibrium solution, but if there are capacity constraints of any kind, then the multipliers will overestimate the total effects, and the final distributional effects will be uncertain. Second, because prices are fixed, there is no allowance for substitution effects anywhere or at any stage, a fact that may also lead to an overestimation of the total response. Third, when prices are not fixed, they may be expected to rise (fall) to offset excess demands (supplies) in any of the markets. Therefore any price changes would tend to mitigate the total effects implied by the fixed-price model. Fourth, the distinction between endogenous and exogenous accounts naturally means that there is a limit to the endogenous responses that are captured in the multiplier model.

Clearly, the exogenous accounts will be affected by the initial shock and by changes in the leakages from the endogenous to the exogenous accounts to balance the exogenous accounts as a group. But other than that, no other responses can occur within the exogenous accounts, whereas in practice they may—government expenditures might change as a result of a trade shock as well as having an effect on the trade balance. So to this extent, the multiplier effects will be underestimated. Overall it is obviously difficult to generalize about the validity of the SAM multipliers in all settings. In some cases the assumption of a perfectly elastic supply of outputs and factors is reasonable, while in others it is not. At best, SAM multipliers provide a first-cut estimate of the effects of a policy or external shock, relying only on the SAM structure. It is an appealing, though somewhat limited, analytical technique, which should not be applied mechanically without due care.

Decomposing Multipliers

The SAM multiplier analysis may, under the circumstances described above, give some indication of the possible resultant effects of an exogenous shock on the functional (factoral) and institutional distributions of income as well as on the structure of output. However, to create more transparency and, in particular, to examine the nature of linkage in the economy that leads to these outcomes, it is possible to decompose the SAM multipliers further.

The simplest decomposition of all can be obtained by reducing the SAM to two endogenous accounts, activities and households (institutions), by solving out the accounts for the factor and commodity markets.[2] In this, and similar cases, the SAM multiplier can be shown to be decomposable into three multiplicative components (Pyatt and Round 1979):

$$(14.2) \qquad dy = M_C dy = M_3 M_2 M_1 dx$$

where M_1, M_2, and M_3 are all "multiplier" matrices.[3] In this case the interpretation of the matrices is direct. M_1 represents the "within-account" effects, that is, the multiplier effects an exogenous injection into one set of accounts (say, either the activities account or the household accounts) will have on that same set of accounts. For activities this component is the input-output multiplier; for households this component will reflect any interdependencies that arise from the patterns of transfers of income between households (such as urban-to-rural remittances). M_2 captures the "cross" (or spillover) effects, whereby an injection of income into one set of accounts (say, activities) has effects on the other set of accounts (say, households), with no reverse effects. M_3 shows the multiplier effects attributable to the full circular flow, these are the "between-account" effects, after extracting the within-account multipliers.

It is of interest to ascertain what might be the relative magnitudes of these component multipliers in order to understand more about the nature of linkage and to identify areas of duality in the economy. For example, the multiplier effects attributable to input-output linkages (activity to activity) may be small relative to the effects attributable to the linkages from activity outputs to factor incomes, through to household incomes and back to activity outputs via household demands for products. Also, these linkages may be stronger for some parts of the economy than for others, showing different values for the different multipliers for rural households, say, than for urban households. Though simple in concept, equation 14.2 is difficult to examine in practice. Therefore Stone (1985) proposed an additive variant that is used in most practical studies:[4]

(14.3) $dy = [I + (M_1 - I) + (M_2 - I)M_1 + (M_3 - I)M_2M_1]dx$

Although this decomposition shows the broad linkage between individual accounts, Defourny and Thorbecke (1984) have argued that even more operational usefulness can be gained by seeking to identify the strength of the various paths along which an injection travels. They proposed an alternative decomposition using structural path analysis that identifies a whole network of paths by which an exogenous injection into one account reaches its endogenous destination account. Thus, in understanding how the incomes of a particular household group, say small-scale farmers, may be affected by an exogenous increase in, say, textile output, the method identifies all the various paths from origin to destination. It may be that the income effects arise directly (through the hiring of unskilled labor supplied by these households in the textile sector) or indirectly (through a stimulus from increased spending on food crops resulting from the increased incomes of unskilled labor, the increased production of which also needs unskilled labor) (Thorbecke 1995). Structural path analysis computes the importance of the various paths relative to the global influence. For example, the global influence of a one-unit increase in textile output on the incomes of small-scale farmers may be computed (from the multiplier matrix M_C) to be, say 0.05. Of this total increase in small-scale farmer household incomes, 35 percent might be attributable to the relatively direct path of the hiring of unskilled labor, 10 percent to a more indirect path of the increased spending on food crops and the hiring of unskilled labor in its production, and the remaining 55 percent to a variety of other indirect paths.

One major limitation of the application of SAM multipliers for poverty analysis is that, no matter how disaggregated the accounts of a SAM, the multiplier effects are confined to determining the income effects of (socioeconomic) household groups. The intragroup income distributions are not generated directly. Clearly, if poverty is largely identifiable with certain socioeconomic groups and not with others then the group effects can be informative. At the same time, it is necessary to try to link the multiplier effects on household group incomes to possible changes in poverty within groups. To do so usually requires some assumption to be made about the income distribution parameters within household groups (variance or Lorenz parameters). Thorbecke and Jung (1996) proposed such a method based on estimated poverty elasticities (in their case for Indonesia) that are in turn defined for the three FGT (P_α) poverty ratios. Elasticities of the poverty ratios P_0, P_1, and P_2, defined with respect to the mean per capita income of each household group, assuming distributionally neutral effects, are estimated independently of the SAM. These elasticities are then linked through the household group incomes and fixed-price multipliers to unit expansions in the output of each activity. As a result Thorbecke and Jung (1996) were able to derive a set of activity-specific poverty elasticities, which they termed "poverty alleviation effects." These show the poverty alleviation responses that arise from unit expansions of each activity, taking account of the various multiplier effects described above. This is a good illustration of a practical use of SAM-based multipliers in the context of poverty analysis.

Application of SAM Multiplier Analysis

Many SAMs have now been compiled, and it is a fairly routine procedure to compute the SAM-based multipliers at an early stage of analysis. The methodology is so straightforward (an Excel spreadsheet will suffice to compute multipliers for even moderately large dimensional SAMs) that few multiplier analyses are now published but are often available as unpublished studies. Four studies selected here illustrate some best-practice methods and provide examples of some results.

Sri Lanka

A pioneering study that computed not only accounting and fixed-price multipliers but also the multiplier decompositions outlined earlier (equations 14.2 and 14.3) was based on an early and quite rudimentary SAM for Sri Lanka for 1970 (Pyatt and Round 1979). The methodology has since been replicated on numerous occasions using SAMs for other economies. The SAM was fairly aggregative by current standards; only three labor accounts and three household groups were distinguished—representing urban, rural, and estate households and workers—alongside twelve production sectors. In 1970 poverty incidence in Sri Lanka was especially high among the estate workers, and one notable outcome from the multiplier analysis was to demonstrate just how dualistic the structure of the economy was. The income multiplier was considerably lower for estate households than for urban or rural households, except when the injection was in the tea or rubber sectors (such as an increase in exports of tea or rubber). This finding suggested that indirect effects could not be relied upon to alleviate poverty in this, the poorest, sector and that estate households needed to be targeted directly. A second observation, again repeated since, was to show that the input-output multipliers (M_1) were low relative to the between-account multipliers (M_3). This finding further suggested that more emphasis needed to be placed on tracing and mapping the income generated to factors and the transmission of this factor income to households, rather than estimating interindustry linkages as the latter are so weak.

Ghana

The general features of the SAM multiplier and multiplier decomposition analysis can be illustrated by a study based on a 1993 SAM for Ghana by Powell and Round (2000). Table 14.3 shows an extract from the results using the Stone additive decomposition procedure (equation 14.3). Consider the first panel for illustration. On the basis of the linkage structure shown in the SAM, an exogenous injection of an extra 100 units of income into the cocoa sector (arising, say, from additional cocoa exports) might lead to additional household incomes of 107 in urban areas and 71 in rural areas, after taking into account the various transfer (within-account), spillover, and feedback effects. In this case the cross-effects (M_2, or spillover effects) account for income effects of 40 (urban) and 28 (rural), while the between-account (M_3) multipliers account for a further 67 and 43, respectively. The effects of the injection on factoral incomes are also shown; again the M_3 multipliers account for the largest component, and the effects of 83 through the "mixed income" category is particularly noteworthy. The second panel shows that the effect on household incomes from an exogenous injection into mining is far lower; the incomes of urban households rise by 63 and of rural households by only 43. This is largely explained by the reduced effects on the mixed income category of factor incomes, which amount to 58. In both cases (cocoa and mining), notice how large the between-account (M_3) effect is relative to the spillover effect from the receipts of factor incomes (M_2).

Now consider the third panel, which looks at the impacts of social expenditures. In terms of overall income effects, the SAM structure suggests that an exogenous injection of 100 units of income into the health and education sector would have larger effects on household incomes than an injection into either cocoa or mining (urban 132 and rural 84). But this finding illustrates the need to exercise caution in interpreting the results. Clearly, the public expenditure injections

Table 14.3 Selected Multiplier Effects Derived from the Ghana SAM (Injections of 100 Units of Income)

Account in which injection originates	Account affected by injection	I	$M_1 - I$	$(M_2 - I)M_1$	$(M_3 - I)M_2M_1$	M
Cocoa	Employees: skilled, male			10	9	18
	Employees: unskilled, male			21	13	34
	Employees: skilled, female			1	1	3
	Employees: unskilled, female			4	2	6
	Mixed income			31	83	115
	Operating surplus			8	12	20
	Urban households			40	67	107
	Rural households			28	43	71
	Cocoa	100			7	108
	Total activity impact	100	62		244	406
Mining	Employees: skilled, male			9	6	15
	Employees: unskilled, male			17	8	25
	Employees: skilled, female			1	1	1
	Employees: unskilled, female			1	2	3
	Mixed income			9	50	58
	Operating surplus			32	7	40
	Urban households			22	41	63
	Rural households			17	26	43
	Mining	100	3		4	107
	Total activity impact	100	36		148	284
Education and health	Employees: skilled, male			33	11	44
	Employees: unskilled, male			15	15	30
	Employees: skilled, female			19	2	21
	Employees: unskilled, female			13	3	15
	Mixed income			1	101	102
	Operating surplus			13	15	28
	Urban households			50	81	132
	Rural households			32	52	84
	Health and education	100			9	109
	Total activity impact	100	14		296	410

Source: Powell and Round (2000, table 5).

have to be financed in a way that the increased exports of cocoa or minerals do not. At the same time, the income effects of the health and education injections indicated here are quite separate from, and additional to, the health and education benefits that might accrue to the recipients of these services. Finally, it can be noted that, as in the cases of cocoa and mining, the overall results indicate relatively low input-output linkages. The input-output multiplier for health and education is zero, and the total activity multiplier for all sectors attributable to this injection is only 14. Thus, in general, for the sectors in which the injections take place, the multipliers are extremely small and the total activity multipliers are also small (M_1), substantially boosted in each case by the between-account effects (M_3).

Korea

Defourny and Thorbecke (1984) have computed detailed structural path multipliers based on a 1968 SAM for Korea. One significance of their study is to demonstrate the methodology, which is far more complex than the calculation of the matrix multipliers in the Pyatt-Round procedure. A key table in Defourny and Thorbecke (1984) shows a selection of global influences (total multipliers) for various paths of injections and account destinations. For each global influence, there may be several alternative loops (elementary paths), and the method computes the percentage of the global influence accounted for by one or more elementary paths. In particular the loops that define connections between an exogenous injection and the effects of a particular household group (such as a poor household) help to provide insights into the income transmission channels.

For example, Defourny and Thorbecke show the relative importance of paths of the multiplier effects on households headed by unskilled workers that arise from an injection in the processed foods sector. They show first that it matters whether the injection is through a large-scale or a small-scale activity. Not surprisingly, the multiplier is higher in the latter case, but not by much. Second, in each case the direct elementary path to unskilled worker households, through the activity demand for unskilled labor, allowing for multiplier effects along the way, accounts for no more than 25 percent of the global effect. The remaining portion of the global effect is attributable to the contribution of indirect paths.

Indonesia

As part of a series of country case studies on "Adjustment and Equity" by the Development Centre of the Organisation for Economic

Co-operation and Development, Keuning and Thorbecke (1992) used SAM-based multipliers to trace through the effects of government budget retrenchment in Indonesia in the 1980s on each of ten socioeconomic household groups. The SAM is more disaggregated, the income mappings are more detailed, and the effects on income distribution are therefore much more sensitive to the exogenous shocks. A further novelty is that, unlike the Ghana example given earlier, the study also builds in the loss of imputed benefits to households attributable to a reduction of health and education expenditures; it therefore attempts to construct a more complete estimate of the impact of budget retrenchment on households. Finally, the analysis of base-year structure is extended to show the relative influence of the different components of exogenous expenditures on different household groups.

The results show, for instance, that higher-income rural and urban households were more influenced by government current expenditure injections than by exports. They contrast with the results for the rural and urban poor, who were more equally affected by all components. Finally the extension by Thorbecke and Jung (1996), based on the same Indonesian SAM, sought to determine the poverty-alleviation consequences of sectoral growth, taking into account the SAM-based multiplier effects and the poverty elasticities. As noted earlier the poverty elasticities define the P_α responses caused by changes in mean per capita incomes and are derived independently of the SAM. The case study for Indonesia showed that growth in agriculture and agriculture-related activities tends to do more to alleviate poverty than growth in industrial, or even service, activities, even after accommodating the various multiplier effects.

Conclusions

This chapter has shown how a social accounting matrix can be used to provide a bridge between macroeconomic and microeconomic analysis of the poverty impacts of policy through socioeconomic household groups. As a data and economic accounting framework, which integrates the macroeconomic accounts with key microeconomic data sets, especially household and labor force surveys, many of its virtues are self-evident. As a single-entry accounting system in which the transactions between agents are traced through explicitly, the SAM has additional appeal as a basis for simple macro- and mesoeconomic-level analysis and multiplier modeling. Nevertheless some important limitations should be borne in mind by a new analyst.

First, there is no single, definitive SAM: the framework is flexibly set around a standard core structure. The detailed classifications should be chosen according to country-specific criteria to best reflect the economy in question. That means that a SAM can be compiled quite readily and without too much difficulty given the main data ingredients, using the (by now) standard procedures described above. However, to be really informative, the mapping of income around the system needs to be relatively detailed and complete; otherwise the information content will be constrained by the weakest link in the chain.

Second, it should be emphasized that the data sets cannot always be used without a certain amount of adjustment. For instance, because the national accounts are not always compiled from household survey data, it is not easy to rationalize the two data sources, and this difficulty applies not only to household expenditures but also (and especially) to incomes. Although the tendency is to calibrate a disaggregated SAM to a macroeconomic SAM that is consistent with the national accounts, it may well be that it is the national accounts that ought to be adjusted in some circumstances.

Third, SAM-based multiplier models do have a role to play in examining the nature of the socioeconomic structure of an economy. Their main virtue is simplicity and transparency, and the decomposition analyses certainly assist further. The models provide a simple structure for examining the potential effects of exogenous policy (or external) shocks on incomes, expenditures, and employment (among other things) of different household groups, in a fixed-price setting. It is tempting to assume that these models work out the broad orders of magnitude and directions of effect. But whether they do so depends crucially upon whether the underlying assumptions are met. There are circumstances when they are not. If an economy is constrained or faces bottlenecks in any sector in the supply of goods or services or in key factors of production, then the multiplier analysis needs to be viewed with caution. Also, multipliers are only useful in examining the real-side effects of quantity-based shocks, they are not especially good at handling price shocks or ascertaining price effects.

Notes

1. Even if within-group distributions are available only for one (base-year) SAM, then the multiplier models subsequently discussed, based on constant within-group distributional patterns, would provide some means of linking macroeconomic shocks with poverty and distributional analysis.

2. The four simultaneous equations can be reduced to two by eliminating two of the variables (factors and commodities) by substitution.

3. M is a multiplier matrix if $M \geq 1$.

4. Unlike the multiplicative decomposition, the additive decomposition is not unique.

References

The word *processed* describes informally reproduced works that may not be commonly available through library systems.

Adelman, Irma, and Sherman Robinson. 1989. "Income Distribution and Development." In Hollis Chenery and T. N. Srinivasan, eds., *Handbook of Development Economics,* vol. II. Amsterdam: North-Holland.

Byron, Ray P. 1978. "The Estimation of Large Social Account Matrices," *Journal of the Royal Statistical Society,* Series A, 141(3): 359–67.

Chander, Ramesh, S. Gnasegarah, Graham Pyatt, and Jeffery Round. 1980. "Social Accounts and the Distribution of Income: The Malaysian Economy in 1970." *Review of Income and Wealth* 26(1): 67–85.

Chung-I Li, Jennifer. 2002. "A 1998 Social Accounting Matrix (SAM) for Thailand." Trade and Macroeconomic Division Discussion Paper 95. International Food Policy Research Institute, Washington D.C. Processed.

Defourny, Jacques, and Erik Thorbecke. 1984. "Structural Path Analysis and Multiplier Decomposition within a Social Accounting Matrix." *Economic Journal* 94: 111–36.

Hayden, Carol, and Jeffery Round. 1982. "Developments in Social Accounting Methods as Applied to the Analysis of Income Distribution and Employment Issues." *World Development* 10: 451–65.

Keuning, Steven, and Erik Thorbecke. 1992. "The Social Accounting Matrix and Adjustment Policies: The Impact of Budget Retrenchment on Income Distribution." In Thorbecke and others (1992).

Leadership Group on Social Accounting Matrices. 2003. *Handbook on Social Accounting Matrices and Labour Accounts.* Eurostat Working Papers 3/2003/E/23. Luxembourg.

Miyazawa, Kenichi. 1976. *Input-Output Analysis and the Structure of Income Distribution.* Berlin: Springer.

Powell, Matthew, and Jeffery Round. 1998. *A Social Accounting Matrix for Ghana, 1993.* Accra: Ghana Statistical Service.

———. 2000. "Structure and Linkage in the Economy of Ghana: A SAM Approach." In Ernest Aryeetey, Jane Harrigan, and Machiko Nissanke, eds., *Economic Reforms in Ghana: The Miracle and the Mirage.* Oxford, U.K.: James Currey Press.

Pyatt, Graham. 1988. "A SAM Approach to Modelling." *Journal of Policy Modeling* 10(3): 327–52.

———. 2001. "Some Early Multiplier Models of the Relationship between Income Distribution and Production Structure." *Economic Systems Research* 13(2): 139–64.

Pyatt, Graham, and Jeffery Round. 1977. "Social Accounting Matrices for Development Planning." *Review of Income and Wealth* 23(4): 339–64.

———. 1979. "Accounting and Fixed Price Multipliers in a SAM Framework." *Economic Journal* 89: 850–73.

Pyatt, Graham, and Jeffery Round, with Jane Denes. 1984. "Improving the Macroeconomic Database: A SAM for Malaysia, 1970." Staff Working Paper 646. World Bank, Washington, D.C. Processed.

Pyatt, Graham, and Jeffery Round, eds. 1985. *Social Accounting Matrices: A Basis for Planning.* Washington, D.C.: World Bank.

Pyatt, Graham, and Erik Thorbecke. 1976. *Planning Techniques for a Better Future.* Geneva: International Labour Organization.

Reinert, Kenneth A., and David Roland-Holst. 1997. "Social Accounting Matrices." In Joseph F. Francois and Kenneth A. Reinert, eds., *Applied Methods for Trade Policy Analysis: A Handbook.* Cambridge, U.K.: Cambridge University Press.

Robinson, Sherman. 1989. "Multisectoral Models." In Hollis Chenery and T. N. Srinivasan, eds., *Handbook of Development Economics,* vol II. Amsterdam: North-Holland.

Robinson, Sherman, Andrea Cattaneo, and Moataz El-Said. 2001. "Updating and Estimating a Social Accounting Matrix Using Cross Entropy Methods." *Economic Systems Research* 13(1): 47–64.

Round, Jeffery. 2003. "Constructing SAMs for Development Policy Analysis: Lessons Learned and Challenges Ahead." *Economic Systems Research* 15(2): 161–83.

Sadoulet, Elisabeth, and Alain de Janvry. 1995. *Quantitative Development Policy Analysis.* Baltimore: Johns Hopkins University Press.

SNA. 1993. *System of National Accounts.* Washington, D.C.: Commission of the European Communities, International Monetary Fund, Organisation for Economic Co-operation and Development, United Nations, World Bank.

Stone, Richard. 1985. "The Disaggregation of the Household Sector in the National Accounts." In Graham Pyatt and Jeffery Round, eds. (1985).

Tarp, Finn, David Roland-Holst, and John Rand. 2002. "Trade and Income Growth in Vietnam: Estimates from a New Social Accounting Matrix." *Economic Systems Research* 14(2): 157–84.

Thorbecke, Erik. 1995. *Intersectoral Linkages and Their Impact on Rural Poverty Alleviation: A Social Accounting Approach.* Vienna: United Nations Development Organization.

Thorbecke, Erik, and Hong-Sang Jung. 1996. "A Multiplier Decomposition Method to Analyse Poverty Alleviation." *Journal of Development Economics* 48(2): 279–300.

Thorbecke, Erik, with Roger Downey, Steven Keuning, David Roland-Holst, and David Berrian. 1992. *Adjustment and Equity in Indonesia.* Paris: OECD Development Centre.

15

Poverty and Inequality Analysis in a General Equilibrium Framework: The Representative Household Approach

Hans Lofgren, Sherman Robinson, and Moataz El-Said

This chapter presents a technique for evaluating the impact of economic "shocks"—policy changes and exogenous events—on poverty and inequality. The technique is based on a computable general equilibrium (CGE) model with representative households (RHs) that are linked to a household module.

Any analysis of the impact of major economic shocks (for example, a significant change in the world price of a major export) on poverty and inequality requires an economywide framework that incorporates considerable detail on how households earn and spend their incomes. Figure 15.1 presents a simple schema delineating the links between households and the economic context within which they operate. The framework must incorporate the sorts of shocks that are of interest. Since most household income typically stems from production factors, the framework should capture the impact of shocks on the distribution of incomes across disaggregated factors (for example, labor differentiated by skill, education, sex,

Figure 15.1 Households in a General Equilibrium Framework

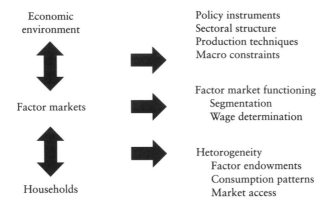

Economic
environment

Factor markets

Households

Policy instruments
Sectoral structure
Production techniques
Macro constraints

Factor market functioning
Segmentation
Wage determination

Hetorogeneity
Factor endowments
Consumption patterns
Market access

Source: Authors.

region, or sector of employment; capital by type, sector or region; and land by region, type, or quality)—the "extended" functional distribution. It is important not only to disaggregate the factors, but also to capture the details of the operation of their markets. Finally, the framework must map from the extended functional distribution to household incomes with enough detail to provide information about the size distribution (the distribution of incomes across households) needed to compute poverty and inequality indexes.[1]

At the economywide level, a CGE model is a good starting point. This class of models explicitly incorporates markets for factors and commodities and their links to the rest of the economy, providing a natural framework for generating the extended functional distribution as well as data on employment, wages, and commodity prices.

There are basically two different approaches to modeling the links between the extended functional distribution and the size distribution, a microsimulation (MS) approach and a representative household (RH) approach. Under an MS approach, the size distribution of incomes is generated by a household module (typically estimated with econometric techniques) in which the units correspond to individual household observations in a survey (see chapter 6). Different approaches may be followed when linking the MS module to the CGE model. The module may be fully integrated with the CGE model, permitting full interaction between the two levels of analysis. Alternatively, under a sequential approach, the CGE model supplies a separate MS module with data on employment, wages, and consumer prices.

Under an RH approach, the RHs that appear in the CGE model (corresponding to aggregates or averages of groups or households in a survey) play a crucial role: the size distribution is generated by feeding data on the simulated outcomes for the RHs into a separate module that contains additional information about each RH, either summary statistics or disaggregated survey data where each household observation is mapped to an RH.

This chapter provides a detailed description of the RH approach. First, we describe a "standard" CGE model developed at the International Food Policy Research Institute (IFPRI), which provides the framework for capturing the extended functional distribution (Lofgren and others 2002). We then describe how the standard model, which incorporates RHs, can feed a separate household module to provide measures of poverty and inequality. Software is available from IFPRI for both the standard CGE model and the separate household module.

A Standard CGE Model

CGE models are solvable numerically and provide a full account of production, consumption, and trade in the modeled economy. Since the first applications in the mid-1970s, this class of models has become widely used in policy analysis in developing countries. IFPRI has developed a standard CGE model written in the GAMS (General Algebraic Modeling System) software with the aim of making CGE analysis more cost effective and more accessible to a wider group of analysts. The computer code separates the model from the database—with a social accounting matrix (SAM) as its main component (box 15.1)—making it easy to apply the model in new settings.[2] Since its introduction in 2001, the model has been applied to a large number of countries, a development that reflects a rapid increase in the number of developing countries for which SAMs are available.[3]

The standard model follows the disaggregation of a SAM and explains all payments that are recorded in the SAM. It is written as a set of simultaneous equations, many of which are nonlinear. There is no objective function. The equations define the behavior of the different actors. In part, this behavior follows simple rules captured by fixed coefficients (for example, value added tax rates). For production and consumption decisions, behavior is captured by nonlinear, first-order optimality conditions of profit and utility maximization. The equations also include a set of constraints that have to be satisfied by the system as a whole but that are not necessarily considered

Box 15.1 Social Accounting Matrices as Databases
Supporting Poverty and Inequality Analysis

A social accounting matrix (SAM) provides much of the data needed
to implement a computable general equilibrium (CGE) model. A SAM
is a square matrix that, for a period of time (typically one year),
accounts for the economy-wide circular flow of incomes and payments. It summarizes the structure of an economy, its internal and
external links, and the roles of different actors and sectors. Its disaggregation is flexible and may depend on data availability and the purposes for which the SAM will be used. If the SAM is to support analyses of poverty and inequality, it must include a detailed disaggregation
of households and the factors, activities, and commodities that are
important in their income generation and consumption. The households may be classified on the basis of their income sources or other
socioeconomic characteristics. A SAM brings disparate data (including input-output tables, household surveys, producer surveys, trade
statistics, national accounts data, balance of payments statistics, and
government budget information) into a unified framework. In order
to overcome data inconsistencies, IFPRI has extended estimation
methods in maximum entropy econometrics (appropriate in data-
scarce contexts) and applied them to SAM estimation (Robinson and
others 2001). Entropy methods have also been used to reconcile
national accounts and household survey data (Robillard and Robinson 1999). Reconciliation of data of these two types is important, not
only for analyses based on economywide models, but also for microeconomic-level policy analyses based on survey data since their results
may be misleading if the data used do not aggregate to plausible
national totals.

by any individual actor. These "system constraints" define equilibrium in markets for factors and commodities as well as macroeconomic aggregates (balances for savings and investment, the government, and the current account of the rest of the world).

The standard model is characterized by flexible disaggregation,
preprogrammed alternative rules for clearing factor markets and
macroeconomic accounts, transactions costs, and household home
consumption. Transactions costs, which tend to be high and a source
of significant welfare losses in developing countries, are incurred
when commodities are marketed (with separate treatments for
exports, imports, and domestic sales of domestic output), leading to
gaps between supply and demand prices. Home-consumed outputs
are demanded at supply (farm- or factory-gate) prices. All other
commodities (domestic output and imports) enter markets and are

demanded at prices that include transactions costs. The inclusion in the model of home consumption and (often high) transactions costs allows the model to capture structural features characteristic of many developing countries that condition the impact of economic shocks on the poor. [4]

Figure 15.2 provides a simplified picture of the links between the major building blocks of the model. The disaggregation of activities, (representative) households, factors, and commodities—the blocks on the left side and in the middle of the figure—is determined by the disaggregation of the SAM. When the model is applied to analysis of poverty and inequality, the disaggregation must be sufficiently detailed to be able to discern, for the shock(s) of interest, the patterns of impacts across different real-world categories of activities, commodities, factors, and households. The arrows represent payment flows. With the exception of taxes, transfers, and savings, the model also includes "real" flows (a factor service or a commodity) that go in the opposite direction.

The activities (which carry out production) allocate their income, earned from output sales, to intermediate inputs and factors. The producers are assumed to maximize profits subject to prices and a nested technology in two levels. At the top of the nest, output is a Leontief or constant elasticity of substitution (CES) function of aggregates of value added and intermediate inputs. At the bottom, aggregate value added is a CES function of primary factors, whereas

Figure 15.2 Structure of Payment Flows in the Standard CGE Model

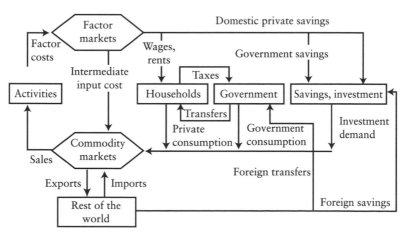

Source: Authors' depiction.

the aggregate intermediate input is a Leontief function of disaggregated intermediate inputs. This specification supports a detailed specification of factors of production, which is required to generate the extended functional distribution. Each activity produces one or more commodities, and any commodity may be produced by more than one activity. The model thus supports disaggregation of production activities (for example, by region, firm size, formal versus informal, or land category) that permits analysis of "livelihood strategies" by different groups of producers—an important issue in the analysis of distributional issues.

Given the assumption that they are small relative to the market, producers take prices as given when making their decisions. After meeting home consumption demands, the outputs are allocated between the domestic market and exports in shares that respond to changes in the ratio between the prices that the producers receive when selling domestically and the prices they receive when selling abroad. In the world markets, the supplies of exports are absorbed by infinitely elastic demands at fixed prices (the small country assumption). Domestic market demands (for investment, private consumption, government consumption, and intermediate input use) are met by supplies from domestic producers and the rest of the world (imports). For any commodity, the ratio between the demand for imports and demand for domestic output responds to changes in the relative prices of imports and domestic output that is sold at home. In world markets import demand is met by an infinitely elastic supply of imports at fixed prices. In the domestic markets for products of domestic origin, flexible prices ensure that the quantities demanded and supplied are equal.[5]

For the factors, alternative mechanisms for market clearing have been preprogrammed. The alternatives, which have different implications for the effects of shocks on the extended functional distribution of income, cover situations with fixed (possibly full) employment (the standard neoclassical assumption), unemployment, and different degrees of mobility or segmentation within the market for any given factor.

The factor costs of the producers are passed on as receipts to the household block in shares that reflect endowments. The household block is defined broadly. Apart from RHs, it may also include other nongovernmental institutions—most important, one or more "enterprises" (which also may be labeled "firms" or "corporations"). In addition to factor incomes, the different entities within the block may receive transfers from the government (which are indexed by the Consumer Price Index, or CPI), the rest of the world (fixed in foreign currency), and other institutions within the household block. These incomes may be spent on savings, direct taxes, transfers to other institutions, and, for the RHs, consumption. Savings, direct taxes, and transfers are modeled as fixed income shares. Consumption is split across different commodities, both home-consumed and market-purchased, according to LES (Linear Expenditure System) demand functions (derived from utility maximization). Enterprise transfers to RHs represent distributed profits.

The government receives direct taxes from the households and transfers from the rest of the world (fixed in foreign currency). It then spends this income on consumption (typically fixed in real terms), transfers to households, and savings. The rest of the world (more specifically, the current account of the balance of payments) receives foreign currency for the imports of the model country and then spends these earnings on exports from the model country, on transfers to the model country's government, and on "foreign savings" (that is, the current account deficit). Together the government, enterprises, and the rest of the world may play an important role in the distributional process by "filtering" factor incomes on their way to the RHs and by directly taxing or transferring resources to the RHs. Finally, the savings and investment account collects savings from all institutions and uses these to finance domestic investment.

The user can choose among a relatively large number of preprogrammed alternative closure rules for the three macroeconomic accounts of the model—the (current) government balance, the balance of the rest of the world (the current account of the balance of payments, which includes the trade balance), and the savings-investment balance. These closures can be adapted to incorporate the behavior of most macroeconometric models. The appropriate choice between the different macroeconomic closures depends on the context of the analysis. For example, in welfare analysis, it is commonly assumed that the account-clearing variables are government savings (a residual given the prior specification of rules for the determination of all other government receipts and expenditures), the exchange rate (given a fixed level for the current account deficit), and the savings rates of selected RHs and enterprises (given rules determining all other savings flows and the need to finance a fixed bundle of investment goods).

The standard model is used for comparative static analysis, implying that the impact of the shock (or the combination of shocks) that is being simulated is found by comparing the model solutions with and without the shock(s). It is straightforward to simulate a wide range of shocks, including changes in the rates of direct taxes, trade taxes, other indirect taxes (or subsidies), world prices, factor productivity, technologies, transactions costs, and transfers to households from government or the rest of the world. Each model solution provides an extensive set of economic indicators, including gross domestic product, sectoral production and trade volumes, factor employment, consumption and incomes for representative households, commodity prices, and factor wages. Extensions of the model to dynamic analysis, needed to analyze long-run strategies for poverty reduction, are also available on request from the authors (including computer code).

A Representative Household Module for Poverty and Inequality Analysis

Any simulation with the CGE model generates, for each RH, data on incomes (total and disaggregated by source), consumption (mean quantities, prices, and mean values), and factors (mean employment, wages or rents, and mean incomes). Under the RH approach, the size distribution is generated by feeding selected parts of this database into a separate household module in which the size distribution and selected poverty and inequality indicators are computed, drawing on additional information on the individual units within each RH group. The details depend on the specific approach that is followed.

In essence, there are two approaches to specifying the within-group distributions and generating measures of the overall size distribution. The first is to specify each within-group distribution by a probability distribution such as the lognormal frequency function, which is commonly used to portray the distribution of income. Under this approach, the CGE model supplies the household module with mean income (or mean consumption) for each RH. The household module requires the following additional data for each RH: poverty line (or the information needed to generate it endogenously), population size, and dispersion (for example, the log variance for the lognormal distribution, preferably estimated from household survey data), which is assumed to be fixed across the different simulations. The overall distribution of income is generated empirically by summing the separate within-group distributions and is then used to generate measures of overall inequality and poverty. This approach was first used by Adelman and Robinson (1978) in a model of the Republic of Korea and later by Dervis, de Melo, and Robinson (1982). More recently, Decaluwé and others (1999) have also followed this approach, specifying the within-group distributions by Beta distributions.

The second approach uses disaggregated household survey data (which should be consistent with the more aggregated information that is found in the SAM). Each survey observation is allocated to an RH in the CGE model. Assuming that the stratification of the survey by these groups has enough data points to represent the various within-group distributions accurately, the approach is simply to feed the individual survey observations with information from the CGE model.[6]

In terms of the details, different alternatives are possible under the second approach, depending on the quality and disaggregation of available survey data. The simplest alternative requires household-level data on total consumption spending (or total income) and size, as well as data on the poverty lines. For each simulation, individual household total consumption (or income) data are generated by scaling survey (base-year) observations on individual household total consumption (or income) by the relative real changes from base income (or consumption) for the RH to which the surveyed household belongs. That is, in terms of relative change, each RH is assumed to be representative of all households in its group. Alternatively, if the survey includes disaggregated income data that follow the classification in the CGE model and the SAM (in terms of factor types and transfer sources), individual household income data may be generated by drawing on information on the relative changes for each income type. If, in addition, the survey includes appropriately disaggregated information on household consumption, the commodity prices generated by the CGE model can be used to compute household-specific cost-of-living indexes, used to adjust real incomes. Given data on consumption of home-produced commodities, these can be properly valued at supply (or producer) prices rather than demand (or retail) prices. As the final step, under all RH approaches that use individual observations from a household survey, adjusted individual household data on real consumption or income are used to generate, for each simulation, the overall size distribution, which is used to compute measures of poverty and overall inequality.

The second approach is followed by Coady and Harris (2001) in their analysis of the welfare impact of the cash transfers of the PROGRESA program in Mexico. In a first step, the transfers are fed into the CGE model, which generates the resulting impact on RH incomes and commodity prices. In a second step, RH incomes and commodity prices are superimposed on the household survey data to generate the total impact on household real incomes, poverty, inequality, and a measure of aggregate welfare.

Among the two RH approaches, the first has the advantage of sparseness—the only additional data required are a summary measure of dispersion for each within-group distribution. The CGE model generates changes in the distribution of income between groups, while the within-group distributions are assumed to be unaffected by the shocks under consideration. However, for this assumption to be a close approximation of reality, the RHs in the CGE model must be highly disaggregated (assuring that the relative change in real income for each RH closely matches the relative change for the real-world households that fall under each RH).

The distinctions between the RH and MS approaches are not always sharp. Household data from a survey are assumed to be representative, with weights that represent their estimated share of the overall population. It is certainly feasible to use many representative households in a CGE model, in the limit approaching the full household detail of an integrated CGE-MS model.[7] Moreover, the second RH approach moves closer to an explicit MS model in that it uses household survey data directly, incorporating more information on household heterogeneity. Less information is lost through assuming that the within-group distributions follow a smooth probability distribution. But the household module includes less behavioral detail than under available MS applications. Compared with an integrated MS model, the second RH approach is more "top down" in that it does not capture feedbacks between the household module and the CGE model. At the same time, the RH approach may well be able to capture the important features of the interactions between the households and the rest of the economy at the level of the RHs in the CGE model, which would make the approach less top down.

Table 15.1 lists the poverty and inequality measures that are preprogrammed in the household module that is linked to the standard model.[8] For poverty the module covers the three measures of the Foster, Greer, and Thorbecke family.

Table 15.1 Poverty and Inequality Measures in the Standard Model

Poverty measures	Inequality measures
P_0 – headcount	Squared coefficient of variation
P_1 – poverty gap	Variance of the logarithms of incomes
P_2 – squared poverty gap	Gini coefficient
	Atkinson measure
	Generalized entropy measure
	Theil (normalized and nonnormalized) entropy measures

Source: Authors.

Conclusions

This chapter has presented an approach for evaluating the impact of economic "shocks" on poverty and inequality that is based on a CGE model with RHs linked to a household module. The approach has been contrasted with the alternative of linking (including fully integrating) a CGE model and a household module that includes an MS model.

There are tradeoffs between the two approaches, although these are not yet well understood and blurred by the fact that each approach covers a potentially wide range of alternatives with overlapping boundaries. Additional research is needed, comparing the different alternatives and assessing the costs and benefits of additional complexity. A crucial issue is to determine the degree of household and factor heterogeneity that should be accounted for in order to capture the essential livelihood strategies pursued by different kinds of households in coping with changes in economic structure (production, employment, prices, and wages) arising from economic shocks and policy changes. On one hand, the MS approach may better capture the impact of shocks as long as its household module incorporates heterogeneous household objectives and constraints in a realistic way and is fed income information that is sufficiently detailed. On the other hand, the RH approach requires fewer resources in terms of data, time, and skill, making it feasible to produce timely and cost-effective analyses in a wider range of policy-making settings.

Notes

1. Work on these issues is surveyed by Adelman and Robinson (1989).

2. In addition to a SAM, the standard model requires elasticity data (for production, consumption, and trade). Data on physical factor quantities are optional.

3. A large number of developing country SAMs can be accessed through the Web site of the International Food Policy Research Institute, at www.ifpri.org. Chapter 14 of this volume covers SAMs and SAM-based techniques.

4. The inclusion of home consumption and transactions costs in the model and the database is optional—the model also works in their absence. Note that transactions costs are not value added—the rates (the ratio between the margin and the price without the margin) change when there

are changes in the prices of transactions services or the commodities that are marketed, or both.

5. In terms of functional forms, the standard model uses a constant elasticity of substitution function to capture the aggregation of imports and output sold domestically to a composite commodity, and a constant elasticity of substitution function to capture the transformation of output into exports and domestic sales. Without any change in the General Algebraic Modeling System code, the model can handle databases with commodities that are only exported (no domestic sales of output), only sold domestically (no exports), or only imported (no domestic production).

6. An approach of this type is followed in Agénor, Izquierdo, and Fofack (2002, pp. 50–53).

7. In a CGE model of Denmark, Gørtz and others (2000) include 613 households, each of which corresponds to a scaled observation in a household survey.

8. Cowell (1995) and Fields (2001) list most of the commonly used measures, discuss their properties, and address a number of issues related to the analysis of income distribution. See also Foster, Greer, and Thorbecke (1984) for more on the properties of the P_α poverty measures.

References

The word *processed* describes informally reproduced works that may not be commonly available through library systems.

Adelman, Irma, and Sherman Robinson. 1978. *Income Distribution Policy in Developing Countries: A Case Study of Korea.* Stanford, Calif.: Stanford University Press.

————. 1989. "Income Distribution and Development." In H. Chenery and T. N. Srinivasan, eds., *Handbook of Development Economics.* Amsterdam: North-Holland Publishing Co.

Agénor, Pierre-Richard, Alejandro Izquierdo, and Hippolyte Fofack. 2002. "IMMPA: A Quantitative Macroeconomic Framework for the Analysis of Poverty Reduction Strategies." World Bank Institute, Washington, D.C. (www.worldbank.org/wbi/macroeconomics/modeling/immpa.htm).

Coady, David P., and Rebecca Lee Harris. 2001. "A Regional General Equilibrium Analysis of the Welfare Impact of Cash Transfers: An Analysis of PROGRESA in Mexico." Trade and Macroeconomics Division Discussion Paper 76. International Food Policy Research Institute, Washington, D.C. (http://www.ifpri.cgiar.org/divs/tmd/ tmdpubs.htm).

Cowell, Frank A. 1995. *Measuring Inequality.* 2d ed. LSE Handbooks in Economics Series. London: Prentice Hall.

Decaluwé, Bernard, André Patry, Luc Savard, and Erik Thorbecke. 1999. "Poverty Analysis within a General Equilibrium Framework." Working Paper 99-06. Université Laval, CRÉFA (Centre de Recherche en Économie et Finance Appliquées), Québec, Canada (http://www.crefa.ecn.ulaval.ca/).

Dervis, Kemal, Jaime de Melo, and Sherman Robinson. 1982. *General Equilibrium Models for Development Policy.* Cambridge, U.K.: Cambridge University Press.

Fields, Gary S. 2001. *Distribution and Development: A New Look at the Developing World.* Cambridge, Mass.: Russell Sage Foundation and MIT Press.

Foster, James E., Joel Greer, and Erik Thorbecke. 1984. "A Class of Decomposable Poverty Measures." *Econometrica* 52(3): 761–66.

Gørtz, Mette, Glenn W. Harrison, Claus K. Nielsen, and Thomas F. Rutherford. 2000. "Welfare Gains of Extending Opening Hours in Denmark." Economics Working Paper B-00-03. University of South Carolina, Darla Moore School of Business, Columbia, South Carolina.

Lofgren, Hans, Rebecca Lee Harris, and Sherman Robinson with assistance from Marcelle Thomas and Moataz El-Said. 2002. *A Standard Computable General Equilibrium (CGE) Model in GAMS.* Microcomputers in Policy Research, vol. 5. Washington, D.C.: International Food Policy Research Institute (http://www.ifpri.org/pubs/microcom/micro5.htm).

Robillard, Anne-Sophie, and Sherman Robinson. 1999. "Reconciling Household Surveys and National Accounts Data Using a Cross Entropy Estimation Method." Discussion Paper 50. International Food Policy Research Institute, Washington, D.C. (http://www.ifpri.org/divs/tmd/tmdpubs.htm).

Robinson, Sherman, Andrea Cattaneo, and Moataz El-Said. 2001. "Updating and Estimating a Social Account Matrix Using Cross Entropy Methods." *Economic Systems Research* 13: 47–64.

Conclusion

Where to Go from Here?

François Bourguignon and
Luiz A. Pereira da Silva

The 15 chapters of this volume have shown how active the field of poverty evaluation of economic policies is. Reflecting the general concern for poverty reduction, a great deal has been and continues to be done. A variety of tools are now available or are being developed to meet a wide array of needs. Experience with these tools has already taught several lessons that are summarized here. It has also exposed several limitations. Further experience will no doubt reveal others and will strengthen the need for improving the tools. The priority for more efficient poverty reduction policies must therefore be twofold: more systematic use of all these tools and constant dialogue between users and the designers, aimed at identifying the most promising directions for further research.

It is not necessary to wait for the results of this dialogue to spot obvious weaknesses and omissions in the toolkit that is currently available. After reviewing several findings drawn from the tools and experiences discussed in this volume, this conclusion stresses three needs for further research: a tighter and more rigorous macro-micro linkage; a way for dealing with dynamic issues and integrating long-run growth considerations; and the incorporation of firms into the analysis.

Some General Lessons

The first and most important lesson to be derived from the preceding 15 chapters is that poverty and distributional analysis of most economic policies requires at some point that the effect of the policies be linked to corresponding changes in the income and expenditure of *individual* households as they are observed in household surveys. The link applies to proposed economic policies at different stages of development, including those in the recent Poverty Reduction Strategy Papers. The link can be accomplished in many ways. The suggestion throughout this volume is that a common underlying "incidence" framework can be used as a general "approach."

The second lesson is that that existing tools can carry a researcher quite far in poverty and distributional analysis. This lesson in turn implies that more intensive use could be made of existing household surveys in analyzing both macroeconomic and microeconomic policies. Household surveys not only permit the analyst to measure the extent of poverty and establish poverty profiles, but also can be readily used to evaluate the effect of policies on poverty and distribution. Tax and benefit incidence analysis is an obvious example, which has been conducted in many, but not all, countries and often only at a single point in time.

A related lesson is that poverty evaluation of economic policies often requires planning and preparing for the evaluation before the policy itself is launched. That is certainly the case for all ex post evaluations, as chapter 5 emphasizes. When they are correctly implemented, ex post evaluations are the most robust and precise approach to policy evaluation, but that precision requires that randomized experiments be planned or that appropriate baseline surveys be taken before the policy is implemented so that the observed effects can be corrected for all sorts of bias.

A fourth lesson is that general incidence analysis is also useful for evaluating the effects of macroeconomic policies and shocks on poverty. Applying the changes in prices, earnings, nonlabor incomes, and possibly employment constraints to households observed in a typical household survey may take the analyst a long way in evaluating the poverty impact of a macroeconomic policy. Several macroeconomic frameworks can be used to link macroeconomic events and instruments to those variables that directly affect the real income or welfare of households, and not all of them seem to be consistent with the incidence perspective on poverty evaluation. More is said on this issue of consistency later, but the general organization of the approaches that combine macro- and microeconomic models to evaluate poverty impacts is rather clear, whether the linkage is made through computable general equilibrium (CGE) modeling or some other representation of macroeconomic forces.

This being said, there is room for a great deal of analytical and technical improvement in several areas. By and large, the lack of adequate information is the main limitation on the satisfactory implementation of techniques for evaluating the effects of microeconomic policies. Our main concern, however, is with the evaluation of policies that have some important macroeconomic dimensions. The available analytical tools are raising issues that are not now being handled satisfactorily. Following are brief descriptions of various research directions that might improve the situation.

Improving the Integration of Macroeconomic and Microeconomic Models

The analysis conducted in this book suggests that the main weakness of poverty evaluation of policies lies in the difficulty of integrating macroeconomic models and the heterogeneity of households as observed in household surveys. Such an integration is necessary on the microeconomic side when policies whose distributional incidence is being studied are likely to have sizable macroeconomic effects—as with taxation, for example, but also with educational or infrastructure expenditures. Integration is equally necessary when macroeconomic policies that affect the whole economy are evaluated. An attractive and probably the most obvious way of integrating macroeconomic and distributional issues relies on representative groups of households (RHs)—an approach used in one way or another by many of the tools discussed in part 2 of this volume. However, the RH approach suffers from several limitations, which need to be overcome.

Limitations of the RH Approach and the Difficulty of a True Macro-Micro Integration

Mean income differences across a few RH groups may explain a substantial part of overall inequality at a single point in time but may be unable to do so for changes in inequality at the margin between two points of time. Most decomposition studies of change in inequality suggest that changes in the distribution are attributable largely to changes in the distribution *within* RH groups; see, for example, the pioneer study by Mookherjee and Shorrocks (1982) for the United Kingdom. Decomposition studies of changes in inequality in developing countries—such as the work by Ahuja and others (1997) in

Thailand and Ferreira and Litchfield (2001) in Brazil—show analogous results. The reason is the pronounced heterogeneity of several macroeconomic phenomena; simply put, income or employment shocks do not affect all individuals or households belonging to the same RH group in the same way. Occupational changes, transitions across labor-force status, and migrations from rural to urban areas typically are individual- or household-specific and are likely to be extremely income selective. Likewise, two members of a given household may earn income from different sources or sectors, producing some heterogeneity in the way households in a RH group are affected by a change in the structure of earnings or income with a macroeconomic origin. For all these reasons, in isolation or combined, the assumption that relative incomes are constant within RH groups may be misleading in several circumstances.

This problem is especially serious when studying poverty. For example, a change—a decline, for example—in the mean income of an RH, as simulated by the kind of model sketched in all the chapters of part 2, may be relatively limited. Yet if income is averaged over households among which the macroeconomic shock under scrutiny had very heterogeneous effects, then poverty might be shown to have increased much more than suggested by the fall in the mean income and the corresponding translation of the density curve of the income distribution. Individuals in some households, but not in others, may have lost their jobs, or some households may have had more difficulty diversifying their activity or smoothing their consumption than others. For individuals in those households, the relative fall in real income is necessarily larger than for the whole group. If their initial income was low, then poverty might increase by much more than expected under the assumption of distribution-neutral shocks within RH groups—that is, under the assumptions used by the methodology reviewed in chapters 10 and 11. By assuming that shocks affect the income of all households belonging to the same group in the same proportion as the "average," the RH approach may drive analysts and policymakers to the wrong conclusions regarding the poverty effect of economic policies.

Even when disaggregated macroeconomic models are explicitly designed so that the household population is broken into a large number of RH groups covering a large number of possible distribution effects of policies and shocks, they might run into trouble. On the one hand, the number of RH groups is likely to be much too large for practical purposes. On the other hand, one may want to follow the fate of individuals rather than households, as would be the case if one were studying the effects of macroeconomic shocks and policies on the empowerment of women, for example, or some other specific category of the population. Again, this is something that is not possible with the RH approach.

How can we go further then? The first possibility consists in moving from "representative" to "real" households within the computable general equilibrium–representative households groups (CGE-RH) type of model or any other macroeconomic model with some RH structure. This move is theoretically possible but empirically difficult even though advances in computational capability are likely to make it easier to use such an approach in the future. Indeed, replacing a small number of RHs with all households in a sample survey also requires having individual- or household-level models equivalent to the RH type of models used in the CGE-RH approach. That could be achieved by estimating structural-form microeconomic models of occupational choice, labor supply, and consumption behavior while allowing for appropriate individual fixed effects. To do so would generally require assuming that all individuals are rational, operate in perfect markets, and are unconstrained in their choices. Such assumptions are probably valid for aggregate RH groups but may be quite debatable at a truly individual level.

Full general equilibrium models based on actual households in sample surveys and an adequate representation of heterogeneity in preferences already exist in the literature, but they are generally based on a very simplified representation of unconstrained household behavior and a fully aggregated production side (Browning, Hansen, and Heckman 1999). As such, they are adapted to a specific set of macroeconomic issues and not so much to structural and sectoral problems that are typical of development. From that perspective, a great deal of the work necessary to achieve full integration in these models remains to be done.

The Sequential Macro-Micro Approach (Top-Down)

A second possibility generalizes the household income microsimulation approach (HIMS) developed in recent work to explain observed changes in the distribution of income over time in a specific country (Bourguignon, Fournier, and Gurgand 2001, for Taiwan; and Ferreira and Paes de Barros 1999, for Brazil). The idea behind this approach is to use an income generation model comprising individual occupational choice models as well as individual earning or self-employment equations and individual fixed effects in all these equations. The link with a macroeconomic model is then obtained by changing the coefficients of earning, self-employment income, and occupational choice functions to fit the counterfactual simulated with the macroeconomic model. In addition, consumer prices obtained in the macroeconomic model may be used to define real income in the microsimulation model. Because changes in earning levels and prices are, at the end of the day, accounting operations at the microeconomic level, the main difficulty is to ensure consistency of employment volumes by sector and type of labor between the two levels of analysis. Bourguignon, Robillard, and Robinson (2002a, 2002b) have developed a method for implementing changes in occupation in the microeconomic database—caused, for example, by the contraction of the formal sector and employment substitution in the informal sector in the macroeconomic model—while maintaining the essence of the original microeconomic occupational model. Their model simulated the effects of the 1997–98 financial crisis in Indonesia. Other applications are currently underway (Ferreira and others 2002).

This top-down approach can work with very different types of macroeconomic frameworks. The choice of one particular macroeconomic model to sit at the top depends on the specific issue being studied and the availability of modeling tools. CGE models are typically used to study the effect of "structural reforms" such as trade policies or indirect taxation, whereas disaggregated macroeconometric models might be preferred when dealing with aggregate demand issues, such as financial or exchange rate crises. However, as discussed later, other tools might be necessary for dealing with long-run growth issues.

It is interesting to note that the layered framework discussed in chapters 11, 12, and 13—consisting of a macroeconomic model plus a consistent disaggregation into sectors and RHs—becomes now explicitly the three-layer structure referred to in the introduction to this volume. The top layer is a model providing predictions or counterfactuals on standard macroeconomic aggregates, such as gross domestic product, price levels, exchange rates, and rates of interest. In the middle layer lies a disaggregated, multisectoral, CGE-type of model, whose closures should be consistent with the macroeconomic results in the upper layer. The bottom is the household income microsimulation framework with rules that make its predictions consistent with the predictions or counterfactuals provided by the intermediate layer.

The construction of this three-layer structure results directly from the logic of the phenomenon being studied. In one way or another, the analysis of distributional issues must rely on some kind of HIMS framework. The RH approach is one example of that framework, but as mentioned above, such an approach could hide important changes in the distribution of living standards or in poverty. Changes in household (real) income are derived, by definition, from changes in relative prices, on both the consumption and the production sides, as well as the structure of wages, self-employment income, and occupational shifts. Changes in household income may also result from changes in idiosyncratic income determinants. But it is the first set of changes that a micro-macro bridge must explain. Clearly that requires some disaggregated macroeconomic representation of the economy and the labor markets on top of the HIMS. This role is played by the intermediate layer. For several policy issues, in particular those concerned with structural reforms, this intermediate layer might be sufficient. Other macroeconomic issues may require the top layer that deals with aggregate demand, the credit market, external balance, and the price of domestic and foreign assets.

Dynamics and Long-Run Growth

There are more challenges still. Much of what was said above about the linkage between microeconomic and macroeconomic levels of analysis refers to a static framework. At least, that seems true of the two bottom layers of the three-layer structure just described. Both the intermediate, disaggregated, multisector, CGE-like model and the HIMS framework are likely to rely on some kind of medium-run equilibrium assumptions. That is certainly true for the allocation of flexible factors of production across sectors in the intermediate model, and it is also true for occupational choices and earning equations in the HIMS. Even though the usual residuals of econometric estimation might reflect microeconomic adjustment mechanisms, they are interpreted in the HIMS framework as individual fixed effects and are thus implicitly considered as stationary components of the distribution of standards of living.

Introducing Dynamics

Such a static framework may be inappropriate in situations where the upper layer of the structure is meant to describe phenomena where dynamics are important, as for instance in cases of macroeconomic crises. If the upper layer describes the dynamic adjustment of the economy to a new equilibrium, it might be necessary to have this adjustment path reflected both in the intermediate and the microeconomic part of the model. But analysts do not have the appropriate tools for dealing with dynamic situations. Augmented CGE models, meant to handle this kind of situation, are most often based on ad hoc assumptions, which may not always be consistent with the modeling choices made in the upper layer. Intertemporal CGE models might be a better tool, but they rely on assumptions about expectation formation that may not be very realistic in the short run and that make the models more appropriate for the analysis of long-run phenomena. The microsimulation of household decisions can be made truly dynamic by representing saving behavior or changes in family composition. But then some particular phenomena remain difficult to model given the data that are available. How does one estimate consumption smoothing or migration behavior without panel data, for instance? At the same time, reconciling this dynamic microsimulation with the dynamics of both the intermediate CGE-like model and the upper layer of the three-layer structure is likely to raise difficult issues.

In view of the difficulty of maintaining the three-layer structure in a truly dynamic framework, some might argue that poverty analysis should rely predominantly on the lower layer of this structure after it is made properly dynamic. Townsend (see, for example, Townsend and Ueda 2001) is following such an approach by simulating the dynamics of income, consumption, and labor supply of cohorts of households facing uncertainty and an imperfect credit market. Several policies of interest may be simulated in such a framework, but they are, for the moment, limited in scope. Here again, more work is needed to see how far it is possible to go in that direction.

Introducing Long-Run Growth

It should be possible to use the three-layer structure to analyze medium-run growth and the effects of both its pace and its structure on poverty and the distribution of living standards. However, matters are likely to be more difficult when a longer perspective is needed, as would be the case with any investment of a long maturity.

Education and other human capital policies provide good examples of that difficulty. The main effect of increasing public spending in these areas today—both in terms of the rate of growth of total income and its distribution—will appear only in the distant future, say, at least 10 to 15 years after the policy is implemented. Therefore, a complete analysis of these policies requires a truly dynamic framework in which one can evaluate the effects of such a policy on the distribution today, particularly the negative effect on current income and poverty of financing the policy, as well as on the distribution 10 or 15 years from now. In turn the long-run analysis requires projections about what the economy and the whole household population will look like in 10 or 15 years, depending on some assumptions about the structure of both economic and demographic growth. Here again, such an analysis may rely on dynamic microsimulation analysis, although with a longer horizon than in the case considered above. Such microsimulation techniques are available for a constant economic environment. Linking them satisfactorily with the evolution of the economy and the structure of economic growth requires much effort.

Incorporating Firms into the Evaluation Techniques

As pointed out earlier, all the progress made or envisaged so far with the three-layer framework has consisted of ensuring that adequate, issue-specific, macroeconomic frameworks could be adapted to provide a guide for microsimulations while fully utilizing the heterogeneity found in household surveys. Although it allows for a much more detailed representation of occupational choices, income generation, and the like, the microsimulation layer remains confined to the activity, income, and expenditure of *households* in the economy. In other words, the microsimulation ultimately deals only with private consumption, the labor market, and in some cases wealth accumulation.

Similarly, one may want to apply the same kind of techniques to a population of firms—using industrial survey data, for example, instead of household surveys. Indeed, it is well known that a considerable proportion of the heterogeneity in individual earnings that is not explained by observed individual characteristics, such as age, area of residence, and education, corresponds to heterogeneity in the firms where those individuals are employed, including family firms. The heterogeneity of firms' individual decisions regarding employment, wages, and investment can also affect the overall analysis of poverty in a given economic environment. The effect may be direct through changes in the earnings, number, and characteristics of their employees. It may also be indirect through the contribution of individual firms to aggregate growth.

Extending Incidence Analysis and Microsimulation to a Sample of Firms

The first level of incidence analysis for a sample of firms would simply consist of measuring the effect of subsidies and taxes on their income (profit) and the profitability of their investments. With simple assumptions about average tax rates, the average incidence analysis conducted for households could be replicated for firms. An analyst might ask: by how much is the tax system modifying the structure of prices and possibly the investment and production decision of firms? This kind of analysis might include, but quite distinctly, a study of the direct effect of the cost of "corruption" (or "quasi-tax") when the appropriate data are available, as has been done in the recent microeconomic "investment climate" studies undertaken by the World Bank (Dollar 2002; Batra, Kauffman, and Stone 2003).

The second level would also replicate the path followed for households. Firms' output and demand for inputs (capital and labor) could be modeled as depending upon the levels of subsidies, taxes, and the cost of corruption. In particular, a relationship between firms' output and investment levels could be feeding back into the economy's price levels and hence into the type of analysis conducted with households.

The major caveat to extending the household methodologies to firms is that the demographics of the creation and destruction of firms is more complex than that of a population of households, and data are not always readily available.

Firm Heterogeneity, Institutions, and Investment Climate

The third level of the approach would consist of extending to firms the type of interaction with macroeconomic models currently used for households. Being able to disaggregate the productive sectors in the second layer of models by the size of the firm could be significantly important. In particular, accounting for different investment, borrowing, or hiring behavior by size of firms within the same sector could permit understanding the interaction between small- and medium-size enterprises and larger firms. These interactions could have implications both at the macroeconomic level and for distribution (wage differentiation, profit distribution, exit and entry of firms).

While it could be cumbersome to try to match for firms the exact approach followed for households, one could envisage using the information on firm heterogeneity in the second layer of the framework. There, one would find, for example, that large and small firms in the same sector would react differently to macroeconomic policies and shocks.

This type of analysis could also enable more precise evaluation of the effect of policies that change the institutional environment firms face. Based on the incidence analysis of investment climate variables on firms' investment, pricing, and hiring behavior, one could first measure the different types of effects of the investment climate on the level and structure of economic activity and then, descending to the bottom layer, the effect of these changes on households.

Implicit in this conclusion is a call for additional efforts by the development research community to address analytical issues linked to the poverty evaluation of policies that have some important macroeconomic dimensions. But there also are microeconomically oriented policies that call for additional efforts. A careful perusal of the annex tables that summarize the techniques reviewed in this volume reveals that these analytical tools do not cover some important policies that have been at the center of the development policy debate, including some policies listed in the introduction (see page 351). For instance, how should one evaluate the effect on poverty of privatization policies in the field of utilities? How can we best evaluate the poverty and distribution effects of decentralization policies, empowerment strategies, and more generally all attempts at reforming governance? What is the impact of investing in more infrastructure such as roads, urban transportation, or irrigation?

For some of these policies, extension of the techniques reviewed in this volume might be envisaged. Ex post, and provided that all precautions have been taken, it should be possible to evaluate most kinds of policies, at least if their macroeconomic repercussion is limited. But more or quicker evaluation of these policies may be needed. The 15 preceding chapters show what is available, operationally relevant, and more or less robust in the field of poverty evaluation for some subset of policies. This exercise was probably the easy part. Clearly, many gaps remain that most likely can be filled only with more elaborate techniques. It is hoped that the current attempt at surveying available tools will prove useful in filling the most important of these gaps.

References

The word *processed* describes informally reproduced works that may not be commonly available through library systems.

Ahuja, Vinod, B. Bidani, Francisco H. G. Ferreira, and M. Walton. 1997. *Everyone's Miracle? Revisiting Poverty and Inequality in East Asia.* Washington, D.C.: World Bank.

Batra, Geeta, Daniel Kauffman, and Andrew H. W. Stone. 2003. *Investment Climate Around the World: Voices of the Firms from the World Business Environment Survey.* Washington, D.C.: World Bank.

Bourguignon, François, M. Fournier, and M. Gurgand. 2001. "Fast Development with a Stable Income Distribution: Taiwan, 1979–94." *Review of Income and Wealth* 47(2): 139–63.

Bourguignon, François, Anne-Sophie Robillard, and Sherman Robinson. 2002. "Representative vs. Real Households in the Macroeconomic Modeling of Inequality." International Food Policy Institute, Washington, D.C. Processed.

Browning, Martin, Lars Hansen, and James J. Heckman. 1999. "Micro Data and General Equilibrium Models." In *Handbook of Macroeconomics*. Volume 1A: 543–633. New York: Elsevier Science, North-Holland.

Dollar, David. 2002. "Investment Climate Assessments, A Global Initiative," World Bank, Washington, D.C. (http://www.worldbank.org/html/fpd/privatesector/ic/).

Ferreira, Francisco H. G., and J. A. Litchfield. 2001. "Education or Inflation? The Micro and Macroeconomics of the Brazilian Income Distribution during 1981–1995." *Cuadernos de Economía* 38: 209–38.

Ferreira, Francisco H. G., and R. Paes de Barros. 1999. "The Slippery Slope: Explaining the Increase in Extreme Poverty in Urban Brazil, 1976–1996." *Revista de Econometrica* 19(2): 211–96.

Ferreira, Francisco H. G., P. Leite, Luiz A. Pereira da Silva, and P. Picchetti. 2002. "Financial Volatility and Income Distribution: Assessing Winners and Losers of the Brazilian 1999 Devaluation Using a Macro-financial Econometric Model Linked to Microsimulations." Paper presented at the FIPE (Fundação Instituto de Pesquisas Econômicas) World Bank Conference, July, São Paulo. Processed.

Mookherjee, Dilip, and Anthony F. Shorrocks. 1982. "A Decomposition Analysis of the Trend in U.K. Income Inequality." *Economic Journal* 92 (December): 886–902.

Townsend, Robert M., and Kenichi Ueda. 2001. "Transitional Growth with Increasing Inequality and Financial Deepening." IMF Working Paper WP/01/108. International Monetary Fund, Research Department, Washington, D.C. Processed.

ANNEX

Summary of Evaluation Techniques and Tools

Related information and interactive Web tools are available on the World Bank's Development Economics Research Web site: http://econ.worldbank.org/.

Note: See chapters and references cited for discussion of country applications mentioned in this annex.

Chapter 1
Estimating the Incidence of Indirect Taxes in Developing Countries
David E. Sahn and Stephen D. Younger

Contact: des16@cornell.edu; sdy1@cornell.edu

The first-order effect of a price change on the welfare of a consumer is the resulting change in the consumption budget when consumption is kept constant, that is, when demand responses are ignored. This intuitive property is used to evaluate, in a very simple way, the distributional incidence of indirect taxation or reforms in it. Basic tools for that evaluation are introduced here, along with the limitations of the first order approximation and some other simplifying assumptions implicit in the tools.

Use of the Tool	
Most important policy application	To assess the distributional impact of indirect taxes or subsidies.
Other important uses	To assess the distributional impact of direct taxes, publicly provided services, and exogenous changes in prices (see also chapter 2).
Main transmission to poverty/distribution	First-order effect of changes in prices and incomes on households' real purchasing power.
Requirements	
Most important requirement	Information on tax and subsidy changes of interest, along with data cited below.
Data	Nationally representative household income or expenditure survey data, including information on specific items to be taxed or subsidized.
Development timeframe	One month, provided data are clean and include a calculated welfare variable (household income or expenditures).
Necessary skills	Familiarity with statistical software.
Software	Any statistical software can easily calculate the point estimates. A matrix programming language (Gauss, Matlab, SAS IML) is useful to calculate variances although the DAD software package also calculates variances in a canned program.
Country Applications	Ghana, ISSER; Madagascar, INSTAT; Uganda, EPRC.

Chapter 2
Analyzing the Incidence of Public Spending
Lionel Demery

Contact: ldemery@worldbank.org

Public spending in social services such as education and health care is generally considered to be the main redistributive or antipoverty policy instrument in developing countries. Yet evaluating the redistribution or poverty reduction that is actually achieved through these so-called social expenditures raises several important problems. Benefit incidence analysis techniques can be used to determine who actually benefits from public transfers and subsidies. .

Use of the Tool	
Most important policy application	To assess whether public spending that is allocated to transfers and subsidies benefits poorer households. Such an evaluation is crucial when public spending reforms are included in policy reforms.
Other important uses	To assess whether sectoral reform programs benefit the poor and which subsectors benefit the poor the most.
Main transmission to poverty/distribution	Estimates the distributional impact of public transfers and subsidies. Transfers can be direct and conditional on entitlement (income transfers, for example), or they can be obtained by consuming subsidized goods and services (such as food subsidies and health spending benefits).
Requirements	
Most important requirement	Information about the use of public services. Best obtained from a household survey or census so that usage can be linked to household characteristics such as income.
Data	Data from household surveys on the use of public services and receipts of public subsidies; information on the allocation of public expenditure.
Development timeframe	Household survey data can take time to analyze, depending on how clean and accurate the data are. Obtaining reliable estimates of public spending incidence can take four to eight weeks, depending on the condition of the household survey data and the accessibility of public sector accounts. If a household survey must be conducted before the analysis can begin, then the project could take as long as two years.
Necessary skills	Good data handling skills, and experience with analyzing large household survey data sets. Familiarity with statistical software.
Software	SPSS, SAS, STATA
Country Applications	Madagascar, 2001, local team and researchers from Cornell University.

Chapter 3
Behavioral Incidence Analysis of Public Spending and Social Programs
Dominique van de Walle

Contact: dvandewalle@worldbank.org

Standard benefit incidence analysis, as presented in chapter 2, is concerned with the distribution of total expenditures or subsidies provided by some specific program. Chapter 3 reviews various techniques that have been used to incorporate behavioral responses into such assessments. Responses can take many forms, ranging from changes in the labor supply or savings of beneficiaries to actions by political or bureaucratic agents that influence the final spending or program incidence. Behavioral responses can greatly influence spending incidence. For example, average incidence can differ appreciably from the incidence of the marginal dollar being added to or subtracted from the budget once one takes account of the political economy of fiscal adjustment. Incorporating the responses of beneficiaries or other agents can sometimes be done with single cross-sectional surveys, though this often requires restrictive assumptions. It is better to have two or more household surveys (taken before and after the policy change) or, better still, panel data.

Use of the Tool	
Most important policy application	To introduce behavioral responses into the incidence analysis discussed in chapters 1 and 2 and to examine the marginal incidence across households and individuals or geographic areas of increases or cuts in spending on social programs such as education, health, and cash transfer programs.
Other important uses	To evaluate the distributional impact of policies such as land reform, pension reform, and microfinance reform allowing for behavioral responses.
Main transmission to poverty/distribution	Assesses the incidence of public spending policies allowing for behavioral responses and examining marginal, rather than average, incidence.
Requirements	
Most important requirement	Data on program participation and welfare for individuals and households or geographic areas; data allowing an imputation of program and policy benefits.
Data	Behavioral marginal incidence analysis can be done using a single household survey cross-section with sufficient regional disaggregation and variance in participation; two or more comparable household cross-sections; household-level panel data; or geographical-level data for dynamic marginal incidence.
Development timeframe	A few weeks to a month depending on the state of the data and the number of public programs to be analyzed.
Necessary skills	Working with large household data sets.
Software	EXCEL and STATA (or other spreadsheet and microeconomic software).
Country Applications	India, 1994 NSS; Indonesia, 1981, 1987 SUSENAS; Vietnam, panel data from 1993, 1998 VLSS; Argentina, public spending and census data, Ministry of Labor team.

Chapter 4
Estimating Geographically Disaggregated Welfare Levels and Changes (Poverty Maps and Impact Maps)
Peter Lanjouw

Contact: planjouw@worldbank.org

Public spending has an important geographical dimension such as the spacial distribution of health care clinics, schools, roads, or water projects. Evaluating the impact of this dimension on poverty involves examining the overlap between the geographical distribution of poverty and that of public services or infrastructure or changes in them. Household surveys contain too few data points to be of much use in this respect. Censuses would seem more promising, but they often do not include the information needed to convincingly assess the welfare level of households or individuals. The matching techniques between household surveys and censuses presented in this chapter can compensate for these information gaps. In particular, these techniques permit estimating with a reasonable degree of accuracy poverty and welfare distribution statistics for relatively small localities. Reliable poverty maps can thus be drawn that may be used to study the geographical incidence of public spending.

Use of the Tool	
Most important policy application	To assess geographic targeting of public resources.
Other important uses	To simulate the geographic effect of policy reforms such as decentralization schemes, community-based targeting initiatives, other community-driven development schemes, and the removal or imposition of trade barriers.
Main transmission to poverty/distribution	Policy reforms lead to a projected change in income or consumption at the household level. These welfare levels are then "imputed" into the population census and assessed at the local level.
Requirements	
Most important requirement	Availability of concurrent population census and household survey data.
Data	Census and household survey data.
Development timeframe	A minimum of two months; six months on average.
Necessary skills	Full grounding in poverty and inequality measurement; extensive experience with statistics and econometric analysis.
Software	SAS, STATA, purpose-written software produced in DECRG.
Country Applications	Bolivia, Ecuador, Guatemala, Mexico, Nicaragua, Panama; Kenya, Madagascar, Malawi, Mozambique, South Africa, Tanzania, Uganda; Albania, Bulgaria; Cambodia, China, Indonesia, Thailand, Vietnam.

Chapter 5
Assessing the Poverty Impact of an Assigned Program (Ex Post Evaluation Methods)
Martin Ravallion

Contact: mravallion@worldbank.org

Ex post analysis of the effects of public programs on poverty or any other dimension of individual welfare or behavior must take into account that the program participants or public service beneficiaries being evaluated are not selected randomly in the population. Under these conditions, it is difficult to distinguish the outcomes of the programs from the effects of the selection process. Evaluating a program by simply comparing participants and nonparticipants, without any correction for the "selection bias" may thus be extremely misleading. An ideal situation is where the program is offered only to a random segment of the population. Comparing that segment with a sample taken in the rest of the population would eventually reveal the true effects of the program. When this "randomization" procedure is not feasible, however, other ex post impact evaluation methods can be used.

Use of the Tool	
Most important policy application	To assess the impact in situations where a policy, program, or economic shock is assigned to some observational units but not others, and the units not assigned are largely unaffected. The units might be people, households, firms, communities, provinces, or even countries.
Other important uses	To understand behavioral responses to a program.
Main transmission to poverty/distribution	Can be used to assess program impacts on poverty or other welfare objectives, but a common feature is that behavioral responses by participants or intervening agents are involved in the linkage. These responses may or may not be identified in the evaluation design.
Requirements	
Most important requirement	Data on relevant outcome indicators for those units who participate versus those who do not, plus an identification strategy for inferring impact from the data. The identification strategy establishes the assumptions under which observed outcomes for participants and nonparticipants can be used (often in combination with other data) to infer impact. Examples include, randomization, propensity-score matching, "difference-in-difference," and instrumental variables.
Data	Survey or census data covering participants and nonparticipants. The data must include relevant outcome indicators and (depending on the identification strategy) other relevant covariates for either participation or outcomes.
Development timeframe	Evaluation ideally begins at the earliest stage of project design and continues through the disbursement cycle and beyond.
Necessary skills	Knowledge of statistics and econometrics and quantitative data skills. Knowledge of the program being studied and its setting is important. Knowledge of microeconomics is often helpful.
Software	STATA or similar standard statistical software programs. Several special-purpose STATA routines are available.
Country Applications	See references in chapter.

Chapter 6
Ex Ante Evaluation of Policy Reforms Using Behavioral Models (Microeconomic Behavior and Ex Ante Marginal Incidence Analysis of Policies)
François Bourguignon and Francisco H.G. Ferreira

Contact: fbourguignon@worldbank.org; fferreira@worldbank.org

The tools for policy evaluation and analysis reviewed so far are essentially ex post, in that they compare the distribution of welfare in the presence of a given policy or program, some suitable counterfactual for the absence of the program. These tools are therefore not very helpful in designing new policies and programs so as to maximize their effect on poverty or to minimize their cost, since experimentation before implementation is usually too costly. Program planning can be aided by ex ante evaluation techniques that rely on the estimation and simulation of structural econometric models of household behavior. The archetypal example of such techniques is the modeling of the labor supply effect of tax-benefit systems in industrial countries and the simulation of reforms in those systems. The development of conditional transfer programs currently observed in developing countries is likely to make these behavioral microsimulation techniques increasingly relevant there, too.

Use of the Tool	
Most important policy application	To assess all types of transfer programs with an expected impact on some dimension of household behavior, such as occupational choices, schooling, or demand for various goods or services.
Other important uses	To evaluate any exogenous changes in the environment of a household likely to trigger a non-negligible behavioral response. Such changes might include accessibility of various types of services, conditions in the labor market, or changes in producer and consumer prices.
Main transmission to poverty/distribution	Linked to chapters 1, 2, 3, and 5. The main difference is that the approach is ex ante, rather than ex post, and that the emphasis is on behavioral response.
Requirements	
Most important requirement	Microeconomic modeling of various dimensions of household or individual economic behavior.
Data	Household surveys, plus specific surveys or questions, depending on the area of interest.
Development timeframe	Six months with an experienced microeconomic modeler.
Necessary skills	Microeconometric modeling
Software	STATA , SAS, or similar software used in microeconometrics.
Country Applications	Brazil, based on 1999 household survey.

Chapter 7
Generating Relevant Household-Level Data:
Multitopic Household Surveys
Kinnon Scott

Contact: kscott1@worldbank.org

All poverty evaluation techniques in the preceding chapters rely on the use of household or individual level data. Several microeconomic data sources may be available in a given country: labor force surveys, income and expenditure surveys, demographic and health surveys. In general, however, these surveys do not cover all of the information needed for accurately measuring individual welfare and evaluating microeconomically oriented public policies. Multipurpose surveys that gather information not only on households' welfare, but also on their economic and social environment are thus highly desirable. This chapter summarizes characteristics of the range of surveys available to the analyst in developing countries and outlines the key features of multitopic household surveys and their advantages for evaluating the poverty impacts of policies and programs.

Use of the Tool	
Most important policy application	For use with Poverty Assessments and Poverty Reduction Strategies. Measuring and monitoring Millennium Development Goals: the fundamental goal of halving poverty as well as three other MDGs can only be done if such survey data are available.
Other important uses	To provide inputs for incidence analysis, poverty mapping, ex ante and ex post assessments of programs and policies, sectoral specific analysis, *inter alia*.
Main transmission to poverty/distribution	Understanding the causes of poverty and observed social sector outcomes.
Requirements	
Most important requirement	Trained survey team, including members of data users' community, to ensure relevance of questionnaire content to policymakers.
Development timeframe	Depends on team expertise (national statistical office or other institution implementing the survey) but, if starting from scratch, 18 months. The time frame can be reduced with an experienced team.
Necessary skills	Expertise in questionnaire design, sampling, field work, and data entry management (to collect data); standard household survey skills; solid grounding in micro-economic theory; and sectoral specialization (to ensure relevant questionnaire content). Analysis requires sectoral knowledge and grounding in economics.
Software	For analysis, SPSS, SAS, or STATA.
Country Applications	Multitopic household surveys along the lines of LSMS surveys have been done in over 60 countries, with the resulting data applied widely. Examples include: Colombia, 1998, used to establish eligibility for social assistance programs; Bosnia and Herzegovina, 2001, data a key input to the Poverty Reduction Strategy; Bangladesh, 2000, data used to evaluate the effectiveness of the public social safety net; Albania 2003, data used with census data to construct poverty maps used to target resources; Guatemala 2002, data used to evaluate transportation and poverty linkages.

Chapter 8
Integrating Qualitative and Quantitative Approaches in Program Evaluation
Vijayendra Rao and Michael Woolcock

Contact: vrao@worldbank.org; mwoolcock@worldbank.org

In evaluating the poverty reduction impact of development programs and policies, the quantitative methods emphasized in previous chapters, while enormously useful, have some important limitations. In particular, many of the most important issues facing the poor that policy tries to remedy cannot be meaningfully reduced to mere numbers or adequately understood without reference to the immediate context in which the poor live. The tools discussed here to integrate qualitative and quantitative approaches in program evaluation can yield insights that neither approach would produce on its own.

Use of the Tool	
Most important policy application	For use with poverty assessments, social assessments, community-driven development projects, and Poverty Reduction Strategy Papers.
Other important uses	To evaluate education and health programs, policies to redress social exclusion, impact of structural adjustment programs or economic crises, microcredit programs, and the like.
Main transmission to poverty/distribution	Understanding processes by which reforms and interventions supplement quantitative measurement of the impact of a program.
Requirements	
Most important requirement	Skilled and experienced qualitative teams.
Data	Primary qualitative and quantitative data at the community and household level. The minimum requirement is qualitative data combined with existing representative household surveys.
Development timeframe	Minimum of four to six months.
Necessary skills	Experience with qualitative work and quantitative surveys; may require multidisciplinary teams.
Software	For qualitative data: not essential, but Ethnograph or QSR-Nudist can be used; for quantitative data: STATA, SAS, SPSS, etc.
Country Applications	Indonesia: (a) evaluation of Urban Poverty Project 2, 2003, local team in place; (b) evaluation of impact of Kecamatan Development Program on local conflict resolution, 2003, local team in place. India: (a) evaluation of Democratic Decentralization in Rural India, 2003, local team in place; (b) understanding urban poverty, 2000, local team in place; (c) social and economic interdependence in poor rural households, 1992–2003, local teams employed. Jamaica: evaluation of Jamaica Social Investment Fund, 2001, local team employed. Guatemala: poverty assessment, 2001–02, local team employed.

Chapter 9
Survey Tools for Assessing Performance in Service Delivery
Jan Dehn, Ritva Reinikka, and Jacob Svensson

Contact: jandehn@yahoo.com; rreinikka@worldbank.org; jakob.svensson.iies.su.se

In countries with weak accountability systems, budget allocations tend to be poor proxies for the services that beneficiaries receive, and data on actual spending are seldom available. Two new survey tools—the public expenditure tracking survey and the quantitative service delivery survey—have been designed to generate such data on actual public spending and a variety of aspects of provider behavior on the frontlines (such as schools and health clinics). Beyond measuring actual spending or aspects of provider behavior, these survey techniques allow a study of the mechanisms responsible for the observed spending outcomes (including leakage of funds) and patterns of provider behavior, in both public and private sectors.

Use of the Tool	
Most important policy application	To assess efficiency of public spending and service delivery, in public and private sectors. Can be used in public expenditure reviews, sector analyses, and poverty assessments.
Other important uses	To assess aspects of service provider behavior (such as motivations or absenteeism), and to measure and explain corruption at the micro level.
Main transmission to poverty/distribution	To assess benefit incidence of public expenditure using actual spending data instead of budget allocations, which tend to be poor proxies for the services beneficiaries receive.
Requirements	
Most important requirement	Skilled and experienced teams to design surveys and collect quantitative data from frontline service providers, including information on actual spending, sources of finance, user fees, inputs, service outputs (such as outpatients and enrollment), and staffing. Public expenditure tracking also requires spending and other data on different levels of government.
Data	Quantitative survey data from frontline service providers (see above), which can be linked to surveys of households and/or individuals and to surveys of public officials. Multi-angular data collection (data on same units are collected from different sources to avoid misreporting) often required in the public sector, including local governments, facilities, and users.
Development timeframe	Three months for survey design, implementation, and data entry once the scope and sector have been defined. One month for data analysis, provided data are clean.
Necessary skills	Micro survey skills, including design of questionnaires and data sheets, survey implementation, and data management. Familiarity with statistical software for data analysis.
Software	EXCEL, STATA, SPSS, SAS
Country Applications	Albania, Bangladesh, Brazil, Chad, Ecuador, Ethiopia, Honduras, India, Kenya, Laos, Madagascar, Mozambique, Nigeria, Papua New Guinea, Peru, Rwanda, Tanzania, Uganda, and Zambia.

Chapter 10
Predicting the Effect of Aggregate Growth on Poverty
(SimSIP Poverty)
Quentin Wodon, Krishnan Ramadas,
and Dominique van der Mensbrugghe

Contact: qwodon@worldbank.org; kramadas@worldbank.org;
dvandermensbrugg@worldbank.org

Predicting the effect of aggregate economic growth on poverty can be done through a procedure where the change in poverty can be decomposed into the change related to the uniform growth of income and the change in relative incomes. Two softwares are based on this idea. One, SimSIP Poverty can be useful to analysts who do not have access to the unit-level records of household surveys but do have at their disposal a population breakdown by level of income.

Use of the Tool	
Most important policy application	To evaluate changes in poverty over time using various decompositions. To simulate future poverty and inequality following exogenous changes in sector-level output and employment growth rates.
Other important uses	To assess changes in inequality due to sectoral patterns of changes in income or consumption and in occupational distribution across sectors; to assess whether growth patterns (observed in the past or simulated for the future) are pro-poor.
Main transmission to poverty/distribution	Differential output (and employment) growth across sectors translates into differential growth in per capita income or consumption of households across those sectors. Changes in occupational distribution are accommodated by reweighting sample households.
Requirements	
Most important requirement	Group-level household survey data (typically by quintile or decile) on population shares and mean income or consumption by group.
Data	Apart from data listed above, macroeconomic variables at a nationally aggregated or sectorally disaggregated level are necessary to make simulations realistic. Examples are past or expected growth rates of income or consumption, employment, and population by sector. The population level is also necessary to calculate the number of poor.
Development timeframe	One day to gather data on population shares and mean income or consumption by group, check realism of scenarios, and enter the data in SimSIP Poverty.
Necessary skills	Basic familiarity with EXCEL is sufficient. The goal is for noneconomists to be able to use this tool.
Software	EXCEL
Country Applications	SimSIP has been used so far mainly in Latin America, Africa, and South Asia, but the tool has no defined geographical limits.

Chapter 10
Predicting the Effect of Aggregate Growth on Poverty
(PovStat)
Gaurav Datt and Thomas Walker

Contact: gdatt@worldbank.org; walkert@rba.gov.au

PovStat is another tool that can be used to predict the effect of aggregate economic growth on poverty by decomposing the change in poverty into the change related to the uniform growth of income and the change in relative incomes. This tool uses country-specific household survey data and a set of user-supplied projection parameters for that country.

Use of the Tool	
Most important policy application	To evaluate exogenous changes in sector-level output and employment growth rates and their impact on poverty and inequality.
Other important uses	To evaluate changes in within-sector inequality and changes in occupational distribution across sectors.
Main transmission to poverty/distribution	Differential output (and employment) growth across sectors translates into differential growth in per capita consumption of households across those sectors. Changes in occupational distribution are accommodated by reweighting sample households.
Requirements	
Most important requirement	Unit-record household survey data. Alternatively, synthetic data from a grouped distribution, which can be generated in PovCal.
Data	Macroeconomic variables at a nationally aggregated or sectorally disaggregated level; growth rates of income, employment, and population; and, optionally, changes in CPI and GDP deflator, changes in relative price of food and shares of food in CPI and poverty-line consumption bundle, changes in ratio of private consumption to GDP, and changes in within-sector inequality. A population level is needed to calculate the number of poor.
Development timeframe	One to two days to format the household survey data, collate and check exogenous economic variables, and enter the data into PovStat.
Necessary skills	Familiarity with EXCEL and appropriate household data-handling software, such as STATA. Familiarity with PovCal is necessary if synthetic data from a grouped distribution is used.
Software	EXCEL
Country Applications	Used in East Asia poverty projections, but the tool has no defined geographic limits.

Chapter 11
Linking Aggregate Macroconsistency Models to Household Surveys: A Poverty Analysis Macroeconomic Simulator (PAMS)
Luiz A. Pereira da Silva, B. Essama-Nssah, and Issouf Samaké

Contact: lpereiradasilva@worldbank.org; bessamanssah@worldbank.org; isamake@worldbank.org

Predicting the effect of disaggregated sectoral growth rates on poverty can be done with the Poverty Analysis Macroeconomic Simulator (PAMS). This tool provides a framework that links household surveys with macroeconomic frameworks to allow macroeconomic forecasts that yield consistent poverty and inequality indicators. The key feature of PAMS is that it enables the analyst to infer changes in disposable income levels for specific categories of workers from expected changes in aggregate variables, especially changes in the gross domestic product by sectors. The only requirement for the aggregate variables is that they be consistent, as in a national accounts framework. The user of PAMS has to translate a set of economic reforms, such as those proposed in Poverty Reduction Strategy Papers, into a GDP growth rate, a change in the sectoral structure of output, and a new set of taxes and government transfers. The cornerstone of the PAMS is a series of independent labor market models, whereby the demand for labor in each sector is derived from the corresponding output level, and the unit labor cost in each sector is affected by the gap between this demand and the (exogenous) labor supply. Changes in the earnings of other factors of production (capital) are obtained as a residual. Finally, the new income levels for each labor category are used to generate poverty and inequality indicators, using microeconomic data from household surveys. This is done by shifting the distribution of income or consumption for each unit of the household survey and within each labor category in the same proportion as the corresponding income level of the sector to which the unit belongs.

Use of the Tool	
Most important policy application	To evaluate poverty and distributional impact of changes in sector-level output, employment, and unit labor cost or income consistent with a macroeconomic growth path.
Other important uses	To evaluate the impact of changes in average income tax rates or average transfers to a homogeneous group of households.
Main transmission to poverty/distribution	Macro-consistent differential output, employment, and labor revenue growth across sectors translates into differential growth in revenue or consumption of households across these sectors. Changes in occupational distribution are obtained by reweighting the relative size of the group in the sample households.
Requirements	
Most important requirement	A household survey with income or expenditure data by unit, and an available macroeconomic model with output, labor income, and employment by sector.
Data	A household survey with income or expenditure data by household unit, national accounts broken down by sector, and labor income and employment by sector.
Development timeframe	Assuming the availability of a macroeconomic model that can be used to ensure consistency, about two weeks to select and extract categories of households from the survey and match the economic sectors from the macroeconomic model; about one week to link the model to the survey data; and about two weeks to run the macroeconomic and survey data together and make adjustments.
Necessary skills	Knowledge of national accounts-based macroeconomic models, basic labor demand models, and the structure of household surveys.
Software	EXCEL, EVIEWS
Country Applications	Burkina Faso, using a 1998 household survey, with a team from the Ministry of Planning. PAMS has also been used in Albania, Cameroon, Indonesia, and Mauritania.

Chapter 12
Partial Equilibrium Multimarket Analysis
Jehan Arulpragasam and Patrick Conway

Contact: jarulpragasam@worldbank.org; patrick_conway@unc.edu

Predicting the effect on poverty of changes in some markets without using a macroeconomic general equilibrium model can be done using a multimarket analysis. The effect on poverty and distribution of changes in the price and quantity of a small group of commodities—produced and consumed—can be assessed through "partial equilibrium" or "multimarket models." These models are most appropriate for evaluating policies that change the relative price of a specific good, such as the removal of a subsidy or the elimination of a tariff or quota. The starting point is identification of the direct effect on a market (or markets) of a policy reform. Then one can use data examination, survey of experts, or other prior knowledge to figure out which other markets are strongly interlinked in demand or supply with the market(s) in which the direct effect is measured. The next step is to rely on household survey information to estimate the share(s) of income that is affected by these changes through own-price and cross-price elasticities of demand for the entire set of interlinked markets. The impact of the policy reform in this system of equations is then calculated.

Use of the Tool	
Most important policy application	To analyze the effect of any imposition or change in taxes, subsidies, quotas, tariffs on specific commodities, or change in the price of an imported or exported commodity.
Other important uses	To assess the impact of any factor that shifts the demand or supply curve for the commodities of interest or exogenously changes their prices.
Main transmission to poverty/distribution	Changes in demand and supply of interlinked markets results in changes in the vector of prices, which can reduce or increase welfare and poverty.
Requirements	
Most important requirement	Partial equilibrium modeling of the key interlinked markets in question; supply and demand parameters for relevant markets.
Data	Aggregate data (such as social accounting matrix-type data) and supply and demand parameters for the commodity markets in question; household survey data to estimate these parameters, if necessary.
Development timeframe	One week using existing or "borrowed" supply and demand parameters; one to two months if estimating supply and demand parameters from household survey data.
Necessary skills	Familiarity with basic partial equilibrium modeling and microeconomic estimation techniques.
Software	STATA, SAS, and GAMS
Country Applications	Vietnam, 2001; Malawi and Madagascar, 2002; Guinea, 1993.

Chapter 13
The 123PRSP Model
Shantayanan Devarajan and Delfin S. Go

Contact: sdevarajan@worldbank.org; dgo@worldbank.org

This technique captures the effects of macroeconomic policies and shocks on poverty by linking a simple static computable general equilibrium (CGE) model, long- and short-term growth models, and household surveys. Designed to respond to the new demands created by the Poverty Reduction Strategy Paper (PRSP) process, the 123PRSP Model represents the middle ground between two approaches: existing macroeconomic-consistency frameworks that take the two most important determinants of poverty—economic growth and relative prices—as exogenous; and more sophisticated approaches, such as multisector CGE models, that can capture the poverty impacts of policies but that are too data intensive and difficult to employ in the timeframe of most policymakers. The 1-2-3 model (the model name stands for one country, two sectors, three commodities, such as exports, a domestic good, and imports) is a simple, static CGE model that captures the effects of policies and shocks on the real exchange rate of resource allocation between tradable and nontradable goods. The model is calibrated with aggregate data normally released by governments, such as national income, fiscal, and balance-of-payments accounts, and can be solved numerically by widely available spreadsheet programs in a user-friendly format. For a given set of macroeconomic policies or external shocks, the 1-2-3 model generates a set of wages, sector-specific profits, and relative prices that are mutually consistent. The same policies and shocks generate a set of short- and long-term GDP growth rates for the economy from the two growth models in the framework. The link with poverty analysis is made when the projected changes in prices, wages, profits, and growth rates are plugged into household data on wages, profits, and commodity demands for representative groups (or segments of the distribution, say deciles). In principle, the model can also calculate the impact on each household in the sample so as to capture the effect on the entire distribution of income or on the poverty rate. In sum, the 123PRSP framework allows for a forecast of household welfare measures and poverty outcomes consistent with a set of macroeconomic policies and shocks.

Use of the Tool	
Most important policy application	To evaluate general equilibrium effects of fiscal and trade policies and exogenous shocks such as changes in terms of trade and changes in foreign capital inflows or outflows.
Other important uses	
Main transmission to poverty/distribution	Policy changes or external shocks produce changes in short- or long-term aggregate economic growth and in the real exchange rate between aggregate tradable and nontradable goods that affect households' real incomes and consumption.
Requirements	
Most important requirement	Shell or prototype EXCEL file, plus data and skills listed below.
Data	Readily available national income, fiscal, and balance-of-payments accounts from government, World Bank's RMSM-X or IMF's Financial Programming framework, and household income and expenditure data.
Development timeframe	Less than a day to set up with minimal data and make simulations. Additional time may be needed to tabulate household data, to estimate short- and long-term growth models, and to gain expertise in use or to add features.
Necessary skills	Familiarity with EXCEL at a minimum; familiarity with EVIEWS or other econometric packages to estimate vector autoregression for short-term growth analysis.
Software	Prototype EXCEL implementation of the 123PRSP Model; optional software includes EVIEW file available for standard short-term growth estimation. Other long-term growth regressions from the growth literature may also be added.
Country Applications	Cameroon, Malawi, Mauritania, Mozambique, Senegal, and Zambia, all from 2000 or later.

Chapter 14
Social Accounting Matrices and SAM-Based Multiplier Analysis
Jeffery Round

Contact: j.i.round@warwick.ac.uk

Social accounting matrices (SAMs) have been used for more than three decades as an integrating framework for data and as a basis for modeling. It is a macro-meso-level accounting framework embracing both the macroeconomic accounts and detailed household and labor force survey data. A SAM is usually quite explicit in portraying the structural features of an economy, in particular how different household groups derive their incomes from different sources and their spending patterns. A SAM can be used to construct simple multiplier models to help assess the impacts of policy and external shocks on household incomes and expenditures and on poverty. SAMs also have some important limitations; although simple and transparent the multipliers may not be useful in all circumstances and at all times.

Use of the Tool	
Most important policy application	To evaluate the distributional impact of real shocks, such as government expenditures, investment, and exports, across incomes of factors and socioeconomic groups of households.
Other important uses	To evaluate distributional effects of changes in income transfers (such as those from government programs), actual or imputed.
Main transmission to poverty/distribution	Fixed-price multiplier effects based on existing structural patterns, and economywide linkages derived from the social accounting matrix.
Requirements	
Most important requirement	A comprehensive range of economywide data and a household income and expenditure survey with a labor force survey module.
Data	Macroeconomic data, commodity supply and use tables, household income and expenditure survey, labor force survey, and balance-of-payments and detailed external accounts. Ideally these data should be for the same or contiguous years.
Development timeframe	At least three months for a moderately detailed SAM, but the time required varies because the SAM compilation depends on data availability and the level of detail and degree of reliability desired.
Necessary skills	Familiarity with large household data sets, strong knowledge of national accounts, and familiarity with EXCEL and maybe GAMS (for using dedicated software).
Software	EXCEL and GAMS-based dedicated software, SAS or SPSS for working with household data sets.
Country Applications	Bangladesh, 1997, SHD and Planning Commission; Ghana, 1997, Ghana Statistical Service; Vietnam, 1999, CIEM Hanoi.

Chapter 15
Poverty and Inequality Analysis in a General Equilibrium Framework: The Representative Household Approach
Hans Lofgren, Sherman Robinson, and Moataz El-Said

Contact: h.lofgren@cgiar.org; s.robinson@cgiar.org; m.el-said@cgiar.org

This tool can be used to evaluate the impact of a wide range of economic shocks—policy changes and exogenous events—on poverty and inequality. The approach is based on a standard computable general equilibrium model with representative households that is linked to a household module. An economywide approach with considerable detail on how households earn and spend their incomes is needed to understand how households are affected by shocks. In the computation of poverty and inequality indexes, the household module uses additional information about each representative household, either the parameters of a probability distribution or disaggregated survey data where each household observation is mapped to a representative household. Compared with this approach, the alternative microsimulation approach may better capture the impact of shocks on poverty and inequality if the income information that is fed to the microsimulation module is sufficiently disaggregated and if its household module adequately captures heterogeneous household objectives and constraints. Still, the representative household approach requires fewer data, time, and skill resources, making it feasible to produce timely analyses in a wider range of policymaking settings.

Use of the Tool	
Most important policy application	To evaluate the impact of a wide range of "shocks"—changes in taxes, subsidies, world prices, production technologies, transfers to households from government and the rest of world, and transaction costs—on macro and micro (including poverty and inequality) indicators.
Other important uses	If data are available, the tool may be used to analyze more specific issues in different areas (such as agriculture or gender). In addition to the country level, it may also be applied to villages or other regions within countries.
Main transmission to poverty/distribution	A change in policy leads to changes in factor and commodity prices and in factor employment, which in turn lead to changes in household real incomes and consumption.
Requirements	
Most important requirement	The International Food Policy Research Institute's standard CGE model in GAMS, including module for generating poverty and inequality indicators.
Data	SAM; population and income or consumption distribution data for each representative household in the SAM or a household survey with income, consumption, and size data.
Development timeframe	Only a few days are needed to generate a base solution if data and skills listed below are available. Substantial time input is needed in the postdevelopment "use" phase: selection and implementation of simulations, analysis, and write-up.
Necessary skills	Familiarity with GAMS and EXCEL, and CGE modeling (including IFPRI's standard model).
Software	GAMS, EXCEL
Country Applications	Malawi, 1998, local team in place; similar applications and teams exist for many Latin American and Caribbean countries.

Bibliography and References

The word *processed* describes informally reproduced works that may not be commonly available through library systems.

Aaron, Henry, and Martin C. McGuire. 1970. "Public Goods and Income Distribution." *Econometrica* 38: 907–20.

Ablo, Emmanuel, and Ritva Reinikka. 1998. "Do Budgets Really Matter? Evidence from Public Spending on Education and Health in Uganda." Policy Research Working Paper 1926. World Bank, Development Research Group, Washington, D.C.

Addison, Douglas. 2000. "A Preliminary Investigation of the Impact of UEMOA Tariffs on the Fiscal Revenues of Burkina Faso." In Shantayanan Devarajan, Lyn Squire, and F. Halsey Rogers, eds., *World Bank Economists Forum*. Washington, D.C.: World Bank.

Adelman, Irma, and Sherman Robinson. 1978. *Income Distribution Policy in Developing Countries: A Case Study of Korea*. Stanford: Stanford University Press and Oxford University Press.

———. 1988. "Macroeconomic Adjustment and Income Distribution: Alternative Models Applied to Two Economies." *Journal of Development Economics* 29(1): 23–44.

———. 1989. "Income Distribution and Development." In Hollis Chenery and T. N. Srinivasan, eds., *Handbook of Development Economics*, vol. II. Amsterdam: North-Holland.

Agénor, Pierre-Richard. 2002. "Macroeconomic Adjustment and the Poor: Analytical Issues and Cross-Section." Policy Research Working Paper 2788. World Bank, Washington, D.C. Processed.

Agénor, Pierre-Richard, and Joshua Aizenman. 1999. "Macroeconomic Adjustment with Segmented Labor Markets." *Journal of Development Economics* 58 (April): 277–96.

Agénor, Pierre-Richard, Alejandro Izquierdo, and Hippolyte Fofack. 2003. "IMMPA: A Quantitative Macroeconomic Framework for the Analysis of Poverty Reduction Strategies." World Bank Institute, Washington, D.C. (www.worldbank.org/wbi/macroeconomics/modeling/immpa.htm).

Aghion, Philippe, E. Caroli, and C. Garcia-Penalosa. 1999. "Inequality and Economic Growth: The Perspective of the New Growth Theories." *Journal of Economic Literature* 37: 1615–60.

Ahluwalia, M., and Hollis Chenery. 1974. "The Economic Framework." In Hollis Chenery, M. Ahluwalia, C. Bell, J. Duloy, and R. Jolly, eds., *Redistribution with Growth*. London: Oxford University Press for the World Bank.

Ahmad, Ehtisham, and Nicholas Stern. 1984. "The Theory of Reform and Indian Indirect Taxes." *Journal of Public Economics* 25(3): 259–98.

———. 1987. "Alternative Sources of Government Revenue: Illustrations from India, 1979–80." In David Newbery and Nicholas Stern, eds. *The Theory of Taxation for Developing Countries*. Oxford, U.K.: Oxford University Press.

———. 1990. "Tax Reform and Shadow Prices for Pakistan." *Oxford Economic Papers* 42(1): 135–59.

———. 1991. *The Theory and Practice of Tax Reform in Developing Countries*. Cambridge, U.K.: Cambridge University Press.

Ahuja, Vinod, B. Bidani, Francisco H.G. Ferreira, and M. Walton. 1997. *Everyone's Miracle? Revisiting Poverty and Inequality in East Asia*. Washington, D.C.: World Bank.

Alderman, Harold, and Carlo del Ninno. 1999. "Poverty Issues for Zero Rating VAT in South Africa." *Journal of African Economies* 8(2): 182–208.

Alderman, Harold, and Victor Lavy. 1996. "Household Responses to Public Health Services: Cost and Quality Tradeoffs." *World Bank Research Observer* 11(1): 3–22.

Alreck, Pamela L., and Robert B. Settle. 1995. *The Survey Research Handbook*, 2d ed. Chicago: Irwin.

Anand, Ritu, and Ravi Kanbur. 1993. "Inequality and Development: A Critique." *Journal of Development Economics* (Netherlands) 41(June): 19–43.

Angrist, Joshua, and A. Krueger. 1992. "The Effect of Age of School Entry on Educational Attainment: An Application of Instrumental Variables with Moments from Two Samples." *Journal of the American Statistical Association* 87: 328–36.

Angrist, Joshua, Guido Imbens, and Donald Rubin. 1996. "Identification of Causal Effects Using Instrumental Variables." *Journal of the American Statistical Association* 91: 444–55.

Angrist, Joshua, Eric Bettinger, Erik Bloom, Elizabeth King, and Michael Kremer. 2001. "Vouchers for Private Schooling in Colombia: Evidence from a Randomized Natural Experiment." NBER Working Paper 8343. Cambridge, Mass.: National Bureau of Economic Research.

Arellano, M., and C. Meghir. 1992. "Female Labour Supply and on the Job Search: An Empirical Model Estimated Using Complementary Data Sets." *Review of Economic Studies* 59: 537–59.

Artus, P., M. Deleau, and P. Malgrange. 1986. *Modélisation macroéconomique*. Paris: Economica.

Arulpragasam, Jehan, and Carlo del Ninno. 1996. "Do Cheap Imports Harm the Poor? Rural-Urban Tradeoffs in Guinea." In David Sahn, ed., *Economic Reform and the Poor in Africa*. Oxford, U.K.: Oxford University Press.

Arulpragasam, Jehan, and David Sahn. 1997. *Economic Transition in Guinea: Implications for Growth and Poverty*. New York: New York University Press.

Ashenfelter, Orley. 1978. "Estimating the Effect of Training Programs on Earnings." *Review of Economic Studies* 60: 47–57.

Atkinson, Anthony B. 1981. *Handbook on Income Distribution Data*. World Bank, Economic and Social Data Division, Washington, D.C.

———. 1983. *The Theory of Tax Design for Developing Countries*. New York: Social Science Research Council.

——— 1987. "On the Measurement of Poverty." *Econometrica* 55: 749–64.

Attanasio, O., C. Meghir, and A. Santiago. 2002. "Education Choices in Mexico: Using a Structural Model and a Randomized Experiment to Evaluate Progresa." University College, London. Processed.

Auerbach, Alan J., and Laurence J. Kotlikoff. 1987. *Dynamic Fiscal Policy*. Cambridge, U.K.: Cambridge University Press.

Auerbach Alan J., Laurence J. Kotlikoff, and Willi Leibfritz, eds. 1999. *Generational Accounting around the World*. Chicago: University of Chicago Press.

Bagchi, Amaresh, and Nicholas Stern. 1994. *Tax Policy and Planning in Developing Countries*. Oxford, U.K.: Oxford University Press.

Bamberger, Michael. 2000. *Integrating Qualitative and Quantitative Research in Development Projects*. Washington, D.C.: World Bank.

Banerjee, Abhijit V., and Andrew F. Newman. 1993. "Occupational Choice in the Process of Development." *Journal of Political Economy* 101: 274–98.

Banks, James, Richard Blundell, and Arthur Lewbel. 1996. "Tax Reform and Welfare Measurement: Do We Need Demand System Estimates?" *Economic Journal* 106: 1227–41.

Bardhan, P. 2002. "Decentralization of Governance and Development." *Journal of Economic Perspectives* 16(4): 185–205.

Barnum, Howard, and Joseph Kutzin. 1993. *Public Hospitals in Developing Countries: Resource Use, Cost, Financing*. Baltimore: Johns Hopkins University Press.

Barro, Robert J. 1997. *Determinants of Economic Growth—A Cross-Country Empirical Study*. Cambridge: MIT Press.

Batra, Geeta, Daniel Kauffman, and Andrew H.W. Stone. 2003. *Investment Climate Around the World: Voices of the Firms from the World Business Environment Survey*. Washington, D.C.: World Bank.

Benabou, R. 1996. "Inequality and Growth." In *NBER Macroeconomics Annual 1996*. Cambridge, Mass.: MIT Press.

Benjamin, Nancy. 1996. "Adjustment and Income Distribution in an Agricultural Economy: A General Equilibrium Analysis of Cameroon." *World Development* 24(6): 1003–13.

Bernheim, B. Douglas, and Michael D. Whinston. 1986. "Common Agency." *Econometrica* 54(4): 923–42.

Berry, Sara. 1993. *No Condition Is Permanent: The Social Dynamics of Agrarian Change in Sub-Saharan Africa.* Madison: University of Wisconsin Press.

Bertrand, M., S. Mullainathan, and D. Miller. 2002. "Public Policy and Extended Families: Evidence from South Africa." University of Chicago. Processed.

Bigman, D., and Hippolyte Fofack. 2000. "Geographical Targeting for Poverty Alleviation." World Bank: Regional and Sectoral Studies, Washington, D.C.

Blanchflower, D., and A. Oswald. 1994. *The Wage Curve.* Cambridge, Mass.: MIT Press.

Blank, Lorraine, and Colin Williams. 1998. "Reanalysis of the First Impact Evaluation Study of 1996." Students Loan Bureau, Kingstown, Jamaica, Processed.

Bliss, Christopher, and Nicholas Stern. 1982. *Palanpur: The Economy of an Indian Village.* New York: Oxford University Press.

Bloch, Francis, and Vijayendra Rao. 2002. "Terror as a Bargaining Instrument: A Case Study of Dowry Violence in Rural India." *American Economic Review* 92(4): 1029–43

Blundell, Richard, and Monica Costa Dias. 2000. "Evaluation Methods for Non-Experimental Data." *Fiscal Studies* 21(4): 427–68.

Blundell, Richard, and T. MaCurdy. 1999. "Labor Supply: A Review of Alternative Approaches." In Orley Ashenfelter and D. Card, eds., *Handbook of Labor Economics,* vol. 3A. Amsterdam: Elsevier.

Blundell, Richard, A. Duncan, J. McCrae, and C. Meghir. 2000. "Evaluating In-Work Benefit Reforms: The Working Families' Tax Credit in the U.K." Discussion Paper, Institute for Fiscal Studies, London. Processed.

Bonnel, René. 2000. "HIV/AIDS and Economic Growth: A Global Perspective." *South African Journal of Economics* 68(5): 820-35.

Bourguignon, François. 2001. "The Distributional Effects of Growth: Micro vs. Macro Approaches." Paper presented at the Prebisch centennial conference, CEPAL (Comisión Económica para América Latina y el Caribe), Santiago, July.

Bourguignon, François. 2003. "The Growth Elasticity of Poverty Reduction: Explaining Heterogeneity across Countries and Time Periods." In T. Eicher and S. Turnovsky, eds., *Inequality and Growth.* Cambridge, Mass.: MIT Press.

Bourguignon, François, W. Branson, and Jaime de Melo. 1989. "Macroeconomic Adjustment and Income Distribution: A Macro-Micro Simulation Model." OECD Technical Paper 1. Organisation for Economic Co-operation and Development, Paris.

Bourguignon, François, Jaime de Melo, and C. Morrisson. 1991. "Poverty and Income Distribution during Adjustment: Issues and Evidence from the OECD Project." *World Development* 19(1): 1485–1508.

Bourguignon, François, Francisco H.G. Ferreira, and P. Leite. 2002. "Ex Ante Evaluation of Conditional Cash Transfer Programs: The Case of *Bolsa Escola*." Policy Research Working Paper 2916. World Bank, Washington, D.C.

———. Forthcoming. *Demand for Schooling, Public Policy, and Income Distribution.* Washington, D.C.: World Bank.

Bourguignon, François, Francisco H. G. Ferreira, and Nora Lustig. 1998. "The Microeconomics of Income Distribution Dynamics in East Asia and Latin America." World Bank Research Proposal 638-18. The World Bank, Washington, D.C. Processed.

Bourguignon François, M. Fournier, and M. Gurgand. 2001. "Fast Development with a Stable Income Distribution: Taiwan, 1979–94." *Review of Income and Wealth* 47(2): 139–63.

Bourguignon, François, Luiz A. Pereira da Silva, and Nicholas Stern. 2002. "Evaluating the Poverty Impact of Economic Policies: Some Analytical Challenges." World Bank, DECVP, Washington, D.C. Processed.

Bourguignon, François, Anne-Sophie Robillard, and Sherman Robinson. 2002. "Representative vs. Real Households in the Macroeconomic Modeling of Inequality." International Food Policy Research Institute, Washington, D.C. Processed.

Braverman, Avishay, and Jeffrey Hammer. 1986. "Multimarket Analysis of Agricultural Pricing Policies in Senegal." In Inderjit Singh, Lyn Squire, and John Strauss, eds., *Agricultural Household Models: Extensions, Applications and Policy.* Baltimore: Johns Hopkins University Press.

Braverman, Avishay, Jeffrey Hammer, and Anne Gron. 1987. "Multimarket Analysis of Agricultural Price Policies in an Operational Context: The Case of Cyprus." *World Bank Economic Review* 1(2): 337–56.

Brennan, Geoffrey. 1976. "The Distributional Implications of Public Goods." *Econometrica* 44: 391–99.

Brock, Karen, and Rosemary McGee. 2002. *Knowing Poverty: Critical Reflections on Participatory Research and Policy.* London: Earthscan Publications.

Browning, Martin, Lars Peter Hansen, and James J. Heckman. 1999. "Micro Data and General Equilibrium Models." In Handbook of Macroeconomics. vol. 1A. New York: Elsevier Science.

Buffie, Edward. 1984. "Financial Repression, the New Structuralists, and Stabilization Policy in Semi-Industrialized Countries." *Journal of Development Economics* 14(3): 305–22.

Burgess, Robin, and Nicholas Stern. 1993. "Taxation and Development." *Journal of Economic Literature* 31(June): 762–830.

Burtless, Gary. 1985. "Are Targeted Wage Subsidies Harmful? Evidence from a Wage Voucher Experiment." *Industrial & Labor Relations Review* 39: 105–15.

Byron, Ray P. 1978. "The Estimation of Large Social Account Matrices." *Journal of the Royal Statistical Society,* Series A, 141(3): 359–67.

Castro-Leal, Florencia. 1996. "Poverty and Inequality in the Distribution of Public Education Spending in South Africa." PSP Discussion Paper 102. World Bank, Poverty and Social Policy Department, Washington, D.C. Processed.

Castro-Leal, Florencia, Julia Dayton, Lionel Demery, and Kalpana Mehra. 1999. "Public Spending in Africa: Do the Poor Benefit?" *World Bank Research Observer* 14(1): 49–72.

Chander, Ramesh, S. Gnasegarah, Graham Pyatt, and Jeffery Round. 1980. "Social Accounts and the Distribution of Income: The Malaysian Economy in 1970." *Review of Income and Wealth* 26(1): 67–85.

Chattopadhyay, Raghabendra, and Esther Duflo. 2001. "Women as Policy Makers: Evidence from an India-Wide Randomized Policy Experiment. NBER Working Paper w8615. National Bureau of Economic Research, Cambridge, Mass.

Chaudhury, Nazmul, and Jeffrey S. Hammer. 2003. "Ghost Doctors: Absenteeism in Bangladeshi Health Facilities." Policy Research Working Paper 3065. World Bank, Development Research Group, Washington, D.C.

Chen, Duanije, John Matovu, and Ritva Reinikka. 2001. "A Quest for Revenue and Tax Incidence." In Ritva Reinikka and Paul Collier, eds., *Uganda's Recovery: The Role of Farms, Firms and Government.* Washington, D.C.: World Bank.

Chen, Shaohua, and Martin Ravallion. 2003. "Are the Income Gains from a Development Project Consumed or Saved?" World Bank, Development Research Group, Washington, D.C. Processed.

———. 2003. "Hidden Impact? Ex-Post Evaluation of an Anti-Poverty Program." Policy Research Working Paper 3049. World Bank, Development Research Group, Washington, D.C.

———. 2002. "Household Welfare Impacts of China's Accession to the WTO." Paper presented at the Fourth Asia Development Forum, Seoul, Korea, November 3–5, 2002. In *East Asia Integrates: A Trade Policy Agenda for Shared Growth.* Washington, D.C.: World Bank. Forthcoming.

Chenery, Hollis, M. Ahluwalia, C. Bell, H. Duloy, and R. Jolly. 1974. *Redistribution with Growth.* New York: Oxford University Press for the World Bank.

Chu, Ke-young, Hamid Davoodi, and Sanjeev Gupta. 2000. "Income Distribution and Tax and Government Social Spending Policies in Developing Countries." IMF Policy Working Paper WP/00/62. International Monetary Fund, Washington, D.C.

Chung-I Li, Jennifer. 2002. "A 1998 Social Accounting Matrix (SAM) for Thailand." Trade and Macroeconomic Division Discussion Paper 95. International Food Policy Research Institute, Washington D.C. Processed.

Coady, David P., and Rebecca Lee Harris. 2001. "A Regional General Equilibrium Analysis of the Welfare Impact of Cash Transfers: An Analysis of PROGRESA in Mexico." Trade and Macroeconomics Division Discussion Paper 76. International Food Policy Research Institute, Washington, D.C. (http://www.ifpri.cgiar.org/divs/tmd/tmdpubs.htm).

Collier, David, and Robert Adcock. 2001. "Measurement Validity: A Shared Standard for Qualitative and Quantitative Research." *American Political Science Review* 95(3): 529–46.

Cooke, Bill, and Uma Kothari. 2001. *Participation: The New Tyranny?* London: Zed Books.

Cornes, Richard. 1995. "Measuring the Distributional Impact of Public Goods." In Dominique van de Walle and Kimberly Nead, eds., *Public Spending and the Poor: Theory and Evidence.* Baltimore: Johns Hopkins University Press for the World Bank.

Cowell, Frank A. 1995. *Measuring Inequality.* 2d ed. LSE Handbooks in Economics Series. London: Prentice Hall.

Cox, David, and Emmanuel Jimenez. 1992. "Social Security and Private Transfers: The Case of Peru." *World Bank Economic Review* 6 (January): 155–69.

Creedy, J., and A. Duncan. 2002. "Behavioral Micro-simulation with Labor Supply Responses." *Journal of Economic Surveys* 16(1): 1–39.

Das, Jishnu, Stefan Dercon, James Habyarimana, and Pramila Krishnan. 2002. "Rules vs. Discretion: Public and Private Funding in Zambian Basic Education. Part I: Funding Equity." World Bank, Development Research Group, Washington, D.C. Processed.

Datt, Gaurav, and Martin Ravallion. 1992. "Growth and Redistribution Components of Changes in Poverty Measures: A Decomposition with Applications to Brazil and India in the 1980s." *Journal of Development Economics* 38(2): 275–95.

Datt, Gaurav, and Thomas Walker. 2002. "PovStat 2.12: A Poverty Projection Toolkit, User's Manual." World Bank, East Asia Poverty Reduction and Economic Management Unit, Washington, D.C. Processed.

———. 2002. "PovStat 2.10: A Poverty Projection Toolkit, User's Manual." World Bank, Washington, D.C. Processed.

Davidson, Russell, and Jean-Yves Duclos. 1997. "Statistical Inference for the Measurement of the Incidence of Taxes and Transfers." *Econometrica* 65: 1453–66.

Deaton, Angus. 1989. "Household Survey Data and Pricing Policies in Developing Countries." *World Bank Economic Review* 3(2): 183–210.

———. 1989. "Rice Prices and Income Distribution in Thailand: A Non-Parametric Analysis." *Economic Journal* 99: 1–37.

Deaton, Angus, and Margaret Grosh. 2000. "Consumption." In Margaret E. Grosh and Paul Glewwe, eds., *Designing Household Survey Questionnaires for Developing Countries: Lessons from 15 Years of the Living Standards Measurement Study.* Washington, D.C.: World Bank.

Deaton, Angus, and J. Muellbauer. 1980. "An Almost Ideal Demand System." *American Economic Review* 70(3): 312–26.

Deaton, Angus, and Salman Zaidi. 2002. "Guidelines for Constructing Consumption Aggregates for Welfare Analysis." Living Standards Measurement Study Working Paper 135. World Bank, Development Economics Research Group, Washington, D.C. Processed.

Decaluwé, Bernard, André Patry, and Luc Savard. 1998. "Quand l'eau n'est plus un don du ciel: Un MEGC appliqué au Maroc (When Water Is No Longer a Gift of God: A CGE Applied to Morocco)." Revue d'Economie du Developpement 0(3-4, December): 149–87.

Decaluwé, Bernard, André Patry, Luc Savard, and Erik Thorbecke. 1999. "Poverty Analysis within a General Equilibrium Framework." Working Paper 99-06. Université Laval, CRÉFA (Centre de Recherche en Économie et Finance Appliquées), Quebec, Canada (http://www.crefa.ecn.ulaval.ca/).

Defourny, Jacques, and Erik Thorbecke. 1984. "Structural Path Analysis and Multiplier Decomposition within a Social Accounting Matrix." Economic Journal 94: 111–36.

Dehejia, R. H., and S. Wahba. 1999. "Causal Effects in Non-experimental Studies: Re-evaluating the Evaluation of Training Programs." Journal of the American Statistical Association 94: 1053–62.

Dehn Jan, Ritva Reinikka, and Jakob Svensson. 2001. "Basic Service Delivery: A Quantitative Survey Approach." World Bank, Washington, D.C. Processed.

Deininger, Klaus, and Lyn Squire. 1998. "New Ways of Looking at Old Issues: Inequality and Growth." Journal of Development Economics 57(2): 259–87.

de Janvry, Alain, and Elisabeth Sadoulet. 2000. "Growth, Poverty, and Inequality in Latin America: A Causal Analysis, 1970–94." Review of Income and Wealth 46(3): 267–87.

de Melo, Jaime, and Sherman Robinson. 1992. "Productivity and Externalities: Models of Export-Led Growth." Journal of International Trade and Economic Development 1:41–68.

Demery, Lionel. 2000. "Benefit Incidence: A Practitioner's Guide." World Bank, Poverty and Social Development Group, Africa Region, Washington, D.C. Processed.

Demery, Lionel, Shiyan Chao, René Bernier, and Kalpana Mehra. 1995. "The Incidence of Social Spending in Ghana." PSP Discussion Paper Series 82. World Bank, Poverty and Social Policy Department, Washington, D.C. Processed.

Demombynes, G., C. Elbers, J. O. Lanjouw, P. Lanjouw, J. A Mistiaen, and B. Özler. Forthcoming. "Producing an Improved Geographic Profile of Poverty: Methodology and Evidence from Three Developing Countries." In Rolph van der Hoeven and Anthony Shorrocks, eds., Growth, Inequality and Poverty. Oxford, U.K.: Oxford University Press.

Dervis, Kemal, Jaime de Melo, and Sherman Robinson. 1982. General Equilibrium Models for Development Policy. Cambridge, U.K.: Cambridge University Press.

Devarajan, Shantayanan. 1997. "Real Exchange Rate Misalignment in the CFA Zone." *Journal of African Economies* 6(10): 35–53.

———. 1999. "Estimates of Real Exchange Rate Misalignment with a Simple General-Equilibrium Model." In Lawrence E. Hinkle and Peter J. Montiel, *Exchange Rate Misalignment: Concepts and Measurement for Developing Countries.* Washington, D.C.: World Bank and Oxford University Press.

Devarajan, Shantayanan, and Delfin S. Go. 1998. "The Simplest Dynamic General Equilibrium Model of an Open Economy." *Journal of Policy Modeling* 29(6): 677–714.

———. 2002. "A Macroeconomic Framework for Poverty Reduction Strategy Papers, with Application to Zambia." Africa Region Working Paper 38. World Bank, Washington, D.C.

Devarajan, Shantayanan, and Shaikh I. Hossain. 1995. "The Combined Incidence of Taxes and Public Expenditures in the Philippines." Policy Research Working Paper 1543, World Bank, Policy Research Department, Washington, D.C. Processed.

———. 1998. "The Combined Incidence of Taxes and Public Expenditures in the Philippines." *World Development* 26(6): 963–77.

Devarajan Shantayanan, and Jeffrey D. Lewis. 1991. "Structural Adjustment and Economic Reform in Indonesia: Model-Based Policies vs. Rules of Thumb." In Dwight H. Perkins, and Michael Roemer, eds., *Reforming Economic Systems in Developing Countries.* Cambridge, Mass.: Harvard Institute for International Development.

Devarajan, Shantayanan, and Dominique van der Mensbrugghe. 2000. "Trade Reform in South Africa: Impact on Households." World Bank, Development Research Group, Washington, D.C. Processed.

Devarajan, Shantanayan, and Ritva Reinikka. 2002. "Making Services Work for Poor People." Paper presented at the African Economic Research Consortium, Nairobi, May. Processed.

Devarajan, Shantayanan, Hafez Ghanem, and Karen Theirfelder. 1997. "Economic Reform and Labor Unions: A General Equilibrium Analysis Applied to Bangladesh and Indonesia." *World Bank Economic Review* 11(1): 145–70.

———. 1999. "Labor Market Regulations, Trade Liberalization, and the Distribution of Income in Bangladesh." *Journal of Policy Reform* 3(1): 1–28.

Devarajan, Shantayanan, Delfin S. Go, and Hongyi Li. 1999. "Quantifying the Fiscal Effect of Trade Reform: A General Equilibrium Model Estimated for 60 Countries." Policy Research Working Paper 2162. World Bank, Development Research Group, Washington, D.C.

Devarajan, Shantayanan, Jeffrey D. Lewis, and Sherman Robinson. 1990. "Policy Lessons from Trade-focused, Two-sector Models." *Journal of Policy Modeling* 12(4): 625–57.

———. 1993. "External Shocks, Purchasing Power Parity, and the Equilibrium Real Exchange Rate." *World Bank Economic Review* 7(1): 45–63.

Devarajan, Shantayanan, Delfin S. Go, Jeffrey D. Lewis, Sherman Robinson, and Pekka Sinko. 1997. "Simple General Equilibrium Modeling." In Joseph F. Francois and Kenneth A. Reinert, eds., *Applied Methods for Trade Policy Analysis: A Handbook*. Cambridge: Cambridge University Press.

Devarajan, Shantayanan, Sherman Robinson, A. Yúnez-Naude, Raúl Hinojosa-Ojeda, and Jeffrey D. Lewis. 1999. "From Stylized to Applied Models: Building Multisector CGE Models for Policy." *North American Journal of Economics and Finance* 10 (1999): 5–38.

Devarajan, Shantayanan, William R. Easterly, Delfin S. Go, C. Petersen, L. Pizzati, C. Scott, and Luc Serven. 2000. "A Macroeconomic Framework for Poverty Reduction Strategy Papers." World Bank, Washington, D.C. Processed.

Dixit, Avinash. 1996. *The Making of Economic Policy: A Transaction-Cost Politics Perspective*. Cambridge, Mass.: MIT Press.

———. 1997. "Power of Incentives in Public Versus Private Organizations." *American Economic Review Papers and Proceedings* 87(2): 378–82.

———. 2000. "Incentives and Organizations in the Public Sector: An Interpretative Review." Revised version of paper presented at the Conference on Devising Incentives to Promote Human Capital. National Academy of Sciences, Irvine, Calif., December 17–18. Processed.

Dollar, David, and Art Kraay. 2000. "Growth Is Good for The Poor." Policy Research Working Paper 2587. World Bank, Development Research Group, Washington, D.C. Processed.

Dorosh, Paul A., and David E. Sahn. 2000. "General Equilibrium Analysis of the Effect of Macroeconomic Adjustment on Poverty in Africa." *Journal of Policy Modeling* 22(6): 753–76.

Dorosh, Paul A., Carlo del Ninno, and David E. Sahn. 1995. "Poverty Alleviation in Mozambique: A Multimarket Analysis of the Role of Food Aid." *Agricultural Economics* 13: 89–99.

Dubin, Jeffrey A., and Douglas Rivers. 1993. "Experimental Estimates of the Impact of Wage Subsidies." *Journal of Econometrics* 56(1–2): 219–42.

Duclos, Jean-Yves, and Quentin Wodon. 2003. "Pro-poor Growth." World Bank, Africa Poverty Reduction and Economic Management Department, Washington, D.C. Processed.

Easterly, William R. 1998. "The Ghost of Financing Gap: Testing the Growth Model Used in the International Financial Institutions." *International Monetary Fund Seminar Series* 1998-2:1–29.

———. 2001. "The Lost Decades: Developing Countries' Stagnation in Spite of Policy Reform 1980–1998." *Journal of Economic Growth* 6(2):135-57.

Elbers, C., J. O. Lanjouw, and Peter Lanjouw. 2002. "Welfare in Villages and Towns: Micro-Level Estimation of Poverty and Inequality." Policy

Research Working Paper 2911. World Bank, Development Economics Research Group, Washington, D.C. Processed.

———. 2003. "Micro-Level Estimation of Poverty and Inequality." *Econometrica* 71 (January): 355–64.

Elbers, C., Jean O. Lanjouw, Peter Lanjouw, and P. G. Leite. 2002. "Poverty and Inequality in Brazil: New Estimates from Combined PPV-PNAD Data." World Bank, Development Economics Research Group, Washington, D.C. Processed.

Elbers, C., Peter Lanjouw, J. A. Mistiaen, B. Özler, and K. Simler. 2002. "Are Neighbours Equal? Estimating Local Inequality in Three Developing Countries." Paper presented at the conference on Spatial Distribution of Inequality, sponsored by the London School of Economics, Cornell University, and the World Institute for Development Economics Research, London, U.K.

Epstein, Scarlet. 1962. *Economic Development and Social Change in South India*. Manchester, U.K.: University of Manchester Press.

Fallon, Peter R., and Luiz A. Pereira da Silva. 1994. "South Africa: Economic Performance and Policies." Southern African Department Discussion Paper 7. World Bank, Washington, D.C. Processed.

Fallon, Peter R., and D. Verry. 1988. *The Economics of Labor Markets*. Oxford, U.K.: Philip Allan

Feres, Juan Carlos. 1998. "Falta de Respuesta a las Preguntas Sobre el ingreso. Su magnitud y efectos en las Encuestas de Hogares en América Latina." Programa para el Mejoramientos de las Encuestas y la Medición de las Condiciones de Vida en América Latina y el Caribe, 2° Taller Regional, Buenos Aires, Argentina, November 10–13, 1998.

Ferreira, Francisco H.G., and J.A. Litchfield. 2001. "Education or Inflation?: The Micro and Macroeconomics of the Brazilian Income Distribution during 1981–1995." *Cuadernos de Economía* 38: 209–38.

Ferreira, Francisco H.G., and R. Paes de Barros. 1999. "The Slippery Slope: Explaining the Increase in Extreme Poverty in Urban Brazil, 1976–1996." *Revista de Econometria* 19(2): 211–96.

Ferreira, Francisco H.G., Peter Lanjouw, and M. Neri. Forthcoming. "A New Poverty Profile for Brazil Using PPV, PNAD and Census Data." *Revista Brasileira de Economía*.

Ferreira, Francisco H.G., P. Leite, Luiz A. Pereira da Silva, and P. Picchetti. 2002. "Financial Volatility and Income Distribution: Assessing Winners and Losers of the Brazilian 1999 Devaluation Using a Macro-financial Econometric Model Linked to Microsimulations." Paper presented at the FIPE (Fundação Instituto de Pesquisas Econômicas) World Bank Conference, July, São Paulo. Processed.

Fields, Gary S. 2001. *Distribution and Development: A New Look at the Developing World*. Cambridge, Mass.: Russell Sage Foundation and MIT Press.

Filmer, Deon, and Lant Pritchett. 1998. "The Effect of Household Wealth on Educational Attainment around the World: Demographic and Health Survey Evidence." Policy Research Working Paper 1980. World Bank, Development Economics Research Group, Washington, D.C. Processed.

———. 1998. "Estimating Wealth Effects without Expenditure Data—or Tears: An Application to Educational Enrollments in States of India." Policy Research Working Paper 1994. World Bank, Development Economics Research Department, Washington, D.C. Processed.

Filmer, Deon, Jeffrey Hammer, and Lant Pritchett. 1998. "Health Policy in Poor Countries: Weak Links in the Chain." Policy Research Working Paper 1874. World Bank, Policy Research Group, Washington, D.C. Processed.

Fofack, Hippolyte. 2000. "Combining Light Monitoring Surveys with Integrated Surveys to Improve Targeting for Poverty Reduction: The Case of Ghana." *World Bank Economic Review* 14 (January): 195–219.

Fofack, Hippolyte, Robert Ngong, and Chukwuma Obidegwu. 2003. "Rwanda Public Expenditure Performance: Evidence from a Public Expenditure Tracking Study in the Health and Education Sectors." Africa Region Working Paper 45. World Bank, Washington, D.C. Processed.

Foster, James E., and Anthony F. Shorrocks. 1988. "Poverty Orderings." *Econometrica* 56: 173–77.

Foster, James E., Joel Greer, and Erik Thorbecke. 1984. "A Class of Decomposable Poverty Measures." *Econometrica* 52(3): 761–66.

Frankenberg, Elizabeth. 2000. "Community and Price Data." In Margaret E. Grosh and Paul Glewwe, eds., *Designing Household Survey Questionnaires for Developing Countries: Lessons from 15 Years of the Living Standards Measurement Study.* Washington, D.C.: World Bank.

Gacitua-Mario, Estanislao, and Quentin Wodon, eds. 2001. "Measurement and Meaning: Combining Quantitative and Qualitative Methods for the Analysis of Poverty and Social Exclusion in Latin America." Technical Paper 518. World Bank, Washington, D.C. Processed.

Galasso, Emanuela. 2002. "The Geographical Dimension of Public Expenditures and Its Link to Poverty: The Case of Madagascar." Paper presented at the conference on Public Expenditures and Poverty Reduction: Issues and Tools, sponsored by the World Bank Poverty Reduction and Economic Management Network, Cape Town, South Africa. Processed.

Galasso, Emanuela, Martin Ravallion, and Agustin Salvia. 2001. "Assisting the Transition from Workfare to Work: A Randomized Experiment." Policy Research Working Paper 2738. World Bank, Washington, D.C. Processed.

Galor, Oded, and Joseph Zeira. 1993. "Income Distribution and Macroeconomics." *Review of Economic Studies* 60: 35–52.

Gerring, John. 2001. *Social Science Methodology: A Criterial Framework.* New York: Cambridge University Press.

Gertler, Paul, and Paul Glewwe. 1990. "The Willingness to Pay for Education in Developing Countries: Evidence from Rural Peru." *Journal of Public Economics* 42(3): 251–75.

Gertler, Paul, and Jacques Van der Gaag. 1990. *The Willingness to Pay for Medical Care: Evidence from Two Developing Countries*. Baltimore: Johns Hopkins University Press for the World Bank.

Ghosh, M., and J. N. K. Rao. 1994. "Small Area Estimation: An Appraisal." *Statistical Science* 9(1): 55–93.

Gibson, John. 1998. "Indirect Tax Reform and the Poor in Papua New Guinea." *Pacific Economic Bulletin* 13(2): 29–39.

Giovanni, Andrea Cornia, Richard Jolly, and Frances Stewart. 1987. *"Adjustment with a Human Face."* Oxford, U.K.: Oxford University Press for UNICEF.

Glewwe, Paul, and Phong Nguyen. 2002. "Economic Mobility in Vietnam in the 1990s." Policy Research Working Paper 2838. World Bank, Development Economics Research Group, Washington, D.C. Processed.

Go, Delfin S. Forthcoming. "Public Expenditure, Growth, and Poverty in Zambia."

Go, Delfin S., and Pradeep Mitra. 1999. "Trade Liberalization, Fiscal Adjustment, and Exchange Rate Policy in India." In G. Ranis and L. Raut, eds., *Trade, Growth, and Development (Essays in Honor of Professor T.N. Srinivasan)*. New York: North-Holland.

Goletti, Francesco, Karl Rich, and C. Wheatley. 2001. "The Cassava Starch Industry in Viet Nam: Can Small Firms Survive and Prosper?" *International Food and Agribusiness Management Review* 2 (3/4): 345–57.

Gørtz, Mette, Glenn W. Harrison, Claus K. Nielsen, and Thomas F. Rutherford. 2000. "Welfare Gains of Extending Opening Hours in Denmark." Economics Working Paper B-00-03. University of South Carolina, Darla Moore School of Business, Columbia, South Carolina.

Government of Tanzania. 1999. "Tanzania Public Expenditure Review: Health and Education Financial Tracking Study. Final Report, Vol. III." Report by Price Waterhouse Coopers, Dar es Salaam. Processed.

———. 2001. "ProPoor Expenditure Tracking." Report by Research on Poverty Alleviation and Economic (REPOA) and Social Research Foundation to Tanzania PER Working Group. March. Dar es Salaam. Processed.

Grosh, Margaret. 1997. "The Policymaking Uses of Multi-topic Household Survey Data: A Primer." *World Bank Research Observer* 12(2): 137–60.

Grosh, Margaret. E., and Paul Glewwe, eds. 2000. *Designing Household Survey Questionnaires for Developing Countries: Lessons from 15 Years of the Living Standards Measurement Study*. Washington, D.C.: World Bank.

Grosh, Margaret, and Juan Munoz. 1996. "A Manual for Planning and Implementing the Living Standards Measurement Study Survey." Living Standards Measurement Study Working Paper 126. World Bank, Development Economics Research Group, Washington, D.C. Processed.

Grosskoff, Rosa. 1998. "Comparación de las estadísticas de ingresos provenientes de encuestas de hogares con estimaciones externas." Programa para el Mejoramientos de las Encuestas y la Medición de las Condiciones de Vida en América Latina y el Caribe, 2° Taller Regional, Buenos Aires, Argentina, November 10-13, 1998.

Hamermesh, Daniel S. 1993. *Labor Demand*. Princeton, N.J.: Princeton University Press.

Hammer, Jeffrey, Ijaz Nabi, and James Cercone. 1995. "Distributional Effects of Social Sector Expenditures in Malaysia, 1974 to 1989." In Dominique van de Walle and Kimberly Nead, eds., *Public Spending and the Poor: Theory and Evidence*. Baltimore: Johns Hopkins University Press for the World Bank.

Harding, Ann. 1993. *Lifetime Income Distribution and Redistribution: Applications of a Microsimulation Model*. Amsterdam: North-Holland.

Hausman, Jerry. 1980. "The Effect of Wages, Taxes, and Fixed Costs on Women's Labor Force Participation." *Journal of Public Economics* 14: 161–94.

Hayden, Carol, and Jeffery Round. 1982. "Developments in Social Accounting Methods as Applied to the Analysis of Income Distribution and Employment Issues." *World Development* 10: 451–65.

Heckman, James, Hedehiko Ichimura, and Petra Todd. 1997. "Matching as an Econometric Evaluation Estimator: Evidence from Evaluating a Job Training Programme." *Review of Economic Studies* 64: 605–54.

Heckman, James, Hedehiko Ichimura, James Smith, and Petra Todd. 1998. "Characterizing Selection Bias Using Experimental Data." *Econometrica* 66: 1017–99.

Hellerstein, J., and G. Imbens. 1999. "Imposing Moment Restrictions from Auxiliary Data by Weighting." *Review of Economics and Statistics* 81(1): 1–14.

Hentschel, Jesko. 1999. "Contextuality and Data Collection Methods: A Framework and Application to Health Service Utilization." *Journal of Development Studies* 35(4): 64–94.

Hentschel, Jesko, Jean Olson Lanjouw, Peter Lanjouw, and Javier Poggi. 1998. "Combining Census and Survey Data to Study Spatial Dimensions of Poverty: A Case Study of Ecuador." Policy Research Working Paper 1928. World Bank, Washington, D.C. Processed.

———. 2000. "Combining Census and Survey Data to Trace the Spatial Dimensions of Poverty: A Case Study of Ecuador." *World Bank Economic Review* 14(1): 147–65.

Howes, Stephen. 1996. "The Influence of Aggregation on the Ordering of Distributions." *Economica* 63(250): 253–72.

Hoynes, H. 1996. "Welfare Transfers in Two-Parent Families: Labor Supply and Welfare Participation under AFDC-UP." *Econometrica* 64 (2): 295–332.

Isham, Jonathan, Deepa Narayan, and Lant Pritchett. 1995. "Does Partici-pation Improve Performance? Establishing Causality with Subjective Data." *World Bank Economic Review* 9(2): 175–200.

Jalan, Jyotsna, and Martin Ravallion. 1998. "Are There Dynamic Gains from a Poor-Area Development Program?" *Journal of Public Economics* 67(1): 65–86.

———. 2003. "Does Piped Water Reduce Diarrhea for Children in Rural India?" *Journal of Econometrics* 112: 153–73.

———. 2003. "Estimating the Benefit Incidence of an Antipoverty Program by Propensity Score Matching." *Journal of Business and Economic Statistics* 21(1): 19–30.

Jha, Saumitra, Vijayendra Rao, and Michael Woolcock. 2002. "Gover-nance in the Gullies: A Mixed-Methods Analysis of Survival and Mobil-ity Strategies in Delhi Slums." World Bank, Development Research Group, Washington, D.C. Processed.

Kakwani, N. 1993. "Poverty and Economic Growth with Application to Côte d'Ivoire." *Review of Income and Wealth* 39: 121–39.

Kanbur, Ravi, ed. 2003. *Q Squared: Qualitative and Quantitative Methods of Poverty Appraisal.* New Delhi: Permanent Black Publishers.

Katz, Lawrence F., Jeffrey R. Kling, and Jeffrey B. Liebman. 2001. "Mov-ing to Opportunity in Boston: Early Results of a Randomized Mobility Experiment." *Quarterly Journal of Economics* 116(2): 607–54.

Keane, M. P., and R. Moffitt. 1998. "A Structural Model of Multiple Wel-fare Program Participation and Labor Supply." *International Economic Review* 39(3): 553–89.

Keuning, Steven, and Erik Thorbecke. 1992. "The Social Accounting Matrix and Adjustment Policies: The Impact of Budget Retrenchment on Income Distribution." In Erik Thorbecke, with Roger Downey, Steven Keuning, David Roland-Holst, and David Berrian, *Adjustment and Equity in Indonesia.* Paris: OECD Development Centre.

Khan, Mohsin S., Peter Montiel, and Nadeem U. Haque. 1990. "Adjust-ment with Growth: Relating the Analytical Approaches of the IMF and the World Bank." *Journal of Development Economics* 32: 155–79.

Khiem, N., and P. Pingali. 1995. "Supply Response of Rice and Three Food-crops in Vietnam." In G. Denning and V. Xuan, eds., *Vietnam and IRRI: A Partnership in Rice Research.* Manila: International Rice Research Institute.

King, Gary, Robert Keohane, and Sidney Verba. 1993. *Designing Social Inquiry: Scientific Inference in Qualitative Research.* Princeton, N.J.: Princeton University Press.

Kumar, Somesh, and Robert Chambers. 2002. *Methods for Community Participation.* London: Intermediate Technology Publications.

Kuznets, Simon. 1955. "Economic Growth and Income Inequality." *Amer-ican Economic Review* 45(1): 1–28.

Lalonde, Robert. 1986. "Evaluating the Econometric Evaluations of Training Programs." *American Economic Review* 76: 604–20.

Lambert, Peter. 1993. *The Distribution and Redistribution of Income: A Mathematical Analysis.* 2d ed. Manchester, U.K.: Manchester University Press.

Lanjouw, Peter, and Martin Ravallion. 1999. "Benefit Incidence, Public Spending Reforms, and the Timing of Program Capture." *World Bank Economic Review* 13: 257–73.

Lanjouw, Peter, and Nicholas Stern. 1998. *Economic Development in Palanpur over Five Decades.* New York: Oxford University Press.

Laroque, G., and B. Salanie. 1984. "Estimation of Multi-Market Fix-Price Models: An Application of Pseudo Maximum Likelihood Methods." *Econometrica* 57(4): 831–60.

Leadership Group on Social Accounting Matrices. 2003. *Handbook on Social Accounting Matrices and Labour Accounts.* Eurostat Working Papers 3/2003/E/23. Luxembourg.

Lindelöw, Magnus, and Adam Wagstaff. 2003. "Health Facility Surveys: An Introduction." Policy Research Working Paper 2953. World Bank, Development Research Group, Washington, D.C.

Lindelöw, Magnus, Ritva Reinikka, and Jakob Svensson. 2003. "Health Care on the Frontline: Survey Evidence on Public and Private Providers in Uganda." African Region Human Development Working Paper 38. World Bank, Africa Region, Washington, D.C.

Lofgren, Hans, Rebecca Lee Harris, and Sherman Robinson with assistance from Marcelle Thomas and Moataz El-Said. 2002. *A Standard Computable General Equilibrium (CGE) Model in GAMS. Microcomputers in Policy Research,* vol. 5. Washington, D.C.: International Food Policy Research Institute. (http://www.ifpri.org/pubs/microcom/micro5.htm).

Lusardi, A. 1996. "Permanent Income, Current Income and Consumption: Evidence from Two Panel Data Sets." *Journal of Business and Economic Statistics* 14(1): 81-90.

Lysy, Frank J., and Lance Taylor. 1979. "Vanishing Income Redistributions: Keynesian Clues About Model Surprises in the Short Run." *Journal of Development Economics* 6: 11–29.

———. 1980. "The General Equilibrium Model of Income Distribution." In Lance Taylor, E. Bacha, E. Cardoso, and Frank J. Lysy, eds., *Models of Growth and Distribution for Brazil.* Oxford, U.K.: Oxford University Press.

MaCurdy, T., D. Green, and H. Paarsch. 1990. "Assessing Empirical Approaches for Analyzing Taxes and Labor Supply." *Journal of Human Resources* 25(3): 415–90.

Mahoney, James. 2000. "Strategies of Causal Inference in Small-N Analysis." *Sociological Methods and Research* 28(4): 387–424.

Malec, D., W. Davis, and X. Cao. 1999. "Model-based Small Area Estimates of Overweight Prevalence Using Sample Selection Adjustment." *Statistics in Medicine* 18: 3189–3200.

Mansuri, Ghazala, and Vijayendra Rao. 2003. "Evaluating Community Driven Development: A Review of the Evidence." World Bank, Development Economics Research Group, Washington, D.C. Processed.

McPake, Barbara, Delius Asiimwe, Francis Mwesigye, Mathias Ofumbi, Lisbeth Ortenblad, Pieter Streefland, and Asaph Turinde. 1999. "Informal Economic Activities of Public Health Workers in Uganda: Implications for Quality and Accessibility of Care." *Social Science and Medicine* 49(7): 849–67.

Meerman, Jacob. 1979. *Public Expenditure in Malaysia: Who Benefits and Why?* New York: Oxford University Press for the World Bank.

Meier, G. M., and Joseph E. Stiglitz J. 2001. *Frontiers of Development Economics.* New York: Oxford University Press.

Mercenier, Jean, and Maria da Conceicao Sampaio de Souza. 1994. "Structural Adjustment and Growth in a Highly Indebted Market Economy: Brazil." In Jean Mercenier and T. N. Srinivasan, eds., *Applied General Equilibrium and Economic Development: Present Achievements and Future Trends.* Ann Arbor: University of Michigan Press.

Mikkelsen, Britha. 1995. *Methods for Development Work and Research: A Guide for Practitioners.* New Delhi: Sage Publications.

Mills, Bradford, and David E. Sahn. 1996. "Life after Public Sector Job Loss in Guinea." In David Sahn, ed., *Economic Reform and the Poor in Africa.* Oxford, UK: Oxford University Press.

Mills, C. Wright. 1959. *The Sociological Imagination.* New York: Oxford University Press.

Minot, N., and Francesco Goletti. 1998. "Export Liberalization and Household Welfare: The Case of Rice in Vietnam." *American Journal of Agricultural Economics* 80(4): 738–49.

Mistiaen, J. A. 2002. "Small Area Estimates of Welfare Impacts: The Case of Food Price Changes in Madagascar." World Bank, Development Economics Research Group, Washington, D.C. Processed.

Mistiaen, J. A., B. Özler, T. Razafimanantena, and J. Razafindravonona. 2002. "Putting Welfare on the Map in Madagascar." World Bank, Development Economics Research Group, Washington, D.C. Processed.

Miyazawa, Kenichi. 1976. *Input-Output Analysis and the Structure of Income Distribution.* Berlin: Springer.

Moffitt, Robert. 1991. "Program Evaluation with Nonexperimental Data." *Evaluation Review* 15(3): 291–314.

Montgomery, Mark, Kathleen Burke, Edmundo Paredes, and Salman Zaidi. 2000. "Measuring Living Standards with Proxy Variables." *Demography* 37(2): 155–74.

Mookherjee, Dilip, and Anthony F. Shorrocks. 1982. "A Decomposition Analysis of the Trend in U.K. Income Inequality." *Economic Journal* 92 (December): 886–902.

Mosley, Paul. 1999. "Micro-Macro Linkages in Financial Markets: The Impact of Financial Liberalization on Access to Rural Credit in Four African Countries." Finance and Development Research Programme Working Paper 4. University of Manchester, Manchester, U.K. Processed.

Narayan, Deepa. 1995. *Toward Participatory Research*. Washington, D.C: World Bank.

Newbery, David M. G., and Nicholas H. Stern, eds. 1987. *The Theory of Taxation for Developing Countries*. Oxford, U.K.: Oxford University Press.

Obermeyer, Carla Makhlouf, Susan Greenhalgh, Tom Fricke, Vijayendra Rao, David I. Kertzer, and John Knodel. 1997. "Qualitative Methods in Population Studies: A Symposium." *Population and Development Review* 23(4): 813–53.

Omoregie, E. M., and K. Thomson. 2001. "Measuring Regional Competitiveness in Oilseeds Production and Processing in Nigeria: A Spatial Equilibrium Modelling Approach." *Agricultural Economics* 26(3): 281–94.

Patton, Michael. 1987. *How to Use Qualitative Methods in Evaluation*. Newbury Park, Calif.: Sage Publications.

Pearce, David W. 1986. *The MIT Dictionary of Modern Economics*. 3d ed. Cambridge, Mass.: MIT Press.

Pereira da Silva, Luiz, B. Essama-Nssah, and Issouf Samaké. 2002. "A Poverty Analysis Macroeconomic Simulator (PAMS): Linking Household Surveys with Macro-models." Working Paper 2888. World Bank, DEC-PREM (Poverty Reduction and Economic Management Network), Washington, D.C. Processed.

Persson, Torsten, and Guido Tabellini. 1994. "Is Inequality Harmful for Growth? Theory and Evidence." *American Economic Review* 94: 600–21.

Powell, Matthew, and Jeffery Round. 1998. *A Social Accounting Matrix for Ghana, 1993*. Accra: Ghana Statistical Service.

———. 2000. "Structure and Linkage in the Economy of Ghana: A SAM Approach." In Ernest Aryeetey, Jane Harrigan, and Machiko Nissanke, eds., *Economic Reforms in Ghana: Miracle or Mirage*. Oxford, U.K.: James Currey Press.

Pradhan, Menno, and Martin Ravallion. 2000. "Measuring Poverty Using Qualitative Perceptions of Consumption Adequacy." *Review of Economics and Statistics* 82: 462–71.

Pritchett, Lant. 2002. "It Pays to Be Ignorant: A Simple Political Economy of Program Evaluation." Harvard University, Kennedy School of Government, Cambridge, Mass. Processed.

PROGRESA. 1998. *Metodología para la Identificación de los Hogares Beneficiarios del PROGRESA*. Mexico City, Mexico.

Pyatt, Graham. 1988. "A SAM Approach to Modelling." *Journal of Policy Modelling* 10(3): 327–52.

———. 2001. "Some Early Multiplier Models of the Relationship between Income Distribution and Production Structure." *Economic Systems Research* 13(2): 139–64.

Pyatt, Graham, and Jeffery Round. 1977. "Social Accounting Matrices for Development Planning." *Review of Income and Wealth* 23(4): 339–64.

———. 1979. "Accounting and Fixed Price Multipliers in a SAM Framework." *Economic Journal* 89. 850–73.

Pyatt, Graham, and Jeffery Round, with Jane Denes. 1984. "Improving the Macroeconomic Database: A SAM for Malaysia, 1970." Staff Working Paper 646. World Bank, Washington, D.C. Processed.

Pyatt, Graham, and Jeffery Round, eds. 1985. *Social Accounting Matrices: A Basis for Planning.* Washington, D.C.: World Bank.

Pyatt, Graham, and Erik Thorbecke. 1976. *Planning Techniques for a Better Future.* Geneva: International Labour Organization.

Quizón, J., and Hans Binswanger. 1986. "Modeling the Impact of Agricultural Growth and Government Policy on Income Distribution in India." *World Bank Economic Review* 1(1): 103–48.

Ragin, Charles. 1987. *The Comparative Method: Moving Beyond Qualitative and Quantitative Strategies.* Berkeley: University of California Press.

Ragin, Charles, and Howard Becker, eds. 1992. *What Is a Case? Exploring the Foundations of Social Inquiry.* New York: Cambridge University Press.

Rajemison, Harivelo, and Stephen D. Younger. 2000. "Indirect Tax Incidence in Madagascar: Estimations Using the Input-Output Table." CFNPP Working Paper 106. Cornell University, Cornell Food and Nutrition Policy Program, Ithaca, N.Y. Processed.

Rao, J.N.K. 1999. "Some Recent Advances in Model-Based Small Area Estimation." *Survey Methodology* 25(2): 175–86.

Rao, Vijayendra. 1997. "Can Economics Mediate the Link between Anthropology and Demography?" *Population and Development Review* 23(4): 833–38.

———. 1998. "Wife-Abuse, Its Causes and Its Impact on Intra-Household Resource Allocation in Rural Karnataka: A 'Participatory' Econometric Analysis." In Maithreyi Krishnaraj, Ratna Sudarshan, and Abusaleh Shariff, eds., *Gender, Population, and Development.* Oxford, U.K.: Oxford University Press.

———. 2000. "Price Heterogeneity and Real Inequality: A Case-Study of Poverty and Prices in Rural South India." *Review of Income and Wealth* 46(2): 201–12.

———. 2001. "Celebrations as Social Investments: Festival Expenditures, Unit Price Variation and Social Status in Rural India." *Journal of Development Studies* 37(1): 71–97.

———. 2001. "Poverty and Public Celebrations in Rural India." *Annals of the American Academy of Political and Social Science* 573: 85–104.

———. 2002. "Experiments in 'Participatory Econometrics': Improving the Connection Between Economic Analysis and the Real World." *Economic and Political Weekly* (May 18): 1887–91.

Rao, Vijayendra, and Ana María Ibáñez. 2003. "The Social Impact of Social Funds in Jamaica: A Mixed-Methods Analysis of Participation, Targeting and Collective Action in Community-Driven Development." Policy Research Working Paper 2970. World Bank, Development Research Group, Washington, D.C. Processed. (http://econ.worldbank.org/files/24159_wps2970.pdf).

Rao, Vijayendra, Indrani Gupta, Michael Lokshin, and Smarajit Jana. Forthcoming. "Sex Workers and the Cost of Safe Sex: The Compensating Differential for Condom Use in Calcutta." *Journal of Development Economics.*

Ravallion, Martin. 1994. *Poverty Comparisons, Fundamentals in Pure and Applied Economics,* vol. 56. Chur, Switzerland: Harwood Academic Publishers.

———. 1999. "Is More Targeting Consistent with Less Spending?" *International Tax and Public Finance* 6: 411–19.

———. 1999. "Appraising Workfare." *World Bank Research Observer* 14(1): 31–48.

———. 2000. "Monitoring Targeting Performance When Decentralized Allocations to the Poor Are Unobserved." *World Bank Economic Review* 14(2): 331–45.

———. 2001. "Growth, Inequality and Poverty: Looking Beyond Averages." Policy Research Working Paper 2558. World Bank, Development Research Group, Washington, D.C. (www.econ.worldbank.org/files/2717_Beyond_Averages.pdf).

———. 2001. "The Mystery of the Vanishing Benefits: An Introduction to Impact Evaluation." *World Bank Economic Review* 15(1): 115–40.

———. 2001. "Tools for Monitoring Progress and Evaluating Impact." Paper presented at the World Bank-IMF Workshop, Processed.

Ravallion, Martin, and Shaohua Chen. 1997. "What Can New Survey Data Tell Us about Recent Changes in Distribution and Poverty?" *World Bank Economic Review* 11(2): 357–82.

Ravallion, Martin, and Monika Huppi. 1991. "Measuring Changes in Poverty: A Methodological Case Study of Indonesia during an Adjustment Period." *World Bank Economic Review* 5(1): 57–82.

Ravallion, Martin, and Michael Lokshin. 2001. "Identifying Welfare Effects Using Subjective Questions." *Economica* 68: 335–57.

———. 2002. "Self-Rated Economic Welfare in Russia." *European Economic Review* 46(8): 1453–73.

Ravallion, Martin, and Menno Pradhan. 2000. "Measuring Poverty Using Qualitative Perceptions of Consumption Adequacy." *Review of Economics and Statistics* 82(3): 462–71.

Ravallion, Martin, Emanuela Galasso, Teodoro Lazo, and Ernesto Philipp. 2001. "Do Workfare Participants Recover Quickly from Retrenchment?" Policy Research Working Paper 2672. World Bank, Washington, D.C. Processed.

Ravallion, Martin, Dominique van de Walle, and Madhur Gautam. 1995. "Testing a Social Safety Net." *Journal of Public Economics* 57: 175–99.

Reinert, Kenneth A., and David Roland-Holst. 1997. "Social Accounting Matrices." In Joseph F. Francois and Kenneth A. Reinert, eds., *Applied Methods for Trade Policy Analysis: A Handbook.* Cambridge, U.K.: Cambridge University Press.

Reinikka, Ritva. 2001. "Recovery in Service Delivery: Evidence from Schools and Health Centers." In Ritva Reinikka and Paul Collier, eds., *Uganda's Recovery: The Role of Farms, Firms, and Government.* World Bank Regional and Sectoral Studies. Washington, D.C.: World Bank.

Reinikka, Ritva, and Jakob Svensson. 2002. "Explaining Leakage of Public Funds." CEPR Discussion Paper 3227. Centre for Economic Policy Research, London, U.K.

———. 2003. "The Power of Information: Evidence from an Information Campaign to Reduce Capture." World Bank, Development Research Group, Washington, D.C. Processed.

———. 2003. "Working for God? Evaluating Service Delivery of Religious Not-for-Profit Health Care Providers in Uganda." Policy Research Working Paper 3058. World Bank, Development Research Group, Washington, D.C. Processed.

Republic of Uganda. 2000. "Tracking the Flow of and Accountability for UPE Funds." Ministry of Education and Sports. Report by International Development Consultants, Ltd., Kampala.

———. 2001. "Study to Track Use of and Accountability of UPE Capitation Grants." Ministry of Education and Sports. Report by International Development Consultants, Ltd., Kampala.

Robb, Caroline. 2002. *Can the Poor Influence Policy? Participatory Poverty Assessments in the Developing World.* Rev. ed. Washington, D.C.: International Monetary Fund.

Robillard, Anne-Sophie, and Sherman Robinson. 1999. "Reconciling Household Surveys and National Accounts Data Using a Cross Entropy Estimation Method." Discussion Paper 50. International Food Policy Research Institute, Washington, D.C. (http://www.ifpri.cgiar.org/divs/tmd/tmdpubs.htm).

Robillard Anne-Sophie, François Bourguignon, and Sherman Robinson. 2001. "Crisis and Income Distribution, A Micro-Macro Model for Indonesia." World Bank, Washington, D.C. Processed.

Robinson, Sherman. 1989. "Multisectoral Models." In Hollis Chenery and T. N. Srinivasan, eds., *Handbook of Development Economics*, vol. II. Amsterdam: North-Holland.

Robinson, Sherman, Andrea Cattaneo, and Moataz El-Said. 2001. "Updating and Estimating a Social Accounting Matrix Using Cross Entropy Methods." *Economic Systems Research* 13(1): 47–64.

Robles, Marcos, Corinne Siaens, and Quentin Wodon. Forthcoming. "Poverty, Inequality and Growth in Paraguay: Simulations Using SimSIP Poverty." *Economía & Sociedad.*

Rosenbaum, Paul, and Donald Rubin. 1983. "The Central Role of the Propensity Score in Observational Studies for Causal Effects." *Biometrika* 70: 41–55.

———. 1985. "Constructing a Control Group using Multivariate Matched Sampling Methods that Incorporate the Propensity Score." *American Statistician* 39: 35–39.

Rossi, Peter H., and J. D. Wright, eds. 1983. *Handbook of Survey Research, Quantitative Studies in Social Relations.* New York: Wiley.

Round, Jeffery. 2003. "Constructing SAMs for Development Policy Analysis: Lessons Learned and Challenges Ahead." *Economic Systems Research* 15(2): 161–83.

Rubin, Donald B., and N. Thomas. 2000. "Combining Propensity Score Matching with Additional Adjustments for Prognostic Covariates." *Journal of the American Statistical Association* 95: 573–85.

Ryten, Jacob. 2000. " The MECOVI Program: Ideas for the Future: A Midterm Evaluation." Consultant Report to the Inter-American Development Bank. Processed.

Sadoulet, Elisabeth, and Alain de Janvry. 1995. *Quantitative Development Policy Analysis.* Baltimore: Johns Hopkins University Press.

Sahn, David E., ed. 1994. *Adjusting to Policy Failure in African Economies.* Ithaca, NY: Cornell University Press, 1994.

———. 1996. *Economic Reform and the Poor in Africa.* Oxford: Clarendon Press.

Sahn, David E., and Stephen D. Younger. 1999. "Dominance Testing of Social Expenditures and Taxes in Africa." IMF Working Paper WP/99/172. International Monetary Fund, Fiscal Affairs Department, Washington, D.C. Processed.

Salmon, Wesley. 1997. *Causality and Explanation.* New York: Oxford University Press.

Saposnik, Rubin. 1981. "Rank-Dominance in Income Distributions." *Public Choice* 36: 147–51.

Scott, Kinnon, Diane Steele, and Tilahun Temesgten. Forthcoming. "Living Standards Measurement Study Surveys." In Ibrahim-Sorie Yansaneh, ed., *The Analysis of Operating Characteristics of Surveys in Developing Countries.* United Nations Technical Report, New York.

Selowsky, Marcelo. 1979. *Who Benefits from Government Expenditure? A Case Study of Colombia.* New York: Oxford University Press.

Shorrocks, Anthony F. 1983. "Ranking Income Distributions." *Economica* 50: 3–17.

Shoven, John B., and John Whalley. 1984. "Applied General Equilibrium Models of Taxation and International Trade: An Introduction and Survey." *Journal of Economic Literature* 22(3): 1007–51.

Singerman, Diane. 1996. *Avenues of Participation*. Princeton, N.J.: Princeton University Press.

Singh, Inderjit, Lyn Squire and John Strauss. 1986. "A Survey of Agricultural Household Models: Recent Findings and Policy Implications." *World Bank Economic Review* 1(1): 149–80.

Skoufias, Emmanuel, and B. McClafferty. 2001. "Is PROGRESA Working? Summary of the Results of an Evaluation by IFPRI." FCND Discussion Paper 118. International Food Policy Research Institute, Washington, D.C. Processed.

Skoufias, Emmanuel, Benjamin Davis, and Sergio de la Vega. 2001. "Targeting the Poor in Mexico: An Evaluation of the Selection of Households into PROGRESA." *World Development* 29(10): 1769–84.

Slack, Enid, and Richard M. Bird. 2002. "Land and Property Taxation." World Bank, Washington, D.C. Processed.

Smith, Jeffrey, and Petra Todd. 2001. "Reconciling Conflicting Evidence on the Performance of Propensity-Score Matching Methods." *American Economic Review* 91(2): 112–18.

SNA. 1993. *System of National Accounts*. Washington, D.C.: Commission of the European Communities, International Monetary Fund, Organisation for Economic Co-operation and Development, United Nations, World Bank.

Somanathan, A., K. Hanson, B. A. Dorabawila, and B. Perera. 2000. "Operating Efficiency in Public Sector Health Facilities in Sri Lanka: Measurement and Institutional Determinants of Performance." Sri Lankan Health Reform Project (USAID). Processed.

Stern, Nicholas. 2002. "Strategy for Development." In Boris Pleskovic and Nicholas Stern, eds., *Annual World Bank Conference on Development Economics, 2001/2002*. Washington, D.C.: World Bank.

Stifel, David, David E. Sahn, and Stephen D. Younger. 1999. "Inter-Temporal Changes in Welfare: Preliminary Results from Ten African Countries." CFNPP Working Paper 94, Cornell University, Cornell Food and Nutrition Policy Program, Ithaca, N.Y. Processed.

Stone, Richard. 1985. "The Disaggregation of the Household Sector in the National Accounts." In Graham Pyatt and Jeffery Round, eds., *Social Accounting Matrices: A Basis for Planning*. Washington, D.C.: World Bank.

Tarp, Finn, David Roland-Holst, and John Rand. 2002. "Trade and Income Growth in Vietnam: Estimates from a New Social Accounting Matrix." *Economic Systems Research* 14(2): 157–84.

Tashakkori, Abbas, and Charles Teddlie. 1998. *Mixed Methodology: Combining Qualitative and Quantitative Approaches*. Thousand Oaks, Calif.: Sage Publications.

Thorbecke, Erik. 1995. *Intersectoral Linkages and Their Impact on Rural Poverty Alleviation: A Social Accounting Approach*. Vienna: United Nations Development Organization.

Thorbecke, Erik, and Hong-Sang Jung. 1996. "A Multiplier Decomposition Method to Analyse Poverty Alleviation." *Journal of Development Economics* 48(2): 279–300.

Thorbecke, Erik, with Roger Downey, Steven Keuning, David Roland-Holst, and David Berrian. 1992. *Adjustment and Equity in Indonesia.* Paris: OECD Development Centre.

Todd, Petra, and Kenneth I. Wolpin. 2002. "Using Experimental Data to Validate a Dynamic Behavioral Model of Child Schooling and Fertility: Assessing the Impact of a School Subsidy Program in Mexico." Department of Economics, University of Pennsylvania. Processed.

Townsend, Robert M., and Kenichi Ueda. 2001. "Transitional Growth with Increasing Inequality and Financial Deepening." IMF Working Paper WP/01/108. International Monetary Fund, Research Department, Washington, D.C. Processed.

Tuck, Laura, and Kathy Lindert. 1996. "From Universal Food Subsidies to a Self-Targeted Program: A Case Study in Tunisian Reform." Discussion Paper 351. World Bank, Agricultural Operations Division, Middle East and North Africa Region, Washington, D.C. Processed

UNICEF. *Adjustment with a Human Face.* Giovanni Andrea Cornia, Richard Jolly, and Frances Stewart. Oxford, U.K.: Oxford University Press.

van de Walle, Dominique. 1992. "The Distribution of the Benefits from Social Services in Indonesia, 1978–87." Policy Research Working Paper 871. World Bank, Country Economics Department, Washington, D.C. Processed.

———. 1994. "The Distribution of Subsidies through Public Health Services in Indonesia 1978–87." *World Bank Economic Review* 8(2): 279–309.

———. 1998. "Assessing the Welfare Impacts of Public Spending." *World Development* 26(March): 365–79.

———. 2002. "Choosing Rural Road Investments to Help Reduce Poverty." *World Development* 30(4): 575–89.

———2002. "Poverty and Transfers in Yemen." Middle East and North Africa Working Paper Series 30. World Bank, Office of the Chief Economist, Middle East and North Africa Region, Washington, D.C. Processed.

———. 2002. "The Static and Dynamic Incidence of Viet Nam's Public Safety Net." Policy Research Working Paper 2791. World Bank, Development Research Group, Washington, D.C. Processed.

———. 2002. "Viet Nam's Safety Net: Protection and Promotion from Poverty?" World Bank, Development Research Group, Washington, D.C. Processed.

van de Walle, Dominique, and Kimberly Nead, eds. 1995. *Public Spending and the Poor: Theory and Evidence.* Baltimore: Johns Hopkins University Press for the World Bank.

van de Walle, Dominique, Martin Ravallion, and Madhur Gautam. 1994. "How Well Does the Social Safety Net Work? The Incidence of Cash

Benefits in Hungary 1987–89." Living Standards Measurement Study Working Paper 102. World Bank, Washington, D.C.

Van Soest, A. 1995. "A Structural Model of Family Labor Supply: A Discrete Choice Approach." *Journal of Human Resources* 30: 63–88

van Wijnbergen, Sweder. 1983. "Credit Policy, Inflation and Growth in a Financially Repressed Economy." *Journal of Development Economics.* 13(1): 45–65.

Wagstaff, Adam. 1989. "Econometric Studies in Health Economics: A Survey of the British Literature." *Journal of Health Economics* 8: 1–51.

Wagstaff, Adam, and Howard Barnum. 1992. "Hospital Cost Functions for Developing Countries." Policy Research Working Paper 1044. World Bank, Development Research Group, Washington, D.C.

Watts, H. W. 1968. "An Economic Definition of Poverty." In Daniel Patrick Moynihan, ed., *On Understanding Poverty.* New York: Basic Books.

Wetterberg, Anna, and Scott Guggenheim. 2003. "Capitalizing on Local Capacity: Institutional Change in the Kecamatan Development Program, Indonesia." World Bank, East Asia Department, Jakarta, Indonesia. Processed.

White, Howard. 2002. "Combining Quantitative and Qualitative Approaches in Poverty Analysis." *World Development* 30(3): 511–22.

Wodon, Quentin, Krishnan Ramadas, and Dominique van der Mensbrugghe. 2002. "SimSIP Poverty: Poverty and Inequality Comparisons Using Group Data." World Bank, Washington, D.C. (www.worldbank.org/simsip).

Wodon, Quentin, Krishnan Ramadas, and Dominique van der Mensbrugghe. 2003. "SimSIP Poverty Module." (www.worldbank.org/simsip).

Woodbury, Stephen, and Robert Spiegelman. 1987. "Bonuses to Workers and Employers to Reduce Unemployment." *American Economic Review* 77: 513–30.

Woolcock, Michael. 2001. "Social Assessments and Program Evaluation with Limited Formal Data: Thinking Quantitatively, Acting Qualitatively." Social Development Briefing Note 68. World Bank, Social Development Department, Washington, D.C. Processed.

World Bank. 1992. "The Social Dimensions of Adjustment Integrated Survey: A Survey to Measure Poverty and Understand the Effects of Policy Change on Households." Social Dimensions of Adjustment in Sub-Saharan Africa Working Paper 14. Washington, D.C. Processed.

———. 1993. "Indonesia: Public Expenditures, Prices and the Poor." Report 11293-IND. World Bank, Country Department III, East Asia and Pacific Region, Washington, D.C. Processed.

———. 1994. *User's Guide, World Bank RMSM-X.* Washington, D.C.

———. 1995. "Ghana: Poverty Past, Present and Future" Report 14504-GH. World Bank, West Central Africa Department, Washington, D.C. Processed.

———. 1996. "Madagascar: Poverty Assessment." Report 14044 (vols. I and II). World Bank, Central Africa and Indian Ocean Department, Washington, D.C. Processed.

————. 1999. "Bangladesh: From Counting the Poor to Making the Poor Count." Country Study 19648. Washington, D.C. Processed.

————. 2000. *World Development Report: Attacking Poverty.* Washington, D.C.

————. 2000. "Nicaragua: Ex-Post Impact Evaluation of the Emergency Social Investment Fund (FISE)." Report 20400-NI. Washington, D.C. Processed.

————. 2001. "Honduras: Public Expenditure Management for Poverty Reduction and Fiscal Sustainability." Report 22070. Poverty Reduction and Economic Sector Management Unit, Latin America and the Caribbean Region, Washington, D.C.

————. 2001. "Nicaragua Poverty Assessment Challenges and Opportunities for Poverty Reduction." Report 20488-NI. Poverty Reduction and Economic Management Sector Unit, Latin America and the Caribbean Region, Washington, D.C. Processed.

————. 2001. "Poverty in the 1990s in the Kyrgyz Republic." Report 21721-KG. Human Development Department, Country Department VIII, Europe and Central Asia Region, Washington, D.C. Processed.

————. 2001. *Zambia Public Expenditure Review: Public Expenditure, Growth and Poverty.* Report 22543-ZA. Washington, D.C. Processed.

————. 2002. "Poverty in Bangladesh: Building on Progress." Report 24299-BO. Poverty Reduction and Economic Management Sector Unit, South Asia Region, Washington, D.C. Processed.

————. 2002. "Social Analysis Sourcebook: Incorporating Social Dimensions into Bank-Supported Projects." World Bank, Social Development Department, Washington, D.C. Processed. (http://www.worldbank.org/socialanalysissourcebook/Social%20AnalysisSourcebookAug6.pdf).

————. 2002. "User's Guide to Poverty and Social Impact Analysis of Policy Reform." World Bank, Poverty Reduction Group and Social Development Department, Washington, D.C. Processed. (http://www.worldbank.org/poverty/psia/draftguide.pdf).

————. 2003. "Bosnia and Herzegovina: Poverty Assessment." Report 25343-BIH. Poverty Reduction and Economic Management Sector Unit, Europe and Central Asia, Washington, D.C. Processed.

————. 2003. "Poverty in Guatemala." Report 24221-GU. World Bank, Washington, D.C. (http://wbln0018.worldbank.org/LAC/LACInfoClient.nsf/Date/By+Author_Country/EEBA795E0F22768D85256CE700772165?OpenDocument).

Xiao, Ye, and Sudharshan Canagarajah. 2002. "Efficiency of Public Expenditure Distribution and Beyond: A Report on Ghana's 2000 Public Expenditure Tracking Survey in the Sectors of Primary Health and Education." Africa Region Working Paper Series 31. World Bank, Washington, D.C.

Yao, Shujie, and Aying Liu. 2000. "Policy Analysis in a General Equilibrium Framework." *Journal of Policy Modeling* 22(5): 589–610.

Yitzhaki, Shlomo, and Joel Slemrod. 1991. "Welfare Dominance: An Application to Commodity Taxation." *American Economic Review* 81:480–96.

Younger, Stephen D. 1993. "Estimating Tax Incidence in Ghana: An Exercise Using Household Data." CFNPP Working Paper 48. Cornell University, Cornell Food and Nutrition Policy Program, Ithaca, N.Y.

———. 2002. "Public Social Sector Expenditures and Poverty in Peru." In Christian Morrisson, ed., *Education and Health Expenditure and Development: The Cases of Indonesia and Peru.* Paris: Organisation for Economic Co operation and Development, Development Center Studies.

———. 2003. "Benefits on the Margin: Observations on Marginal versus Average Benefit Incidence." *World Bank Economic Review* 17(1): 89–106.

Younger, Stephen D., David E. Sahn, Steven Haggblade, and Paul A. Dorosh. 1999. "Tax Incidence in Madagascar: An Analysis Using Household Data." *World Bank Economic Review* 13: 303–31.

Contributors

François Bourguignon is director of research in the Development Economics Vice-Presidency of the World Bank. He is on leave from Ecoles des Hautes Etudes en Sciences Sociales where he has been a professor since 1985. He holds a Ph.D. in economics from the University of Western Ontario and a Doctorat d'Etat en économie from the Université d'Orléans, France. His work is both theoretical and empirical and bears mostly on distribution and redistribution of income and economic development.

Luiz A. Pereira da Silva is currently a lead economist in the Research Department of the World Bank, and his areas of work are macroeconomic modeling of financial crises and poverty. He holds a Ph.D. in economics from the University of Paris-I (Sorbonne). He has worked for the French central statistical office (INSEE) and the governments of South Africa, Brazil, and Japan, and has been a visiting professor at the University of São Paulo, Brazil.

Jehan Arulpragasam is a senior economist at the World Bank, where he has worked at the Bank's Poverty Reduction Group and as a country economist since 1995. He was a researcher at the Cornell University Food and Nutrition Policy Program from 1988 to 1993, where he published a book, journal articles, and chapters of edited volumes on the impacts of economic reforms on the poor in several African countries. He received a Ph.D. in economics from the University of North Carolina.

Patrick Conway is professor of economics at the University of North Carolina at Chapel Hill, where he has been on the faculty since 1983. His research has focused on the international aspects of trade and finance with developing countries. His current research interests include the impact of IMF lending programs on developing country welfare, the development of financial markets in transition economies, and the welfare impact of exchange rate depreciation in developing countries. He holds a Ph.D. in economics from Princeton University.

Gaurav Datt is senior economist at the Poverty Reduction and Economic Management Unit in East Asia and the Pacific Region at the World Bank. He has a Ph.D. in economics from the Australian National University. His research interests are in the areas of poverty, income distribution, and labor markets.

Jan Dehn currently works as an economist in Latin America Research at Credit Suisse First Boston in New York. Previously, he worked for the World Bank's Research Department. He has also worked as an economic advisor to the Ministry of Finance and Economic Development in Uganda. He holds a doctorate in economics from Oxford University with emphasis on applied econometrics. His research interests include public sector service delivery and the macroeconomic effects of commodity price shocks.

Lionel Demery works in the Africa Region of the World Bank, specializing on poverty issues. Previously he taught economics at University College Cardiff and at the University of Warwick in the United Kingdom. He has also worked for the International Labour Organization in Bangkok and at the Overseas Development Institute in London. He holds a master's degree in economics from the London School of Economics, and has published widely on policy reform, inequality, and poverty.

Shantayanan Devarajan is chief economist of the World Bank's Human Development Network and editor of the *World Bank Research Observer*. His recent research has focused on various aspects of public expenditures in developing countries, including the links with growth, project appraisal, and foreign aid. Before joining the Bank, he was on the faculty of Harvard University's John F. Kennedy School of Government. He has a Ph.D. in economics from the University of California at Berkeley.

Moataz El-Said is a research analyst in the Development Strategy and Governance Division of the International Food Policy Research Institute (IFPRI), where he works on research projects related to agricultural development, income distribution, poverty, and international trade. He received a master's degree in economics from the American University in Cairo.

B. Essama-Nssah is a senior economist with the Poverty Reduction Group at the World Bank, working on the distributional implications of public policy. He is the author of a book on analytical and normative underpinnings of poverty, inequality, and social well-being. He was a senior research associate with the Cornell University Food and Nutrition Program from 1990 to 1992. From 1984 and 1989 he was vice dean of the Faculty of Law and Economics, and head of the Economics Department at the University of Yaoundé (Cameroon). He holds a Ph.D. in Economics from the University of Michigan.

Francisco H.G. Ferreira is currently a senior economist in the Research Department of the World Bank and a regular visiting professor at the Pontifícia Universidade Católica do Rio de Janeiro. His research focuses on income distribution dynamics during economic development. He sits on the boards of the Latin American and Caribbean Economic Association (LACEA), the Instituto de Estudos do Trabalho e da Sociedade (Rio de Janeiro, Brazil) and the Institute for Public Policy and Development Studies (Puebla, Mexico), and is an associate editor of *Economia*, the journal of LACEA. He holds a Ph.D. in economics from the London School of Economics.

Delfin S. Go is a senior country economist for South Africa at the World Bank, specializing in macroeconomics, public finance, and Southern Africa. He was formerly with the Development Economics Research Group of the World Bank, where his principal areas of research were taxation, investment, growth, and economic modeling. He received his Ph.D. in political economy and government from Harvard University.

Peter Lanjouw works in the Poverty and the Rural Development clusters of the World Bank's Development Research Group. His current research focuses on issues in the measurement of poverty and inequality and on the role of the nonagricultural sector in rural economic development. He holds a Ph.D. in economics from the London School of Economics.

Hans Lofgren is a senior research fellow in the Development Strategy and Governance Division of the International Food Policy Research Institute (IFPRI), where he leads a multicountry program, "Macroeconomic Policies, Growth and Poverty Reduction." His research focuses on the analysis of food, agriculture, and trade policies in an economywide context. He received a Ph.D. in economics from the University of Texas at Austin.

Krishnan Ramadas is a consultant in the Poverty Reduction and Economic Management Unit of the Africa Region at the World Bank. He received a master's degree in mechanical engineering from Rensselaer Polytechnic Institute.

Vijayendra Rao is with the Development Research Group of the World Bank. He received his Ph.D. in economics from the University of Pennsylvania and previously worked at the University of Chicago, Michigan, and Williams College. He mixes the field-oriented analysis of qualitative data with quantitative methods to study topics that include dowries, domestic violence, sex work, community development, and the role of culture in development.

Martin Ravallion is research manager for poverty and inequality in the Development Research Group of the World Bank. He holds a Ph.D. in economics from the London School of Economics and has taught economics at a number of universities. His main research interests over the last 20 years have concerned poverty and policies for fighting it. He has advised numerous governments and international agencies on this topic and written extensively on this and other subjects in economics.

Ritva Reinikka is research manager in the Development Research Group of the World Bank and codirector of the 2004 World Development Report, *Making Services Work for Poor People*. Her research has focused on trade policy, public expenditures, and service delivery in developing countries. She previously worked in the World Bank's Eastern Africa Department and, before joining the Bank, in the Helsinki School of Economics and UNICEF. She has a Ph.D. in economics from Oxford University.

Sherman Robinson is an institute fellow at the International Food Policy Research Institute (IFPRI). He received a Ph.D. in economics from Harvard University, and before joining IFPRI in 1993 as director of the Trade and Macroeconomics Division, he taught agricultural and resource economics at the University of California, Berkeley. He has held visiting senior-staff appointments at the Economic Research Service, U.S. Department of Agriculture; the U.S. Congressional Budget Office; and the President's Council of Economic Advisers (in the Clinton administration).

Jeffery I. Round holds a Ph.D. from the University of Wales and is currently a reader in economics at the University of Warwick, U.K.; and has been a visiting associate professor at the Woodrow Wilson

School, Princeton; a Harkness Fellow at Harvard; and a consultant for the World Bank and the Department for International Development. His research interests include social accounting matrices, poverty and inequality analysis, and CGE and regional modeling.

David E. Sahn is a professor of economics at Cornell University. He has published widely on issues of poverty, inequality, education, and health, as well as having worked extensively with numerous international organizations, such as the Organisation for Economic Co-operation and Development, the International Monetary Fund, the World Bank, and the U.S. Agency for International Development. He has a Ph.D. from MIT.

Issouf Samaké is an economist and a consultant in the Africa Region and the World Bank Institute at the World Bank. He is currently completing a Ph.D. in economics at the George Washington University.

Kinnon Scott is a senior economist in the Research Group on Poverty in the Development Economics Vice-Presidency in the World Bank. She manages the Living Standards Measurement Study team in addition to carrying out research on poverty issues.

Jakob Svensson is a senior economist in the Development Research Group (public services team) at the World Bank and an assistant professor in economics at the Institute for International Economic Studies, Stockholm University, Sweden. His research focuses on the political economy of public service delivery and corruption.

Dominique van der Mensbrugghe is senior economist in the Prospects Group of the Development Economics Vice-Presidency at the World Bank. He received a Ph.D. in economics from the University of California at Berkeley.

Dominique van de Walle is lead economist in the World Bank's Development Research Group. She received her Ph.D. in 1989 from the Australian National University. Her research interests are in the general area of poverty and public expenditures. The bulk of her recent research has been on Vietnam, covering rural development, infrastructure (rural roads and irrigation), safety nets, and impact evaluation.

Thomas Walker is an economist in the Economic Research Department at the Reserve Bank of Australia, and a consultant in the East Asia and Pacific Region at the World Bank. His research interests include macroeconomic modeling and forecasting, poverty and inequality analysis, and the role of private transfers in developing countries.

Quentin Wodon is lead specialist in the Poverty Reduction and Economic Management Unit of the Africa Region at the World Bank. He worked in the private sector and spent five years with an international NGO working with families in extreme poverty before completing a Ph.D. in economics at American University. He taught at the University of Namur before joining the World Bank in 1998.

Michael Woolcock is a social scientist in the World Bank's Development Research Group and an adjunct lecturer in public policy at Harvard University's Kennedy School of Government. His work focuses on the role of social institutions in shaping survival and mobility strategies. He received his Ph.D. in sociology from Brown University.

Stephen D. Younger is associate director of the Cornell University Food and Nutrition Policy Program. He holds a Ph.D. from Stanford University. His research interests include the incidence of taxes and public expenditures, poverty and inequality analysis of nontraditional measures of well-being such as health or educational status, and poverty and inequality analysis for multivariate definitions of well-being.

Index

Note: *f* indicates figures, *n* indicates notes (*nn* more than one note), and *t* indicates tables.